Emmanuel Rebold

A general history of free-masonry in Europe

Emmanuel Rebold

A general history of free-masonry in Europe

ISBN/EAN: 9783337277017

Printed in Europe, USA, Canada, Australia, Japan

Cover: Foto ©ninafisch / pixelio.de

More available books at **www.hansebooks.com**

A GENERAL HISTORY

OF

FREE-MASONRY

IN

EUROPE.

Based upon the Ancient Documents relating to, and the Monuments erected by this Fraternity from its foundation in the Year 715 B. C. to the present time.

TRANSLATED AND COMPILED FROM THE MASONIC HISTORIES OF

EMMANUEL REBOLD, M. D.,

Past Deputy of the Grand Orient of France, President of the Academy of Industrial Sciences, and a Member of many Philosophic and Scientific Societies,

BY J. FLETCHER BRENNAN,

EDITOR OF THE AMERICAN FREEMASON'S MAGAZINE.

CINCINNATI:
AMERICAN MASONIC PUBLISHING ASSOCIATION,
114 MAIN STREET,
1868.

Fraternally Dedicated

TO THE

GRAND ORIENT OF FRANCE,

THE SUPREME COUNCIL FOR FRANCE,

AND THE NATIONAL GRAND LODGE OF FRANCE,

at the East of Paris;

TO THE

GRAND ORIENT AND SUPREME COUNCIL OF BELGIUM,

at the East of Brussels;

TO THE

NATIONAL GRAND LODGE OF HOLLAND,

at the East of the Hague;

TO THE

NATIONAL ALPINE GRAND LODGE,

at the East of Zurich;

AND TO

ALL THE LODGES OF THEIR ALLIANCE,

BY THE AUTHOR.

FRATERNALLY DEDICATED

TO THE

Grand and Subordinate Lodges

OF

Free-Masons

IN THE

United States of America,

BY THE TRANSLATOR.

TABLE OF CONTENTS.

Title, Author's Dedication, Translator's Dedication and Introduction, Table of Contents, Preface, and Report of Examining Committee............pp. 1–26

GENERAL HISTORY OF FREEMASONRY.

Introduction..	27
Origin of all the worships...	28
" of Hieroglyphics and Symbols...	29
" of Mysteries, Sybils, Oracles, Magi......................................	30
" of the Roman Colleges of Builders, the Cradle of Freemasonry.	34
The organization and privileges of these colleges................................	35
Origin of the expression "Grand Architect of the Universe"...............	35
Introduction and development of the colleges in Britain.....................	36
Charter of St. Alban, A. D. 292..	40
Origin of the qualification "Free Mason"..	41
" of the title "Worshipful Master"...	46
Charter of York, A. D. 926..	48
Origin of the dedication of lodges to St. John......................................	49
Masonic corporations of Lombardy...	50
Monopolies accorded to the Masonic corporations by the Popes........	51
Organization and development of the Fraternity in Germany............	52
The stone-cutters of Strasburg, A. D. 1459...	53
Influence of the "Reformation" upon the Masonic corporations........	54
Importance of the Fraternity in England in the 17th and 18th centuries.	54
Origin of the "higher" degrees...	54
" of the title "Royal Art" accorded to Freemasonry................	55
Transformation of the Fraternity to a philosophic institution.............	56
Its new constitution as such..	57
Its influence upon social progress..	57
Persecutions directed against it..	57
Divers opinions as to the origin of Freemasonry.................................	59
Explanation of the two Forms of its initiations...................................	60
It is an imitation and not a continuation of ancient mysteries............	61
Object of the initiation into the mysteries of antiquity.......................	62
Object and doctrine of modern Freemasonry,.....................................	62
Approaching ideal of Freemasonry...	63

(vii)

CONTENTS.

HISTORICAL SUMMARY OF THE MOVEMENTS OF THE MASONIC CORPORATIONS IN GAUL, FROM THEIR INTRODUCTION, IN THE YEAR 60 B. C., TO THEIR DISSOLUTION, IN THE 16TH CENTURY.

Establishment of the Roman Colleges of Builders in Trans-Alpine Gaul after its conquest..	64
Establishment of the great military roads from Rome to Gaul..............	66
Erection of Romo-Gallic cities...	67
Re-erection of the destroyed cities and towns...................................	68
Vestiges of ancient Romo-Gallic monuments in France.......................	69
Separation of the Colleges of Builders into different bodies.................	71
Erection of the first Christian churches and monasteries.....................	71
Architectural knowledge of monastic refugees..................................	72
Celebrated architects who go out from the Masonic schools.................	72
Architecture in France under Charlemagne......................................	72
The Masonic corporations directed by the religious orders..................	73
Architecture paralyzed by the terrors of the year 1000.......................	73
General renewal of all the religious edifices.....................................	73
The Masonic corporations of Lombardy extend over Europe.................	74
Their monopolies renewed by all the Popes......................................	74
League of mutual succor among the Masonic brethren........................	74
The architect fraternity of bridge and road builders...........................	74
Conception and erection of the great cathedrals of France..................	75
Unity of plans visible in all buildings by Freemasons..........................	76
Effect of the "Reformation" upon the Masonic corporations................	77
Disintegration of the corporations the origin of trade unions...............	77
Consequences of the disintegration of the Masonic corporations...........	78
Celebrated French architects who succeeded those of the corporations..	78

ABRIDGMENT OF THE HISTORY OF MODERN OR PHILOSOPHIC FREEMASONRY IN FRANCE, FROM ITS INTRODUCTION IN 1721 TO THE ESTABLISHMENT OF THE GRAND ORIENT IN 1772.

First lodges founded at Dunkirk and at Paris.....................................	80
Lord Derwentwater first Provincial Grand Master for France...............	81
Establishment of a Provincial Grand Lodge for France........................	81
Baron Ramsay introduces his Jacobite Masonry.................................	81
Lord Harnwester the second Provincial Grand Master for France,........	82
He is succeeded by the Duke of Antin..	83
The P. G. L. of France takes the title of English G. L. of France...........	83
Difficulties follow and increase constantly.......................................	83
Origin of the chapters of Arras and of Clermont................................	84
Origin of the Rite of Perfection..	85
Incongruities in the accepted history of the A. and A. S. Rite...............	85
Continued disgust and disagreeability among the Fraternity.................	86
English G. L. of France becomes the National G. L. of France..............	86
The Grand Master, to avoid duty, selects deputies.............................	87
They misbehave, and their commissions are revoked..........................	87
Consequent schism of the (Deputy) Lacorne faction...........................	87
Stephen Morin is patented for America..	88

CONTENTS.

A reconciliation but engenders subsequent dissension.................................... 89
The G. L. revokes all *ad vitam* and other patents.. 90
Lacorne's party is expelled and proceed to extremes..................................... 90
The government interferes and interdicts Freemasonry 90
Each party misbehaves in a grievous manner.. 91
Events consequent upon the Grand Master's death.. 91
Election of the Duke of Chartres to the vacant position................................. 92
He is induced to accept the direction of all the bodies.................................. 93
Establishment of the Grand Orient... 94

ABRIDGMENT OF THE HISTORY OF MODERN OR PHILOSOPHIC FREEMASONRY IN ENGLAND, DENMARK, SWEDEN, RUSSIA, POLAND, GERMANY, HOLLAND, BELGIUM, SWITZERLAND, ITALY AND PORTUGAL, FROM ITS INTRODUCTION INTO THOSE COUNTRIES TO THE PRESENT TIME.

Circumstances attending the establishment of the G. L. of London................. 95
Compilation of "Anderson's Constitutions".. 96
The G. L. of London assumes the initiate and sole authority....................... 97
The Freemasons of York and Edinburgh protest... 97
The G. L.'s of Ireland and Scotland are established..................................... 98
Exceptions made by the lodge of Canongate Kilwinning................................. 99
Origin of the Rite of Harodim of Kilwinning... 100
Pope Benedict XIV and others interdict Freemasonry.................................. 101
In London the Grand Lodge of Ancient Masons is organized.......................... 102
Origin of the Royal Arch degree... 103
Union of the two Grand Lodges in 1813... 104
What English Freemasons have accomplished at home................................... 105
Present organization of the G. L. of England.. 105
    "   "   of the G. L. of Scotland.. 107
    "   "   of the G. L. of Ireland... 107
Present condition of Freemasonry in Great Britain..................................... 107
Introduction of Freemasonry into Denmark.. 108
    "   "   into Sweden.. 110
Jesuitical interference with Freemasonry in Sweden.................................. 111
The Templar system introduced by Jesuit emissaries.................................. 112
Introduction of Freemasonry into Russia... 113
Catharine II protects and encourages it... 114
Jesuitical interference causes it to be abused... 115
Interdiction of Paul I revoked by Alexander I, and afterward confirmed.... 115
Introduction of Freemasonry into Poland... 116
The Jesuit system of strict observance is introduced................................. 117
Introduction of Freemasonry into Belgium.. 118
Joseph I, Emperor of Austria, interdicts it.. 119
When Belgium becomes a French province it is revived................................ 119
Prince Frederick, as Grand Master, becomes its protector........................... 120
King Leopold unites the lodges into a Grand Orient................................... 121
Masonry triumphs over Jesuitism... 121
The new Grand Master, Verhaegen, recommends general discussions in the lodges.. 122

CONTENTS.

Introduction of Freemasonry into Holland............ 123
The Jesuits preach against it and excite the people............ 124
Establishment of the Grand Lodge of Holland............ 125
    "   of the G. L. for the Low Countries............ 126
The charter of Cologne is discovered............ 127
Introduction of Freemasonry into Germany............ 128
Freemasonry in Prussia............ 129
Initiation of Frederick the Great at Brunswick............ 130
Present condition of Freemasonry in Prussia............ 131
Freemasonry in Saxony............ 132
    "   in Hanover............ 132
    "   in Bavaria............ 133
    "   in the Grand Duchy of Baden............ 134
    "   in Wurtemburg and Hesse Darmstadt............ 135
    "   in Hesse-Cassel and Brunswick............ 136
Duke Ferdinand of Brunswick becomes head of the Templar system............ 137
He convokes various Masonic congresses............ 138
The Jesuits cause Freemasonry to be interdicted in Austria............ 139
Freemasonry in Bohemia............ 140
Recapitulation of Masonic lodges in Germany............ 140
Introduction of Freemasonry into Switzerland............ 141
Masonic Directories at Basle and Lausanne............ 142
Erection of "Hope" Lodge at Berne to a Prov. G. L. of England............ 143
Establishment of the Alpine Grand Lodge............ 144
Introduction of Freemasonry into Italy............ 145
    "   "   into Sardinia............ 146
Establishment of the Grand Orient at Naples............ 147
General Garibaldi is elected chief the Sup. Council for Sicily............ 148
Introduction of Freemasonry into Portugal............ 149
Acts of the Portuguese "Holy Office"............ 150
Freemasonry is interdicted by John VI, King of Portugal............ 151
Introduction of Freemasonry into Spain............ 152
Ferdinand VI, King of Spain, interdicts its operations............ 153
European countries in which Freemasonry is now interdicted............ 154

HISTORY OF THE ORIGIN OF THE ANCIENT AND ACCEPTED SCOTTISH RITE, AND ORGANIZATION OF THE SUPREME COUNCIL FOR FRANCE.

Partisan evidence as to the origin of the rite............ 156
Reflections upon this evidence............ 159
Impartial evidence as to the origin of the rite............ 160
Proof adduced that Frederick II was not its chief............ 162
Extract from the Book of Gold............ 165
Real origin of the rite............ 166
Its contemptuous disownment by the G. L. of Scotland............ 169
Introduction of the rite into France............ 172
Remarks in connection with the history of this rite............ 174

CONTENTS.

ORIGIN AND HISTORY OF THE "EGYPTIAN RITE OF MISRAIM," FROM ITS CREATION IN 1806 TO THE PRESENT TIME.

Account of its origin by its French agent, M. Bedarride	178
Mark and Michael Bedarride its propagandists	180
Its real author Lechangeur of Milan	181
He denies his highest degrees to the brothers Bedarride	182
They surreptitiously obtain them and establish a council at Paris	183
Description of the rite	185
Difficult to organize lodges—France in mourning (1815)	186
Grave abuses appear in the administration of the executive	187
The rite is interdicted by the G. O. of France	188
The brothers Bedarride obtain a new patent	189
The rite is interdicted by Frederick, G. M. of Netherland lodges	189
The administration and its constituents at war	190
Expulsion of a whole lodge	191
Misappropriation of the funds by the executive	192
The Grand Orient is exhorted to suppress the rite	193
The brothers Bedarride present their little bill of charges	195
It amounts to only $20,550	195
They arrange a new obligation, binding all to pay it	196
Objectors to this obligation are expelled	197
The death of Mark Bedarride lets up nobody	197
The rite is ridiculed by the "Masonic Globe"	198
Funds are demanded to bury a brother	199
Michael Bedarride requires all the funds to pay his bill	200
The applicants protest and denounce the whole swindle	201
Dying, M. Bedarride bequeaths his bill to his successor	201
The successor, an honest man, arranges M. B.'s debts	201
Then stigmatizing the little bill as "a debt accursed," he cancels it	202
Reflections upon the history of this rite	202

CONCISE HISTORY OF THE RITE OF MEMPHIS, FROM ITS CREATION IN 1838 UNTIL ITS FUSION INTO THE GRAND ORIENT OF FRANCE IN 1862.

The author's account of the rite	203
Strictures upon this account	204
Introduction of the rite into France	205
Its author an expelled member of the rite of Misraim	206
Extracts from the Constitution	207
The author begins to operate with his rite in France	208
Meets with difficulties and goes to London	209
In the latter city the rite explodes	210
He then goes to America and founds a lodge at Troy, N. Y.	211
Marshal Magnan's magnanimous decree covers the rite	211
The Grand Orient adopts it, and M. Marconis, its author, is happy	211

A CONCISE HISTORY OF THE ORIGIN OF ALL THE RITES FOR HIGH DEGREES INTRODUCED INTO FREEMASONRY FROM 1736 TO THE PRESENT TIME.

The only true traditional Freemasonry has but three degrees	212

CONTENTS.

The Jesuits first break this arrangement... 213
To support the "Pretender" they create new degrees. 214
They extend their nets over Germany and France.............................. 215
Investigation elicits some important discoveries................................ 216
They denaturalize the institution in France.. 217
They construct the system of Strict Observance................................. 218
The College of Clermont the nest in which new rites are hatched........ 219
The Jesuits divide continental Europe into provinces......................... 220
They erect "Unknown Superiors" for their system.............................. 220
Investigation unmasks the Order of Loyola.. 221
"Modern Freemasons are not the successors of Knights Templar"..... 222
What the Congress of Wilhelmsbad provoked..................................... 223
Fruits of the Jesuits' Masonic systems.. 224
The Order of Modern Templars... 225
The Rite of Rigid Observers... 226
Introduction of Knight Templarism into America................................ 226
The Rite of Unitarian Masonry... 227
Names of Masonic Rites extant.. 228
Rites extinct or absorbed into existing rites.. 229

DOCUMENTARY AND HISTORICAL EVIDENCE BEARING DIRECTLY UPON THE ORIGIN AND GENERAL HISTORY OF FREEMASONRY IN EUROPE.

Documentary Evidence.. 232
Historical Evidence, chronologically arranged.................................... 234
Indications of the causes for diversity of opinions, etc....................... 244

HISTORICAL ENUMERATION OF THE PRINCIPAL MASONIC CONGRESSES AND CONVENTIONS WHICH HAVE HAD PLACE IN EUROPE.

York, Strasburg, and Ratisbonne.. 251
Ratisbonne, Spire, Cologne and Basle... 252
Strasburg, London and Dublin... 253
Edinburgh, the Hague, Jena and Altenburg... 254
Kohlo, Brunswick, Leipsic and Lyons.. 255
Wolfenbuttel and Wilhelmsbad... 256
Paris, Zurich, Berne, Basle and Locle.. 257
Paris in 1848 and in 1856... 258

CHRONOLOGICAL ARRANGEMENT OF THE HISTORY OF FREEMASONRY, BASED UPON THE ANCIENT DOCUMENTS AND THE PRINCIPAL MONUMENTS ERECTED BY THIS FRATERNITY, DIVIDED INTO THREE EPOCHS.

First Epoch, from 715 B. C. to A. D. 1000, comprising the establishment of the Colleges of Builders at Rome; the construction of all the monuments of Ancient Rome; the founding of many cities; the results of the persecutions of such of the builders as became Christians, and, subsequently, the results of the invasions and international wars, and dispersion of the Christian builders into the East; the state of architecture in Gaul and Britain under the Romans, and, after their retreat, under the free and Anglo Saxon kings; the reconstruction of the Masonic corporations at the general assembly in York A. D. 926, and the distress of the Masonic corporations during the terrors invoked by the clergy at the close of the tenth century 259-295

Second Epoch, from A. D. 1000 to A. D. 1717, comprising all the most remarkable facts which signalized this period as connected with the arts and philosophy; the epoch of the construction of all the great cathedrals and other religious monuments in Europe; the organization of the Masonic corporations in Germany, its Grand Lodges, its congress and results; the influence of the Reformation upon religious architecture; the dissolution successively of all the Masonic corporations except those of England; and the transformation there, in 1717, of the Masonic corporations into a philosophic institution 296-311

Third Epoch, from A. D. 1717 to A. D. 1850, comprising all the most remarkable occurrences connected with Philosophical or Modern Freemasonry during this period; the causes and results of the schisms; the different congresses and their results; the dates, the places, and the countries where Freemasonry was persecuted; and the statistics indicating its numbers wherever its exists 312-339

Text of the Edict of Pope Pius VII against the Freemasons 340

PRIMITIVE MASONIC LAWS AND CHARTERS.

Observations concerning the Charter of York 347
Its non-recognition of a Divine Trinity 348
Its evident religious tolerance 348
It became the basis of all modern Masonic constitutions 349
Its caption and opening prayer 350
Note explanatory of its text 351
Its " Fundamental Laws of the Brother Masons " 352-355

Summary of the Ancient Masonic Charters, comprising the Roman Charter, Charter of St. Alban, Charter of York, Charter of Edward III, Charter of Scotland, Charters of Strasburg, Charter of Cologne, Charters of Scotland and London 355-558

EPITOME OF THE WORSHIP AND THE MYSTERIES OF THE ANCIENT EASTERN WORLD.

Introduction—Origin of all the worships 359
Sabeism, or sun worship, and its legends 363
The Mysteries of India 364
Mysteries of the Persians 367
Mysteries of Isis and Osiris 370
Mysteries of the Hebrews 373
Mysteries of Eleusis 375
Mysteries of Samothracia 375
Mysteries of the Phrygians and Phenicians 377
Mysteries of the Romans 377
Sybils and Oracles most celebrated 379

LEGISLATORS, REFORMERS AND FOUNDERS OF WORSHIPS AND MYSTERIES, WITH A SUMMARY OF THEIR DOCTRINES IN INDIA, CHINA, PERSIA, ETHIOPIA, EGYPT, GREECE, ROME AND JUDEA 380-385

CONTENTS.

NOTES ILLUSTRATIVE AND AUTHORITATIVE OF SUNDRY PASSAGES IN THE TEXT OF THE WORSHIPS AND MYSTERIES OF THE ANCIENT EASTERN WORLD.

Worships and Mysteries	384
Theology of the Ancients	384
Sacred Books of all the peoples	385
Cosmogonies	386
Symbols	389
Hiram of the Freemasons	392
The Angels	393
Magnificent monuments of the Hindoos	393
Bhudda (Bood, Boudd)	393
The Magi	394
Temple of Bel, or Tower of Babel	394
Ecbatana, Babylonia, Persepolis	396
Caves or Retreats of Mithra	397
In the throat of a bull	397
Zoroaster	398
Zendavesta	399
Temple of Ammon	399
Ethiopia, once a powerful state	400
Egypt in civilization	400
Pyramids of Ghizza	401
Hermes	402
Sybils	402
The avenues of Thebes	403
Subterranean cities	403
Jehovah	403
Tyre	404
The Jews driven from Egypt	404
The Pentateuch	405
The Prodigies of Moses	408
Dogma of an only God	408
Worship of the Stars	413
The Essenians	413
Christianity	413
Mysteries of Christianity	419
Eleusis, Athens	420
Temple of Balbek	420
Temple of Tadmor (Palmyra)	420
Janus	421

APPENDIX.

Recapitulation	422
The Commandments of the Ancient Sages	425
The Precepts of Modern Freemasonry	426

TRANSLATOR'S INTRODUCTION.

A connection of several years with the Masonic press, during two of which he edited and published *The American Freemason's Magazine*, afforded the translator of this work opportunities for reading all that in the English language had been published concerning the origin and history of Freemasonry, of valuing all that was reasonable, and rejecting much that was traditional, apochryphal, romantic and false. In 1861, and after he had, in consequence of the then disturbed condition of the country, suspended the publication of his magazine, he accidentally became introduced by a brother of rank and education in the Fraternity at New York to the earlier work of BRO. REBOLD, and after a hasty perusal, stored it among the few effects of a citizen soldier for future and, should opportunity offer, more leisure study. From that study, within the past year, the decision to translate and publish had been evolved, when he became possessed of the later work of BRO. REBOLD, and from both he has compiled that which he now presents and dedicates to the Fraternity in America. In doing so, his conviction is fixed that at no previous time has he been able to benefit that Fraternity to so great a degree as he now does, by translating and publishing this work.

PREFACE.

BEFORE I make known to the reader the motives which inspired this history of Freemasonry, I beg permission to give here a succinct confession of faith.

Since the moment when the principles of Freemasonry were shown me, I have made this institution a particular study, with much more fervor than that with which I have studied the religion taught me in my youth; because, by the light of reflection and experience, I found the latter crowded with contradictions and puerilities, while the former offered logic and harmony according with the idea of a Divinity imbued with wisdom, clemency, power, and love.

When circumstances occasioned me to take up my residence in this celebrated city, (Paris), at a time when its Masonic temples were recovering from the effects of the political tumults of 1847, my heart found itself going out toward that fraternal society, wherein, of all others, I most expected to enjoy the pleasures of morality and brotherly love. But I am free to confess, as then conducted, the labors of the lodges left much to desire; and I found that the reproaches addressed to Masonry in Paris by the most serious authors, such as Thory, Bazot, Chemin-Dupontés Ragon, Clavel, Des Etangs, Juge, and Moreau, were entirely justifiable.

And, notwithstanding that there are few places upon the globe where the Masonic fraternity has produced results more powerful and efficacious than at Paris—where the concentration of sixty-one lodges in the same locality permit the most complete unity in a financial point, and present moral and intellectual resources so powerful to accomplish so much, not alone in the connection of educating the people, but also of founding other humanitarian institutions—yet it is necessary to state that there is no place in the world where the dissipation of moral strength is so manifest, and where the Masonic fraternity has done so little for suffering humanity, as in this same Paris, when we consider the great number of Freemasons who here reside.

But that which struck me above all, in assisting at the work of the lodges of Paris, was the total want of intelligent Masonic instruction—a reproach which the authors named have so often made—the labors of the lodges being altogether confined to the ceremonies of initiation, the regular lectures, and the administration of their affairs. And it is to this circumstance, principally, that it is necessary to attribute the indifference so generally manifested for Freemasonry among the wealthy and intellectual Parisians; for the greater portion of the intellectual initiates, finding nothing in the society, such as they expected, to attract their attention, after attending a few meetings, fall off, in the belief that Freemasonry has no moral signification to justify the consideration they had been induced to accord to it.

These observations are painful to Freemasons convinced of the high object and deep signification of Freemasonry, and who believe it destined to become one day the religion of all nations; and these observations apply happily but to Paris, for, in all other portions of France, Masonry is much better estimated, and consequently its value is much better appreciated than in the capital.

This lack of instruction of which I speak is more apparent in the superior initiations called "high degrees," or, to speak more correctly, it is there entirely absent. By all, however, by whom Masonry is estimated, Masonic instruction is looked upon as a sacred duty due to those who are received into its bosom, and that instruction should be extended not only to all that concerns its history, its object, and the doctrines of the institution, but to all that is interesting to the friend of humanity and the lover of his race. And here we can not refrain from quoting a passage which we find proceeding from the pen of brother Cesar Moreau, of Marseilles, and published in his journal, *The Masonic World:*

"From this state of things there resulted an Order[1] which, while it embraced the universality of the nations, and drew within its bosom many of the notabilities of all races, is compelled to ignore its nature, its origin, its spirit, and its object; and to acknowledge that its traditions are forgotten or altered; that we have substituted some novelties contrary to the genius of Masonry; that the initiated fail to perceive any thing of mystery beyond the ceremonies and the ornaments of the lodge, and do not suspect that a hidden meaning is attached to the knowledge conveyed by the symbols. Thus Masonry is unfaithful to its high destiny. This society, which, according to the ideas of its founders, is entitled to the first place in the system of civilization, is allowed to march in the rear of that system. While progress in every other condition is manifest, it alone is stationary, if not falling behind in the march of human improvements. The most powerful of all human agencies, by reason of its immense association and the facilities afforded by its multiple correspondence, Freemasonry is

---

[1] The editor of the Masonic World is the only French author who has admitted that material architecture has probably given birth to moral architecture; and yet, making of Freemasonry an Order, finds himself in accord with all of his predecessors. This opinion, however, so generally that of the French Masons, is entirely erroneous; for Freemasonry never was an Order. Its origin was a fraternity; and that its transformation, from a corporation of artisans to a philosophical institution, did not change its character, is proven in the most incontestible manner by its own Constitution, which, adopted in 1717, and published by the Grand Lodge of England in 1723, is entitled "Constitution of the Ancient and Respectable *Fraternity* of Freemasons."

to-day utterly powerless to enlighten its own members, to say nothing of enlightening the rest of mankind."

All the French authors, except Moreau, have placed the origin of Freemasonry in the mysteries of the East; and the Masters of our lodges, as well as the commonly received lecture of its history, tend to perpetuate this erroneous idea. The work of Alexander Thory, entitled "*Acta Latomorum*," and that of B. Clavel, entitled "*Histoire Pittoresque de la Franc-maçonnerie*," must be placed among the most remarkable of Masonic publications; but they are, nevertheless, incomplete and fragmentary. In the history by B. Clavel, it is true he mentions the colleges of Roman architects; but, always preoccupied, in common with his predecessors, in seeking a remoter origin for Freemasonry in the mysteries of the East, he fails to perceive that it was precisely within these colleges that the birth of Freemasonry took place.

The authors who pretend—and their number is very great—that Masonry originated at the construction of Solomon's Temple, are led into this error by the numerous allusions to that construction which have place among the lectures of our lodges of to-day. Those authors who believe that Freemasonry proceeded from the society of the Rose-Cross, founded in 1616, by Valentine Andrea, a profound philosopher,[1] who, in founding it, had in view the beautiful design of reforming the world—a society which was propagated by Christian Rose-Croix,[2] renewed afterward by the renowned philosopher, Lord Bacon, and put in practice by the famous antiquary, Elias Ashmole, in 1646—are led into this error by the fact that this society was resuscitated, under Masonic forms,

---

[1] See his work, "*La Reformation*," etc.
[2] There appeared, in 1616, a new work, entitled "*La Noce Chemique de Christian Rose-Croix.*" This name of Rose-Cross is itself allegorical. The cross represented the sanctity of union, and the rose the image of discretion; these two words united signifying a holy discretion.

in Germany, in 1767; and yet others, who attribute its foundation to the partisans of the Stuarts,[1] or to Christopher Wren, architect, in 1690, are led into this error by the transformation of Freemasonry from an exclusively operative to an exclusively philosophic institution having taken place about this time.

Independently of the serious authors mentioned, there may be found a certain number of pretending historians, who, concerning the origin of Freemasonry, have advanced assertions as absurd as ridiculous. Among them we find those who represent God himself as the first Freemason,[2] and Paradise as the first sanctuary of the lodge! We find another author who pretends that the archangel Michael was Grand Master of the first lodge that the children of Seth held after the murder of Abel![3] Others, who maintain that Noah was the founder of Masonry; and yet others, who as stoutly assert that it originated at the construction of the Tower of Babel on the plains of Shinar. From this mass of contradictory opinions, A. Thory, in the preface to his work already named, deduced an opinion which he thus expresses:

"The general opinion among the most distinguished Freemasons is, that it is impossible to write a general history of Freemasonry which will bear any approach to correctness in dates and authenticated facts. M. De Bonnville has asserted that ten ages of mankind would not suffice for such a work. Others have expressed, and yet others have repeated the same idea, while to-day those of

---

[1] See, in the "*Acta Latomorum*," by A. Thory, the fragment upon the origin of the Society of Freemasons, translated from the second volume of the work "*Versuch über die Beschuldigungen wider den Tempelherrenorden*," etc., by Nicolaï. This fragment of a German work, extracted and admitted by Thory, proves that he himself had no settled opinion upon the origin of Freemasonry; for otherwise we can not comprehend how, to give a just idea in his work of the origin of the institution, he could have chosen to copy from a work which, in his opinion, had no historic value in this connection.

[2] See the work of Le Franc, entitled "*Voile levé pour les Curieux.*"

[3] "*Le vrai Franc-Maçon,*" by Enoch, 1773.

the members of the association who, by their talents and their lights, could be expected to undertake the task with success, have never essayed it, persuaded that it is beyond their strength.

"In seeking for the true cause of such discouragement, we believe it consists in the extreme difficulty of procuring the proper documents, the secret memoirs, the polemic and didactic writings; in fact, the necessary manuscript and printed information as to the history of the institution. This obstacle, if not insurmountable, is certainly exceedingly difficult; and we are free to state that, were it not that the extensive library of the mother lodge of the Scotch Rite had, with its rare and valuable manuscripts, been placed at our disposal, we never would have attempted the labor of which this our work is the result."

It is, in fact, to the insufficiency of the materials that it is necessary to attribute the fact that since the work of Dr. Anderson, first published in London in 1723, and subsequently to the number of five separate editions, no writer has attempted to produce a general history of Freemasonry, believing the problem of its origin insoluble; and, therefore, they have been forced to treat it from a philosophical point of view, and place its origin among the mysteries of antiquity.

It is these considerations which determined me to extract from the numerous materials which I have gathered, during a number of years, with the intention of one day filling a void in Masonic literature, and publish a history of our institution free from the superstitions and traditions with which it has been continually surrounded; and, in this object, I have resolved to unite, in a synoptic table, all that is afforded the most interesting, to the end that the erroneous opinions upon its origin may be dissipated, and a just and instructive idea of the principles and object of Freemasonry be afforded.

In treating in a manner indicative of my own convictions this general history of Freemasonry, I have endeavored to demonstrate—

1. That India is not only the cradle of the human race, but the country wherein may be found the source of all the religions of the world.

2. That, in her antiquities, India offers us a civilization the most advanced, as is abundantly proven by her colossal monuments, which have existed for at least six thousand years.

3. That from India have proceeded science and philosophy.

4. That we find in her sacred books, the Vedas, a sublime doctrine, practiced by the Buddhist Samaneens, and which presents the most striking resemblance to the primitive Christian doctrine.

5. That these same Vedas recount the creation of the world in a manner corresponding to the description contained in the sacred books of the Persians and the Hebrews, but with the difference that in the Vedas the description has an entirely figurative sense, while the sense conveyed by the Hebrew Scriptures, as given to us, is actual.

6. That the religion of the Hindoos—their science and philosophy—passed into Persia and Chaldea, and subsequently to Ethiopia, and from thence to Egypt. Afterward, returning invested with other forms, it is found to exist at present in the former countries.

My readers may be assured that intentions the most pure have guided me in this work, and that, while I have communicated the results of the philosophical researches of the most profound thinkers, I have to my readers awarded the task of harmonizing these truths with their own Masonic and religious ideas.

In this work I believe I have omitted nothing which would interest a young Mason. Herein he will find the origin of the mysteries of antiquity, as also the origin of all religions, and the connections which the ancient religions and mysteries bear to those of the present day; also, the degrees of civilization of the ancient peoples, the true origin of Freemasonry, its history, and in that history each historic fact, each important monument—whether of antiquity or of the middle ages—which appertain to that history, each document, each usage, each important name of which mention should be made; and, having done this, I leave to the reader to judge of the actual condition and importance of this institution from the tables of the lodges existing on the globe, and the countries wherein Freemasonry has spread and its doctrines are practiced.

EMMANUEL REBOLD.

EAST OF PARIS, *November*, 1860.

REPORT

OF THE COMMITTEE INTRUSTED WITH THE EXAMINATION OF THE WORK OF BRO. REBOLD, ENTITLED "GENERAL HISTORY OF FREEMASONRY."

BRO. REBOLD having requested the undersigned to examine his History of Freemasonry, and report their opinion thereof, it is with the most lively interest that we comply with his wishes.

In our opinion it is impossible to put together, in a manner more instructive and more concise, so many facts and dates in so few pages. All is comprised in the work of Bro. Rebold—facts, historical and geographical, as well as chronological; all is arranged by the hand of a master; and we can, without exaggeration, say that it is the first Masonic history truly worthy of this name which has ever appeared in France.

All the works that we possess speak of Masonry as an institution of an illusory character, and its origin merely traditional, if not apocryphal; but Bro. Rebold, on the contrary, taking hold of it at its birth, follows its growth and extension through the different phases of its career, from nation to nation, and from century to century, and supports his every statement with facts and dates and names, and the edifices and monuments of antiquity.

Many pages might be profitably filled with even a cursory analysis of the work of our brother, but this we will leave to the reader, being satisfied with saying, for ourselves, that nearly every line is the substance of a volume; every word carries with it a portion of instruction. We have read and re-read the manuscript with the most intense interest, and we can return to it again and again with pleasure, for it nobly fills the deplorable vacuum that exists in all of our Masonic libraries.

An immense success is reserved for this book—we had almost

said this library in epitome—a success enthusiastic, merited, and durable. To every brother who, animated with true religious sentiments, seeks instruction at the source of the most solid information, we recommend this work; and, after the most conscientious examination—*after the most attentive study, and with our hands, as Freemasons, upon our hearts, we express this our opinion of the work of Bro. Rebold; and regret our inability, by so limited an expression of our feelings, to do that justice to this really meritorious production that it is so richly entitled to.*

Du Planty, M. D.,
Wor. Mas. of Trinity Lodge.

Auguste Humberte,
Wor. Mas. Star of Bethlehem Lodge.

B. Limeth,
Wor. Mas. of Commanders of Mt. Lebanon Lodge.

East of Paris, *June,* 27 1860.

GENERAL HISTORY OF FREEMASONRY.

INTRODUCTION.

When man, placed upon this earth, saw himself surrounded with so many differently formed beings, of which the producing cause and motive for their existence were to him unknown, his thoughts were necessarily concentrated in one sentiment—intense *admiration*. Unable to comprehend the cause, he attached more importance to the effect. He studied the physical qualities of all, to the end that he might be enabled to select for his use those which were useful, and reject those which were hurtful.

But that which struck him with most surprise was the constant return of day and night, light and darkness—the brilliance and warmth of summer, and the cold and gloom of winter—to see the earth for a season ornamented with flowers and fruits, whilst during a corresponding period it languished and labored in sterility. He sought to ascertain the cause of those phenomena which regularly reproduced themselves around him, and to whose influence he found his own nature subjected; and little by little, in the laws, first of physics, and next of astronomy, he discovered the explanation.

He saw that, regulated by these laws, nature existed; that the sun and moon and earth moved in common accord. In fact, whilst all else lived and died around him—and died forever—these alone abated not in the regularity of their movements nor perpetuity of their existence: without beginning, and, apparently, without end, they seemed uncreated and immutable. To feelings, therefore, of admiration for all, were added feelings of gratitude and thanks for the beneficence of that star of day whose brilliance and heat ripened for his use fruits and vegetables; for that lesser light which seemed arranged, when the greater disappeared, to take its place; and for the earth, the great nurse, always attentive, supporting all living creatures, and offering each year, for their use, the abundance of her varied and bounteous products.

Those sentiments of admiration and gratitude begot yet another—their natural product—worship; and from that time man began to reverence good and evil. He made of light and darkness spirits of good and spirits of evil, regarding the former as the good being, and the latter as the evil one; light the benefactor; darkness the destroyer. And this worship of light of every degree necessarily led to sun worship or *Sabeism*, which we see diffused among all the primitive peoples of the earth—as well in Europe as in Asia, in Africa, and among the Incas of America.

It is thus that the Hindoos adored in Brahma the sun of summer, the creator, the genius of good; and in Shiva the sun of winter, the destroyer, the genius of evil; that the Persians reverenced the good principle in Oromaze, and the bad in Ahrimane; that the Egyptians adored these same principles in Osiris and Typhon; and the Israelites in Jehovah and the Serpent, without stopping to consider that this adoration was a worship of stars, or a worship of the changes of nature. Every-where, in fact, and among all peoples—even among the Jews themselves—we find, from the earliest times, man prostrated before material nature, confounding continually, in one and the same worship, the being who suffers the action and the principle that caused it.

This primitive worship was not entirely abolished, but maintained itself among the elect, and was, consequently, the fundamental dogma taught in the mysteries of antiquity by the gymnosophists of India and the hierophant of Memphis. And, as it was the duty of those sages to notice and record natural phenomena, to the end that the dates of feasts and the movements of the planets should be known, as well as a record kept of memorable events, and the knowledge of their doctrines, sciences, and discoveries be communicated among themselves, the system of hieroglyphics and symbols was invented—a system which has been found to exist, as the earliest style of record, among priests and peoples of the most remote ages.

These priests were the intercessors before the divinities, the counselors and guides of the people; and to perpetuate their numbers, men were admitted who proved themselves capable and worthy of the position by submitting, after a long and careful training, to the ordeal of a severe examination. It was in this manner that the initiations, so celebrated among the peoples of antiquity, were instituted.

These civilizers and early instructors of the human race, believing that it was impossible for the mass of mankind—the ignorant and illiterate—to perceive the truths of science, religion, and philosophy, except when represented by material symbols, instituted such symbols for that purpose, and, in consequence, two forms of religion began to prevail; viz.: the one the religion of the multitude, who, in great numbers, perceived nothing beyond the exterior object or symbol; and the other the religion of the learned, who perceived in the symbol but the emblem of the moral truth or natural effect, of which the symbol was but the type.

All these mysteries and their initiations, having a common object, resembled each other in their rites and symbols, and differed but in degree, according to the genius and manners of the particular peoples among whom they were practiced, and the talents, more or less brilliant, of their priests and founders. Those among the Chaldeans, the Ethiopians, and the Egyptians taught the arts and sciences in secret, particularly architecture. Among the Egyptians the priests formed a distinct class, and devoted themselves to teaching special branches of human knowledge. The youth who by them were instructed were initiated into the mysteries of religion, and during their novitiate formed an outer class or corporation of artisans, who, according to the designs drawn by the priests, erected the temples and other monuments consecrated to the worship of the gods. It was this class that gave to the people kings, warriors, statesmen, and useful citizens.

The favor shown to the priests by the people of Egypt was due in part to their wisdom, in part to the elevated conditions of science and morality which they taught, but more particularly to their study and application of an occult science practiced by the magicians of Persia. In this study they were aided by a class of assistants, called sybils or oracles, to whom they were indebted for the knowledge of a great number of plants and their therapeutic properties—of which the priests affixed the names at the gates of their temples—as, also, for their knowledge of chemistry, anatomy, and many of the secrets of nature.[1]

---

[1] This occult science, designated by the ancient priests under the name of regenerating fire, is that which at the present day is known as animal magnetism—a science that for more than three thousand years was the peculiar possession of the priesthood, into the knowledge of which Moses

INTRODUCTION. 31

Thus we see the most illustrious men of Greece—Thales, Solon, Pythagoras, Democritus, Orpheus, Plato, Theodosius, Epicurus, Herodotus, Lycurgus—these great philosophers of antiquity, binding their stoutest sandals upon

---

was initiated at Heliopolis, where he was educated, and Jesus Christ among the Essenian priests of Jerusalem.

This science, that an illustrious Dominican calls "a piece broken from a grand palace, a ray from the Adamic power, destined to confound human reason and to humiliate it before God, a phenomenon belonging to the prophetic order"—is that same science which has been resuscitated by Bro. Mesmer, whose disciples to-day spread every-where, and, by the application of it as a therapeutic agent, are every-where alleviating the physical condition of the sick and the afflicted.

Magnetism, the vital principle of all organized beings, soul of all who respire, made a part, under various names, of the secret teachings of the priests. The titles of regenerating fire, living fire, magic, were given to it by them, and the initiation into this divine science was participated in but by a small number of the elect. Believing it to be our duty to define the meaning of this science in as clear and distinct a manner as possible, we have chosen for this purpose to select a passage that we find in the work of our friend and brother Henry Delage, entitled "Perfection of the Human Race," in which he expresses himself upon this subject as follows:

"The knowledge of this magnetic fluid is the most precious gift of Divine Providence. It is the mysterious key that opens to our dazzled intelligence the world of truth and of light, and joins the finite to the infinite. It is the chain of gold so often chanted by the poet, the basis of that secret philosophy that Democritus, Plato, and Pythagoras traveled to Egypt to demand of the hierophants of Memphis and of the gymnosophists of India. Invisible to the eyes of the senses, it must be studied by the vision of the soul as seen in the rapt gaze of the somnambulist. In other days the truth was heard proceeding from the lips of the initiating priest; to-day we see it in the eyes of the *clairvoyant.* A magnetic fluid, very subtle, placed in the human race between the soul and the body, it circulates in all the nerves; and, particularly abundan in the great sympathetic of the healthy subject, it constitutes the spiri of the living being. Its color, that of fire or the electric spark, induces the name of *living fire* given to it in the works of the magicians of Persia, and of *intimate star* in those of the alchymists and astrologers of

their feet, and taking the pilgrim's staff within their hands, leaving their country and going forth to visit the vast sanctuaries of Egypt, there to be initiated into the mysteries of Isis and Osiris.

These mysteries were transported into Greece, where Orpheus founded those of Samothracia, and Triptoleme those of Eleusis. The Greeks drew upon these mysteries and initiations for a part of their mythology. Homer drew upon them for his ingenious fictions, and clothed his songs with their allegories. The descent into a well, made by the aspirant for initiation, led to the saying that truth was concealed at the bottom of a well. The judges of the dead, before whom they were conducted by the ferryman Charon across the lake Acheron, the urn that contained the ballots, and after an examination of which the judges pronounced sentence and again intrusted the initiates to the care of Charon, who alone appeared to have the right or ability of traversing the subterranean obscurity through which they passed, the barking of dogs, the monsters, the hideous specters, the flitting shades, the furies, the dog Cerberus—the sight of all those objects which the Egyptians and the Greeks had invented to try the nerves of the initiates—made in their imagination a real hell. While the Elysian fields, lighted up by a mimic sun, was evidently the place to which the initiate was conducted after his initiation; and Tartarus, where shades groaned plaintively at their own feebleness, the place where those who had succumbed in terror before these hideous spectacles were congregated. The braziers and flames, between which the initiate was compelled to pass, evidently gave

---

the middle ages. One of its principal virtues is the generative power; hence the sacred books give it the name of *regenerating fire*. Soul of the world, universal spirit permeating all nature, it is the essence and the vital spark of all that it animates, of all orders of beings, classes, and races in which it is incarnated, and is profoundly modified by all through which it passes."

rise to the saying that men who would be elevated to the rank of the gods must first pass through fire and be purified of all of earth that attaches to humanity. In fine, to descend into hell, and to be initiated into the mysteries, were, among the ancients, one and the same operation.

FOUNDATION OF THE COLLEGES OF BUILDERS,

THE CRADLE OF FREEMASONRY.

The mysteries of the Egyptians, passing through Moses to the Jewish people, afterward disseminated among the Greeks and the Romans, were, among the latter, introduced in part into the Colleges of Builders, instituted by Numa Pompilius, in the year 715 before our era.[1]

These colleges were, at their organization, as well religious societies as fraternities of artisans, and their connection with the state and the priesthood were by the laws determined with precision. They had their own worship and their own organization, based upon that of the Dyonisian priests and architects, of whom many were to be found anterior to this period in Syria, in Egypt, in Persia, and in India; and the degree of sublimity to which they had carried their art is revealed to us by the ruins which yet exist of the monuments which they there erected. Besides the exclusive privilege of constructing the temples and public monuments, they had a judiciary of their own, and were made free of all contributions to the city and state.

The members of these colleges, usually after the labors of the day, convened in their respective lodges—wooden houses, temporarily erected near the edifice in course of construction—where they determined the distribution and

---

[1] Numa Pompilius also instituted Colleges of Artisans (*Collegia Artificum*) to the number of one hundred and thirty-one; at the head of which were the Colleges of Architects or Constructors, otherwise Builders (*Collegia Fabrorum.*) The latter were designated under the name of Fraternities (*Fraternitates.*)

execution of the work upon such edifice, the decisions being made by a majority of votes. Here, also, were initiated the new members into the secrets and particular mysteries of their art. These initiates were divided into three classes: apprentices, companions or fellow-workmen, and masters; and they engaged themselves by oath to afford each other succor and assistance. The presidents of those colleges, elected for five years, were named masters or teachers (*magistri*); their labors in their lodges were always preceded by religious ceremonies, and, as the membership was composed of men of all countries, and consequently of different beliefs, the Supreme Being necessarily had to be represented in the lodges under a general title, and therefore was styled "The Grand Architect of the Universe"—the universe being considered the most perfect work of a master builder.

In the beginning the initiations into these corporations appear to have been confined to but two degrees, and the ritual of these degrees limited to, 1st, some religious ceremonies; 2d, imparting to the initiate a knowledge of the duties and obligations imposed upon him; 3d, to explaining certain symbols, the signs of recognition, and the inviolability of the oath: the workman or fellow-craft being, in addition, carefully instructed in the use of the level and the square, the mallet and chisel. To become a master, the elected had to submit to proofs such as were exacted at the initiation of the priest architects of Egypt, and in which he underwent a searching examination of his knowledge of art and moral principles.

By the protection that these colleges of builders accorded to the institutions and worships of other countries, there were developed among them doctrines and rules of conduct very much in advance of their age, and which they clothed in symbols and emblems, which were thus charged with a double signification; and, like the Dyonisian priest architects, they had words and signs of recognition.

These colleges of artisans, and principally those who professed excellence in ability to execute civil and religious, naval and hydraulic architecture, at first extended from Rome into Venice and Lombardy, afterward into France, Belgium, Switzerland. and Britain; and more lately into Spain, Arabia, and the East: and a great number of these colleges, which at this time were known by the name of Fraternities, followed the Roman legions. Their business was to trace the plans of all military constructions, such as intrenched camps. strategic routes, bridges, aqueducts, arches of triumph. etc. They also directed the soldiers and the laborers in the material execution of their works. Composed of artisans, educated and studious men, these corporations extended the knowledge of Roman manners and a taste for Roman art wherever the legions carried victorious the Roman arms. And as, in this way, they contributed more largely to the victories of peace than to those of war, they carried to the vanquished and to the oppressed the pacific element of the Roman power— the arts and civil law.

These colleges existed, in all their vigor, almost to the fall of the Roman empire. The irruption of the peoples called barbarians dispersed and reduced their number, and they continued to decline while those ignorant and ferocious men continued to worship their rude gods; but when they were converted to Christianity, the corporations flourished anew.

The Masonic Corporations in Britain.

Many of the corporations of builders who were with the Roman legions in the countries bordering on the Rhine were sent by the Emperor Claude, in the year 43, into the British Isles, to protect the Romans against the incursions of the Scots. Before their arrival in that country, there were to be found neither towns nor villages. Here, as elsewhere, the Masonic corporations constructed for the legions camps, which they surrounded with walls and fortifications; and, as time advanced, the interior of these colonies was beautified with baths, bridges, temples, and palaces, which, in a great degree, rivaled even those of Rome herself.

Wherever the legions established intrenched camps, the Masonic corporations erected cities more or less important. It is thus that York, called by the Romans *Eboracum*, and subsequently celebrated in the history of Freemasonry, became one of the first that acquired importance and elevation to the rank of a Roman city.

The native population who aided the Romans in those different constructions were incorporated into the operative bodies of workmen, and taught their art; and, in a short time, towns and villages were in course of erection on every side. The rich inhabitants of the country, imitating the Romans, constructed equally sumptuous habitations, which the architects ornamented with the same sentiments of art they had exhibited on the temples of the most powerful Romans. Daily in contact with the most elevated people of the civilized world, the inhabitants acquired a humanitarian tolerance for the manners of foreigners, and for religious ideas so different from their own. And, in their turn, the Romans discovered that there existed in every people a portion of true humanity; and this they sought to increase rather than unveil the barbaric and disagreeable in local manners and national prejudices.

The irruptions of the mountaineers of Scotland obliged the Romans to erect on the north of Britain three immense walls, in three different directions,[1] one of which traversed the country from the east to the west.

---

[1] The first great wall was constructed by the Masonic Corporations.

The corporations being inadequate for the construction of such immense works, the Britons, who were devoted to their service, aided them in their labors, and thus became partakers of all the advantages and privileges which were enjoyed by the corporations themselves. Their constant intercourse, during the execution of the same constructions, and particularly in foreign countries, always resulted in individual advantage, and the enjoyment in common of the same privileges cemented this intercourse. The same art, the unity in plans of action, combined to create in their intimacy the greatest tolerance for religious and national peculiarities, and a feeling of common brotherhood was thus developed among them. All the workmen of every degree employed upon a construction called themselves a lodge—sleeping and taking their meals in buildings resembling tents, which were temporarily erected in the vicinity of the work in course of construction, and which served them as dwellings until its completion only.

The erection of these houses and palaces, bridges and aqueducts, castles and walls, contributed to elevate architecture in Britain to a degree of perfection it had not attained in any other Roman province; so that, as early as the third century, this country was celebrated for the great number and the knowledge of her architects and of their workmen; and their services were called for wherever, upon the continent, great constructions were about to be erected. Christianity, too, from the first hour of its introduction, spread in Britain, and gave to the Masonic lodges the peculiar characteristics which distinguished them at this period. These same military roads,

---

under the orders of Agrippa, the Roman general in command of the legions in Britain, in the year 90 of our era. The second under the Emperor Adrian, A. D. 120. This crossed the country from the river Tyne to the Gulf of Solway, and thus traversed Britain from east to west. And the third was constructed further north, by order of Septimus Severus, in the year 207.

so immense in their extent, and upon which chains and slavery had been carried to people as free as they were ignorant, served now to carry to enslaved humanity, wearied of life, that new and inspiring liberty preached by Christ. Men now traveled these roads who, filled with the new faith, believed it to be their mission to impart to ll whom they met or overtook in their journeyings a knowledge of the true God and the gospel of his Son. And although, when alone, these missionary converts were exposed to bloody persecutions in the towns and villages through which they passed, they were invariably permitted to accompany unmolested the Masonic corporations, who now, sometimes alone and sometimes in the retinue of the Roman legions, were continually threading the immense empire.

Britain, too, by a favorable fortune, had more kind and humane governors at this period than any other Roman province. The example of the nobility, in becoming converts to the new faith, was swiftly followed by the people. If, in consequence, in the other provinces, the persecutions of the Christians were, by order of the emperors, executed with rigor the most appalling, in Britain a certain refuge was offered to the persecuted, by the connivance of her governors, among the building corporations. Hence it was that many among those who became advocates and public propagandists of the gospel, for the certain protection afforded them by these corporations, sought for and obtained admission among those fraternities of builders; and thus, in the hearts of the lodges, they associated with auditors more freely disposed to listen to their doctrines, at once so humane and so pure; for that love of the human race which characterized the primitive Christians entirely accorded with the spirit of those cultivated workmen who composed the Masonic corporations. When, therefore, a humane governor shrank from the disagreeable function of ordering the execution of Christians under imperial decree, those who were thus menaced sought refuge among the Scots, or in the Orkney Islands; or, aided by the builders who accompanied them, they fled to Ireland, and there remained until the death of the emperor who had ordered their execution.

In this manner Scotland became the most accessible resort of these refugees, who, in return for the security awarded them, carried into that country a knowledge of Roman architecture; and from this period may be dated the construction of those magnificent castles of the Romanesque or Etruscan style of architecture, whose grand remains, braving even until to-day the destructive hand of time, attest the architectural knowledge and artistic genius of their builders.

When Carausius, as commander of the Roman navy, found himself upon the coast of Belgium, he revolted, and, making sail for Britain, landed on that island in the year 287, when he declared his independence of Rome and took the title of emperor; but, ever fearful of an attack by the Emperor Maximilian, whom Diocletian had chosen for co-emperor, and to whom he had awarded the western empire, Carausius sought, above all, to conciliate that society—then the most influential and important in the island—the Masonic corporations. These were then composed not alone of the descendants of those Greeks and Romans whom the Emperor Claude had, in the year 43, ordered into the country, as already mentioned, but, in major part, of the natives of Britain.

With this object in view, Carausius, at the ancient city of Verulam, afterward known as St. Albans, where he had taken up his abode and established his court, conveyed and confirmed to the Masonic corporations—through the instrumentality of Albanus, a Roman knight, and Amphiabulus, a Roman architect—all those ancient privileges accorded to them by Numa Pompilius, and the kings, his successors, more than a thousand years before, but which in later years had been greatly curtailed by the subsequent Roman emperors. And it is to this renewal of those privileges—the greatest among which was the right of making laws for their own government, and thus, in establishing their own judiciary, becoming independent of all other legal tribunals—to which may be attributed the title *Freemason*, which, since that time, has distinguished the members of these corporations in contradistinction to the other workers in wood and stone who composed no part of such bodies.

Not having been interfered with by the Emperor Maximilian, Carausius employed all his wealth to augment the well-being of the country. He engaged the Masonic corporations in the erection of magnificent public edifices, which were rivaled but by those of Rome herself. His death, however, which occurred by assassination, in the year 295, brought these plans to an abrupt close.

Immediately after the death of Carausius, Maximilian appointed Constance Clorus to the vacant governorship of Gaul and Britain. He, selecting *Eboracum*, subsequently known as the city of York, for his residence, found there the oldest and most influential lodges of the Masonic corporations; and this city, from that time, became the center of all the lodges of Freemasons in Britain.

After the death of Constance, called the Great, an event that took place in the year 306, his son Constantine succeeded him. He stopped at once the persecution of the Christians, and declared himself their protector. After his victory over his rival, Licinius, he adopted Christianity himself—more, it is believed, from political motives than from a conviction of its truth—and declared it the religion of the state.

Among the earliest Christian communities the true doctrines of Christ were, from the first, exhibited in the lives of their members—the first apostles having been found in Britain among the Masonic corporations. These true priests and propagandists of the religion of Jesus were entire strangers to all thought of temporal power; and the unfortunate disputes of the four bishops who had arrogated to themselves the government of all Christendom had not, as yet, affected the primitive doctrine recognized in that declaration of the Redeemer: "He who serves me with most devotion upon earth shall be greatest in the kingdom of heaven." The confiding and susceptible spirit of the artist easily became impressed with the beauties of that morality which embraced humanity as a whole. The sentiments of art with which his soul was imbued repulsed all sophism, and the social life of the lodges resembled the earliest Christian associations, with this exception, that, instead of that contemplative idleness that saw no religious labor save in fasting and prayer, was exercised a robust and manly energy that found, in the acquirement of useful knowledge and the engagement in actual labor, a fitting outlet for that love of beauty and perception of the sublime which are never better directed than in the creations of art when employed for the glory of God.

The early Christian missionaries, not being actuated by feelings of ambition, their doctrines were simple, pure, and easily understood and appreciated by those whom they addressed. Hence, to make themselves intelligible and beloved by their companions in the lodge, they had but to unfold before them the pure ordinances of primitive Christianity; and when, as was often the case, they were obliged to seek refuge in Scotland, in Ireland, or among the Orkney Islands, there to live the lives of Couldeans,[1] it was necessary, when the most simple interpreta-

---

[1] Many Christians who had sought refuge in Ireland, in Gaul, and the Orkneys, habituated to every privation during their apostolical excursions, lived in solitude in those same caves and grottoes, in the sides of rocks and mountains, which had been, before their time, inhabited by the Druids, who there assembled to celebrate their religious rites; and from which those Christians went forth only for the purpose of spreading the

tion of their doctrines was desired, to seek for it among those northern heroes of the truth. It was in this manner that Christianity in its greatest purity was better preserved in Great Britain than in any other country.

As Christianity, in its new relations to the state, daily increased in power, and demanded for its exercise the erection of suitable buildings, the Freemason corporations found ample employment. Every-where Christian Churches sprang up under the direction and active operations of these workmen. Constantine himself, who, imitating his father in many of his acts and determinations, made York his residence during the first years of his reign, knew personally the principal members of those corporations, extended to them every privilege they had ever possessed or were at any time deprived of, and thus they became the most effective and influential arm of the public service.

The approaches of the Germans upon the Roman Empire of the West became from day to day more menacing. They did not content themselves, as was once their custom, with pillaging and retiring from such provinces as they overran, but commenced to definitely establish themselves therein. Succeeding hordes pushed past those who had arrived before them, and penetrated even beyond the country possessed by the Romans; and it was from this cause that Britain, finding herself more and more isolated from the protection of the continental empire, began to look forward with more of fear than pleasure upon a day of freedom from the Roman sway.

From the beginning of the third century the Romans had to contend almost constantly with the mountaineer of Scotland, a warlike people, the aborigines of their

---

Gospel among the people. It was from the name of those solitary habitations that the title of Couldeans was given to those preachers of Christianity; as, in the Gaelic language, the word *couldean* signifies "hermit," or dweller in solitude

country, and who, like the Welsh or Cambrians, had never been conquered;[1] and at length, menaced on every hand, and wearied with the continued strife, the Western emperor considered it prudent to remove to the southern portion of his empire those forces which had hitherto been reserved for the protection of Britain; and, by degrees, as they were required to protect his empire from the inroads of the Goths, he withdrew his legions, and with them his jurisdiction over the country—a jurisdiction which he finally abdicated in the year 406. Thus deserted by the Romans, the Britons called to their assistance the Anglii and the Saxon pagans of the neighboring continent, to protect them from the assaults of the Picts and Scots and the northern pirates who infested their coasts. These auxiliaries, however, became as injurious in one sense as they were useful in another. They repulsed the Scots, it is true, but they also fixed themselves in the land and founded the seven Anglo-Saxon kingdoms. Their gross barbarities made them the enemies of all civilization. Cities and villages were destroyed, and the flourishing prosperity that Britain enjoyed under the Roman sway disappeared. The Christian and civilized inhabitants fled to the mountains of Wales, to Scotland, or to the isles beyond. It was among these refugees that the ancient language of Britain was preserved, and with it primitive Christianity and the knowledge of architecture as practiced by the Masonic corporations.

After the first barbarous impetuosity of the Anglo-Saxons had been calmed, and the more peaceful pursuits of agriculture replaced the wars of robbers, some of these Christian refugees withdrew from their mountain caves and fortresses, and, returning to what were once their homes, converted many among the pagan nobles and people,

---

[1] It was not until between the years 1273 and 1307 that the Welsh were finally conquered by Edward I, son of Henry III, and grandson of John, the Nero of English kings.—TRANS.

but as yet dreaded to approach the kings. And thus, toward the close of the sixth century, the mild and fruitful light of the primitive Christian doctrine began to diffuse its gentle rays almost to the center of the seven kingdoms. It was reserved for the Benedictine monks, whom Pope Gregory I sent to England, to convert th Anglo-Saxons, and at whose head presided Austin, a celebrated priest-architect, to succeed in gradually converting all the kings. It is true that these monks, prompted by that spirit of temporal dominion which even at that early age began to manifest itself in the Church, exerted their best efforts to strengthen the power of the Pontiff and enhance the possessions of the Holy See; but in these operations they were at once met by the returned refugees and their pupils, who had kept the early faith, doctrine, and practices of the primitive Church; and thus, to a great extent, were the encroachments on that early doctrine prevented, and abuses of power corrected. And to this preservation of the primitive teachings of Christian apostles, in the midst of the Masonic corporations, it is proper to attribute that better and more liberal spirit that rendered the converts of the British Isles more favorably disposed toward the arts and sciences of those days than were the inhabitants of the neighboring continent.

In accordance with the teachings of their founder, the Benedictine monks worked more than they fasted or prayed. Austin himself, the apostle of England and first Archbishop of Canterbury, was no less celebrated for his knowledge of architecture than for his other powers of mind and varied acquirements; and it was he who, at this time, began to rebuild and re-establish the ancient Masonic corporations, now reduced, it may well ne believed, to a very small number—indeed, entirely inadequate for those immense constructions projected by the new apostles of Christianity. It was in this manner that at this time, in England as upon the continent, the lodges became attached to the convents, and were more or less governed by monks, according as the leading architects were monks or lay brethren; and from this fact arose the condition that lodges held their meetings almost exclusively in the convents, where, if an abbot was proposed as Master or Warden of a lodge, they addressed him as *Worshipful Brother* or *Worshipful Master*, thus establishing a mode of address which has descended even to our own day as the usual one in speaking to or of the first officer within a lodge.

After the close of the seventh century, both bishops and abbots made frequent journeys to Rome, as well for the purpose of collecting pictures and relics of saints as to induce superior workmen to return with them and settle in England. Such as did so, and all others who erected for the nobles their castles and for the clergy their convents and churches, were treated with the greatest consideration by the principal men of the country, who concerted means for establishing a taste for the arts and sciences. And in this undertaking it was soon discovered that the sentiments of early art, as taught by Vitruvius, in the reign of Cæsar Augustus, had been better preserved among the Masonic refugees from Anglo-Saxon murder and robbery in the mountains of Wales and of Scotland, than among any other of the peoples of either islands or continent. In consequence of this discovery, it became necessary to arrange anew the British lodges, and to compose them not alone of companion architects and masons, but also of influential men; and men who, advanced in civilization, protected and loved the arts, began to take a position in these lodges as *accepted masons*. The lodge at York was revived and became the most important one in the country, and into it none were received as companions but *free men*—thus establishing what is yet the principal characteristic of this institution, to the end that no person, when once admitted into its membership as an equal, could in any manner be impeached in his possession of Masonic privileges. It was at this time, also, that he who desired elevation to the rank of master or teacher had to make three voyages into strange countries, and prove to the chief workmen, when he returned, that he had perfected himself in a knowledge of the architecture peculiar to those countries.

The superior knowledge of the workmen who had practiced their art among the early refugees in Scotland began to be generally recognized at the beginning of the eighth century, and to stamp its expression upon the buildings erected in Britain. This fact produced a particular modification in the constitution of the lodges. While the general assemblies of Masons occupied themselves with architecture of a general character, particular members of the fraternity formed themselves into a separate organization, that aimed to copy exclusively after the Scottish models, and, for each important work, these admirable models were most rigorously followed. From York, therefore, these select masters, as they might properly be called, made frequent journeys to Scotland, where a rendezvous was fixed upon at which each of them might deliberate, after he had arrived, upon the observations made by others during their travels in the country, and record his own. For this purpose was chosen the valley of Glenbeg, on the north-east coast of Scotland, opposite the Isle of Skye. Here there were two old castles, built in a remarkable manner, of stone, with neither lime nor mortar, and which appeared to have served as places of refuge in the wars of earlier times. It was in these castles that the masters assembled in council, and consequently they received the name of *Masters of the Valley*, or *Scottish Masters*. In lodge assembled, when they returned, all deference was paid them, as the most learned members of the fraternity, and to them were intrusted the most particular parts of each construction, or, in other words, the conscientious adaptation and rendering of the Scottish models.

In this way, the Masonic corporations, in connection with the convents and abbeys, became, after the fall of the Roman empire, the great conservators of science and art; and in so great esteem were the members of these corporations held, that, notwithstanding the political inferiority of Britain at this time, these corporations were found to create, by their invincible hardihood, a circle of activity and influence that embraced nearly the whole west of Europe. Whenever an apostle of the Christian religion was sent to a distant mission, a body of builders invariably accompanied him, and thus it was that a material edifice soon bore witness to the advent of the spirit of truth.

During the invasion of the Danes, between the years 835 and 870, nearly all the convents, churches, and monasteries were destroyed by fire, and with them the records and ancient documents of the lodges which had been preserved in those convents. Fifty years afterward, the king, Athelstan, desirous to rebuild these monuments of the religion of his heart, directed his adopted son Edwin, who had been taught the science of architecture, to assemble, in the year 926, in the city of York, all the lodges of Freemasons scattered throughout the country, to the end that they would reconstitute themselves according to their ancient laws. This done, he confirmed to them all the privileges which were possessed by the free Roman colleges in the time of the republic. The constitution that was at this time presented by the king to the assembly of Masons, and which is called the Charter of York, is imbued with the spirit of the first Christian communities, and proves, in its introduction, that the Masonic corporations at this time were but little affected by any of the peculiar doctrines which subsequently were promulgated by councils of the Church dominant.[1]

---

[1] See the text of this Constitution, under the title "Charter of York."

In those days it was customary to dedicate and consecrate to some saint every erection intended for the worship of God, and with the like idea all the corporations of artists, artisans, and trades chose patron saints. The Freemasons chose St. John the Baptist for theirs, because his feast fell on the 24th of June, date of the summer solstice. This day had always been celebrated by the peoples of antiquity and by the Masons, since the foundation of their fraternity, as the period of the year when, the sun having attained its greatest height, nature is clothed and disports herself in the greatest abundance of her richest products. As successors of the ancient colleges of the Romans, the Freemasons of England conserved these cherished feasts; but, not to come in conflict with the dominant clergy, they were obliged to give their celebration a name not calculated to give offense. It was on this account they were known not exclusively by the name of Freemasons, but often as the Fraternity of St. John, and, upon the continent, almost exclusively as St. John Brothers, or Brothers of St. John.

The Masonic Corporations in Gaul.

In the transalpine provinces of Gaul, the Masonic corporations, cotemporaneous with those of Britain, increased in a no less extraordinary manner. After the Roman provinces were abandoned in the year 486, all the countries which had been subject to the Roman sway received with delight the attention of these builders. In those countries they were called Free Corporations, their membership being composed entirely of brother Masons.[1] Com-

---

[1] See, for all that relates to the history of the society in France, first the Chronological Table, and then the Summary of the History of Freemasonry in Gaul.

posed of the remains of the ancient colleges of constructors, they maintained their antique organization in Lombardy, where Cosmo had a celebrated school of architecture. Here they multiplied to such an extent that they failed to find occupation in that country, and consequently spread over the continent. After obtaining from the Popes the renewal of their ancient privileges, and the exclusive monopoly of erecting, in all Christendom, the monuments dedicated to religious worship, they spread into all Christian countries. And although the members of these corporations had but little fear of, or respect for, either the temporal or spiritual power of the Popes—a fact which they took no care to hide—so useful were they in enhancing the grandeur and dignity of religion, this monopoly was, nevertheless, renewed and confirmed by Pope Nicholas III, in the year 1277, and continued until the year 1334, when Pope Benedict XII accorded to them special diplomas. These diplomas made them free of all local laws, all royal edicts, all municipal regulations, and every other obligation to which the other inhabitants of the country had to submit, thus rendering the title by which they were known, of free corporations, peculiarly appropriate. In addition to this freedom, these diplomas conceded to them the right of communicating directly with the Popes, of fixing the amounts of their own salaries or wages, and of regulating in their general assemblies all subjects appertaining to their interior government. All artists and artisans who were not members of these corporations were interdicted from every act which would in any wise interfere with the work of the builders, and all sovereign rulers were commanded, as they dreaded the thunders of the Church, to suppress, with the strong arm of their power, any combination of such artists and artisans as might rebel against this provision.

During the middle ages, in all the kingdoms and principalities of Europe, do we find these corporations or fraternities—in Germany, in France, Italy, Spain, and Portugal, where, under the title of St. John Brothers, or Brothers of St. John, they have erected these sublime monuments, which, for all time, seem destined to remain as mementoes of their architectural skill and genius. Wherever these corporations established themselves, they there increased their influence by adopting, as patrons, the eminent men of the locality, and initiating them as *accepted* Masons into the bosom of their society. These, generally laying aside the material object of the institution, which for them had no charms, attached themselves to its mystical sense, and founded, outside of the lodges of workmen, lodges whose labors were entirely moral and philosophic. But, almost immediately after becoming known to the clergy, these lodges were met by that intolerant spirit which superior knowledge, if unauthorized by the Church, did, in those days of general ignorance, receive at their hands, and the members of these lodges were accused of introducing schisms among the laity, and troubles and sedition into the temporal sovereignty, disaffection toward the Pontiff and all other sovereigns, and, in fine, of the wish to re-establish the Order of the Knights Templar, and to revenge the death of the last Grand Master and other officers of that Order upon the descendants of the kings and princes who were accessory thereto. In consequence of these charges, it is stated by a document the authenticity of which has not yet been entirely established, that the representatives of nineteen of those philosophic lodges, located in different portions of Europe, assembled at Cologne, in the year 1535, under the direction of Hermann V, Bishop of Cologne.[1] At this meeting there was prepared a confession of faith, in which were enunciated the purposes and doctrines of these Masonic societies. This document, called the "Charter of Cologne,"

---

[1] For presiding at this assembly, he was, some years subsequently, put under the ban of the Church.

is dated 24th of June, 1535, and thereto are signed nineteen illustrious names, among which appear Philip Melancthon, Bruce, Coligni, Falk, Visieux, Stanhope, Jacobus Prepositus, Van Noock, and Noble—names of those present at this assembly, as delegates from the Masonic lodges of London, Edinburgh, Amsterdam, Hamburg, Paris, Vienna, and other cities, to assist at this general assembly convoked at Cologne. This charter is written upon a sheet of parchment in Masonic characters, which are contracted into the Latin of the middle ages, and the writing of which is so much defaced as to render some of the words unintelligible. This charter, together with a document, said to be the records of a lodge called the "Lodge of the Valley of Peace," from its organization to the year 1519, after the death of a member of the lodge, named Boetzlaar, fell into the hands of Prince Frederick, Grand Master of the lodges of Holland, who had copies of them prepared and sent to the principal looges of Europe. The persecutions of the ultramontane clergy, however, eventually destroyed the philosophic lodges of Southern and Western Europe.

The Masonic Corporations in Germany.

During the fifteenth century there existed in Germany a great number of lodges of operative Masons which, following the example of the English lodges of the same period, recognized a few principal lodges of master workmen and architects, to whom they accorded the title of high or grand lodges. These were in number five, and were established at Cologne, Strasburg, Vienna, Zurich, and Madgeburg. That at Cologne was from at first considered the most important, and the master of the work upon the cathedral at Cologne was recognized as the chief of all the masters and workmen of Lower Germany, as was the master of the work on the cathedral of Strasburg[1] considered as occupying a similar position of honor in Upper Germany. Subsequently there was established a central mastership, and Strasburg, when the work upon its great cathedral was continued to its completion, disputed the pre-eminence with Cologne, whose cathedral is yet unfinished, and became the seat of the grand mastership. The grand lodge of Strasburg counted within her jurisdiction the lodges of France, Hesse, Swabia, Thuringia, Franconia, and Bavaria; while to the grand lodge of Cologne were subordinate the lodges of Belgium and neighboring portions of France. The grand lodge of Vienna exercised jurisdiction over the lodges of Austria, Hungary, and Styria; while those of Switzerland were attached to the grand lodge of Berne during the construction of the cathedral in that city, and subsequently to that of Zurich, where its seat was transferred in 1502. The lodges of Saxony, which from at first recognized the supremacy of the grand lodge of Strasburg, were subsequently placed under that of Madgeburg.

These five grand lodges had a sovereign and independent jurisdiction, and adjudged, without appeal, all causes brought before them, according to the statutes of the society. These ancient laws, revised by the chiefs of the lodges, assembled at Ratisbonne on the 25th of April, 1459, and, for the first time, printed in 1464,[2] were entitled "*Statutes and Rules of the Fraternity of Stone-cutters of Strasburg.*" Sanctioned by the Emperor Maximilian in the year 1498, the constitution, composed of those statutes and rules, was confirmed by Charles V in 1520, by Ferdinand in 1558, and their successors.

---

[1] Erwin of Steinbach. He called together, at Strasburg, the Masonic Congress of 1275. His seal is mentioned by Brother Clavel as being the oldest arrangement of the compass, square, and letter G extant.—TRANS.

[2] This was about twenty-five years after the discovery of the art of printing with moveable types.—TRANS.

Toward the close of the fifteenth century, however, the crying abuses of the clergy and the Popes having cooled the religious fervor and unsettled the faith of the people, the construction of many churches was arrested for want of necessary means to erect them. This led to the dispersion of the men engaged in erecting them, and immediately following this change in public sentiment, burst forth the reformation, led by Luther, which rent for the time, almost to its foundation, the temporal and spiritual power of the Popes, and, forever arresting the work upon the vast monuments of worship, gave the death-blow to the Masonic corporations in every portion of the European continent. Gradually thenceforth the German lodges dissolved—those of Switzerland had been by an order of the Helvetian Diet disbanded in 1522—the jurisdiction of the five grand lodges was narrowed to very confined limits, and with nothing to construct, and nothing to adjudicate, the Diet of the Empire, sitting at Ratisbonne, abrogated, by a law of the 16th of March, 1707, the authority of these lodges, and ordained that the differences between the workmen builders which might thereafter arise should be submitted to the civil tribunals.

General Transformation of Freemasonry from an Operative to a Speculative or Philosophic Institution.

During the troubles which desolated England about the middle of the seventeenth century, and after the death of Charles I, in 1649, the Masonic corporations of England, and more particularly those of Scotland, labored in secret for the re-establishment of the throne destroyed by Cromwell; and for this purpose they instituted many degrees hitherto unknown and totally foreign to the spirit and nature of Freemasonry, and which, in fact, gave to this time-honored institution a character entirely political. The discussions to which this country was a prey had already produced a separation between the operative and accepted Masons. The latter were honorary members, who, according to long established usage, had been accepted into the society for the advantage which their generally influential position in the country might effect; but this very position made them at this time naturally the adherents of the throne and the strong supporters of Charles II, who during his exile was received as an accepted Mason by their election, and, in consequence of the benefits he derived from the society, gave to Masonry the title of *Royal Art;* because it was mainly by its instrumentality that he was raised to the throne and monarchy restored to England.

Notwithstanding, however, the favor with which it was regarded by the king, Freemasonry, during the latter part of the seventeenth century, decreased to such a degree that in 1703 but four lodges existed in the city of London, while throughout Great Britain at that time none other were known to the members, who, reduced to the smallest number, attended the meetings of these. In fact, with the completion of St. Paul's Cathedral, the city of London was considered rebuilt, and the occupation of the operative Masons seemed to have been brought to a close; while the accepted Masons, having obtained the object of their desire in the restoration of the monarchy, neglected the communion they had previously kept up with the operative members of the institution. Hence we find that in the year 1703 the lodge of St. Paul—so named because the operative Masons engaged in the erection of the cathedral held their lodge in a building situated in the churchyard or grounds thereof—passed an important resolution the object of which was to augment the numbers of the fraternity, and to give the Masonic institution some of its former importance in public estimation. Here, having agreed that they should continue the existence of so praiseworthy an institution to be used as the conservator of religion and tradition, and perpetuate, by the beautiful allegories of its legends and symbols, its eminently humanitarian doctrines, they for this purpose adopted the following memorable resolution:

"RESOLVED, *That the privileges of Masonry shall no longer be confined to operative Masons, but be free to men of all professions, provided that they are regularly approved and initiated into the fraternity.*"

This important decision changed entirely the face of the society, and transformed it into what we find it to-day; but many difficulties had to be removed, many years of probation had to be passed before this form of its workings could be successfully adopted. This was owing, first, to the want of union among the four lodges; second, to the exceedingly disreputable character which, for many years, had attached to the society—it having degenerated from an influential and privileged institution to little better than a pot-house companionship, with here and there a proud few who remembered its glories of other days—but perhaps, above all, the determined opposition of the Grand Master, Sir Christopher Wren, the architect of the new city of London, to the spirit of the innovating resolution. This opposition he maintained until his death; so that it was not until after that event, which occurred in 1716, that the four lodges which still existed, more in name than in fact, felt themselves at liberty to assemble their membership with the primary object of electing a new Grand Master, but more particularly to detach themselves from all connection with the lodge at York, that had for fifty years enjoyed but a nominal existence, and to put into active operation the decision involved in the resolution of 1703.

In that assembly, after electing the Master of St. Paul's Lodge, Anthony Sayre, to the office of Grand Master, there were gathered up the "*Constitution and Charges of a Freemason,*" which, subsequently prefaced by a " History of

Freemasonry," prepared by Dr. Anderson, were accepted, sanctioned, and printed in 1723, under the title of "*The Constitution and Charges of the Ancient and Respectable Fraternity of Freemasons.*" And it is the date of this publication that may properly be considered the commencement of exclusively speculative or modern Freemasonry. The principle of civilization indwelling in the doctrines and pursuits of Masonry, after having burst the bonds which kept it grasped in the stiff embrace of a mechanical association, at once abandoning itself to all its powers of expansion, almost immediately penetrated the heart of the social system, and animated it with a new life. The new Freemasonry, in the short space of twenty-five years, spread itself in a manner but little less than miraculous into nearly every portion of the civilized world. It passed from England to France as early as 1725, thence to Belgium, to Holland, to Germany, to America, subsequently to Portugal, Spain, Italy, Switzerland, to Sweden, and to Poland; and, as early as 1740, were to be found lodges in Denmark, in Bohemia, in Russia, in the Antilles, in Africa, and in the British possessions in Hindostan.

If Freemasonry has ceased to erect temples; if it has ceased to engage in material architecture; if it no longer exhibits itself in the elevation of spires and turrets as points from which eyes may be directed and hopes ascend toward a better and a happier world, it has not less continued its work of moral and intellectual culture; and its success in this respect has been far more satisfactory than those who planned its design as a speculative institution ever hoped to achieve. In all time it has exercised a powerful and happy influence upon social progress; and if today, instead of holding itself at the head of all secular societies, it is known in some countries but to be rejected and despised, this condition is owing to the destruction of that uniformity and oneness of purpose which constituted its fundamental recommendation; and this destruction is due to the innovations introduced by ambitious and designing men for motives of personal influence and advancement, and in defiance of their solemn asseverations that it was not within the power of its membership to introduce innovations into the body of Freemasonry. But even here it has shown the immortality of its spirit; for, notwithstanding the multiplicity of rites which have been forced upon it, and the ceremonial degrees which have been added to it—thus dividing its strength, causing grave inconvenience, choking the sources of accurate information as to its origin and history, and creating useless and unsatisfactory distinctions among its members—that excellent spirit which its earliest teachings engender and subsequent culture fosters is ever exhibited in a fraternal regard for each other when the brethren meet in their popular assembly, and there lay aside "all distinctions save that noble distinction, or rather emulation, of who can best work and best agree."

DIVERS OPINIONS UPON THE ORIGIN OF FREEMASONRY—ITS DOCTRINES, ITS OBJECT, AND ITS FUTURE.

The origin of Freemasonry has been, for a long time, vague and obscure. And while it is to this obscurity in its history, augmented by the multiplicity of systems which have been introduced, that it is necessary to attribute the contradictory opinions as to its origin held by those who have written upon that subject, it is, however, due to the scientific researches of a few Masonic historians who have entered this field of darkness with the determination to lay aside all the commonly received opinions and traditions upon the subject, that at the present day this obscurity has disappeared.

By the connection that its forms of initiation present with the Egyptian Mysteries, and with many societies and philanthropical schools of antiquity—the Dyonisian, the Therapeutic, the Essenian, the Pythagorean—some authors have believed that within one or several of those societies might be found the cradle of Freemasonry; while others, led into error by the symbols and passwords of Hebrew origin, have pretended that its birth had place at the building of Solomon's Temple, of which the books of Kings and of Chronicles, as found in the Old Testament, afford us such precise details. This temple, erected in the year 1012, before the Christian era, by king Solomon, who was, no doubt, Master of the Hebrew Mysteries—a type of the Egyptian—and nine years afterward dedicated by him to the glory of the *one only and ever-living God*, was the first national manifestation of an only God ever erected. From the pointed bearing of this fact, and as a masterpiece of gorgeous architecture, representing in perfection the image and harmony of the universe, this temple has ever symbolized in Freemasonry the moral excellence to which every brother is in duty bound to carry his perfected work. Losing sight, however, of this aspect of the matter, as well as of the fact that all the teachings of antiquity were invariably clothed in allegories and illustrated by symbols, many authors, and following them the mass of the brethren, have accepted the teachings of Masonry and the legends of the degrees not as allegories, but as actual occurrences, and have inextricably entangled themselves in their endeavors to explain them as such.

Another peculiarity which has, above all, contributed to induce error in the researches into the origin of the society, is the difference presented by the forms of initiation; that of the first degree being evidently borrowed from the Egyptian, while those of the second and third belong entirely to the Hebrew mysteries. This difference, however, will be easily understood, when it is known that Numa Pompilius organized his colleges of constructors as a fraternity of artists and artisans, and, at the same time, as a religious society. When so organized, the greater number of the colleges, finding themselves composed of Greeks who had been initiated into the mysteries of their country, imitated in their worship the form of initiation practiced in those mysteries; but when, some seven hundred years afterward, in the time of Julius Cæsar, the Jews were protected at Rome and granted many immunities, among which were the privilege of setting up their synagogues, a great many Hebrew artists and artisans were affiliated in those colleges, and in their turn introduced a part of the Hebrew mysteries, and with them their own beautiful allegories, among which that of the third degree was chief.

It is true that the forms of initiation practiced in our day probably bear very little resemblance to those which were in use among the Roman colleges of builders, and that these forms have often been changed or modified to suit the country and the men who found themselves at the head of the fraternity; nevertheless, it is certain tha a fixed and unchanged foundation has always religiously been preserved. The rituals which were established at London in 1650, as well as those of 1717, seem to have been based upon the Anglo-Saxon documents, arranged by the General Assembly at York in the year 926. It will be remembered that the fraternity in 1650, the year after the bloody execution of Charles I, and when the accepted Masons had acquired such influence in the institution, had, to some considerable extent, and, in 1717, to a far greater degree, abandoned the material object of the association, and the members thereof having submitted, at their initiation into the two first degrees, to all the proofs required of the Master, the allegory of Hebrew origin and the summit of Hebrew mystery was always preserved as the proper illustration for the third degree, susceptible, as it is, of a local interpretation that satisfies men of every worship.[1]

Notwithstanding the connection that so evidently exists between the ancient mysteries and the Freemasonry of our day, the latter should be considered an imitation

---

[1] Such historians as attribute to the partisans of the Stuarts the institution of Freemasonry, and who constantly believe that this allegory portrays the violent death of Charles I, are in error; for it requires but a very limited knowledge of the ancient mysteries to see in Hiram, the master workman, the Osiris of the Egyptians, the Mithras of the Persians, the Bacchus of the Greeks, the Atys of the Phrygians, or the Balder of the Scandinavians, of whom these people celebrated the passion, violent death, and resurrection as the Roman clergy of to-day, in the sacrifice of the Mass, celebrate the passion, violent death, and resurrection of Jesus Christ. Otherwise, this is the type eternal of all the religions which have succeeded each other upon the earth.

rather than a continuation of those ancient mysteries; for initiation into them was the entering of a school wherein were taught art, science, morals, law, philosophy, philanthropy, and the wonders and worship of nature; while the mysteries of Freemasonry are but a *resumé* of divine and human wisdom and morality—that is to say, of all those perfections which, when practiced, bring man nearest to God. Freemasonry of to-day is that universal morality that attaches itself to the inhabitants of all climes—to the men of every worship. In this sense, the Freemason receives not the law, he gives it; because the morality Freemasonry teaches is unchanging, more extended and universal than any native or sectarian religion can be; for these, always exclusive, class men who differ from them as pagans, idolaters, schismatics, heretics, or infidels; while Masonry sees nothing in such religionists but brothers, to whom its temple is open, that by the knowledge of the truth therein to be acquired they may be made free from the prejudices of their country or the errors of their fathers, and taught to love and succor each other. Freemasonry decries error and flies from it, yet neither hates nor persecutes. In fine, the real object of this association may be summed up in these words: To efface from among men the prejudices of caste, the conventional distinctions of color, origin, opinion, nationality; to annihilate fanaticism and superstition; extirpate national discord, and with it extinguish the firebrand of war; in a word, to arrive, by free and pacific progress, at one formula or model of eternal and universal right, according to which each individual human being shall be free to develop every faculty with which he may be endowed, and to concur heartily and with all the fullness of his strength in the bestowment of happiness upon all, and thus to make of the whole human race one family of brothers, united by affection, wisdom, and labor.

Slowly and painfully does the highest condition of

human knowledge accomplish its great revolution around the glittering axis of truth. The march is long, and since it began nations and peoples have lived and died; but when that journey is accomplished, and the incarnation of truth, now robed but in its symbol, shall appear in all the splendor of its brilliant nudity, truth's torch itself shall then enlighten the world, the doctrine that has just been announced shall become the religion of all the peoples of the earth, and then, and not till then, will be realized that sublime ideal now mysteriously hidden in the symbol of Freemasonry.

That day is, without doubt, yet far distant; but it will arrive. Its coming is marked by destiny and in the order of the centuries. Already, in the sacred balance of eternal justice, is seen each day to diminish a portion of the errors of the people, and to increase the body of light, of principle, and those truths which are preparing the way for its triumph, and which, one day, will give assurance of its reign.

HISTORICAL SUMMARY OF THE MASONIC CORPORATIONS IN GAUL, FROM THEIR INTRODUCTION IN THE YEAR 60 B. C., TO THEIR DISSOLUTION IN THE SIXTEENTH CENTURY.

AFTER ten years of unavailing war, the old Gallic nationality perished. All had to submit to the great genius of Julius Cæsar—the most beautiful devotion as well as the most indomitable courage. It was in vain that the three hundred and fifty tribes of the Gauls, the Bellovici and the Carnutes, the Aedui and the Bituriges, the Treviri and the Arverni, had disputed with him, step by step, the possession of their territory. The Roman legions, surmounting every obstacle, filling up swamps, breaking out roads, and traveling securely through dense forests, took possession of nearly every town and village to which they laid siege, and gained nearly every battle which they fought. After having exhausted themselves in vain efforts for the defense of Alise and Uxellodunum,[2] Gaul

---

[1] Shortly before this period, some brigades of Companion Constructors, with their masters at their head, accompanied the Roman legions into the middle of Gaul and into Spain, and there had erected some towns: Cordova, for example. But it was not until Cæsar's time that the colleges, complete in all their appointments, were called by him to reconstruct the destroyed cities.

[2] *Alise* is supposed by some to be now called *Iselburg*, or, according to Junius, *Wesel*, in the duchy of Cleves, but more probably *Elsen*—*Index to Cæsar's Comments*. The situation of *Uxellodunum* is not now known, though, in the opinion of some geographers, it was the modern *Ussoldun*. —*Ibid*. (Note by Translator.)

forced into her last intrenchments, was obliged to submit to the yoke of the conqueror; and thus, despite of herself, she became one of the most rich and beautiful provinces of the vast Roman Empire.

According to Plutarch, Cæsar, for the purpose of bringing to a successful conclusion his long and perilous enterprise, had taken more than eight hundred towns, conquered more than three millions of men—of whom one million perished in battle, and another million was reduced to captivity—but, finally, in the year 60 B. C., the work of conquest was achieved.

Cæsar treated the conquered country with extreme moderation. He left to Gaul her territory, her habitations, and the essential forms of her government. He accorded to her people even the title and rights of Roman citizens, with the sole condition that they should pay tribute.

Little by little the old Gauls abandoned their rude and savage manners for those soft and polished of their conquerors. They forsook their antique *oppida*, difficult of access, for cities embellished and adorned with elegant constructions, and upon favorable spots, desolated by war, arose cities and towns equaling those of Italy. Augustodunum replaced Bibracte, and Augusto-nemetum was built near Gergovia. The new cities, built under the direction of the corporations of constructors, who were partly attached to the Roman legions, took names from the language of their builders, and received from Rome priests and magistrates. Immediately sumptuous edifices arose upon the sacred places; beautiful statues, modeled by Graeco-Latin art, are substituted for the rude effigies of the Celtic divinities; swamps filled with reeds, and lands covered with briars, are converted into beautiful fields and meadows; the forests are cleared and the soil cultivated to rival the most beautiful countries on the thither side of the Alps. Numerous roads open up communication with all parts; the rivers are furrowed with boats, and the ocean with richly-laden ships, like those of the Mediterranean; commerce is extended, fabrics of every kind begin to be manufactured; and, in fine, the various products of the country are carried into every province of the vast empire.

Since the time of Cæsar, Gaul had been furrowed with oads, but it remained until the reign of Augustus to connect them with those which had been constructed in the neighboring provinces. That Emperor, for the immense work that the conquest reclaimed, ordered from beyond Cisalpine Gaul, (Venice and Lombardy,) and even from Rome itself, all the builders and artisans, members of the colleges of constructors, which could be spared. These corporations conserved their important privileges, and in Gaul considerably augmented their organization. One portion occupied themselves with the construction of the roads, and directed the Roman soldiers in their labors. Another was more particularly charged with the work on fortifications and intrenched camps, and the latter were generally attached to the legions. Other colleges, composed of artist constructors in wood, and mechanics, built, at Massilia (Marseilles), and at Frejus, ships and boats for the service of the state; while another class of those colleges were occupied exclusively in the erection of public temples and monuments; and, finally, yet another in constructing bridges and aqueducts. It was under the orders of Agrippa that the latter class constructed the most beautiful paved roads which crossed Gaul in every direction. Among these may be reckoned the *Via Domitia*, that traversed Savoy and Provence (this road was originally constructed under the directions of Pompey, in the year 45 B. C., and extended from Italy almost into Gaul, toward the Alps); the *Via Aurelia*, which starting from Civita Vecchia (Forum Aurelia), to Arles; that of Emporium, from near the Pyrenees to the passage of the Rhone; finally the road which, ending at Lyons, after having passed through the valley of Aosta, continued, by order of Agrippa, in four different directions—viz.: the first into Aquitania (Guienne and Gascony), by the Auvergne; the second to the Rhine, by the mouth of the Meuse; the third to Laon, by Burgundy and Picardy, and the fourth to Marseilles, by Narbonne. These were the principal roads; but there were a great many others which connected the different towns and villages. Lugdunum (Lyons) was to Gaul what the City of Rome was to the rest of the universe, the center wherein terminated all the principal roads of the country. As at Rome was there to be seen at Lyons the great milestone or column from which all roads were measured, and upon which the distance to every point along each road was marked. The great Roman roads were marked at regular distances, by milestones (*milliarii lapides*), of from five to eight feet high, upon which was indicated the number of the stone, and the distances given in miles and leagues.

A means of pacification employed by the Roman Emperor was to found a great number of military colonies. Entrusted with the task of keeping quiet their most turbulent neighboring countries, and with the defense of their frontier against the aggressions of the Germans, these colonies, which have given birth in nearly all the provinces to the cities of the present day, were in daily communication with the inhabitants of the neighboring country, transmitting to them their ideas of taste and cultivation. Composed of Roman citizens, they enjoyed the same rights and privileges to which they were accustomed in Italy.

The Emperor Augustus, after having regulated, at Narbo-Martius (Narbonne), in the year 27 B. C., the assessment of imposts and the administration of the interior, after having established schools and adapted the laws to the wants of the people, occupied himself in directing the construction, in many of the cities, in Narbonne and Lyons, particularly, by the colleges of architects, roads, aqueducts, entrenched camps, etc. From that date the prosperity of Lyons may be said to have begun. Under the Roman rule this city became the capital of Gaul, the seat of government, the imperial residence during the voyages of Augustus, and those of most the successors to his reign.

Cæsar and Augustus, moreover, accepted the patronage of a number of towns which took their names from the Julian and Augustan families, and which enjoyed many privileges.

The ancient cities, such as Marseilles, Arles, Aix, Narbonne, etc., were ornamented, in a considerable degree, by monuments; while, by the prodigious activity of the colleges of constructors, upon the sites of ancient towns, destroyed in the wars, arose new cities, in the construction of which both Roman soldier and native population lent their aid.

Among this crowd of cities, the most important were Rheims, Rouen, Bourges, Sens, Bourdeaux, Besançon, Lyons, Vienne, Toulouse, Paris, and Treves, and the last-named was chosen latterly as the residence of the governors of Gaul. Those cities were organized exactly upon the plan of Rome, wherein reposed the center of government. Each of them had its forum, its capitol, its theaters, its amphitheater, its temples, its cathedrals, its streets and aqueducts, and also its schools, wherein were taught polite literature, science, and art with a success that rivaled that of Athens under Pericles, and Rome under Augustus himself.

The spectacle that Gaul presented under the dominion of the twelve Cæsars is of the highest interest. The colleges of architects, composed generally of artists and men versed in all the sciences, had contributed to this elevated degree as much by the great number of monuments which they had erected in the principal Gallic cities, under the reign of Augustus, as by their learning and their humanitarian principles. In this manner the fraternity had attained to a condition of such consideration that men the most distinguished regarded it a high privilege to be accepted among them as honorary members. At this time many of the most illustrious patricians, prefering Gaul to Italy as a residence, Agrippa, Drusus, Tiberias, and the richest among the citizens of Rome, sought governorships in that country preferably to any other. In fine, the Roman institutions, manners, letters, and arts transplanted to this soil attained a development as abundant as in the most flourishing of the years known to Italy herself.

It should be remarked that all of these productions of intelligence were forwarded or retarded, however, by the condition of reigning emperor—the good ruler working for the good of the provinces as well as for that condition of Rome herself, while the evil-disposed ruler burdened them with imposts and vexatious grievances.

Almost to the fourth century the arts, and particularly architecture, were very flourishing in the province of Gaul. From the time of Constantine, almost to the defeat of Syagrius, the emperors continued to visit the country to defend it against the incessant invasions of the Germans, Saxons, Burgundians, Herulians, etc. But the Franks, of all its invaders, appeared to be the most redoubtable and persistent. No defeats damped their courage until the year 355, of our era, when Julian, having overthrown them in the most signal manner, removed his residence to Lutesia (Paris), and caused there to be constructed an immense palace, the ruins of the baths of which may be seen, in the Rue de la Harpe, to this day. Under the emperors who succeeded him, however, the aggressions became more active and audacious, and the ravages more terrible. The imperial power lost each year, each day, a portion of its prestige. Stilicon yet sustained the power of Honorius, in Gaul; but, after him, the Sclaves, the Alans, and the Huns pillaged and devastated the country without pity and without mercy. The Visigoths and the Burgundians undertook even to establish themselves in the land. Adolph, king of the Goths, fought the German hordes for some time with variable success, but he was, in his turn, chased from Narbonne and finally driven from the south by Constance, a general commanding the army of Honorius. It was in this war that the greater portion of the beautiful monuments erected by the Roman colleges were destroyed—monuments the beauty and symmetry of which we can yet judge by the existing remains of the amphitheaters at Arles, at Frejus, Nemes, etc., the aqueducts of the Pont du Gard, at Lyons, and those of neighboring cities.

Honorius reorganized the Gauls, and Arles became the capital. In a proclamation, he invited the people to construct twenty-four of their destroyed cities, to rebuild their bridges, and re-establish their roads. For this purpose, he sent into all parts of the country which had been overrun by the barbaric hordes artist constructors, to guide the workmen and direct them in their labors. But all of these ameliorations endured for but a short time; the barbarous nations continued their invasions, and the Franks finally triumphed. It was in vain that Actius fought the Visigoths, repulsed the Burgundians, defied Attila. It was in vain that Majorien retook Lyons from Theodoric; the Franks seized upon Mayence, Treves, and Cologne, destroyed their principal edifices, and heaped ruin upon ruin. They established themselves at Tournay, and from thence advanced, step by step, over the territory of the empire. In fine, Clovis appeared, and Gaul was forever withdrawn from Roman domination. Then it was that a new art erected itself upon the old ruins, established itself upon a new basis, and developed itself, marked with some material elements of the past, but reinvested with another symbol.

The Masonic corporations which had been formed outside of the legions who settled in Gaul—and their number was considerable—after the retreat of the Romans in the year 486, remained in the country. For years they had been in the habit of receiving into their membership many of the Gauls. Many members of these corporations embraced Christianity, which, in Gaul, since the beginning of the third century, had numerous partisans. No longer exclusively employed by the government, and their privileges consequently having decreased, a change operated in their organization. The different arts and trades which, almost to that time, had been united in one fraternity, separated and formed distinct corporations; and it was among these corporations that, much degenerated, were found to exist the manners and customs of the Roman colleges of constructors, and which, subsequently, served as a basis for the *communes* of the middle ages. Among them the corporations of Masons were at all times the most important, because they conserved their primitive organization and privileges, and continued to devote themselves particularly to the construction of religious edifices. Intrusted by the new apostles, who, in the year 257, came from Rome, bearing the title of bishops, with the construction of the religious edifices then in course of erection at Amiens, Beauvais, Soissons, Rheims, and Paris, these Christian Masons, guided by those apostles, and inspired by them with a horror of pagan temples, wrought with zeal in the destruction of the enormous number of edifices and works of art that the wars and the invasions had not yet destroyed, and of which there existed many remains. In this manner the earth became the sepulcher of all the remains of centuries of early art.

Under the reign of Childeric (460–481), of Clovis (481-511), of Clothaire (511–561), many churches were built upon the ruins of the pagan temples, and, at the close of the sixth century, a great many existed. During the international wars, the invasions of barbarians and social struggles of the people, the study of science and the practice of the divers branches of the arts, found place alone in the monasteries, wherein, above all, were cultivated architecture, sculpture, and painting. So that wherever the erection of a church was contemplated, the plan was furnished by an ecclesiastic—a member of the Masonic corporations—and the work was executed under his direction. St. Eloi, Bishop of Noyen (659), St. Ferol, of Limoges, Dalmac, Bishop of Rhodes, and Agricola, Bishop of Chalons (680–700), were the celebrated architects. But the corporations had equally good from among the laity, of which the most renowned had gone to England, having been engaged by the Bishop of Weymouth, who came to Gaul to seek such; and, later, Charles Martel, who ruled (740) in France under the title of "Major of the Palace," sent many masters and workmen to England upon the demands of the Anglo-Saxon kings.

The invasion of the Arabs (718) arrested the flight that the arts had taken in the seventh century, and it was not until the reign of Charlemagne (768–814) that stone-cutters and sculptors were ordered from Lombardy, and architecture was again cultivated with success. The qualification of stone-cutter, or master of the work, was then given to the greatest architects of Europe, and whoever wished to become an architect found it necessary to be received into the corporation to learn the art of stone-cutting—that branch of architecture being considered the basis of the art—not, however, to be considered or received as a master until he had passed through many degrees of apprenticeship. It was in the Latin style that all edifices of the time were erected. The Roman and Roman-ogee, or transition, styles succeeded it.[1]

---

[1] All the monuments constructed by Masonic corporations were erected after certain forms and rules which are called style. The style was adopted by the architects or chiefs, and all the masters had to conform

The year 1000, so much dreaded, arrived. It should have brought the reign of Anti-Christ and the end of the world's existence; but no inundation had flooded nor earthquakes shaken our globe from its axis, although the terror entertained by the Christian world, that its destruction was merely deferred, was not dissipated for nearly three years afterward. At the expiration of that time, however, the most skeptical felt they had nothing further to fear, and this belief was hailed as the aurora of a new earth. Art as well as humanity arose from its long lethargy and gave evidence of the vitality of its being. The desire to repair the disasters of years became general, and soon made itself felt in the reconstruction of nearly all the religious edifices of the Christian world. William the Conqueror, King of England in 1054, influenced in some degree by the stream of Norman priests and architects that flowed into England during his reign—graduates all of the school of the Lombards—built the finest and most stupendous cathedrals of England. A great number of Masons had, at this time, formed an Italian school in Lombardy, which, in the seventeenth century, was an active center of civilization, and where some fragments of the ancient Roman colleges of builders had located themselves, and enjoyed their antique organization

---

to it. There may be enumerated four periods in which each style is marked by a form or style different from the other.

In the first period, it was the Latin style that prevailed, from the fourth to the eleventh century; subsequently the Roman style, during the eleventh and first half of the twelfth.

In the second period, it is the Roman-ogee, or transition Roman style, that prevailed, from 1150 to 1200.

In the third period, it was the primary ogival style that prevailed in the thirteenth century, the secondary in the fourteenth, and the tertiary in the fifteenth centuries.

In the fourth period, it was the style called the Renaissance, or ancient Latin revived, that prevailed to the close of the sixteenth and during the seventeenth centuries.

and privileges, under the name of Free Corporations. The most celebrated were those of Como, which had acquired so great a degree of superiority that the title of *"Magistri Comacini,"* or Masters of Como, had become the generic name of all the members of the architect corporations. They always taught in secret, and had their own judiciary and mysteries.

While they had been laboring to cover Lombardy with religious edifices, their number had so greatly increased that, this work accomplished, the country failed to afford employment for all, and, in consequence, many united in the formation of a great Fraternity, having for its object to travel into all Christian countries, and therein erect religious edifices. This design was earnestly and ably seconded by the Popes, who conferred upon the corporations and upon those who, with the same object, followed in their train, the exclusive monopoly—mentioned in another part of this work—which was respected and sanctioned by the kings of such countries.

In the eleventh century we find them again in France, where they are known under the name of Brother Masons and Brother Bridgers, and sometimes, also, under that of Freemasons. Employed and directed almost exclusively by the religious orders, the abbots and prelates held it an honor to enter into membership with the Fraternity, and to participate in their secrets, and thus greatly promoted the stability and consideration accorded to the institution. The numbers of the Mason Fraternity were united by mutual obligations of hospitality, succor, and good offices, and thus they were enabled to make, at small expense, the most lengthy journeys in the pursuit of employment.

The Bridgers, or Bridge-building Fraternity, who formed a community, civil and religious, resembling that of the ancient Roman colleges, occupied themselves more particularly with that which concerned bridges. It was them who built the bridge at Avignon (1180), and nearly all the bridges of Provence, Lorraine, and Lyons.

The architect-in-chief of the corporation of Freemasons was generally a Benedictine monk, and supported by men of all the principal nationalities—Italy, England, France, Holland, Germany, and Greece—who, during the construction of some more masterly production than usual, found it necessary to travel much from country to country.

The workmen dwelt, upon these occasions, in barracks erected for their convenience, near by the edifice in course of construction, and generally upon a high or rising ground. The master directed all. Ten men were always under the surveillance of a chief, and none but actual Freemasons participated in the work, and who, when their task was in that locality accomplished, sought their fortunes elsewhere. In nearly every instance they were ably seconded by the people of the neighborhood, who freely carried to the spot the necessary materials in the rough which were used in the construction of the edifice, and also by the nobles, who gave them money and provisions necessary for their support. All of the principal cities had their corporations of workmen, who, in addition to their rights as citizens, had their own fundamental and special laws, as corporate societies.

It was in the reigns of Philip Augustus (1180 to 1223), and of St. Louis (1226–1270), that were conceived the majority of these magnificent cathedrals that can be called by no lesser name than sublime sanctuaries of an all-powerful God; grand conceptions of Christian genius as poems written out in the faith and by the hand of those Mason philosophers. In the eyes of the vulgar, these monuments are but masses of stone regularly heaped together; their forms present to such nothing beyond the expression of an idea indicating a temple, a palace, or other form of edifice; but to the eye of the philosopher, this form had a mission more noble and elevated—that of transmitting to future generations the ideas, manners, and civilizing progress of the day and generation, and of faithfully reflecting the image and sentiments indicative of the then civil and religious knowledge of the peoples. Thus the varied genius which had conceived and executed the temples, as well of antiquity as the middle ages, gave expression to the spirit of the times, while each of these monuments seems animated with the soul of its author.

Without entering into the details of these gigantic conceptions, such as we find expressed in the cathedrals of Cologne, Strasburg, Paris, and many others, let us pause a moment to grasp their grandness as majestic edifices, and we will discover ourselves lost in surprise at the hardihood evinced by the builder in his harmonious blending of diametrically opposite elements. But, when we perceive that a principle—individual, original, and ingenious, disposing of even the smallest parts and descending to the arrangement of the most minute details—rules and imparts to the whole an unrivaled strength and beauty, our souls are ravished with unbounded admiration.

The principle of repetition and regular variation from a fundamental form that is observable in the interior of these monuments, has been uniformly followed in the formation of all the other members in the exterior of the edifice. By all the type of the whole is represented in the parts; and thus we find, in the compositions of these architect philosophers, a marvelous principle of development from a few fundamental forms, proceeding from the simple to the composite, such as Haüy, in his treatise on Mineralogy, demonstrates as the principle of crystallization, and such as Goethe, in his "Naturwissenschaft und Morphologie," discovered in plants, as the principle of vegetable metamorphosis.

The ties of union which existed among the membership of Freemasons, explains how and why there appears such a striking identity of expression among the various monuments erected by them in the different countries of Europe, and above all, among those erected during the thirteenth century. The masters of the work (architects) of all the religious edifices of the Latin Church had obtained their knowledge at the same central school; they were obedient to the laws of the same hierarchy; they were directed in their constructions by the same principles, and what was known to one immediately became the property of the whole body. They were obliged to conform to a general plan adopted for all religious edifices, and therefore were not permitted to follow their individual ideas of form, even if the result of their inspirations, as to details, would have been more beautiful in effect or harmonious in ornament. And it is thus that the cotemporary monuments of Alsatia, Poictiers, Normandy, Burgundy, and the province of Auvergne present, in point of decoration, a particular physiognomy, which is generally attributed to local circumstances, and to the nature of the materials, rather than to the facts we have indicated.

The enormous sacrifices that the population had made to erect churches, joined to the crying abuses of the clergy and the popes, had, in the fifteenth century, weakened the popular ardor, and dispelled the popular faith to so great a degree, that new church edifices ceased to be erected, and the work even on these in course of construction was stopped. Then the Reformation completed the destruction of papal power, and forever arrested the erection of vast religious edifices. No more enjoying the protection of the popes, the privileges of the Masonic corporations became of little value, and, having no more religious edifices to construct, the corporations dispersed; and, by the beginning of the sixteenth century, they found occupation but in the erection of civic edifices. Finally, in 1539, Francis I suspended all the corporations of workmen, and thus Freemasonry, in the ancient sense of the term, was extinguished in France.

Since that time, the architects have, in their individual capacity, undertaken and finished, by the aid of workmen engaged in the usual manner, such erections as was ordered or required. The tie of fraternity that heretofore had united master, workman, and apprentice was gradually dissolved, and the workmen formed themselves into separate societies which were imitated by other bodies of tradesmen. This was the origin of the trades-unions which were so prevalent in the seventeenth century, and which at the present day exists, in more or less influence, in every city of Europe and America.

The consequences of the dissolution of the Masonic societies were such that in a few years the art of building the pointed arch was lost, as also the art of constructing those voluted elevations which characterizes the great cathedrals of the middle ages. The Gothic style, prevalent from the thirteenth to the fifteenth centuries, gave place to the style called the Renaissance, as that of the sixteenth and seventeenth centuries; and it is to this last school that belonged the celebrated architects, Delorme and Bullant, who built, in 1577, the Tuilleries; Lescot and Goryon, who built, in 1571, the Louvre; Lemercier, who built the national palace of St. Rock; Blondel and Bullet, who built, between the years 1674 and 1686, the gates of St. Denis and St. Martin; Mansart, who built the castles of Versailles and the Invalides, between the years 1700 and 1725; and J. Soufflot, who built the Pantheon. These architects were not members of the Freemason corporations.

The Masonic corporations never presented in France that distinctive character that they had in England, and more particularly in Scotland; and consequently their influence upon civilization there has been much less than in the latter countries. The practice adopted by the corporations in those countries of affiliating, in the capacity of honorary members or patrons, some eminent men, had, however, in France, the same result; that is to say, the formation of lodges outside of the corporations, whose object was the propagation of the humanitarian doctrines of the institution; for it is certain that, since the Masonic corporations were dissolved in France, there have existed lodges of this character at Marseilles, Lyons, and Paris, similar to those which existed at Anvers, Gand, Brussels, Amsterdam, and Florence. All of these lodges are believed to have had entered into relations of correspondence with each other; but, since the middle of the seventeenth century, no trace of such relationship is discoverable.

The final transformation of this fraternity of artists and artisans to a moral institution, such as went into operation in London in 1717, and as it exists in our own day, took place in France in 1721.

ABRIDGMENT OF THE
HISTORY OF MODERN OR PHILOSOPHIC FREEMASONRY
IN FRANCE, SINCE ITS INTRODUCTION, IN 1721, TO THE ORGANIZATION OF THE GRAND ORIENT OF FRANCE, IN 1772.

In the abridgment of the General History of Freemasonry previously given, we have shown how this ancient fraternity of arts was transformed, in 1717, at London, from a corporation mechanical and philosophic to an institution purely philosophic, abandoning forever its material object—that is to say, the construction of buildings of every kind—but otherwise scrupulously conserving its traditional doctrines and symbols. The first cities of the continent of Europe to which Masonry, thus regenerated, was carried, were Dunkirk,[1] in 1721, and Mons.[2]

It was not until 1725 that the first lodge was founded at Paris, by Lord Derwentwater and two other Englishmen, under the title of "St. Thomas," and constituted by them, in the name of the Grand Lodge of London, on the 12th of June, 1726. Its members, to the number of five or six hundred, held their lodge at the house of the traitor Hurre, in the street of the St. Germain meat-market. A second lodge was established, by the same English gentle-

---

[1] The lodge at Dunkirk was named "Friendship and Brotherly Love," and was reconstituted by the Grand Lodge of France in 1756.

[2] The lodge at Mons was constituted by the Grand Lodge of England. on the 24th of June, 1721, under the title of "Perfect Union." Subsequently it was erected into an English Grand Lodge of the lower country of Austria, and has constituted or chartered lodges since 1730.

men, on the 7th of May, 1729, under the name of "Louis d'Argent." Its meetings were held at the house of the traitor Lebreton, who kept the same as an inn, under the name of *Louis d'Argent*. Upon the 11th of December of the same year a third lodge was constituted, under the title of "Arts Sainte Marguerite." Its meetings were held at the house of an Englishman named Gaustand. Finally, on the 29th of November, 1732, a fourth lodge was constituted, under the name of "Buci," the same being the name of the hotel wherein its meetings were held. This house was located in the *Rue de Buci*, and kept by the traitor Landelle; and the lodge "Buci," after having initiated the Duke of Aumont, took the name of "Lodge of Aumont."

Lord Derwentwater, who had, in 1725, received from the Grand Lodge of London plenary powers to constitute lodges of Freemasons in France, was, in 1735, invested by the same Grand Lodge with the functions of Provincial Grand Master; and when he subsequently quitted France to return to England, (where he perished upon the scaffold, a victim to his adherence to the fortunes of the Stuarts,) he transferred those plenary powers which he possessed to his friend Lord Harnwester, whom he authorized to represent him, during his absence, in the quality of Provincial Grand Master.

The four lodges then existing at Paris resolved to found a Provincial Grand Lodge of England, to which such lodges as should be organized in the future should address themselves directly, as the representative of the Grand Lodge of London. This resolution was put into execution after the death of Lord Derwentwater, and this Grand Lodge regularly and legally constituted itself, in 1736, under the presidency of Lord Harnwester.

Beside the lodges constituted by Lord Derwentwater, under the powers and after the forms of the Grand Lodge of London, there were constituted other lodges by a Scotchman named Ramsay, who styled himself Doctor and Baron of Ramsay, also a partisan of the Stuarts. This celebrated Mason filled for some time the office of Orator to the Provincial Grand Lodge of whose organization we have just spoken, and during that time he sought to introduce and to establish a system of Masonry called Scottish, and which he stated had been created at Edinburgh by a chapter of the lodge "Canongate Kilwinning," but which had a political object no less than to make Masonry subservient to the Stuart party, and an aid to the Catholic Church by the restoration of the Pretender to the throne of England. Not wishing to avow its true origin, the founders of this system attributed its creation to Godfrey de Bouillon, the last Grand Master of Knights Templar. This rite, styled Masonic, had not, however, at this time been accepted either in Scotland or England; but, introduced by Ramsay in France, it served as a basis for all the Masonic systems invented and propagated from that time in France, and exported into the different countries of the globe.

In 1737, Lord Harnwester, the second Provincial Grand Master of Freemasons in France, wishing to return to England, demanded, before his departure, to be replaced in his office by a Frenchman, and the Duke of Autin, a zealous Mason, succeeded him in the month of June, 1738.[1]

---

[1] The Duke of Autin was chosen from among the lords of the Court of Louis XV, as that one who had shown the greatest zeal for Freemasonry. He had, in fact, braved the anger of the King, who had interdicted the lords of his court from attending the meetings of the Freemasons; and he, above all, had shown, in accepting the position of Grand Master, an unusual degree of courage, as he knew that the King had threatened him with arrest and condemned him to the Bastile for so doing. The King, however, contrary to general expectation, took no steps to carry out his threat; but the police of the court continued the proscription against the lords in attendance who would not oppose the weight of their names and influence against the institution. After having, in 1737, condemned the inn-keeper Chapelot to pay a fine of one hundred francs, and to close his tavern, because he had allowed a meeting of Freemasons to take place therein, the year following they brutally dispersed a lodge which had met at the Hotel of Soissons. in the street

After the death of the third Grand Master, which took place in 1743, the Masters of the lodges, at a meeting that was held on the 11th of December of that year, named in his place the Duke of Bourbon, Count of Clermont, and from this time the organization over which he presided took the title of the "English Grand Lodge of France," always recognizing, as it did, the supremacy of the Grand Lodge of London.

From the period of its organization, this English Grand Lodge created difficulties for itself which became the principal cause, eventually, of spreading disorder in the Masonic ranks, by giving, according to the usage of the Grand Lodge of York at this time, and also of chapters established by its lodges, powers to permanent Masters,[1] of

---

of the Two Crowns, and imprisoned many of its members in the Fort L'Eveque. The nomination, in 1743, of the Duke of Bourbon to the Grand Mastership did not even weaken their pursuit of the brethren; for, on the 5th of June, 1744, they issued an order which prohibited the Freemasons to meet in the capacity of a lodge, and by virtue of this order they condemned, shortly afterward, the hotel-keeper Leroy to pay a fine of three thousand francs, for having allowed a lodge session to take place at his house.

[1] Alexander Thory, in his *Acta Latamorum*, affords us a very vivid picture of these disorders. On page 70 he says: "The Grand Lodge of France, which was established at Paris, in 1743, under the title of the 'English Grand Lodge of France,' declared itself the Grand Lodge of the Kingdom, and released from the authority of the Grand Lodge of London; but it conserved in the charters which it gave, in like manner with the Grand Lodge of York, the authority to dispose of personal titles to brethren under the style of permanent Masters, or Masters *ad vitam*, and thus empowered such Masters to govern their lodges continually, and according to their individual caprice. These Masters were permitted to dispose of charters to other Masters of lodges, at Paris and in the provinces, who, in their turn, constituted other bodies, which rivaled, in the expression of their authority, the Grand Lodge; and which bodies organized themselves, under the titles of chapters, colleges, counsels, and tribunals, at Paris and in many of the cities of France, wherein they established additional lodges and chapters. From these disorders there resulted such a complication of evil consequences, that it soon became

whom a great number had already been created by the first delegates of the Grand Lodge of York. The English Grand Lodge of France also organized local and federal administrations, under the name of Provincial Grand Lodges, which were presided over by the Masters of subordinate or operative lodges. These Provincial Grand Lodges, equally with the power that created them, had the right to create lodges and grant charters. From this general distribution of the creative power, it resulted that at this time there existed in Paris more than sixty lodges, and over one hundred in the provinces.

Independently of these Provincial Grand Lodges, there were also established in France other constituent bodies, some professing the rite introduced by Ramsay, and others analagous rites under other names. From among these we will mention the Chapter of Arras, constituted on the 15th of April, 1747, by the Prince Pretender, Charles Edward Stuart; and another, under the title of the "Mother Lodge of St. John of Scotland," organized at Marseilles, in 1751, by a Scotchman of the Pretender's suite. Subsequently there was established the Chapter of Clermont, founded at Paris, in 1754, in the college of the Jesuits at Clermont, the refuge of all the partisans of the Stuarts. For the purpose of hiding the true authorship of the system of the Templars, mentioned as having been propagated at Paris by Ramsay, this system was at this time called *Strict Observance*, and the chevalier Bonnville, also a partisan of the Stuarts, was announced as its founder, when he was nothing in connection with it but its propagator. Finally, in 1758, the chapter called "The Emperors of the East and the West," of which the members

---

impossible to ascertain with any readiness what body was really the head of Masonry in the kingdom. The history of Masonry at this period is much more obscure than at any other, as none of these Masters of lodges and chapters kept any minutes of their proceedings or operations—a formality that was often neglected by the Grand Lodge itself.

gave themselves the titles of *Sovereign Prince Masons, Substitutes General of the Royal Art,* and *Grand Wardens and Officers of the Sovereign Grand Lodge of St. John of Jerusalem*—a chapter created by the Jesuits of Lyons.[1]

---

[1] According to the work of Alexander Thory, it should be by this chapter that the Consistory of Princes of the Royal Secret was founded, in 1758, at Bordeaux, and by the members of which the thirty-five articles comprising the rules and regulations of the system styled a *Lodge of Perfection* were prepared. This system comprised the twenty-five degrees which, under the direction of its founders, had been for some short time practiced in France. This assertion of Thory is incorrect; for no proof can be found that a Consistory of Princes of the Royal Secret existed at Bordeaux before the year 1789. No authority of this name existed either in 1758 or in 1761 at Bordeaux; and consequently its membership could not have aided in the compilation of the famous thirty-five articles upon which the Supreme Council of the Scottish Rite for France founded its origin and its rights to the exclusive administration of this rite, and which it called "The Grand Constitutions." How, otherwise, is it reasonable to admit that the council, constituted and composed of the "Emperors of the East and West," created in 1758, at Paris, who are said to have established this Consistory of the Royal Secret in 1759, at Bordeaux, had called in the aid of their members to compile rules and regulations which already were compiled, and under which this very Consistory was organized? All that there is of truth in connection with these "Grand Constitutions" is, that they had no existence in any form prior to 1804, when the Supreme Council was organized by Grasse de Tilly; and they were, in all probability, fabricated by him as complementary to the history of the *Ancient and Accepted Scottish Rite,* invented at Charleston, South Carolina, and carried by him to France. Otherwise the facts which should have been advanced against the authenticity of these Regulations, which we unworthily dignify by calling them Constitutions, would have completely crushed them out of existence. Of these facts, one is that there was not a printed or manuscript copy of these regulations prior to 1804, and the manuscript that appeared at that date rendered it necessary for the reader to suppose that it had been prepared at Berlin; for the name of that city, where a name of production should have appeared, was indicated by the letter B, followed by the three points, (∴). Now, as this manuscript assured the .eader that the king, Frederick of Prussia, had ratified it in his capacity as supreme chief of the rite—an assertion completely and in every particular false, as we shall prove in our history of the Supreme Council—this initial

The establishment of all these independent bodies created gradually such confusion and such disorder that these councils, consistories, tribunals, and chapters knew not themselves which was the true constituting body in France.

Constantly disquieted by these "sovereign" chapters and tribunals, founded, as we have indicated, for the most part by Scotch gentlemen, partisans of the Stuarts, the English Grand Lodge of France resolved, in 1756, to detach itself from all connection with the Grand Lodge of London, and by thus declaring itself independent, hoped to be able to rule the different isolated bodies. In pursuance of this resolve, it declared itself independent of all foreign Masonic alliances, and took the title of "National Grand Lodge of France." Its hopes, however, were not realized, for it continued to be tormented by new creations of Masonic authority it could not impeach, and which, like all elder organizations, attributed to themselves the right of supremacy over it. The Grand Lodge, they asserted, in conformity with its character, delivered to it by Lord Derwentwater and confirmed by Lord Harnwester, conferred but the three degrees of symbolic Masonry, while these "chapters and lodges of perfection" believed themselves alone possessed of the right to confer what they styled the "higher" degrees. Following their lead, many councils and chapters were constituted by masters *ad vitam*, who obtained, and very often purchased, their privileges from others of their own rank; and these last affected equally a supremacy toward the Grand Lodge of France, by reason of their pretended knowledge and their right to confer "high" degrees—a right which, though usurped, the no less obtained general recognition. Repeatedly did

---

should have indicated Berlin, and not Bordeaux. Was it by design, or through ignorance, that subsequently the word was completed by writing it Bordeaux? We are unable to decide. But it is plain that Thory has believed and repeated the fable invented by the creators of the rite, to give it an importance that age alone would confer.

the Grand Lodge denounce the administration and the acts of these usurpers, as abusive of the trust reposed in those who enabled them to act in this manner; but this denunciation, as also the efforts put forth by the Grand Lodge from time to time, to demonstrate the inutility of these "higher" degrees, were all in vain; for a great many of the lodges, recognizing its authority and jurisdiction, had adopted those degrees, and conferred them in chapters organized by and under the control of those lodges.

The Grand Lodge, unhappily, was powerless to enforce the execution of its edicts against these illegitimate powers. The chapters continued to issue charters, and the Grand Lodge, in consequence of the carelessness of its Grand Master, the Count of Clermont, fell into anarchy. To relieve himself from the administration of its affairs, the Grand Master substituted a deputy named Baure, who, soon misbehaving himself, was replaced by a person even less worthy—a dancing-master named Lacorne. Impressed with the belief that the possession of all the degrees in vogue was necessary to add to his dignity, in the new position into which he was thrust, Lacorne had himself initiated into a lodge of perfection. He then convoked many assemblies, from which every member of the Grand Lodge abstained to attend. Irritated at this desertion, he assembled a number of lodge masters, whom he recruited in the taverns, to organize a Grand Lodge, and of these he chose his officers in accordance with his caprice. Finally, upon the representations which were made to the Count of Clermont on the subject, he revoked the appointment of Lacorne, and named in his stead the brother Chaillou de Joinville, as his substitute or Deputy General. From this state of things there arose a schism in the Grand Lodge, and it became divided into two parties who occupied themselves in tearing each other, each pretending to represent the constituent body of French Masonry and perform its functions. To aid the disorder, each party published constitutions,[1] and the masters of the lodges, composing a portion of the party of Lacorne, and equally desirous of gain, sold the right of holding lodges, and thus the mysteries and the constitutions becoming an object of traffic, outside of the lodges Masonry fell into contempt, while inside anarchy reigned supreme.

---

[1] We believe it proper here to give in full one of these constitutions, which was delivered, in 1761, to Stephen Morin, an Israelite, both because that it is at once a document authentic and curious, as well as that it served, some forty years afterward, as the foundation of the "Ancient and Accepted Scottish Rite of Thirty-three Degrees," created at Charleston, South Carolina, by five other Jews, and introduced into France, in 1804, by the establishment of the Supreme Council for France, situated at Paris, and which is to-day the rival authority of the Grand Orient of France. This constitution reads as follows:

"To the glory of the Grand Architect of the Universe, etc. Under the good pleasure of his serene highness, the very illustrious brother, Louis of Bourbon, Count of Clermont, prince of the blood, Grand Master and protector of all the lodges at the Orient, etc., the 27th of August, 1761. *Lux e tenebris, unitas, concordia fratrum.* We, the undersigned, Substitutes General of the Royal Art, Grand Wardens of the Grand and Sovereign Lodge, President of the Grand Council, a request to us made by the brother Lacorne, substitute of the T. M. G. M., read at a meeting: That our dear brother Stephen Morin, grand elect, perfect and ancient sublime Master of all the orders of the Masonry of Perfection, member of the Royal Lodge of the Trinity, etc., having, upon his departure for America, desired the power to travel regularly, etc.; that it has pleased the Supreme Grand Council and Grand Lodge to accord to him letters patent for constitutions, etc. For these causes, etc., are given plenary and entire powers to the said brother to form and to establish a lodge for to receive and to multiply the royal art of the Freemasons in all the degrees perfect and sublime, etc.; to regulate and to govern all the members who may compose the said lodge which he may establish in the four quarter parts of the world whither he shall arrive or he may reside, under the title of 'Lodge of St. John,' and surnamed 'Perfect Harmony;' giving him power to choose such officers to aid him in the government of his lodge as he shall judge suitable; deputing him, in the quality of our Grand Inspector in all parts of the new world, for to reform the observance of our laws in general; constituting him our Grand Master Inspector; giving him full and entire power to create inspectors in all places where the sublime degrees shall not be established.

After remaining in this condition for some time, a reconciliation took place between the two parties composing the Grand Lodge, and a union was ratified on the 24th of June, 1762. But the old masters, who made no portion of the Lacorne faction, and who were persons belonging some to the nobility of the kingdom, some to the bar, and some to the most distinguished of the people, seeing themselve. confounded with mechanics and men of no education, as also men infamous and utterly unworthy of a place in the Grand Lodge, took exceptions constantly to such men being members of that body; and hence constant dissensions arose, and which were envenomed by the pretensions, growing more and more intolerable, set up by the other constituent bodies. Finally, worn out with the inces-

"In witness of which we have delivered these presents, signed by the Substitute General of the Order, Grand Commander of the Black and White Eagle, Sovereign Sublime Prince of the Royal Secret, and Chief of the eminent Degree of the Royal Art, and by our grand inspectors, sublime officers of the Grand Council and of the Grand Lodge established in this capital, and have sealed them with the great seal of his serene highness, our illustrious Grand Master, and with that of our Grand Lodge and Sovereign Grand Council at the Grand East of Paris, the day and year, etc.

[Signed] "CHAILLOU DE JOINVILLE,

"Substitute General of the Order, Worshipful Master of the first Lodge in France, called 'St. Thomas,' Chief of the eminent Degrees, Commandant and Sublime Prince of the Royal Secret. -

"PRINCE DE ROHAN,
"Member of the Grand Lodge 'Intelligence,' Prince Mason.

"LACORNE,
"Prince of Masonry, Substitute of the Grand Master.

"SAVALETTE, DE BUCKOLY, TAUPIN, and

"BREST DE LA CHAUSSEE,
"Grand Knights and Prince Masons.

"DE CHOISEUL,
"Count, Grand Knight, Prince Mason, and Orator.

"BOUCHER DE LENONCOURT,
"Grand Knight and Prince Mason, by Order of the Grand Lodge; and

"DAUBANTIN,
"Grand Knight and Prince Mason, Grand Secretary of the Grand Lodge and of the Sublime Council of Perfect Masons in France, etc."

sant complaints which were addressed to it by a great number of the lodges organized by councils, colleges, and tribunals of the "high" degrees, the Grand Lodge resolved to choke all these pretensions, and on the 14th of August, 1766, decided to publish a decree by which was revoked all the capitulary constitutions, and all the symbolic lodges prohibited from recognizing the authority which was arrogated to themselves by these councils and chapters.[1] A certain number of the members of the Grand Lodge of the old Lacorne party, infamous men, and who were, at the same time, members of the chapters, protested against this decree and compromised the authority of the Grand Lodge. Consequently, in the re-election of the officers of the lodges which took place in 1766, in accordance with the regulations, those members who belonged to the Lacorne faction were not renominated. From that sprang protestations on their part and defamatory writings against the Grand Lodge and against the acts of its officers, until, finally, it became incumbent upon the Grand Lodge to expel these factious members, and publish them as deprived of all their Masonic rights.

The brethren thus expelled from the Grand Lodge responded to its decision by new libels, personalities, and other injuries, and even went so far, at the feast of St. John, 1767, as to make it necessary for the government to interfere and forbid, after that day, the meetings of the Grand Lodge.

This rigorous measure, which struck as well at the innocent as the guilty, paralyzed all the efforts of the Grand

---

[1] Though the Grand Lodge of France, in 1756, declared itself independent of the Grand Lodge of London, which had, through its agent, Lord Derwentwater, constituted it, it nevertheless subsequently sought to renew its amicable relations with the latter, and in 1767 proposed and concluded an agreement, by the terms of which each of these constituent Masonic bodies agreed to respect the rights of the other, and constitute no Masonic organization within each other's jurisdiction.

Lodge membership. The expelled brethren who had been the cause of the interdiction, and who were always under the direction of Lacorne, profiting by the dispersion of a great many members of the Grand Lodge, held secret meetings and constituted operative lodges, to which they delivered constitutions ante-dated to a time previous to the division in the Grand Lodge. Upon the other hand, the legal party of the Grand Lodge, represented by the brother Chaillou de Joinville, Substitute General of the Grand Master, the Count of Clermont, also delivered constitutions to organize working lodges in the provinces, which documents were also ante-dated, and of which no less than thirty-seven of these constitutions, so delivered by the latter party during the period of the interdiction, were subsequently annulled.

The Lacorne party eventually conceived the plan of overthrowing the Grand Lodge and replacing it by a new power, in order to re-establish in their Masonic rights all the honorable members who should once more compose such authority; and they awaited but a favorable occasion to put this design into execution. Some approaches made to the Lieutenant-General of Police were not attended with success; and the state of interdiction was prolonged until the death of the Count of Clermont, which took place in 1771. This event raised the courage of the factions, who had not ceased to intrigue; and, in the hope of reassuming power, they addressed the Duke of Luxembourg, falsely announcing that they had formed the nucleus of the ancient Grand Lodge of France, interdicted since 1767, and desired to offer the Grand Mastership to the Duke of Chartres. The proposition was agreed to, and the Duke of Chartres, nephew of the Count of Clermont,[1] designated the Duke of Luxembourg for his substitute. The faction who had thus obtained so important a success convoked

---

[1] Since Duke of Orleans, Philip Equality.

a general assembly of the Masters of all the lodges of Paris, and even invited the members of the Grand Lodge who had expelled them. At this assembly they submitted the acceptance of the Grand Mastership, signed by the Duke of Chartres, and offered to present this document to the Grand Lodge, provided that it would revoke its decree of expulsion made against them. The unfavorable circumstances in which the Grand Lodge found itself at this time, joined to the advantageous considerations which would result to it by its acceptance of the Duke of Chartres as its Grand Master, determined the members to accept the conditions which were proposed; and they decided that a report should be submitted to the Grand Lodge, upon the demand for a revocation of the decrees rendered against the expelled brethren, in order that these decrees should be revoked in due form. This being done, at the feast of St. John, in the year **1771**, the Duke of Chartres was nominated for the Grand Mastership, and the Grand Lodge thereupon proceeded to annul all the charters, or constitutions, delivered during the suspension of its privileges, in the name of the Grand Lodge of France. A commission, composed of eight members, was thereupon appointed to elaborate a project of reorganization of the Masonic fraternity. There were also named twenty-two Provincial Grand Inspectors, with the mission to visit all the lodges in the kingdom and direct the administration of the rules and regulations, etc.

The party who had obtained the revocation of the decrees of expulsion had, in the reorganization of the Grand Lodge, exerted their influence to obtain the admission of their partisans; and the success which had attended their first operation favored the accomplishment of the latter designs. Therefore, in the interval, this party, reinforced by all the councils and chapters of the Scottish Rite, who had reserved to themselves the privilege of avenging the injury they had sustained from the decrees directed against them by the Grand Lodge, resolved to equally offer to the Duke of Chartres the honorable position of Grand Master of all the lodges, chapters, and councils of the Scottish Rite in France. This honor the Duke accepted.[1]

In submitting this request to the Duke of Chartres, they made him believe that he had already attained the position, by his nomination in 1771, to the Grand Mastership of the Grand Lodge of France. The Duke knew nothing of Masonic forms, and never supposed that any nomination of this kind should be made in an assembly of the Grand Lodge, an authority that had repudiated and proscribed the "high" degrees. He, therefore, accepted the office which to him was offered, and signed the article of acceptance presented to him by the Duke of Luxembourg, on the 5th of April, 1772. The latter, as substitute of the Duke of Chartres, wished to concentrate in his own hands the control of all the Masonic bodies in the kingdom, as, by the parties who had proposed the matter, he had been advised; but he did not perceive that he had made

---

[1] We here give the text of this acceptance, because this document is not without historic interest:

"The year of the great Light, 1772, third day of the moon John, 5th day of the 2d month of the Masonic year 5772, and from the birth of the Messiah the 5th day of April, 1772, in virtue of the proclamation made in Grand Lodge assembled the 24th day of the 4th month of the Masonic year 5771, of the very high, very powerful, and very excellent prince, his most serene highness Louis Phillipe Joseph d'Orleans, Duke of Chartres, prince of the blood, for Grand Master of all the regular lodges of France; and of that of the Sovereign Council of the Emperors of the East and West, sublime mother lodge of the Scottish (rite), of the 26th day of the moon Elul, 5771, for sovereign Grand Master of all the Scottish councils, chapters, and lodges of the great globe of France, offices which his said most serene highness has been pleased to accept for the love of the royal art, and in order to concentrate all the Masonic labors under one only authority.

"In guarantee of which, his said most serene highness has signed this minute of the transaction of acceptance.

[Signed]   "LOUIS PHILIPPE JOSEPH D'ORLEANS."

himself, in this respect, the instrument of but a faction. Unhappily having once lent himself to such a scheme, all the remonstrances addressed to him by the enlightened and respectable portion of the Grand Lodge, who pointed out to him the awkwardness of his position, and his stultification of theirs, were not sufficient to induce him to resign he powers thus accorded to him, and his adhesion to which ultimately caused the extinction of the Grand Lodge of France, and the organization of the Grand Orient, whose history we propose to give an another volume.

ABRIDGMENT OF THE

HISTORY OF MODERN OR PHILOSOPHIC FREEMASONRY

IN ENGLAND, DENMARK, SWEDEN, RUSSIA, POLAND, GERMANY, HOLLAND, BELGIUM, SWITZERLAND, ITALY, AND PORTUGAL, FROM ITS ORGANIZATION IN THOSE COUNTRIES TO THE PRESENT DAY.

England.

We have seen, at the conclusion of our summary of the origin and general history of Freemasonry, in what manner the transformation of the corporation of Freemasons from an operative to a philosophic institution took place in England, in the year 1717, and under what circumstances the Grand Lodge of London, in constituting itself, put into execution the decision made, in 1703, by the Lodge of St. Paul.

The new Grand Lodge directed George Payne, who had been elected its Grand Master, to collect all the documents, manuscripts, charters, rituals, etc., relating to the ancient usages of the fraternity, for the purpose of connecting them with the registers and Anglo-Saxon deeds written in the Gothic and Latin languages, and of the whole to form a body of laws and doctrines, and to publish so much of the same as might be judged proper and necessary.[1]

---

[1] Some members of the Lodge of St. Paul, alarmed at the prospective publicity of their archives, believed it to be their duty, imposed upon them by the oath which they had taken, to publish nothing which par-

After the careful examination of all these deeds, and a report made of their subjects by a commission composed of fourteen brethren, chosen from the most erudite Masons of London, the Grand Lodge directed the brother Anderson, a doctor of philosophy and eminent minister of the Presbyterian Church at London, to compile from these documents a constitution, to be preceded by a history of the corporation, which would in the future serve us as a guide to modern Freemasonry.

Brother Anderson, having acquitted himself of the task, in 1722 submitted his work to the commission, who approved it, and caused it to be sanctioned by the Grand Lodge on the 25th March, 1723. This constitution is entitled, "The Book of Constitutions for Freemasons, containing the History, Charges, and Regulations, etc., of that Most Ancient and Right Worshipful Fraternity, for the use of the Lodges."

This constitution is based upon the charter of York, which, of all others, has served as a guide for all those which have been established since A. D. 926. Into this constitution were carried otherwise the changes and the developments which were rendered indispensable by the new object of the society, and properly above all was caused to predominate the supremacy of the Grand Lodge of London. This last tendency, so much to be, in this our own day, deprecated, but proves that its authors were not penetrated by the true spirit of the Charter of York.

This collection of laws, published for the first time in 1723,[1] has been printed many times, and for the last time

---

took of the character of corporate information, delivered the greater part f the documents in the possession of their lodge to the flames, thus causing, by their exaggerated scruples, an irreparable loss to the Masonic historian.

[1] Translations of this work were made and published in Germany in the years 1741, '43, '44, '62, '83, and 1805. In London it was reprinted in 1756, '57, and '75.

by the Grand Lodge of England, in 1855. Beginning with the year 1723, the organization of the new Masonry was seated upon a solid foundation, and its prosperity continued to increase. By virtue of this constitution, the new Grand Lodge of England placed itself in legitimate and sole authority over the entire Masonic fraternity, and settled from that time all contradictions on the part of English lodges constituted previous to that date. This constitution in fact attainted the ancient liberties of Freemasons, and in particular prohibited the formation of any lodges which should not receive the confirmation of the Grand Lodge of London. In this manner protests against this new authority were excited in the Grand Lodges of York and Edinburgh.

The activity displayed by the Grand Lodge of London, and the great number of operative lodges that it constituted, stimulated the zeal of the Masons of Ireland and Scotland, who, up to this time, had not assembled but at distant and irregular periods. Soon Masonic temples opened on all sides in the two kingdoms, and the initiations were multiplied in great number, which fact resulted in the convocation of a general assembly of the Masons of Ireland by the lodges of Dublin, with the object of organizing Freemasonry upon the same basis as sustained the lodge of London. A central power was constituted at this assembly, which took place in 1729, under the title of the Grand Lodge of Ireland, and the Viscount Kingston was elected Grand Master.

The Grand Lodge of York, jealous of the prosperity of the Grand Lodge of London, and pretending that it was the most ancient and legitimate power, and solely endowed with the right to direct Freemasonry, contested the supremacy claimed by the latter, and thereby caused for a time some considerable embarrassment; but it could not arrest the progress of that body, nor interrupt its success, and soon found itself under the necessity of revising its laws and conforming its regulations to the object of the modern Freemasonry, as had already been done by its successful rival, the Grand Lodge of London.

The ancient Grand Lodge of Scotland, at Edinburgh, considering the prosperity and aggrandizement of the new English lodges as the consequence of their adoption of new regulations and the election of new Grand Masters, desired to introduce these changes into its system; but the hereditary trust of patron, of which James I had conceded the honor to the family of Roslin, in 1430, was an obstacle to this innovation. However, the Baron Sinclair of Roslin, then Grand Master under this concession, acceded to the general wish expressed for him to renounce this authority, and the four oldest lodges of Edinburgh convoked, on the 24th of November, 1736, all the other lodges and all the Masons of Scotland in a general assembly, with the object of organizing a new Masonic power. After reading the act of renunciation of the Baron Sinclair of Roslin to the dignity of hereditary Grand Master, as also to all the privileges thereto appertaining, the assembly, composed of the representatives of thirty-two lodges, constituted itself the "Grand Lodge of St. John of Scotland," and named the Baron Sinclair of Roslin its first Grand Master for 1737. Some of the ancient lodges, that of Kilwinning among others, had conserved the two political degrees—Templar and Scottish Master—and by so doing introduced troubles which had agitated England from 1655 to 1670, and which degrees were not conferred at this time but upon brethren adjudged to be worthy of being initiated into the political designs favorable to the Stuarts, and they had been maintained subsequently, by a decision of King Charles II, from the time of the general assembly of Masons at York, in 1663. It was the chapter named Canongate Kilwinning, composed of partisans of the Stuarts, who propagated, between the years 1728 and 1740, these anti-masonic degrees, created with a political object, and delivered to their partisans—among whom was the Doctor Baron Ramsay, and other emissaries—by diplomas, authorizing them to confer those degrees wherever they found suitable persons to receive them. It is in this manner those degrees became to be known as the Scottish Rite. Ramsay, not finding the collection extensive enough, added to it, and others who succeeded him continued so profitable an occupation, until the Scottish Rite comprised in France lodges, chapters, and councils, the membership of which being composed mainly of intriguing politicians.

After the organization of the Grand Lodge of Scotland, the thirty-two lodges of which it was constituted ranked by number in the order of their claims to age, and the lodge "Mary's Chapel," exhibiting an act in due form, which carried its origin to the year 1598, was placed at the head of the list of operative lodges, and took the rank of No. 1. The lodge "Canongate Kilwinning" had claimed this first place, stating that its origin went back as far as the year 1128—a circumstance very generally admitted in the country; but this lodge, having lost its papers during a sleep of a century and a half, could not now produce them, and consequently was refused the preference; and this refusal caused this lodge to desire no connection with the new Grand Lodge, but, on the contrary, to set itself up as an independent constituent power, which it did, at Edinburgh, in 1744, at first under the name of the "Mother Lodge of Kilwinning," and subsequently as the "Royal Grand Lodge and Chapter of the Order of Herodim of Kilwinning," abandoning the administration of the three symbolic degrees to the Grand Lodge of Scotland, and reserving to itself the right to confer the two high degrees (Templar and Scottish Master) that it already possessed, and also those which by this time were in use, the invention of Ramsay and others, in France. Not meeting with any success at home in its assumption of the right to propagate its high degrees, this lodge created, through its emissaries upon the continent, a number of chapters, and thus returned to France the degrees which it had imported, by establishing at Rouen, on the 1st May, 1786, in the lodge of "Ardent Amitie," a Grand Chapter of Herodim, to propagate, as a provincial grand lodge, this false Masonry.

Such is the origin of the Rite of Herodim of Kilwinning, about which, as an important and valuable adjunct to Freemasonry, so much noise has been made. Finally, after having, during half a century, been instrumental in producing as much disorder as it could in the Masonic ranks at home and abroad, this lodge of "Canongate Kilwinning" quietly proposed a union with the Grand Lodge of Scotland, and in the year 1807 was placed on the list of the operative lodges of Scotland, under the jurisdiction of the Grand Lodge of Scotland, as "Canongate Kilwinning, No. 2."

The three Grand Lodges of Great Britain, thus constituted, propagated the new Freemasonry upon every portion of the globe, so that, in 1750, we find it extended into nearly every civilized country; but its humanitarian doctrines, like the dogma of "Liberty, Equality, Fraternity," which it exhibited, frightened the kings and the clergy, who sought to arrest its progress by issuing decrees and edicts against it. In Russia, in 1731, in Holland, in 1735, in Paris, in 1737, 1738, 1744, and 1745, the meetings of lodges of Freemasons were interdicted by the government; while at Rome and in Florence its members were arrested and persecuted, and in Sweden, Hamburg, and Geneva they were prohibited from meeting or assembling themselves in the capacity of lodges. The Holy Inquisition threw Freemasons into prison, burnt; by the hand of the public executioner, all books which contained Masonic regulations, history, or doctrines; condemned at Malta to perpetual exile, in 1740, a number of knights who had organized a lodge on that island; in Portugal it exercised against them cruelties of various kinds, and condemned them to the galleys; while in Vienna and Marseilles, as also in Switzerland, in the canton of Berne, the iron hand of that "Holy" institution was felt in 1743. In 1748, at Constantinople, the sultan endeavored to destroy the Masonic society. In the states of the Church, the King of Naples prohibited Masonry, and Ferdinand VII, King of Spain, issued an edict that prohibited the assembly of Freemasons within his kingdom, under penalty of death. In 1751, Pope Benedict XIV renewed the bull of excommunication promulgated against the Fraternity by Clement XII, while the threat of death menaced all who should be known to attend Masonic meetings.

But all these exhibitions of the rage of kings, princes, and potentates were ineffectual to stop the onward course of Freemasonry, which continued to be propagated upon all the surface of the earth with a rapidity that no power could arrest. Braving the bull of Benedict XIV, Freemasonry is openly practiced in Tuscany, at Naples, and in many other parts of the Italian peninsula. At Rome even the partisans of the Stuarts founded some lodges, which they took but feeble pains to hide from the authorities.[1]

The activity of the three Grand Lodges of Great Britain, and, above all, of that of London, was not confined to the establishment of lodges in Europe between the years 1727 and 1740; they had already transplanted Masonry to Bengal, to Bombay, the Cape of Good Hope, New South Wales, New Zealand, and Java, and as early as 1721, lodges of Masons were established in Canada. Before 1740 Masonry existed in the principal colonies of

---

[1] It may well be believed that the reason for the blindness which pressed upon the vision of the authorities at Rome, in connection with these lodges, was, that the Jesuits, whose cause those lodges served, did not wish to see.

the now United States of America, such as Massachusetts, Georgia, South Carolina, and New York. In those colonies the lodges had created Grand Lodges independent of the Grand Lodges of England, of whom they had in the beginning received their authority. Massachusetts had a Grand Lodge in 1777, Vermont in 1774, Virginia and North Carolina in 1778, Maryland in 1783, Pennsylvania, Georgia, and New Jersey in 1786, and New York in 1787.

The Lodge of London, notwithstanding its astonishing prosperity, was not permitted to enjoy that prosperity without great internal struggles, caused first by the Grand Lodge of York, and subsequently by the schism of a great many brethren, who, adhering to the claims of the latter, went out from the former and took the name of "Ancient Masons," in contradistinction to the membership of the Grand Lodge of London, who remained true to their engagements, and whom this schismatic party styled "Modern Masons." These schismatic lodges, composed in great part of Irish Masons—who accused the Grand Lodge of altering the rituals and introducing innovations—and of Masons who had been expelled, in 1751, constituted a rival power to the Grand Lodge, under the title of "The Grand Lodge of Ancient Masons of England." Notwithstanding its inferiority, and the few lodges which it represented or was enabled to establish, this schismatic party, in 1772, requested the Duke of Athol, who had already filled that office in the Grand Lodge of Scotland, to become its Grand Master, a request with which he complied.

To give itself importance, and to influence to its ranks the nobility, this schismatic party added to the degrees with which it had started some of the high degrees created in France by the partisans of the Stuarts, and which they imported into England about the year 1760, and combined them with the symbolic degrees into a rite of seven degrees, the highest of which they called the Royal Arch.[1] This Grand Lodge of self-styled Ancient Masons transplanted its rite into the lodges which it constituted in America, and there produced the same disorders and the same schisms among the Fraternity that the "high" degrees had already provoked in all the states of Europe.[2]

---

[1] This degree is founded entirely upon the biblical legend of the Jewish ark of the covenant; but, in England, they give it another signification, and call it the "Holy Arch."

[2] In this statement I beg leave to correct brother Rebold. The only disorders or schisms created by "Lawrence Dermott's Grand Lodge"—by which name the schismatic organization styled "Ancient Masons" is known, at this time, in America—were at an early stage checked in their growth by the organization of what is also known as the "American System of Freemasonry," comprising a rite of twelve degrees, in which, while the different State Grand Lodges have exclusive jurisdiction over the three degrees of symbolic Masonry, the operative Royal Arch Chapters, Councils, and Encampments, (or, as more lately styled, Commanderies), have in charge the conference of the other degrees known as Capitular, Cryptic, and Christian Masonry; and they, in their turn, are subject to State organizations, and the latter to a general organization for each, styled, respectively, the "General Grand Chapter of Royal Arch Masons for the United States," organized in 1808, and the "General Grand Encampment of Knights Templar for the United States," organized in 1816. In this manner the different degrees are utilized and kept apart, every Master Mason being allowed to "take" as many or as few of them as he may deem necessary for his enlightenment.

While the object of these higher degrees in Europe, according to our author, was entirely of a political character, in this country no such character, or even tendency, has ever been attributed to them. The anti-masonic excitement, which prevailed in this country from 1826 to 1836, or thereabouts, had no effective origin within a Masonic body of any rite. William Morgan, it is true, in the former year, took umbrage at being refused membership in a Royal Arch Chapter about to be organized in the town of Batavia, his residence, in the State of New York and thereupon resurrected an old copy of "Jachin and Boaz," published in London in 1750, and republished shortly afterward in the then colony of New York. With this book, and what he knew of Masonic rituals, he made an "Exposition of Freemasonry;" and, by the aid of an evil-disposed person named Miller, published the same. His subsequent

This unhappy division in the bosom of English Masonry, commenced in 1736, was continued for a long time, by the Grand Lodges of Ireland and Scotland recognizing the schismatic "Grand Lodge of Ancient Masons," to which they in this manner gave a character that it did not merit, but which continued until the year 1813, when at his time it ceased, by the schismatic Grand Lodge, which then had as its Grand Master the Duke of Kent, and the Grand Lodge of London, styled by these schismatics "Modern Masons," and which had as its Grand Master his brother, the Duke of Sussex, uniting under the title of the "United Grand Lodges of England." In this union the ancient laws, as well written as traditional, were taken as the basis, and the spirit that influenced the organization of 1717 was recognized, and it was then and there announced and proclaimed that the ancient and true Freemasonry was composed of but three degrees, viz: *Apprentice*, *Fellow-craft*, and *Master Mason*. Unhappily, however, the legitimate Grand Lodge conceded to the party self-styled "Ancient Masons," who necessarily had to abandon their rite of seven degrees, a division of the degree of *Master Mason* practiced by this party, and taught as a supplementary portion of this degree, under the name

---

sudden disappearance from the town of his residence was made use of by what was then in this country a lesser political party, for the purpose of increasing its strength and numbers, by raising a cry against the Freemasons, and branding them as a secret society which stopped not even at the sacrifice of human life to accomplish its purposes. The cry was successful; the life of Morgan was asserted to have been taken by the Freemasons, and, in the summer of 1828, the body of a drowned man having been found in the neighborhood of Morgan's disappearance, it made, in the language of one of the leaders of the anti-masonic party ' a good enough Morgan until after the [then pending presidential] election." For some years after this the Fraternity remained in comparatively a dormant condition; but, during the last twenty-five years, its progress has been as rapid and its ranks as united as its most ardent admirers could desire.—TRANSLATOR

of *Royal Arch*. This concession, which the schismatic party exacted as a *sine qua non* of their union with the legitimate Grand Lodge and surrender of their rights to that body, was an act of feebleness, on the part of the Grand Lodge of London, which has destroyed, in a great degree; the unity and the basis of true Masonry, as it had been practiced by that body, up to that time, with a laudable firmness.

If English Freemasonry has remained, for a long time, in a consumptive condition, and has not, as it did for the first century of its existence, continued to extend its civilizing and progressive character, it has practiced always in a generous manner one of the essential dogmas of the institution; viz., solidarity. Among the numerous beneficent establishments created by it, we may particularly mention three which are due to the efforts of the Grand Lodge of London.

1. The Royal School of Freemasons for girls, of which the capital fund, in March, 1863, amounted to about $145,000.

2. The Royal Masonic Institute for the sons of indigent Freemasons, which possessed, at the same date, a capital fund of over $100,000.

3. The Royal Beneficiary Institution for aged Freemasons and their widows, of which the capital was, at the same date, about $75,000 for the men's department, and $35,000 for that of the women.

After having recorded the most important events in the history of English Freemasonry, we will now briefly indicate the composition of the three Grand Lodges and their importance as Masonic powers.

The Grand Lodge of England is composed of a Grand Master and his deputy, of all the Past Grand Masters and Provincial Grand Masters, of all the officers of the Grand Lodge, and of all the Past and Acting Worshipful Masters. In it resides the legislative and judiciary power for jurisdiction of England and the British colonies. A general committee, composed of twenty-four masters of lodges, of a first Professor (*Expert*), of the Grand Master and his representative, exercise the administrative and executive power. The decisions are made by a majority of votes. All the offices, even that of Grand Master, are submitted to an annual election. The Grand Lodge holds quarterly communications upon the first Wednesday of the months of March, May, September, and December; in the latter, the election for Grand Master takes place. Charles, Earl of Zetland, who has filled the office of Grand Master since 1850, has been re-elected for the thirteenth time since his first nomination. The Earl Grey and Ripon is the Deputy Grand Master.

Under the jurisdiction of the Grand Lodge of London there are sixty-three Provincial Grand Lodges, of which forty-two are in the counties of England, and twenty-one are elsewhere in British possessions. Under these there are nine hundred and eighty-nine operative lodges, who report themselves in the manner following: Four hundred and ninety-one in the counties, one hundred and fifty-four in London, one hundred and forty-three in America, twenty in Africa, eighty-seven in Asia, eighty-three in Oceanica, and fourteen in other countries. It possesses a Grand Chapter of Royal Arch Masons—a degree which, as we have stated, comprehends the second part of the degree of Master Mason, but which forms really a fourth degree, having its own officers and its special meetings. This Grand Chapter directs two hundred and eighty-seven operative chapters in England and sixty-one in the British possessions. No advantage or privilege is accorded to its members in the ordinary or extraordinary meetings of the Grand Lodge.

Independently of the Grand Chapter, there also exists at London, but having no connection with the Grand Lodge, a Grand Conclave of "High Knights Templar," at the head of which presides the brother F. W. Stuart. Neither this authority nor any other of the kind are recognized by the Grand Lodge; they are the remains of the systems which were imported from France to England by the partisans of the Stuarts, and by whom these poisonous germs have been introduced into the body of English Masonry.

The Grand Lodge of Scotland, sitting at Edinburgh, which has for its Grand Master the Duke of Athol,[1] counts under its jurisdiction thirty-eight Provincial Grand Lodges, and two hundred and ninety-seven operative lodges in Scotland and elsewhere in British possessions. Like the Grand Lodge of London, it tolerates the Royal Arch Chapters, which have been engrafted upon a great number of its lodges from the time that the schismatic Grand Lodge at London propagated its rite of the Royal Arch, and for the direction of which there was established, in 1817, a Supreme Grand Chapter; but, like the Grand Lodge of London, it does not accord to the members of these chapters the least privilege; for, like the lodges which constitute it, the Grand Lodge does not practice, confer, or recognize but the three symbolic degrees.

The Grand Lodge of Ireland, held at Dublin, of which the Duke of Leinster is the Grand Master, has under its jurisdiction ten Provincial Grand Lodges, with three hundred and seven operative lodges in Ireland and other countries outside of Great Britain. Independently of the Grand Lodge of Ireland, which confers, in like manner with the other Grand Lodges, none but the symbolic degrees, there is established, at Dublin, a Supreme Council of Rites, founded in 1836, which confers all the "high" degrees of such rites, a Grand Royal Arch Chapter, which is under the direction of the same Grand Master, and constitutes, like those of England and Scotland, operative

---

[1] George Augustus Frederick John, Duke of Athol, died at Blair Castle, his residence, on the 16th of January, 1864.

chapters of the Royal Arch degree;[1] also a Grand Conclave of Knights Templar; but these three authorities have no connection with the Grand Lodge of Ireland.

The three Grand Lodges of Great Britain, consequently, control one hundred and nine Provincial Grand Lodges, with one thousand five hundred and ninety-seven operative lodges under their jurisdiction, which extend their connections to every part of the globe.

In the connection of its moral effects and civilizing influence, English Freemasonry—we say it with sorrow—has made but slight advances in the last half century; while, as we have seen, it was once the active pioneer every-where. It exercised by its introduction into France an immense influence upon the principles of 1789, and started the development of liberal ideas throughout the whole of Europe; while in Oceanica, Hindostan, and China its principles have modified the religious beliefs of the sectaries of Brahma, of the Persians and the Mussulmans, of whom are composed the majority of the lodges founded in those countries; yet to-day the Grand Lodge of England, like its sisters, those of Scotland and Ireland, seems satisfied to repose under its glories of the past and rest upon its laurels

Denmark.

FREEMASONRY was introduced into the capital of this kingdom, in 1783, by the Baron of Munich, Secretary of the Ambassador of Russia, who organized the first opera-

---

[1] Besides these three grand colleges, all conferring a species of high degrees, there is in Dublin, to complete the hierarchy, a Supreme Council of the Scotch Rite of Thirty-three Degrees, established in 1808, of which the Duke of Leinster is also nominally the Grand Master. A similar institution is established at Edinburgh, founded in 1846, while a third is situated at London since 1845. At the head of the last are the brethren H. B. Leison, Esq., and Colonel Vernon; but these authorities, not being recognized as Masonic, are of very little importance and merely enjoy a vegetating existence.

tive lodge, under the name of "St. Martins Lodge." Shortly afterward several others were established, and, in 1749, the Grand Lodge of London there constituted a Provincial Grand Lodge, of which Count Damekiold Laurvig was named Grand Master, and who, in 1780, erected the same into a Grand Lodge of Denmark. The simplicity of English Masonry had to give way here, as every-where else, to the system of high degrees, which had invaded all Europe and blinded the good sense of the brethren. The system of Strict Observance, invented, as we have seen, by the Jesuits in France, to forward the interests of the Stuart party, was introduced by the Baron of Bulow at Copenhagen, who organized there a prefectship, or commandery, having for Grand Master the Duke Ferdinand of Brunswick. After the Congress of Wilhelmsbad, in 1782, the Grand Lodge of Denmark abandoned the rite of "Strict Observance," or Templar system; but, in returning to the English system, besides the three degrees of symbolic Masonry, she preserved of the abandoned rite two degrees, those of Scottish and Past Master. Immediately after this reformation, lodges were established in all the cities of any importance in the kingdom, and even, in 1785, extended to the Danish colonies, in the archipelago of the Antilles, the islands of St. Croix and St. Thomas.

King Christian VIII, after having named the landgrave, Charles of Hesse, Grand Master for life, solemnly recognized Freemasonry by an official act, dated 2d of November, 1792.

At the death of the landgrave of Hesse, in 1836, the Prince Royal, afterward King Christian VIII, declared himself protector and Grand Master. In 1848, the Grand Mastership passed to King Frederick VII, under whom Danish Masonry has attained a very flourishing condition.

The intimate connection of this country with Sweden, where the Masonry of Swedenborg, subsequently that of Zinnendorf, had taken deep root, and, at an early period, manifested a religious tendency that it has held from the first in a remarkable manner, and toward which evidently the Masons of Copenhagen, including the king, have inclined, decided the Grand Lodge of Denmark to adopt officially, on the 6th of January, 1855, the Swedish rite, or that of Zinnendorf, of seven degrees, and to enforce its adoption upon all the lodges under its jurisdiction.

Danish Masonry enjoys great consideration in the country, and, under the Grand Mastership of the reigning king, prospers from day to day.

In 1863, the Grand Lodge of Denmark exercised jurisdiction over nine operative lodges, of which four are in the capital and five in the provinces.

Sweden.

Masonry was introduced at Stockholm in 1736; but the interdictions pronounced against it by nearly every European state affected in a similar manner the Swedish government against it, and the Masonic meetings were prohibited in 1758. Nevertheless, new operative lodges were subsequently established, and, in the year 1764, a provincial Grand Lodge for Sweden was organized at Stockholm. One of the first acts of the Freemasons of this country was the establishment of an orphan asylum, which is to-day the glory and crown of Swedish Masonry. One donation of $30,000, which was made it by Brother Bohmann, permitted it to be greatly enlarged. As elsewhere, the true Freemasonry did not long exist in this country before the importation from France of the Rite of Perfection of twenty-five degrees; but the progress of this rite was checked by the crusade entered into against the system of Strict Observance. The chivalrous character of the Templars, from the first approaches of that system, met none of the favor in Sweden it had enjoyed in France and Germany. The King, Gustavus III, and his brother, the Duke of Sudermanie, were initiated in 1770; and believing the statement made to him by the officials of the rite, that Sweden was the first country into which it was introduced, the king undertook to re-establish the order of Knights Templar. He was named Grand Master, and exercised the functions of that office until 1780, when the provincial Grand Lodge, declaring itself independent, took the title of Grand Lodge of Sweden, and the king designated his brother, the Duke of Sudermanie, to replace him as Grand Master.

The importers of the system of Strict Observance into Sweden—of whom history has not preserved the names—deposited in the archives of the Grand Chapter of the system, at Stockholm, many documents which, according to them, were of the highest importance to the order of the Templars, and among which they exhibited a will, in the Latin language, which they said was the last will and testament of Jaques de Molay, the last Grand Master; as also an urn, said to contain his ashes, collected, according to the same authority, by his nephew, the Count of Beaujeu. These statements engaged the attention of the Duke of Brunswick, who had been nominated at this time Grand Master of the system, and he repaired to Sweden to examine the documents; but the result proved satisfactory in but a very trifling degree.

The King Gustavus had in the beginning favored the establishment of the system of the Templars, and in some degree discouraged the lodges practicing the English rite; but, having immediately discovered the secret plans which lay hidden under the system of Strict Observance, he mistrusted its tendency; and it is to this fact—thanks to the efforts of the independent Masonic lodges located in the country—that he afterward successfully confounded the projects of the Jesuits, and liberated himself from the tutelage under which he was held by them. Assassinated the 27th March, 1792, his son succeeded him, under the title of Gustavus IV, and was initiated, though yet a minor, into Masonry upon the 22d March of the year following, after he had renounced his right to the throne. His uncle, the Duke of Sudermanie, already Grand Master of Swedish Freemasonry since 1780, succeeded him, under the title of Charles XIII, and exercised the Grand Mastership until 1811, when he delegated the office to Prince Charles Jean Bernadotte.

In Sweden the endeavor was, as it also was in Germany, to discover the truth in relation to the system of the Templars, of which the chiefs had been expelled from the latter country. These researches wrought in the system some modifications, which were due, in great part, to one of the most eminent Masons of the time—the brother Swedenborg—intimate councilor of the king, who had introduced religious principles, impressed with his own mystical creed, and which, in consequence, has imprinted upon Swedish Masonry a particular character, which distinguishes it to the present day.

Beside the Templar system thus transformed, Zinnendorf, surgeon-in-chief of the Swedish army at Berlin, and Grand Prior of the system of the Templars, having abandoned the chiefs of the rite after he had exposed their juggleries, established, in Sweden, a rite of seven degrees, which bears his name, founded, in part, upon the same religious principles, but less mystical than those of Swedenborg. It is this rite that now is found to predominate, and is known in Europe as the Swedish Rite, or Rite of Zinnendorf.

The protection of the king, and the official recognition of Masonry by the government, in 1794, has given to the institution in Sweden an importance which it does not possess elsewhere. On the 27th May, 1811, King Charles XIII founded an order exclusively for meritorious Freemasons, of which the insignia is publicly worn, and thus proved his respect for the institution. The foundation of this order, created from a noble sentiment that greatly honored the king, is, nevertheless, in contradiction to the spirit of Freemasonry, and in opposition with its principles. The same day this order was established, the king announced as his successor the brother Bernadotte, Prince of Ponte-Corvo, and the announcement was sanctioned by the government, and he was proclaimed at the same time Grand Master of Swedish Masonry. Since coming to the throne, in 1818, the new king delegated the Grand Mastership to his son Oscar, Duke of Sudermanie, subsequently Charles John XIV, who directs in person, as the actual king, (Charles XV,) the Masonic labors of the Grand Lodge. The Grand Lodge of Sweden has under its jurisdiction three provincial Grand Lodges, with twenty-four operative lodges. The reigning king is Grand Master in his own right.

Russia.

It was the Grand Lodge of London that established the first lodge at Moscow, in 1731, under the reign of the Empress Anna Ivanowa, and, for the purpose of constituting others in the country, patented John Phillips, Provincial Grand Master. Freemasonry made but little progress in Russia, and it was not until the year 1771 that the first lodge was organized at St. Petersburg. In 1772, the Grand Lodge of London delivered to John Yelaguine, a Senator and Privy Councilor, a patent constituting him Provincial Grand Master for Russia; and, after his death, he was succeeded by the Count Roman Woronsow. At this time the lodges increased to a greater extent in St. Petersburg than in any other portion of the empire, the membership belonging in great part to the nobility. Under the reign of Catherine II, it would have been difficult to find in St. Petersburg a noble who was not a Freemason.

It is true that the Empress often manifested some chagrin when, often finding but a single chamberlain in attendance upon her, she inquired for such and such a one whom she missed, and was told that he had gone to the lodge; but, nevertheless, she was well enough disposed toward the fraternity to have her son, Paul I, initiated immediately upon his becoming of age.

The high degrees, and, above all, those of the system Strict Observance, had invaded, about the year 1775, Russian Masonry, and in which it lacked nothing of creating the same disorders it every-where caused; for many of the lodges, professing only the English Rite, had no desire to accept this Templar parody, which was principally the cause of the interdiction of Freemasonry in 1798.

The system of Strict Observance, under the patronage and Grand Mastership of the Duke of Brunswick, had organized at St. Petersburg a power, under the title of Grand Lodge of the Order of Vladimir, which pretended to direct all the lodges of Russia, and thus came in conflict with a great many operative lodges which practiced only the English Rite.

In few countries did Masonry rise to the splendor it attained under Catharine II, for the Masonic temples at St. Petersburg were indeed palaces. Many beneficial establishments were also founded by her directions and under her patronage.

During the sojourn of the King of Sweden, Gustavus III, at St. Petersburg, who, in his own country, was Grand Master of the Templar lodges, or lodges of the system of Strict Observance, the lodges of this system gave him the most superb feasts, at which he assisted with his whole suite, composed entirely of Freemasons.

Notwithstanding these brilliant appearances, the true Freemasonry, so far from making corresponding progress in Russia, had, on the contrary, degenerated to such a point that the Empress Catharine not only openly expressed her discontent thereat to the gentlemen of her court, in respect to the abuses which were being introduced, but published a pamphlet very severe in its strictures against Freemasons. This pamphlet has been translated into French and German.

Such was the situation of Masonry in Russia upon the accession of Paul I to the throne, in 1796. Although he had been initiated, this prince had allowed himself to be prevailed upon by intriguants, who obtained of him an interdiction, under the most severe penalties, of Masonic assemblies, as well as those of all other secret societies. Subsequently, regarding the Order of Knights of the Temple as the true possessors of Masonic science, he desired to re-establish that Order, and, in fact, in the object of hastening this pretended regeneration of Masonry, he had, the 16th of December, 1798, taken the title of Grand Master of the Order of Malta, as a means of more effectually accomplishing his purpose; afterward, however, he renounced the project, which was, in fact, otherwise impracticable.

To Paul I, assassinated the 23d of March, 1801, succeeded Alexander I. At first he confirmed the interdiction pronounced by his predecessor against Freemasonry; but, in 1803, consequent upon a circumstantial report which he ordered to be made upon the object and principles of Freemasonry, he revoked it, and was himself initiated. We have been unable to ascertain the exact date of this ceremony, the place, or the lodge in which it took place, nor do we know that he ever took any part in the labors of the Fraternity. On the contrary, although he never restricted in any way its existence, he always exhibited a certain degree of mistrust in the institution.

The Grand Lodge of Vladimir, which, with the operative lodges under its jurisdiction, were suspended by the interdiction pronounced by Paul I, after 1803 awoke to renewed activity. From that time the struggle recommenced. The lodges of the English system established a new Masonic code for all the lodges of Russia; but not wishing to recognize certain privileges that the Grand Lodge Vladimir revindicated, and to withdraw forever from the systematic domination of it, they founded, in 1815, another Grand Lodge, under the title of "Astrea," of which the rules and regulations were approved by the government, and which from that time directed all the lodges of Russia.

Though Freemasonry had not greatly extended, it appears that it afforded some unquiet to the Emperor Alexander; for, by a ukase, dated the 21st of August, 1821, he interdicted anew all Masonic assemblies; and, in the autograph rescript that he addressed to his minister charged with the execution of this ukase, he based its promulgation upon the assertion that the lodges occupied themselves with the discussion of political subjects.

None of the successors of Alexander, who died in 1825, having revoked this prohibition, Masonry remains in Russia under the ban of this interdiction.

POLAND.

In consequence of the political troubles which have constantly agitated it, Freemasonry has never attained a permanent position in this country.

In 1839, some nobles, resident at the court of King Frederick I, established a lodge at Varsovia, which was shortly dissolved by the bull of Clement XII; but, notwithstanding this prohibition, the Count Stanislaus Mniszek, Andrew Mocranowski, and Constantine Jablonowski founded, at Viennavitz, in Wolhania, a lodge, in which men the most eminent for their virtue and patriotism came from all parts of Poland to be initiated. In 1744, a French lodge was organized at Lemberg, by a man named

Francis Longchamps, the labors of which were subsequently directed by another Frenchman, named Colonel Jean de Thoux de Salverte. After many vicissitudes, there was organized, at Varsovia, on the 24th June, 1769, under the reign of Stanislaus Augustus—who protected Masonry—a Grand Lodge of Poland, of which the Count Augustus Moszynski was nominated Grand Master. This Grand Lodge organized operative lodges at Cracovia, Wilna, and Lemberg; but, after the first division of Poland, their labors were interrupted.

The system of Strict Observance here, as elsewhere, soon appeared, and established, at Varsovia, a Directory, under the authority of the Duke of Brunswick. Many French lodges were also established at Varsovia, and, among others—by the Grand Orient of France—the lodge "Perfect Silence," which, aspiring to the title of Grand Lodge, sought to win to its direction operative lodges; afterward, by virtue of a patent delivered to it by the Grand Orient of France, and dated 14th May, 1781, it proclaimed itself Mother Lodge, or Grand Lodge of Poland. But it failed in its project, as did many others, which obtained, for this purpose, from the Grand Lodges of England and Germany, patents, constituting them legal powers, for which the necessity was recognized. Finally, thirteen lodges united, and, on the 26th February, 1764, constituted definitely a Grand Orient of Poland, by virtue of a patent delivered to them by the Grand Lodge of England. This Lodge was installed on the 4th of the following March, and chose for its Grand Master the Count Felix Potoski. Its existence was of short duration; for, after the second partition of Poland—which took place in 1784—this Grand Lodge, together with all the operative lodges under its jurisdiction, suspended operations.

The Lodges which were subsequently established in the Grand Duchy of Poland were then organized, under the

Grand Lodges located at Berlin. Finally, on the 22d March, 1810, the Grand Orient of Poland awoke and took charge of the lodges in the country. The political events of 1813 but slightly modified their condition, and but momentarily interrupted their labors; and, in 1818, we find the Grand Orient of Poland directing the labors of thirty-four operative lodges. The ukase of the Emperor Alexander, however, struck with death the lodges of Poland, in common with those of Russia, and since that time (12th August, 1822,) all Masonic labors have ceased in Poland.

The heroic courage with which our Polish brethren fought for their liberty and their nationality, against a despotism the most arbitrary and revolting that any power calling itself Christian ever exercised against a civilized people, has acquired for them the sympathy and admiration of the Freemasons of the whole world.

Belgium.

The history of Freemasonry in Belgium is divided into many periods: that during which Belgium was part of the low country of Austria; that during which it was incorporated in the Empire of France; that of its re-union with Holland; and, finally, the period since the independence of Belgium was established. This was the first continental country that received the new Freemasonry of England. The first lodge was instituted at Mons, the 4th of June, 1721, under the title of "Perfect Union," by the Duke of Montague, then Grand Master of the Grand Lodge of London. It was this lodge that was subsequently erected into an English Grand Lodge for the low countries of Austria; but, in 1785, it shared the fortunes of all other Austrian lodges by the edict of the Emperor Joseph I.

Another lodge was established, in 1730, at Gand, under

the Austrian direction. In common with other lodges organized about the same time, in consequence of the persecutions of the Catholic clergy, who were armed with the bulls of excommunication launched at Freemasons by the popes, it labored in the most profound secrecy. The membership of these lodges were, in most part, composed of the nobility, animated, in a great degree, by the democratic tendencies of that period, and seeking to extend the principles of political liberty among the people. The most zealous patriots were to be found at the head of the lodges—many of the clergy themselves, who then were liberal, exhibiting a strong partisan trait for Masonry. To such a degree was this feeling expressed, that even the Bishop of Liege, and many of his ecclesiastics, were initiated into and directed the labors of the lodges. The Duke of Aremberg, the Duke of Ursel, the princes of Ligne and of Gavre, all took a very active part in the labors of Masonry. At one time fifteen lodges were in operation; but, unhappily, the political manifestations of the population of the low countries of Austria caused, in 1785 and in 1786, the Emperor Joseph I to interdict Masonic assemblies, though elsewhere—in Brussels, for instance—he permitted the lodges to continue their labors. In 1787, however, he ordered, by a new edict, that all the lodges in the empire, without exception, be closed, under the most severe penalties.

When Belgium was incorporated into the French Empire, the Belgian lodges—which at that time, in consequence of the edict of 1787, were in a state of suspended animation—were ordered to place themselves under the jurisdiction of the Grand Orient of France; and, from that time, Masonry in Belgium became an integral part of that of France, which there organized some twenty-two lodges. In 1814, there were in Belgium, in active operation, twenty-seven lodges, which, after the re-union of Belgium with Holland, for three years vainly endeavored to erect a central authority at Brussels. Finally, Prince Frederick, of the Low Countries, second son of the king—who, after the enfranchisement of Holland, had therein constituted a new Grand Orient—proposed to the Belgian lodges the creation of two independent Grand Lodges, which should direct all the operative lodges, each having its own administration and particular jurisdiction: the one to be located at the Hague, to exercise jurisdiction over all the northern lodges and those of the East Indies; the other having its seat at Brussels, to direct the southern lodges and those of the West Indies—the Grand Orient of Holland, thus divided into three sections, to form a Supreme Council, whose object would be to take cognizance of all the great principles affecting Freemasonry in general, etc.

This treaty of union was concluded in 1817, and the installation of the Provincial Grand Lodge at Brussels took place on the 11th April, 1818, at which time Prince Frederick was elected Grand Master of the three independent Grand Lodges, and named, as his representatives, Brother Falk, Minister of State, for the Provincial Grand Lodge of the Hague, and the Prince of Gavre for that of Brussels.

From this time the history of Belgian Freemasonry is confounded with that of Freemasonry in Holland. We will only add that from 1817 to 1832, strenuous attempts were made to establish in Belgium, particularly at Brussels, the different systems of high degrees.

The separation of Belgium from Holland—which took place in 1831—modified anew the condition of Masonry in the former country. The provincial Grand Lodge of Brussels becoming, by the separation, isolated from the Grand Orient of Holland, invited, by a circular, dated the 16th of December, 1832, all the lodges of the new kingdom to recognize it as an independent authority, to unite under its recognition, and to send up their delegates to a general assembly convoked for the 25th of February, 1833. Only four lodges, however, were represented; but the delegates present, nevertheless, decided to declare the provincial Grand Lodge of the Low Countries dissolved, and to constitute in its place a Grand Orient of Belgium. This new authority, placed under the protection of the king, Leopold I—himself a Freemason—succeeded in uniting under its jurisdiction, but not without difficulty, all the lodges of Belgium except four, which were then declared irregular. On the 1st May, 1835, the Baron of Stassart was nominated Grand Master.

The flourishing condition of Masonry, and the influence that its members were exercising over all classes of society, provoked the hate of the Catholic clergy, who recommenced their persecutions; and the Bishop of Malines, in 1837, published a sentence of excommunication—a strange proceeding in our day—against all the Belgian Freemasons. The struggle became more and more lively, and the Catholic party, of whom the "Journal of Belgium" is the organ, surpassed the part it took in the revolution of 1830, in its pretentions to rule the country, and exhibit the intolerance that elsewhere and always is exhibited in seasons of triumph by this party.

The Masonic lodges, pursued, excommunicated, tormented, in their material interests and social position, almost up to the family hearth-stones, by their implacable enemies, who sought to drive to destitution the President of the Senate and the Governor of Brussels himself, because of their adherence to Freemasonry, though the king himself was known to be a member of the institution, were constrained to take an attitude, through their Grand Orient, which was no less an exhibition of dignity and moderation than it was of strength. They opposed universal liberty to universal Romanism, free publications and loyal to anathemas, and the preaching of the eternal truth of their faith to the intolerance of a theocratic ambition. By this course the Freemasons finally triumphed.

To brother, the Baron of Stassart, who abdicated in 1841,

succeeded Brother Defacqz d'Ath, Counselor to the Court of Appeals, and to him succeeded, in 1854, the brother Theo. Verhægen, Advocate and President of the Chamber of Representatives.

The new Grand Master, seeing the institution over which he was called to preside the constant object of the attacks of obscure politicians, backed by the clergy, insisted, in a discourse pronounced upon St. John's day, 1854, and which reflected the profound convictions and eminent talents of the distinguished speaker, that there existed an absolute necessity for Freemasonry to oppose itself more and more energetically to the antagonistic party, and discuss within its lodges such religious and political questions as affected the condition of the country; and, for this purpose, that the regulations of the Grand Orient be so amended as to repeal the laws forbidding such discussion to take place within the lodges. His advice was approved by all the brethren who assisted at the feast, and they decided to publish his discourse. This declaration, consequently, being printed and promulgated, provoked the protest of a portion of the Grand Lodges of Germany, and also that of Sweden, who not only ceased, in consequence of this manifestation, all connection with the Grand Orient of Belgium, but even prohibited their operative lodges from receiving Belgian Masons.

This movement was attended by another deplorable consequence. The chiefs of the Supreme Council of the Scottish (33d) Rite, located at Brussels—a rival authority of the Grand Orient—and some lodges under the jurisdiction of the latter body, protested against the new interpretation of the principles and the rights of Freemasons, as inculcated by the Grand Master Verhægan, and made it the occasion of their passing over to the jurisdiction of the Supreme Council. This factionist condition has remained nearly the same up to the present time.

The statutes of the Grand Orient, promulgated the 19th

of January, 1838, contained but fifteen articles, and made no mention of any other style of Masonry except that of the three symbolic degrees. Each lodge of the union is represented by three delegates, who in general assemblies exercise the legislative power. The Grand Orient of Belgium exercises jurisdiction over sixty operative lodges while the Supreme Council of the Scottish (33d) Rite, which was instituted the 1st of March, 1817, and had for a long time a precarious existence, now counts thirteen lodges within its jurisdiction. These two authorities hold their meetings in the same city, Brussels.

HOLLAND.

THIS country was for a long time preserved from the innovations due to intriguing politicians and other schemers, who every-where have provoked deplorable schisms in the Masonic ranks; nevertheless it finally had to submit to the consequences of allowing the English Rite, which was for years the only one known, to be encroached upon by those anti-masonic productions which have denaturalized our beautiful institution, and which, in place of hastening us forward to the goal of its ideal, have but advanced that goal farther from us.

A lodge was founded at the Hague, in 1725, composed of the *elite* of Dutch society; but the clergy, ever hostile to Freemasons, not having permitted it to be openly constituted, its labors during many years were conducted in the most profound secrecy; and it was not until 1731, when Lord Stanhope, Duke of Chesterfield, was English embassador at the court of William, Prince of Orange, that it was officially constituted. This lodge owed its existence to Brother Vincent de la Chappela, who had been authorized for the purpose of organizing it by the Grand Lodge of England. It was by it that the Emperor Francis I, then Duke of Lorraine, was initiated.

In 1834, many lodges united in a general assembly for the purpose of regularly organizing Freemasonry in Holland, by constituting a provincial Grand Lodge. This Grand Lodge, of which the Count of Wagenaer was proposed as provincial Grand Master, after having been regularly patented by the Grand Lodge of England, was inaugurated in 1735, in an assembly held at the hotel of Niewe-Doelen, under the presidency of the titulary provincial Grand Master, Brother John Cornelius Rademacher. It took the title "Grand Masters' Lodge of General Appeal for the United Provinces;" and, in 1749, it took the name of "Mother Lodge of the Royal Union."

Another lodge, founded in 1734 at the Hague, and composed of eminent men, announced, in the public newspapers of the 24th October, 1735, a Masonic assembly which would be presided over by the new provincial Grand Master Rademacher; but the magistracy of the Hague, on the 30th of the following November, issued an ordinance interdicting all such assemblies.

Notwithstanding this prohibition, a lodge of Amsterdam, which numbered among its members the most eminent men in the city, dared to continue its labors. The Catholic clergy, by the aid of calumnious reports, succeeded in stirring up the ignorant class of the people against it; and its place of meeting being invaded by a crowd of those fanatics, they burned the property of the lodge and exhibited otherwise a disposition, upon any resistance being offered, to proceed to the most violent measures. The general government, with the object of preventing a recurrence of such action, intervened and prohibited Masonic assemblies. One lodge, having, in defiance of this prohibition, continued to meet, it was surrounded, by the order of the magistracy, and its members captured and imprisoned. The master of the lodge and his officers, when brought before the court, explained so clearly the object and principles of the institution, that they were immediately set at liberty, and all the judges of the tribunal solicited the honor of being initiated. Since that time, a great many lodges have been established in the country; but, in 1746, new persecutions, on the part of the Catholic clergy, forced the lodges of the Hague, Nimegue, and Amsterdam to demand the intervention of the general government, which obliged the clergy to retract their calumnies.

The Holland lodges—which held their constitutions, some from the Grand Lodge of England, and others from those of Germany and France—existed isolated from and independent of the provincial Grand Lodge created in 1735. With the object of a more intimate union, the lodge styled "Royal Union" convoked a general assembly, which was attended, on the 27th December, 1756, by representatives from thirteen lodges, and then and there organized, under the patronage of the Grand Lodge of London, a Grand Lodge for the United Provinces, of which the Baron Van Aersen Beyeren was nominated provincial Grand Master.

This Grand Lodge proclaimed, the following year, its general statutes in forty-one articles. In 1770 it declared itself independent; and, by virtue of an agreement with the Grand Lodge of London, it took the title of Grand Lodge of Holland, and notified all the Grand Lodges of Europe of the fact. It at once organized a provincial Grand Lodge, at Brussels, for the low countries of Austria, and nominated the Marquis of Gages provincial Grand Master; but this lodge was obliged, in 1789, in consequence of the edict of the Emperor Joseph I, to suspend active operations. After the removal of this interdiction, in 1798, the Grand Lodge of Holland decreed, on the 17th May of that year, a new administrative code, according to which it ruled only the three symbolic degrees, and intrusted a special chapter, directed by the Grand Master, Baron Van Teylingen, with the conference of the other degrees of its rite.

In 1810, by the aid of the subscriptions made up by the Holland lodges, an asylum for the blind was instituted at Amsterdam.

After the union of Holland with the French Empire, in 1811, the existence of the Grand Orient of Holland was attacked and compromised, by the Grand Orient of France assuming to extend its authority over all the Masons and all the Masonic institutions of Holland. To the decree published by it on the 3d March, 1812, the Grand Orient of Holland responded, on the 21st of the same month, in a manner so dignified that the Grand Orient of France renounced its project of assumption, and the Grand Orient of Holland continued its jursdiction as before, save that the nine operative lodges, instituted by the Grand Orient of France at Amsterdam and the Hague, remained, from 1812 to 1814, under the jurisdiction of the latter.

At the time of the events of 1814, which changed anew the position of Freemasonry in Holland, the Grand Orient had under its jurisdiction, in Holland and the two Indies, seventy-one operative lodges. The direction of the lodges of the Low Countries having been offered to it, the Grand Orient proposed, in 1814, a treaty of union among all the northern and southern lodges of the Low Countries, for the purpose of organizing a Grand Lodge for that kingdom, with the Provincial Grand Lodges,[1] of which the one should be located at the Hague, and comprising within its jurisdiction all the northern lodges, together with those in the East Indies; and the other should be located at Brussels, to take charge of all the southern lodges of the kingdom, together with those of the West Indies. Of the latter, Prince Frederick was elected Grand Master, and

---

[1] See Masonry in Belgium, *ante*.

the Minister of State, Brother Falk, Grand Master of the former.

In 1819, Prince Frederick sent to all the lodges of Europe copies of two documents found in the papers of the defunct Grand Master Boetzelaar. The first of these documents is a species of charter,[1] dated at Cologne, the 24th of June, 1535, and signed by nineteen persons, bearing illustrious names, and who therein are presented as delegates from nineteen Masonic lodges of different countries in Europe. The second is the record-book of the meetings of a lodge which, according to it, should have existed at the Hague in 1637, and whose date of organization is 8th May, 1519. These documents, particularly the charter, have been submitted to the examination of learned Freemasons, some of whom have pronounced them authentic, while others have decided that both documents have been produced for some purpose best known to the manufacturers. The latter decision seems to be best supported.

The lodges under the jurisdiction of the Grand Orient of the Low Countries numbered, in 1820, one hundred and five, of which forty-five in Holland, and fourteen in the East Indies, were borne upon the register of the Grand Lodge of the northern provinces at the Hague; and thirty-two in Holland, and fourteen in the West Indian colonies, on that of the Grand Lodge of the southern provinces at Brussels. The number of operative lodges organized from that time to 1829 augmented the foregoing by thirty-one lodges, thus making the total number one hundred and thirty-six.

The events of 1830 changed anew the Masonic organization in Holland, placing it as we found it in 1818; and the Grand Orient of Holland took under its direction the lodges of the new Dutch territory and the Dutch colonies in the two Indies. As in the past, it continues to fill with dignity, under its noble chief, Prince Frederick William

---

[1] See General History of Freemasonry, p. 51.

Charles, the position that it occupies as one of the most ancient departments of Freemasonry in Europe.

The Grand Orient of Holland at present directs, in all, the labors of sixty-seven operative lodges, of which about twenty are in the East and West Indies.

Germany.

We must give the history of Freemasonry in this vast country, which contains an empire, five kingdoms, and twenty-one principalities, in a manner more succinct than that of any other of the States of Europe. We will commence, therefore, by speaking of that city which, of all others in Germany, was the first in which Freemasonry took root.

Hamburg.—On the 3d of December, 1737, the first Masonic lodge in Germany, under the English dispensation, was established in this city. It was named "Absalom Lodge," and was placed under the direction of Brother Charles Sarey. On the 30th of October, 1740, this lodge was raised, by the Grand Lodge of England, to the rank of the Provincial Grand Lodge of Hamburg and Lower Saxony, and having for its Grand Master, Brother Luttman. It was by a deputation of this lodge that the Prince Frederick of Prussia, subsequently Frederick II, was initiated, in 1738, at Brunswick—a circumstance that has contributed much to the propagation of Freemasonry in Germany. From Hamburg, Freemasonry passed, in 1738, to Dresden; in 1740, to Berlin; in 1741, to Leipsic; in 1744, to Brunswick, and in 1746, to Hanover. The Provincial Grand Lodge established up to 1795 but five lodges, and in that year these united in founding a hospital for house servants, and, subsequently, created a fund for the relief of foreign brethren who might require it. This Grand Lodge had extended its jurisdiction, in 1807, over sixteen lodges, all working the English Rite and remaining faithful to its mother lodge of London. In this respect it shone as a bright example of fidelity in comparison to other Provincial Grand Lodges, which, although established under like circumstances and by the same authority, generally took the first favorable opportunity to become independent of the authority that created them. It was not until the year 1811 that the Provincial Grand Lodge of Hamburg decided to assert its independence. To-day it directs a Provincial Grand Lodge and twenty-one operative lodges, all practicing the English Rite, together with a chapter, created by Shrœder, who was, during many years, its Grand Master.

Prussia.—The "Lodge at the Three Globes," in Berlin, composed of French artists, was constituted on the 23d of September, 1740. This was the first lodge established at that time. On the 24th of June, 1744, Prince Frederick elevated it to the rank of a Grand Lodge, under the title of "Royal Grand Mother Lodge." He was, as a natural consequence, elected Grand Master, and filled the office as such until 1747, from which date he ceased to take any part in Masonic labors.

This mother lodge suffered itself to be from an early period invaded by the high degrees of the rite of "Perfection," as also by those of the rite "Strict Observance." In 1773, desiring to organize a lodge whose membership would be composed entirely of the nobility, it requested permission to do so from the king, Frederick II, but was refused. Such an institution could no better carry out the object of Masonry than those which were charged with the propagation of its doctrines.

Although, like Hamburg, some parts of Germany had received Masonry direct from England, and the lodges thus constituted worked the English Rite, others had received it by the intermediation of France. The institution soon extended in a most extraordinary manner. The lodges there, finding themselves composed, in great part, of the nobility and men devoted to art and the sciences, having a weakness for the French language, many of them conducted their labors in that language, and, for the most part, even took French names. This tendency favored the introduction into the German lodges of the high degrees which the officers of the army of Broglie had imported from France; and it is from this period these innumerable follies which culminated in the introduction of the Templar system may be dated. It was not until after the Congress of Wilhelmsbad that these disorders ceased. The discussions which took place in that assembly broke the chains of the Templar hierarchy, believed to be so firmly riveted by the Jesuits, and relieved the fraternity in all Germany from their drunken enthusiasm for the systems of high degrees.

In no country had the Templar system been extended so generally as in Germany. Nearly all the lodges had adopted it, under the belief that its object was the reestablishment of the ancient Order of Knights Templar. The most elevated classes of society and people the most honorable, among whom were the greater portion of the nobility, became its partisans, notwithstanding the doubts which were thrown out of the sincerity of the assertions of its chief officials. Twenty-six princes of Germany had been initiated into those degrees, and thus became promoters more or less zealous; while many of them took position at the head of the Templar Order in their respective States.

Since Frederick the Great, all his successors have been Freemasons, or have declared themselves in favor and the protectors of Freemasonry. Frederick William III, who had been initiated, confirmed and recognized from the throne, in 1798, the three Grand Lodges of Berlin. At the second Congress of Vienna, in 1833, when Austria and Bavaria demanded, in terms not in any wise equivocal, the extermination of the society of Freemasons, this king declared that they were and always should be in his kingdom, under his protection; and, by his warm defense of the institution, he prevented the other powers represented at this congress from exhibiting any leaning towards the project of extermination advanced by the two powers just named.

It was by his desire and with his consent that the present king, William I, proclaimed himself, during his life, protector of Masonry in Prussia. The latter, without partaking of the favorable opinion of the institution entertained by his father, imitated him, as well from political motives as to continue the custom consecrated by his predecessors of the royal family, in consenting that his son, the prince royal Frederick William, should be initiated and should represent Prussian Masonry. This initiation took place on the 5th of November, 1853. The principles of this prince are known to be at variance, however, with those of his father.

The three Prussian Grand Lodges located at Berlin have each founded some humanitarian establishments in favor of Freemasons and their families.

The Grand Lodge at the Three Globes has under its jurisdiction ninety-nine operative lodges.

The National Grand Lodge of Germany, founded in 1773, registers under its jurisdiction sixty-seven operative lodges.

The Royal York Grand Lodge, founded in 1798, registers twenty-seven operative lodges under its jurisdiction.

Each of these three Grand Lodges has its Grand Master and Deputy Grand Master. The Prince William of Baden has been, since 1859, Grand Master of the Royal York Grand Lodge.

Kingdom of Saxony.—A lodge was established at Dresden, in 1738, by the Count Rotowsky, under whose direction a Provincial Grand Lodge was organized in 1741. This Grand Lodge, with the operative lodges under its jurisdiction, experienced the same embarrassments, by their connection with the high degrees, as all the other legislative Masonic bodies of Germany. We shall pass them by without further notice.

In 1755, this lodge took the title of Grand Lodge of Saxony; and, after having, in 1807, abolished all the degrees above that of Master Mason, it united, in 1811, with the National Grand Lodge of Saxony, which then had been established.

Under the auspices of the first Grand Lodge, there was founded, in 1792, on the 22d of September, at Frederickstadt, a philosophic establishment, which is directed at the present time by the Lodge of the Three Swords, at Dresden, and in which two hundred children are educated.

The Grand Lodge of Saxony has at present under its jurisdiction fifteen operative lodges.

Kingdom of Hanover.—The capital of this country admitted Freemasonry in 1746, and the Grand Lodge of London established there, in 1755, a Provincial Grand Lodge, under the Grand Mastership of Count Kielmansegge. Having detached itself from the Mother Grand Lodge, in 1828 it declared its independence as a Masonic authority, under the Grand Mastership of the reigning king. Its history is intimately connected with that of German Masonry in general.

The king, George V, on ascending the throne on the 18th November, 1851, declared himself—like his father, who was a Freemason—the protector of Masonry in Hanover, and was initiated, on the 14th of January, 1857, in the "Lodge at the Black Bear," in Hanover. From that time he has directed, as Grand Master, the Freemasonry of the country, and taken a very active part in Masonic labors.

The Grand Lodge of Hanover numbers at the present time upon its register twenty-one symbolic lodges.

Kingdom of Bavaria.—In no country of Germany has Freemasonry been subjected to as many restrictions and vexations as in the kingdom of Bavaria. It did not penetrate, until very lately, into the elder Bavaria; and it was not until 1777 that the Royal York Grand Lodge organized a lodge at Munich. But for a long time it has existed in operative lodges, located in countries which, in 1810, were annexed to this kingdom. A lodge had been organized by Prince Frederick of Brandenburg, on the 21st June, 1741, at Beyreuth, the ancient capital of Franconia, where other lodges were said to have existed at this time, but concerning which we know nothing.

The society of the Illuminati, founded by the professor Weisshaupt, and to which was intrusted the noble task of causing virtue to triumph over folly and ignorance, and of carrying instruction and civilization into all classes of society, had found access into some lodges located in the Elder Bavaria, and particularly those of Munich; and thereupon Prince Charles Theodore, moved by the influence of the Jesuits, issued two decrees, the one dated 2d March, and the other 16th August, 1785, interdicting the assemblies of the Illuminati, and also those of the Freemasons. Following these prohibitions, which were renewed from at first by the king, Maximilian Joseph, on the 4th November, 1799, and subsequently on the 5th March, 1804, the lodges of Munich and of Manheim ceased their labors.

Within the Protestant countries annexed to Bavaria—at Beyreuth and Ratisbonne—the lodges were allowed to continue their labors, but under most intolerable restrictions. No employé of the government, either civil or military, was permitted to attend the meetings of or be initiated into them. In a word, these lodges had to contend with the Jesuitical tendencies of the government, and were consequently paralyzed in their actions.

Notwithstanding this pressure, however, the lodge at Beyreuth—constituted, on the 3d of August, 1800, as a Provincial Grand Lodge, under the jurisdiction of the Royal York Grand Lodge at Berlin—made a stand, under the Grand Mastership of Count Giech and Brother Voeldendorf, prefect of the government; and finally, in 1811, it, with four other lodges, created an independent power at Beyreuth, under the title of "Grand Lodge of the Sun." This authority has at present under its jurisdiction, in the northern portion of Bavaria, eleven operative lodges, while in the southern portion, which is entirely Roman Catholic, Freemasonry is completely interdicted.

Grand Duchy of Baden.—The most ancient lodge of this country is the lodge "Charles of Concord," established on the 24th November, 1778, at Manheim, by the Royal York Grand Lodge of Berlin. Its labors were suspended in 1785, in consequence of the interdiction of Masonic assemblies in the states of the elector of Bavaria, in which Manheim was at that time situate. But when this city was, in 1803, incorporated in the Grand Duchy of Baden, Freemasonry awoke, under the direction of the Marquis of Dalberg, and founded, in 1806, a Grand Orient of Baden, of which Prince Charles of Ysenberg was chosen Grand Master.

Another power, under the title of the "National Union of the Lodges," was, upon the 23d of May, 1809, constituted at Manheim by the lodges of Carlsrühe, Friburg, Heidelberg, etc., of which the Marquis Charles Frederick Schilling, of Constadt, was nominated presiding officer.

After the death of the Grand Duke, Charles Frederick,

his successor, under the pressure of political events, on the 16th February, 1813, and on the 7th March, 1814, promulgated two ordinances, prohibiting all assemblies of secret societies, among which, of course, Freemasonry stood first. After this the lodges remained closed for thirty years; and it was not until in 1845 that the reigning Grand Duke authorized anew the assembling of Freemasons. The greater part of the old lodges began their labors, and to-day they are at work, under the jurisdiction of the Grand Lodge of Beyreuth and the Grand Lodge at the Three Globes, in Berlin, respectively.

Kingdom of Wurtemberg.—In 1774 a lodge was instituted at Stuttgart, under the title of "Charles of the Three Cedars," which practiced the rite of "Strict Observance," and having at its head Brother Taubenheim, privy councilor; but it failed to sustain itself, and, by a circular, dated the 16th July, 1784, it was announced that its labors were suspended. It was not until the year 1835 that we see Freemasonry reappear at Stuttgart. The lateness of this reappearance is due to the unfriendly disposition for the institution entertained by the sovereigns who governed Wurtemberg since 1784. To-day we see lodges in active operation, working under the direction of various German Grand Lodges.

Duchy of Hesse-Darmstadt.—The first traces of Freemasonry were exhibited in this country in 1764, when a lodge, under the name of the "White Pigeon," had been organized by the National Grand Lodge of Germany; but this lodge disappeared immediately, and left no sign of Masonic life in Hesse-Darmstadt, where, as in many other portions of Germany, the reigning sovereigns did not have much love for the institution. It was not until the year 1816 that it awoke, thanks to the particular protection of the landgrave Christian of Hesse. A lodge, under the title of "St. John the Evangelist," was constituted at Darmstadt, on the 5th of August of that year, and installed on the 23d of the following October, by the Grand Lodge of the Eclectic Union at Frankfort. This lodge established a fund for the relief of the widows and orphans of deceased brethren.

In 1846 was established at Darmstadt, under the title of "The Union," a Grand Lodge, which now numbers upon its register seven operative lodges, besides the lodge "St. John the Evangelist."

Hesse-Cassel.—Notwithstanding all the members of the ducal family of this duchy were Freemasons, as were also the ruling princes, in this country, Freemasonry has never made any progress. The lodges have never sought to form a central power, but work in an isolated manner, and without ranking under any jurisdiction.

When the country was transformed into a kingdom, under Jerome Buonaparte, in 1808, the lodges organized a legislative authority at Cassel, under the title of the "Grand Orient of Westphalia;" but this organization was dissolved after the events of 1815. Another Masonic authority was constituted at Cassel in 1817. We have no documents to inform us as to what occurred since that date.

Duchy of Brunswick.—Through the agency of the chamberlain De Kisselben, who was by it named Provincial Grand Master for life, the Provincial Grand Lodge of Hamburg, on the 12th of February, 1844, instituted a lodge at Brunswick which was called "Jonathan," and at the installation of which Prince Albert of Brunswick was present. After the introduction of the Templar system into the lodges of Germany, a number of the members of this lodge refused to recognize it as Masonic, or admit the system into the lodge. This circumstance, in 1765, led to a division of the membership into two factions, which, while they continued to work each independent of the other, ceased not to criminate and war upon each other. A third lodge, named "St. Charles of Concord," organized in 1764 by some Frenchmen, who worked in the French language, and conferred the high degrees brought by them from France, having, notwithstanding the protection of the reigning duke, been authorized by the two dissenting lodges just mentioned, Duke Charles, to put an end to this strife and disorder, closed up all the lodges, and subsequently ordered their membership to re-organize into two new lodges, the one to work in the French language, and the other in the German.

In 1770, the Duke Ferdinand of Brunswick, having been nominated, by the Grand Lodge of London, Provincial Grand Master for the lodges of the Duchy of Brunswick, installed the officers of these two lodges on the 10th and 11th of October of that year, in presence of the Duke Charles of Sudermanie, brother of Gustavus III, King of Sweden; Prince Frederick Augustus of Brunswick-Luneburg, and General Rhetz, Deputy Grand Master.

As the Templar system lacked in Germany an influential chief, who could facilitate its propagation and support the secret plans of its founders, the emissaries of the Jesuits sought, not in vain, to gain the Duke Ferdinand to such position. After having consented to their proposition, and being initiated in the Convent of Kohlo in 1772, by the chapter there assembled for that purpose, he was nominated Grand Master of all the lodges of the Templar system in Germany. On the 18th January, 1773, he established a Supreme Directory of Strict Observance at Brunswick, and within the very locality of those lodges which his predecessor had closed to prevent them from practicing the rite of which he now announced himself as chief. Deceived, however, as had been Gustavus III of Sweden, and his brother the Duke of Sudermanie, as to the origin of the Templar system, by the emissaries, who pretended that the object of that system was to re-establish the Order of the Knights Templar, and to claim restitution of the property of that order from the power that had confiscated it, Duke Ferdinand assembled in 1775 at Brunswick, and in 1778 at Wolfenbuttel, conventions of Freemasons, to ascertain the facts in this connection. The consequences were, that while many of the emissaries of the Templar system were unmasked and imprisoned, the object of the inquiry was no further advanced than before. Finally, the Duke Ferdinand convoked, in 1782, a congress at Wilhelmsbad, to which were invited all the Masonic authorities of Europe, in order, first, to ascertain if the Templar system was really directed by the Society of Loyola; second, to discuss the merits of the system, as also its demerits; and, third, to reform it, to the end that Freemasonry might be extricated from the political complications into which this system had drawn it, not alone in all Germany, but also in Sweden, Italy, Poland, and Russia. The discussions which took place during the thirty days this congress continued in session, while they led to no positive assurance beyond the fact that the Templar system was a totally anti-masonic institution, carried the conviction to the minds of the majority present that there was no Freemasonry beyond that of the English Rite, or the three symbolic degrees. The consequences were that all the systems of high degrees were rejected and cast aside as worthless, except the rite of Strict Observance, which was changed into the "Refined Scottish Rite."

The "Supreme Directory" at Brunswick, after the death of Duke Ferdinand, on the 3d July, 1792, returned to the practice of the English Rite, and assumed what it claimed as its original name of "St. Charles of Concord;" and thereafter, for some time, continued to exist isolated and independent.

While Westphalia was a kingdom this lodge was in

danger of losing its independence, in consequence of the Grand Lodge of Westphalia, instituted in 1808 at Cassel, attempting to register it under its direction. But the interference of the king prevented this consummation, and, for the purpose of having some recognized Masonic authority to lean upon, it returned to its obedience to the ancient mother lodge of Hamburg. The 11th and 12th February, 1844, were employed by this lodge—"St. Charles of Concord"—in celebrating the centennial feast of the introduction of Freemasonry into Brunswick.

Empire of Austria.—In all countries wherein the Roman Catholic and apostolic clergy predominate, Freemasonry experiences great difficulty in attaining a permanent foothold. Of this fact Austria is a striking illustration. All the lodges constituted in the Austrian States have had but a brief term of existence, the persecutions on the part of the clergy and the prohibitions of the sovereigns having never given them time to take root.

The Empress Maria Theresa, notwithstanding her husband, the Emperor Francis I, was a Freemason, interdicted Masonry, in 1764, within the Austrian States. It was not until the reign of Joseph II that we find the institution again existing in that country; but, as before, an object of suspicion, and under the strict superintendence of the police.

The system of Strict Observance had been established in all its hierarchy at Vienna; but some very grave complications caused it, in a short time, to abandon its seat. In 1784, however, there were established some ten lodges in Vienna, all working under this system, and which—to judge from the language of a Masonic journal which was there secretly published from 1784 to 1786, and edited with marked ability—were composed of worthy men, and progressive in their principles and practices.

After the death of Joseph II in 1790, his successor,

Francis II, prohibited Masonry anew, and used the greatest severity in enforcing this prohibition, even to demanding a decision from the German Diet, in 1794, then sitting at Ratisbonne, to interdict the institution throughout all Germany. But the representatives of Prussia, Brunswick, and Hanover responded to this demand by saying, that as he was protector of the rights and liberties of his own subjects, they claimed the same privilege with regard to theirs.

Freemasonry penetrated into Bohemia in 1769, and in 1770 four lodges were actively engaged in Prague. They were composed of the most prominent citizens. In 1786, a Provincial Grand Lodge for Bohemia was organized; but the interdiction of Francis II caused the total suspension of Masonic labor in this portion of his empire; and, since 1794, Austria has been shut out from Masonic light.

RECAPITULATION OF THE LODGES EXISTING IN THE SEVERAL STATES OF GERMANY.

Prussia, with 3 G. L.	187	Holstein	1
Saxony, " 1 "	16	Saxe-Coburg-Gotha	2
Hanover, " 1 "	20	Meiningen	1
Bavaria, " 1 "	10	Anhalt Dessau	2
Baden	5	" Bernbourg	1
Wurtemberg	6	Reuss (the elder)	1
Hesse-Darmstadt, 1 G. L.	7	Reuss (the younger)	1
Hesse-Cassel	2	Waldeck	1
Luxembourg, 1 G. L.	2	Lippe-Detmold	1
Mecklenburg-Schwerin	9	Schwartzbourg-Schwerin	2
" Strelitz	2	Lubeck	2
Saxe-Weimar	2	Bremen	2
Oldenbourg	2	Frankfort-on-the-Main and its dependencies, with 1 G. L.	10
Nassau	1	Hamburg and dependencies, 1 G. L.	21
Brunswick	3		
Altenburg	1	Total 10 G. Ls. and 323 Ls.	

SWITZERLAND.

FREEMASONRY penetrated into Switzerland in 1737, when a Provincial Grand Master of England, named George Hamilton, founded the first lodge at Geneva, and shortly afterward the second at Lausanne; but in consequence of its interdiction, in 1738, by the magistracy of Berne, the latter was dissolved. In 1740 a new lodge was organized at Lausanne; but a second prohibition by the government of Berne, dated the 3d March, 1745, closed it. It was not until about 1764 that lodges were organized in Lausanne and in the canton of Vaud; but a third edict, issued by the government, in 1770, against the assembling of Freemasons, dispersed these lodges also.

The Provincial Grand Lodge of Geneva maintained itself with much difficulty; for nearly all the lodges that it constituted, particularly those in the canton of Vaud, were dispersed by the edicts mentioned. Having sought, however, to establish lodges in the cities of German Switzerland, and others in Geneva, it seemed necessary that a Grand Orient of Geneva should be established; and, in 1786, this authority was instituted; but the French Revolution of 1789 caused it to suspend operations. In 1796 it resumed its functions; but, by the union of Geneva with the Empire of France, its operations were set aside by the Grand Orient of France, which immediately commenced instituting lodges within its jurisdiction. In 1765, Masonry having extended into German Switzerland, a lodge was established at Basle, and another at Zurich in 1771. Both of these lodges were instituted by the Provincial Grand Lodge of Geneva.

The system of Strict Observance soon found its way into the valleys of Helvetia; and its anti-masonic distinctions, while producing the same disorder there which they produced elsewhere, culminated in dividing the Masons of Switzerland into two camps. In 1775, the system of

Strict Observance, having organized a Helvetian Scottish Directory, divided itself into two factions. The one, having its seat at Basle, assumed authority over German Switzerland; while the other, sitting at Lausanne, and styling itself the Scottish Directory of Roman Helvetia, took charge of French Switzerland. But this last had to submit to a like fortune with all the lodges of the canton of Vaud; and in consequence of the edict of the Lords of Berne, issued in November, 1782, it suspended its operations. This edict, for the fourth time, prohibited Masonic assemblies in every portion of the canton. The Directory of Basle was not more fortunate; for, in 1785, under the stringent requirements of an edict of the magistrates of Berne, it also had to suspend operations. During the French Revolution all Masonic labors in Switzerland were suspended; and, in 1818, the seat of the Scottish Directory of Basle was transferred, after the death of the Grand Master Burhardt, from that city to Zurich.

The Directory of Roman Helvetia at Lausanne awoke to renewed activity in 1810; but the system of Strict Observance having been abolished after the congress of Wilhelmsbad, it took the title of Grand Orient of Roman Helvetia, on the 15th October of that year, and from that time governed the lodges of the canton of Vaud, until its fusion, in 1822, with the Provincial Grand Lodge of Berne, which then became an independent Grand Lodge.

At Berne Masonry had been introduced, about the year 1740, by the Provincial Grand Lodge of Geneva; but, in consequence of the interdiction of the magistrates of Berne, it had disappeared, and no traces of it could be found in the canton until about 1798, when some Bernese officers, in the service of France, established three lodges, styled, respectively, "Friends of Glory," "Foreign Country," and "Discretion." The first two had but a short existence, and from the remains of the last was formed the "Lodge of Hope," which was constituted by the Grand

Orient of France, on the 14th of September, 1803, and which was then the only lodge in active operation in the whole Swiss Confederation.

A new era now appeared to dawn for Masonry in Switzerland, which, no more persecuted, developed with wonderful rapidity, and lodges were established, within a short time, in the principal towns of the country; but the wars of the empire once more arrested this new growth. The Lodge of Hope was composed of eminent men of all classes of society—nearly all foreign diplomatists, resident at Berne as representatives of foreign powers, having become members of this lodge. In 1812 it initiated Prince Leopold of Saxe-Coburg, since King of the Belgians. On the 12th July, 1818, this lodge applied for a patent to the Grand Lodge of England; and on the 24th June, 1819, it was installed as a Provincial Grand Lodge of England, by the brother Louis de Tavel de Kruiningen, who had been elected to the position of Provincial Grand Master. From that time it abandoned and discredited the chapters and high degrees of all kinds which it had received from France, and thenceforward recognized nothing as Masonic but the three symbolic degrees.

Thenceforth the eminent brethren who directed this authority sought to unite, under one alliance, all the lodges of Switzerland. Having announced their desires upon this subject to the Helvetian Scottish Directory at Zurich, without meeting any favorable response, on the 24th June, 1822, the Provincial Grand Lodge of Berne concluded a treaty of union with the Helvetian Grand Orient[1] at Lausanne, by virtue of which both of these authorities were dissolved, and in their place was instituted a National Grand Lodge of Switzerland, to which, by virtue of the treaty, the six lodges of the Grand Orient and

---

[1] This Grand Orient was, in some sort, the successor of the Roman Helvetian Directory, that suspended operations in 1782.

the three lodges of the Provincial Grand Lodge yielded obedience. In this manner but two Masonic authorities came to exist, viz: the National Grand Lodge of Switzerland, and the Helvetian Scottish Directory at Zurich.

Such new lodges as were subsequently instituted in Switzerland took rank under the National Grand Lodge; and notwithstanding the Zurich Directory had at various times, and particularly in 1830, after the death of the Grand Master De Tavel, made overtures of union to the National Grand Lodge, in consequence of the pretensions to the right of conferring high degrees retained by the former, the latter, having abolished such pretension, would never consent to such union.

Finally, the feelings which prompted a desire for union were renewed in 1835, and, at the twenty-fifth anniversary of the re-opening of the lodge "Liberty with Modesty," in Zurich, the Swiss lodges were invited, and the feast took place on the 20th August, 1836. It was then agreed that the "Lodge of Hope," at Berne, should convoke, in the year 1838, all the lodges of Switzerland in a congress, in which should be discussed the basis of a future union. In accordance with this decision the congress met, the basis of union was discussed, and the decision arrived at that a third congress should assemble at Basle in 1840, to continue the discussion. Subsequently, a fourth congress assembled at Locle in 1842, and finally a fifth, at which were assembled the representatives of fourteen lodges, who ratified the union on the 22d June, 1844, and established the new Alpine Grand Lodge, with the brother Professor Hottinger as Grand Master.

The place of meeting of this body is changed every two years. Governed by a council of administration, having the Grand Master for president, and composed of the members united in a general assembly, this authority exercises legislative powers. Its jurisdiction extends over twenty-seven lodges, which form the Swiss union.

Italy.

In no country has Freemasonry been subjected to such changes of fortune as in Italy. It is at Florence that we find the first traces of the institution. Introduced there in 1729, by the Grand Lodge of England, which established many lodges in Tuscany, in 1731 we find a Provincial Grand Lodge instituted. But Gaston, the last Grand Duke of the family of the Medici, in 1737 interdicted all Masonic meetings, and not until after his death did Freemasons again meet in a lodge capacity. Then, the clergy having complained to Pope Clement XII, he sent an inquisitor to Florence, who arrested and imprisoned all the Masons he could discover, and ceased not in his persecutions until ordered so to do by the successor of Gaston, Francis, Duke of Lorraine, who was subsequently Emperor of Austria. This prince, who had been made a Mason in Holland, protected the institution. Under his reign Masonry extended into all Italy—to Milan, Padua, Venice, and Verona. It existed even at Rome, where, unknown to the Pope, a lodge worked in the English Rite. The bull of excommunication of the 27th April, 1738, published on the 29th of the following May, and which prohibited Masonic meetings in all Catholic countries, under the most severe penalties, closed a portion of the Italian lodges. A new edict of the Cardinal Farras, dated 14th January, 1739, confirmed this bull, and ordered to be burned, by the hands of the public hangman, a pamphlet written in favor of Freemasons. These persecutions, however, had but little effect in interrupting the spread of Masonry in Italy, particularly at Naples; and it was but by the promulgation of the bull of Pope Benedict XIV, on the 18th March, 1751, that the lodges were obliged to close their meetings.

In 1760, the Grand Lodge of Holland instituted a Provincial Grand Lodge at Naples, which, in a short time had organized eight operative lodges. Then detaching itself from the Grand Lodge of Holland, this lodge took rank as a Provincial Grand Lodge, under the Grand Lodge of England. In 1767 this body declared itself independent, under the title of the National Grand Lodge of Italy, with the Duke Demetrio della Rocca in the office of Grand Master; in which condition it existed until 1790, when it was dissolved by the French Revolution.

Masonry was cotemporarily introduced into the kingdom of Sardinia, lodges having been organized at Turin and Chambery, while, in the latter city, the Grand Lodge of London founded a Provincial Grand Lodge.

In 1762 Masonry was imported from England to Venice, where many lodges were established, under the direction of the Provincial Grand Master Manuzzi.

The partisans of the Stuarts, and other political schemers, found in Italy, as elsewhere, means to establish their illegitimate Masonry. In 1775 they had installed at Turin a commandery of the eighth department of the system of Strict Observance, under the direction of the Count of Bernez, steward to the King of Sardinia; and by him were established priories of this system in all the principal towns of that kingdom, as well as in many cities of Italy.

At Chambery English Freemasonry had soon to give way to the system of Strict Observance, and the Provincial Grand Lodge, instituted in that city by the Grand Lodge of London, transformed itself, in 1775, into a Directory of the Masons of Lombardy; but which was dissolved in 1794. At Naples the Prince of Caramanca was placed at the head of the Templar system, which there, as elsewhere, very soon displaced the English Rite.

The interdictions of the Papal authority, as also the clandestine persecutions of the clergy and government, little by little, dispersed the majority of the lodges, and those which survived were closed during the French Revolution.

Under the French government, however, a new era

seemed to dawn for Masonry in Italy. A lodge, organized at Milan in 1801, was followed by the establishment of another at Mantua, and others in the principal cities; when the Scottish Rite, introduced at Paris in 1804, and imported to Milan in 1805, by virtue of a constitution dated at Paris, and bearing the signatures of De Grasse-Tilly, Pyron, Benier and Vidal, organized a Supreme Council for Italy, which extended its ramifications to Sicily. It was this Supreme Council of Milan which gave to one of its members, named Lechangeur, the idea of creating, in 1806, the Rite of Misraim, in accordance with which councils of high degrees were instituted at Naples and Venice.[1]

The Grand Orient, created at Naples in 1807, and having the Prince Eugène for Grand Master, subsequently united itself to the Grand Orient of Italy, which was organized on the 24th June, 1809, under the auspices and Grand Mastership of the king, Joachim Murat.

With the fall of Napoleon I, this portion of the history of Freemasonry in Italy closes. Thereafter all the interdictions, bulls, and edicts were renewed. The decree of Pope Pius VII, dated 15th August, 1814, carried infamy and bodily torture as the penalty incurred by all convicted of assembling as Freemasons. Immediately following this, similar decrees were promulgated by all the crowned heads of Catholic countries, all repeating the absurd charges contained in the decree of the Pope, Pius VII, and prohibiting in their respective states all Masonic assemblies. Finally, on the 8th August, the King of Naples issued his interdiction, and, under penalty of sentence to the galleys, prohibited all participation in the assemblies of Freemasons.

After that time the lodges continued closed in Italy,

---

[1] This rite was imported to Paris in 1814, where it yet exists, and has given, in its turn, birth in that city to the Rite of Memphis.

and it was not until 1856—an interval of forty years—that the Grand Orient of France instituted lodges at Gênes and at Livorne. Since then the lodges have multiplied and extended into all the principal cities of the peninsula. These lodges soon decided to institute an independent Grand Lodge; and, after the elaboration by their delegates of a suitable constitution, on the 1st January, 1862, the Grand Orient of Italy was organized, with its seat at Turin, and the brother Nigra nominated Grand Master. This brother, however, having declined the nomination, the brethren Cordova and General Garibaldi were put in nomination, and the former elected.

In consequence of the severity practiced against it by the new central power, the lodge "Dante Alighieri," which professed the Scottish (33d) Rite—a profession that was unhappily entertained by several other lodges—detached itself from the Grand Orient, and declared itself independent. Similar tendencies having manifested themselves in other parts of Italy, and a Supreme Council for Sicily having been constituted at Palermo, with General Garibaldi as its chief, and some twelve lodges ranking themselves under its banner, on the 12th August, 1863, a convocation of all the Masonic bodies of Italy was called, to meet at Turin, to take into consideration the tendency of these disorders, and devise means to check them. Not being able to agree, the brethren who represented the Grand Orient of Turin withdrew from this assembly, and thus allowed their places in the commission, appointed to draft a new constitution, to be filled by brethren who were all partisans of the Scottish Rite. We know not, at the present time, (close of 1863,) the result of this labor; in no case, however, can we believe this result will be favorable to the interests of true Freemasonry.

The Grand Orient of Italy, having rejected the high degrees which, during the past century, had produced much discord among the lodges of that country, and, under its constitution, recognized nothing as Masonry but the three symbolic degrees of the English Rite, many Masonic authorities hesitated to recognize it, in the belief that the political agitation of the country might cause its early dissolution. The desire to found a Polish and a Hungarian Grand Orient, at the head of which, respectively, should be placed a political chief of these countries, has not a little contributed to strengthen such a belief.

At the close of 1863 the Grand Orient of Italy reckoned under its jurisdiction sixty-eight operative lodges, among which are to be found lodges in Alexandria and Cairo, in Egypt; at Constantinople, in Turkey, and Lima, in South America.

Portugal.

There is one country where Masonic light has penetrated but with the greatest difficulty; for it is the seat of ignorance and superstition. This country is the paradise of monks, who there cease not to build convents, and exercise the exclusive privilege of directing the minds of the people, the king, and his councilors. That country is Portugal.

From the Book of Constitutions, first published by the Grand Lodge of London, in 1723—and subsequently at later periods, to the extent of five separate editions, the last of which was published by order of the Grand Lodge of England, in 1855—we learn that the Grand Lodge of London instituted at Lisbon, in 1735, a Provincial Grand Lodge, by the agency of Bro. George Gordon; but th seeds thus sown fell on barren soil. In the matter of persecution, undergone by all who attempted to disseminate Freemasonry in this country, it stands without a rival, if we may except Spain; but latterly this condition is disappearing.

The Inquisition, here under the protection of the king, tracked every person from far and near who were suspected of being Freemasons. Thus, two lapidaries—the one named John Custos, originally a Protestant from Berne in Switzerland, and the other, named Alexander James Monton, originally a Catholic from Paris—having been accused of having expressed the desire to see a lodge organized in Lisbon, fell into the snares set by the "Holy Office," and were thrown into prison in 1743. The accusation charged them with seeking to introduce Freemasonry into Portugal, in violation of the bull of the Pope, which condemned this detestable doctrine as a heresy, and all Freemasons as impious, sodomists, etc. Under the order of the Cardinal Dacunha, grand inquisitor, they submitted nine times in three months to the most abominable torture that it is possible to imagine; subsequently they were forced to assist at an *auto-da-fé*, and finally condemned to the galleys for life. Thanks to the aid of English Freemasons, however, they were enabled to escape and seek refuge in England. Of the many other Masons who, like those unfortunates, fell into the traps of the Inquisition, and who, no doubt, sunk under the torture inflicted by that detestable institution, we have been unable to discover the least trace.

The Inquisition was no less severe with the natives of the country; for, in 1776, two Portuguese nobles, Major D'Alincourt and Don Oyres D'Ornelles-Parracao, were also imprisoned and tortured, because they were Freemasons. Although all vestige of Masonry had disappeared for twenty-five years, in 1802 an inquest was ordered against Freemasons in Portugal, and all who were suspected even, by this inquest, were charged with conspiracy against the king and the church, and sentenced to the galleys without trial or form of law.

Notwithstanding these severe measures, we find, in 1805, a Grand Orient at Lisbon, with a Grand Master, named

Egaz-Moniz; but its ramifications were not very extended. Dissolved after the events of 1814, it was formed again in 1817, and sought to animate some lodges; but Freemasonry continued to inspire the monks with terror, and, yielding to their solicitations, King John VI issued a decree, dated at Rio Janeiro, the 30th March, 1818, inter dicting Freemasons from assembling together, under pain of death. We know nothing of the lives destroyed under this decree; but, about five years afterward, it was modified by another, which, dated Lisbon, June 20, 1823, stated that it was issued in consequence of remonstrances upon the subject having been, during the interval, addressed to the government by many of the resident embassadors. By the terms of this last decree, the penalty was changed from capital punishment to five years' labor in the galleys in Africa. No proof beyond mere suspicion was necessary to cause the arrest of persons who were punished under the penalties of those edicts. Foreigners as well as natives were proceeded against without any attempt to disguise the act, or the least attention being given to the many protests which were made by the agents of their respective countries.

Notwithstanding these interdictions, however, as well as the cruelties which were exercised under their authority, a Masonic body was constituted at Lisbon, under the title of the Grand Orient of Lusitania, as also a Supreme Council of the Scottish (33d) Rite. The later sovereigns of Portugal, without having revoked the prohibitory decrees against Freemasons, appeared to tolerate the Fraternity; for there has been established another authority at Oporto, under the name of *"Pattos-Manuel;"* and subsequently a Provincial Grand Lodge of Ireland. But in a country where—as in Spain and at Rome—the clergy rule every thing, we can entertain but little hope for the extension or well-being of Freemasonry.

Spain.

In no country, Portugal excepted, has Freemasonry been exposed to persecutions more atrocious than in the Roman Catholic kingdom, *par excellence*, of Spain—persecutions based upon the bulls of Clement XII, of the 27th April, 1738; of Benedict XIV, of the 18th May, 1751, and the edict of Cardinal Consalvi, of the 13th August, 1814, which, as we have seen, pronounced all Freemasons excommunicated, and condemned them to the most severe penalties, even to death itself.

From the Book of Constitutions we learn that in 1727 and in 1728, under the Grand Mastership of the Count of Inchquin and Lord Coleraine, the first warrants were delivered to establish lodges at Gibraltar and Madrid. In 1739 a number of lodges were instituted at these places, and the Grand Lodge of London patented Captain Commerford Provincial Grand Master for all Andalusia.

The Catholic clergy of Spain exhibited themselves at a very early period here, as elsewhere, the bitter enemy of Freemasonry. The better to enable them to discover the members of the Fraternity, and the secret practices and doctrines of the institution, the monk Joseph Torrubia, censor of the Holy Office of the Inquisition at Madrid, was ordered, in 1750, to assume a false name, pass himself as a layman, and be initiated into a Masonic lodge. For this purpose he received from the Pope's legate the dispensations necessary to relieve him from the obligations of the oaths he should have to take upon being made a Freemason. After having thus been enabled to visit the lodges in different parts of Spain, he presented himself before the supreme tribunal of the Inquisition, denounced Freemasonry as the most abominable institution that existed in the world, accused its members of every vice and crime revolting to religion, and submitted a list of ninety-seven lodges established in the kingdom, against which he solicited the most rigorous action of the Inquisition.

The importance of the great number of brethren who were members of these lodges, belonging, as they did, to the nobility and to the rich and influential classes, induced the Holy Office to reflect upon the matter, and decided i to request the king to interdict the institution of Freemasonry. In response to its promptings, Ferdinand VI issued a decree, dated the 2d July, 1751, prohibiting the institution of Freemasonry throughout the extent of his kingdom, under the pretext that it was dangerous to the state and to religion, and pronouncing the penalty of death against all who should profess it. Under this decree many persons were sacrificed by the order of the Inquisition. These cruelties were calculated to suppress all idea of introducing Masonry within the country, and also of restraining any exhibition of life on the part of the lodges already established; so that it was not until after the French Revolution that they emerged again into the light, and began to spread more rapidly than before. After having founded at Xeres a Grand Lodge for Spain, there was established, on the 3d November, 1805, under the government of Joseph Napoleon, a Grand Orient of Spain, having its seat at Madrid, the very stronghold of the Inquisition. The same year was constituted a Supreme Council of the Scottish (33d) Rite, and subsequently a Grand Orient, at Grenada, the Athens of Spain.

In 1814, Ferdinand VII re-established the Inquisition, and, by a decree dated 24th May of that year, ordered all the lodges to be closed, and pronouncing all participation in Masonry a crime against the state. Many lodges, particularly those of Grenada, having braved this ordinance, all their members were arrested and thrown into prison. Of their number was the Marquis of Toulouse, and General Alvada, Adjutant-General to the Duke of Wellington, together with many Frenchmen, Italians, and Germans. The provisional government of 1820 released them all, and in that year many lodges resumed their labors; but, on the 1st August, 1824, the King, Ferdinand VII, renewed his decree of interdiction, and pronounced the penalty of death against all who, being Freemasons, should not announce themselves as such within thirty days; while, after that time, those who should be recognized as such, and had not so declared themselves, should be hung within twenty-four hours without form of law.

So stringent a measure as this would have informed that government, which held no obligations sacred, that eighty thousand of its subjects were banded together as a brotherhood, had any of those subjects been disloyal to his obligations to that brotherhood; but, strange to say, the Inquisition found very few victims.

In 1825, the clergy of Grenada, under the authority of this interdiction, distinguished themselves by the bloody execution of seven Freemasons; and subsequently, in 1829, new traces of Masonry having been discovered in Barcelona, the unhappy brethren fell into the hands of the Inquisition, which ordered the execution of one of them, the brother Galvez, a lieutenant-colonel in the Spanish army, and sentenced the other two to the galleys for life.

Notwithstanding these rigorous measures, there were many Freemasons in Spain; and even a Masonic authority, styled the "Grand Directory," is known to exist somewhere in the kingdom, but where, or what may be the plan of its labors, we are unable to say.

At Cadiz there is a lodge composed entirely of Englishmen, with which the government does not interfere; and at Gibraltar there are four, like that in Cadiz, under the protection of the Grand Lodge of England, at London.

The countries in which Masonry is at present prohibited are: Spain and her colonies, Catholic Bavaria, Austria and its dependencies, and Russia, with the countries under her rule.

HISTORY OF THE ORIGIN

OF THE

ANCIENT AND ACCEPTED SCOTTISH RITE,

AND ORGANIZATION OF THE SUPREME COUNCIL OF THAT RITE FOR FRANCE.[1]

THE Masonic authority which directed a fraction of French Masonry, under the title of the "Supreme Council of Sovereign Grand Inspectors General of the 33d and last degree of the Ancient and Accepted Scottish Rite for France," was organized at Paris, on the 22d of September, 1804, by the Count Alexander Francis Augustus de Grasse-Tilly, son of the admiral of that name; and this organization was formed under a warrant, dated and delivered to him at Charleston, South Carolina, on the 21st February, 1802, by a body styling itself the "Supreme Council of Grand Inspectors General for America," etc., sitting in that city. This warrant conferred upon the brother De Grasse plenary powers to initiate Masons into, and constitute lodges, chapters, and consistories of, this rite in the then (February, 1802,) French colony of St. Domingo.

---

[1] Knowing how much importance will attach to this portion of th General History of Freemasonry, assuming, as it does, to give the real origin of "the Ancient and Accepted Scottish Rite" of thirty-three degrees—how earnestly it will be studied, discussed, and commented upon by some, and probably disbelieved by others of the brethren, who have taken the commonly-received history of the rite and the "grand constitutions" as truth in every particular—I have followed the author so

Without proceeding, in this place, with the history of the first Masonic power created in France under this warrant, and the forms of this rite—the title of which we have already given—and to chronicle the acts of such body from 1804 to the present time—which we propose to do in another volume—we will at this time give our attention to the origin of the Masonic authority by which it was instituted.

We will begin with quoting from the document submitted to the Masonic Fraternity by the partisans of this rite, giving an account of its origin:

"It appears, from authentic documents, that the establishment of the sublime and ineffable degrees of Masonry took place in Scotland, France, and Prussia immediately after the first crusade; but, in consequence of circumstances which to us are unknown, they were neglected from 1658 to 1744. Then a Scotch gentleman visited France, and re-established the Lodge of Perfection at Bourdeaux.[1] . . . In 1761, the lodges and councils of the superior degrees having extended over the continent of Europe, his majesty the King of Prussia, who was Grand Commander of the degree of

---

closely in this department—sentence for sentence and word for word—that I may be said to have waived the right of a translator, and rendered the author's language at the expense of my own. I trust, however, the object will justify the action.—TRANSLATOR.

[1] According to this recital, it would be necessary to admit that the propagation of the Scottish Rite of "these sublime and ineffable degrees" is due to a "Scotch gentleman," unknown both as to his own name as well as the lodge or Masonic authority that authorized him to "re-establish" this rite in France! The fact is, that before 1789 there never was a lodge of the Scottish Rite, neither of twenty-five nor thirty-three degrees, established at Bourdeaux; while that which existed at Arras—a Grand Chapter—was founded by Charles Edward Stuart, in 1747. Subsequently there was, in 1751, a mother lodge of what was then called the Scottish Rite, founded at Marseilles; and in 1756 the Grand Chapter of Clermont was founded, in the convent of Clermont, at Paris. In addition to these so-called Masonic bodies, the dates of whose institution are well known, there were numerous chapters, tribunals, etc., founded by Dr. Ramsay, between the years 1736 and 1740, no details of which are known to us.

Prince of the Royal Secret,[1] was recognized by all as chief of the sublime and ineffable degrees of Masonry in the two hemispheres.

His royal highness Charles, hereditary prince of the Swedes, the Goths, and the Vandals, Duke of Sudermanie, etc., was and continued to be the Grand Commander and protector of sublime Masonry in Sweden; and his royal highness Louis of Bourbon, prince of the blood, the Duke of Chartres, and cardinal prince of Rohan, Bishop of Strasburg, were at the head of these degrees in France. * * *

"On the 25th of October, 1762, the grand constitutions were finally ratified at Berlin, and proclaimed for the government of all the lodges of sublime and perfect Masons, chapters, councils, colleges, and consistories of the royal and military art of Freemasonry upon the whole surface of the two hemispheres, etc.

"In the same year some constitutions were transmitted to our illustrious brother Stephen Morin, who, on the 27th of August, 1761, had been appointed Inspector General of all the lodges, etc., of the New World, by the Grand Consistory of Princes of the Royal Secret, convoked at Paris, and at which presided the deputy of the King of Prussia, Chaillou de Joinville, Substitute General of the Order, Worshipful Master of the first lodge of France, called St. Anthony, Chief of the eminent degrees, etc. Being present the brethren Prince of Rohan, etc.[2]

"By the constitutions of the Order, ratified on the 25th of October, 1762, the King of Prussia had been proclaimed Chief of the high degrees, with the rank of Sovereign Grand Inspector General and Grand Commander. The high councils and chapters not being able to work but in his presence, or in that of the substitute who he might designate; while all the transactions of the Consistory of Princes of the Royal Secret had to be sanctioned by him, or his substitute, for the establishment of their legality; and many other prerogatives being attached to his Masonic rank. No disposition had, however, been inserted in the constitution for the nomination of his successor; and, as this was an office of the highest importance, the greatest precautions were necessary to

---

[1] This was the name of the last degree of the Rite of Perfection, which was composed of twenty-five degrees.
[2] See page 88 for a transcript of this appointment.

protect it, that none but a person entirely worthy should be appointed to it. Realizing the importance of this fact, the king established the thirty-third degree.[1] Nine brethren of each nation formed the Supreme Council of Grand Inspectors General, who, since his decease, have possessed all the Masonic powers and prerogatives enjoyed by him. They constitute the exclusive body of the Society, and their approbation is now indispensable to the acts of the Consistory, to which it gives the force of law. From their decisions there is no appeal. The sublime degrees are at this moment (1802) as they were at the time of their first formation; they have not undergone the slightest alteration—the least addition. The same principles and the same ceremonies have been from all time observed; and this we know by the documents of our archives, which have existed for many centuries of years in their original condition."

The author of these passages has forgotten, no doubt, to quote the documents mentioned in the introduction, as also those extracts from the archives to which he alludes at the close.

This recital we extract from a report which, accompanied by some historical notes, seems to have been submitted to the Supreme Council at Charleston, in 1802, by one of its members, named Frederick Dalcho, and which, in 1808, were printed in Dublin. This curious document is the first that has given the pretended history of the Scottish Rite, and all that has been published since then as to the origin of the rite has been extracted more or less literally from it. The object for which this document was produced is therein explained—it was to be distributed and sent, in the form of a circular, to all the Masonic authorities upon the globe; and to render it more worthy of belief, and to give it greater importance, the Supreme Council at Charleston had it affirmed, or sworn to, by the brethren Isaac Auld and Emmanuel de la Motte, approved

---

[1] It will be remembered that the rite of which it is stated he was chief had but twenty-five degrees.

by the Grand Master, *ad vitam*, Colonel Mitchell, and certified to, as in all particulars true and sincere, by Abraham Alexander, Secretary of the Holy Empire.[1]

The preceding recital concerning the Scottish Rite, so far as quoted, is well worthy of taking rank among the products of that noble army of Masonic authors and fabricators of new rites, who, to give their creations some importance, invent with the greatest facility, time, place, and honorable circumstances attending their origin. If the authors of this new Scottish Rite have not considered it necessary to assign to it a greater antiquity; if they have not, as is customary with most writers upon Masonry, placed the birth of their rite in the cradle of the world, or thereabouts, it is because they have reasoned a little more logically than their imitators. The name of *Scottish* not being any better known to antiquity than was that of *Freemason*, it reasonably became necessary to place the origin of this rite at an epoch which had some connection with history. The majority of our self-styled Masonic historians, in their statements as to the origin of our institution, trouble themselves to the smallest possible extent as to its connection with written history; for, in speaking of its antiquity, they appear to think it entirely unnecessary to describe how it was possible for it to descend intact to our time through forty or fifty centuries, which, they glibly inform us, have elapsed since its birth. The name of *Freemason*, as indicating with decision and in the most incontestable manner the origin of the institution, is not, to this class of writers, of the slightest consequence.

If the inventors of the Scottish Rite of thirty-three degrees have not been as careless as the generality of their predecessors, they have not been much more happy in their

---

[1] It is by this title that the "Ancient and Accepted Scottish Rite" qualifies the country over which it extends its authority.

exposition of its origin. Not being able to found their creation upon any act more or less authentic, or upon any fact of history, the scaffolding erected by them to support it necessarily gives way at the first shock, in the way of an earnest examination, to which they submitted it; and thus left unsupported, it shares the fortune of the creations of their predecessors in the same kind of speculation.

In overturning this scaffolding, we need but advance the facts of history and compare them with the assertions contained in the fragment of the report that we have quoted. As to an examination of the question of fact whether or not the report which he produced, signed by Frederick Dalcho, had not been fabricated by himself subsequently to 1802, in order to destroy the doubts which attached themselves at a later period to the authenticity of this rite, we leave that to one side.

In the beginning, ancient Freemasonry (from 715 B. C. to the year 400 of our era), that of the middle ages (from 400 to 1500), and that which was practiced after that time in England, had never but three degrees of initiation. From 1640 to 1660 the partisans of the Stuarts, abusing the trust reposed in them by the Masonic Fraternity, and using their meetings as a cloak under cover of which to elaborate their schemes of monarchical restoration, created two superior degrees, viz: that of Scottish Master as the fourth, and that of Templar Mason as the fifth degree. When the society was transformed, in 1717, at London, and, from being a corporation more or less mechanical, became an institution entirely philosophic, it adopted but the three primitive or symbolic degrees. Before the year 1717 the lodges of Freemasons had no affiliations outside of England, and it is proven incontestably that the first lodge of the modern or philosophic Freemasonry established outside of Great Britain, was established at Dunkirk, in 1721, with a ritual of three degrees. A third lodge was established in 1725 at Paris. From that time

Freemasonry extended rapidly into all the other countries of the north of Europe, first into Belgium, and subsequently into Holland and Germany.

The rite called Scottish is a bastard child of Freemasonry, to which the policy of the Stuart interest gave birth. It was introduced in France, between 1736 and 1738, by the Baron Ramsay, who was an instrument of the Jesuits.[1] This partisan of the Stuart interest was the first propagandist of this rite in France, wherein he extended it to many parts, in a few years, by the aid of his delegates and those of the Jesuits; but it was not until after the arrival in France of the Pretender, Charles Edward, that the rite called Scottish assumed any importance. The Pretender treated the Chapter of Arras, and the noblemen of his suite immediately besought of this chapter warrants with which to propagate the rite. His scale had then augmented, and from seven degrees it successively arose to twenty-five; for we find, in 1758,[2] a chapter or council of Emperors of the East and West, furnished with this number of degrees, established at Paris.

From this time all the fabricators of new rites, although they increased to a frightful extent, had the good sense not to augment the number of the degrees, but, on the contrary, gradually reduced them—the Scottish Rite alone containing the highest number, and it, from 1755 to 1802, being limited to twenty-five. After the congress of Wilhelmsbad the principal Masonic rites were subjected to great changes, and were every-where modified and reduced to seven, to ten, and to twelve degrees.

From these facts—which are incontestable—it followed that during the space of time that we have named (from 1755 to 1802), there did not exist in any country—no more in England than in France, no more in Prussia than in Sweden—councils of the Scottish Rite of thirty-three de-

---

[1] See the History of the origin of all the Rites. [2] Ibid.

grees. Now, the report that we have quoted explicitly says: "These sublime degrees are at this moment (1802) as they were at the time of their first formation; they have not undergone the slightest alteration—the least addition." This assertion is doubly inexact; because, in the first place, previous to 1801, no Scottish Rite of thirty-three degrees was known; and, in the second place, all the rites and degrees, without regard to name or number, were created between 1736 and 1800, and they had nothing in common with the primitive English Rite.

If, then, there did not exist, before 1802, neither a Scottish Rite of thirty-three degrees, nor councils of Grand Inspectors General and Commanders, it follows that the Prince of Sudermanie could not be the Grand Master of the rite in Sweden, nor, for the same reason, could Frederick the Great be its chief in Prussia.

As to another allegation in the same report—that the King of Prussia had been recognized chief of these councils upon the two hemispheres, conformably to the grand constitutions of this Order, which were ratified on the 25th of October, 1762, at Berlin—it is, like all the others, destitute of foundation in fact; and this we will proceed to prove.

The king, Frederick of Prussia, was initiated into Masonry on the 15th of August, 1738, at Brunswick, being then prince royal.[1] The lodge at the Three Globes, in Berlin, founded by some French artists whom the king had invited to Prussia, was elevated by him to the rank of a Grand Lodge in 1744, and of which he became thereupon Grand Master—a dignity that he exercised until 1747.[2] After that time he never occupied himself actively with Masonry. In his interviews with the brethren who directed the Grand Lodge at the Three Globes, and who kept him informed as to what occurred of a Masonic

---

[1] See Lenning's Encyclopedia of Freemasonry, book 4, page 453, 2d ed.
[2] His name, nevertheless, was borne upon the register of the "Grand Lodge at the Three Globes," as its Grand Master, until 1755.

character, he continued to exhibit his attachment to our institution; but when the different new systems, brought into Prussia by the Marquis of Berny and the officers of the army of Broglie, disseminated themselves in the German lodges, he exhibited himself the enemy of these innovations, and expressed his disdain for these high degrees, as was his manner, freely and in hard terms, prophesying that they would one day be a fruitful source of discord among the lodges and the systems. It seemed that his prediction was to be verified; for these divers systems soon engendered anarchy within the lodges, even in the lodge at the Three Globes itself, to such an extent that disgusted him with Masonry, without, however, changing his preconceived opinions of the institution. After this he authorized the creation of two other Grand Lodges at Berlin; but he never had any other connection with them than to respond with thanks to their complimentary expressions on the occurrence of his birthday. The last letter that King Frederick wrote, under these circumstances, is addressed to the Grand Master of *La Goanerie*, and bears date 7th February, 1778. As has been well remarked, this letter is written in a style very different from what he had been accustomed to use in addressing the lodges.[1] After this letter, he abstained from even thank-

---

[1] We extract from Lenning's Encyclopedia a transcript of this letter, as it appears on page 455 of that work:

"The king has been sensible of the homage that the Lodge of Friendship at Berlin has rendered to His Majesty in the discourse pronounced by its orator on the anniversary of the day of his birth. His Majesty has found such expressions very conformable to the sentiments which he has always attributed to that lodge as sustained toward his person; and he readily assures that lodge, in his turn, that he will always interest himself with pleasure in the happiness and prosperity of an assembly which, like it, places its first glory in the indefatigable and uninterrupted propagation of all the virtues of the honest man and the true patriot. [Signed] "FREDERICK.

"POTSDAM, 7th February, 1778.
"To the Royal York of Friendship Lodge of Freemasons."

ing the lodges, when they felicitated him upon the recurrence of the occasion we have mentioned. During the last thirty years of his reign, King Frederick took no active part whatever in Masonry; this is a notorious fact, and proven by the minutes of the Grand Lodges of Berlin.[1] Then it follows that the revision of the high degrees and the Masonic constitutions which they attribute to him, and which should have taken place, according to the report in question, in 1786—the year of his death—is no more correct than is his augmentation of the degrees.

As to the rituals which he should have prepared himself for these high degrees the same year,[2] they could not

---

[1] We can support these assertions with not only the letters which we have received from the Secretary of the Grand Lodge at the Three Globes in Berlin, but also with the minutes of this authority, bearing date, respectively, the 17th August, 1833, and 19th December, 1861, which declare, in the most formal and positive manner, that the documents sent to it at different times, styled "Grand Constitutions of the Scottish Rite of thirty-third," as well those written in Latin and in French as those written in the English language, and attributed to King Frederick II—documents of which the authenticity is doubtful—are all apocryphal, as, in general, are all the other acts relating to this rite which pretend to have emanated from that prince. (See Lenning's Encyclopedia of Freemasonry, edition of 1862, pages 455 and 456.)

There is other proof not less authentic, which puts to flight the fables invented by the partisans of the Scottish Rite. It is that it is well known that the King Frederick II, on the 9th September, 1785, went to Berlin for the last time, to visit his sister, the Princess Amelia, and the next day he reviewed the artillery at Wedding. From thence he returned to Potsdam, where he passed the whole winter in bodily suffering from the malady that eventually caused his death. He was moved in a very unquiet state, on the 17th April, 1786, to his retreat of *Sans Souci*, and there died four months afterward. (See the same work, page 456.)

We will abstain from any other reflections upon this subject, and merely add, as a last fact in support of our assertions, that, to the knowledge of every lodge in Berlin, the King Frederick II in no manner occupied himself with Masonry during the last thirty years of his life.

[2] See the *Book of Gold* of the Supreme Council for France, printed in 1807, page 7. It is in direct contradiction with the report of the brother Dalcho, who does not attribute to King Frederick but the creation of the

in any case have been drawn up by him, as he was at this time in a dying condition; and, long before his death—which took place on the 17th August, 1786—he was totally incapable of any species of labor.

With regard to the assertions relating to the grand constitutions, or rules and regulations of the rite, of 1762, that King Frederick II should have himself ratified on the 1st of May, 1786, they are equally destitute of foundation, since these rituals did not exist at this time, but were evidently fabricated in 1804. In a word, every thing connected with this rite that pretends to be historic has been invented in part by its creators, and finished by its propagandists.

To all these simple facts, which are truly historic, destructive as they are of the truth of the principal assertions contained in the report of Frederick Dalcho—though that report is affirmed, approved, and certified as true by many high dignitaries of this rite—we could add others not less conclusive, did we not believe such addition superfluous.

We will now enumerate the facts which preceded the establishment of this authority in Paris, and indicate the origin of the Masonic power which constituted it; but to do this we must go back nearly a century.

---

thirty-third degree, and not that of the eight degrees from the twenty-fifth to the thirty-third. This *Book of Gold* (it would be better named the book of *brass*) thus explains the creation of these degrees:

"It *would appear* that the institution of the Supreme Council of the thirty-third and last degree is the work of this prince (Frederick II), who, upon his ascent to the throne, declared himself the protector of the Order in his states; that the dignity of Sovereign of Sovereigns, in the Consistories of Princes of the Royal Secret, resided in his person; that it was him who augmented to thirty-three the twenty-five degrees of the ancient and accepted rite, as they were decreed in 1762: and, finally, that he delegated his sovereignty to the Supreme Council, who named it 'of the thirty-third and last degree,' for the purpose of exercising it after his death."

In 1761, a brother named Stephen Morin, by confession an Israelite, a member of the then National Grand Lodge of France, and also of a chapter of high degrees, having been called to America by some private interests, manifested the desire to establish in those countries the Masonry of the higher degrees, then called "Masonry of Perfection;" and, with this object, he addressed himself to the brother Lacorne, dancing-master, and at that time a deposed substitute of the Grand Master, the Count of Clermont. Upon the proposition made by the latter for this purpose to the Sovereign Grand Council of Princes of the East and West, there was, on the 27th August, 1761, delivered to the brother Morin a patent or warrant, by which he was created Inspector General of all the lodges of the New World, etc.[1]

Arrived at St. Domingo, the brother Stephen Morin named, by virtue of his patent, one of his co-religionists, the brother Moses M. Hayes, Deputy Inspector for North America. He afterward conferred the same dignity upon a brother Frankin for Jamaica and the English windward islands, and upon the brother Colonel Prevost for the English leeward islands and British army. Some time afterward the brother Frankin transferred his authority to the brother Moses Hayes, Grand Master at Boston, Mass. In his turn, the brother Moses M. Hayes named, as Inspector General for South Carolina, another of his co-religionists, the brother Isaac Da Costa, who established, in 1783, a Sublime Grand Lodge of Perfection at Charleston. To this brother, after his death, succeeded another Israelite, named Joseph Myers. There were successively created by these self-styled Grand Inspectors General other inspectors for the different States of America. The brother Bush was appointed for Pennsylvania, and the brother Barend M. Spitzer for Georgia.

---

[1] See the text of this patent in the History of Freemasonry in France, page 88.

On the 15th May, 1781, these brethren assembled in council, at Philadelphia, the different inspectors for those States. It was by this council that the degree of Inspector General was conferred for Jamaica on the brother Moses Cohen. It also appointed to this dignity Isaac Long and the brethren De La Hogue, Croze-Magnan, St. Paul, Petit, and Marie—all residents of Charleston—to propagate the rite in the different countries of America.

There existed, as we have already stated, at Charleston, a Grand Lodge of Perfection, with a Council of Princes of Jerusalem, founded by the brother Da Costa in 1783. To this Grand Lodge, on the 27th February, 1788, was united the Royal Arch Chapter, founded by authority of a chapter of this title at Dublin; and it was by this body that the brother Colonel Mitchell was appointed, on the 2d of August, 1795, a Deputy Inspector General for the State of South Carolina, who, in the plenitude of his powers, in 1797 conferred this title on the Count De Grasse-Tilly, a resident of St. Domingo, and assigned to him the same power for the French colonies of America.

This council of Inspectors General styled itself the Grand Council of Princes of Jerusalem, and all the constitutions delivered by it to its inspectors were always given in this name, seeing that the first patent delivered to Stephen Morin, in 1761, emanated from an authority which had given itself this name.

This council of Princes of Jerusalem, sitting at Charleston, created some inspectors of lodges and chapters, whom it liberally remunerated. In 1801 it was composed of the brethren Colonel Mitchell, Frederick Dalcho, Abraham Auld, Isaac Auld, Emmanuel de la Motte, and some others of less mark, who all belonged to the Jewish religion.[1]

It may readily be believed that the constitutions granted by this council, composed, as we have indicated, of breth-

---

[1] See Ragon's *Masonic Orthodoxy*, page 181, which represents the members of this council as audacious jugglers.

ren belonging to the Jewish religion, were not as extensive as they probably desired; and it was this feeling, without doubt, that suggested the idea of creating something new—something striking, and of a nature to procure them some advantage not offered by their position. The abuse that they had already made of the powers conferred upon them—although the conferring authority itself was more or less illegal, emanating, as it did, from a self-created body—should have induced all earnest Masons and honest men to have shunned a similar work, and particularly one that they dared not avow; but personal ambition and self-interest prevailed over the Masonic principles and common honesty which these brethren had sworn to observe, the speculation was engaged in, and, unhappily for the character of Freemasonry, it has, to some extent, proved a success.

A new Masonic power was combined and created under the title of "Supreme Council of the Grand Commanders Inspectors General of the thirty-third and last degree of the Ancient and Accepted Scottish Rite."

This new creation naturally bore the same illegal character, and was accompanied by the same deplorable circumstances which had already signalized the factious period from 1740 to 1770—a period of false titles, illegal constitutions, antedated regulations, etc.

The new authority lost no time in constituting itself. It elected its own members to the highest dignities of their new order of knighthood, and delivered to them patents with which they were empowered to institute this new rite wherever their fortunes should carry them. The brother Colonel Mitchell was nominated the first Grand Commander. He died at Charleston, in 1841.

But to facilitate the progress of the new rite, it was necessary to give it a respectable origin, and support it with some historic names as those of its originators and protectors. This trust was committed to the brethren

Dalcho, Auld, and La Motte, and we have seen by the report from which we have quoted how they discharged it.

Probably among the first deliverances of the new power was the warrant sent to De Grasse-Tilly—who had some time previously been appointed as Inspector General of the Rite of Perfection for the French colonies in America—to enable him to establish, in the Island of St. Domingo, a Supreme Council of the new rite. This patent conferred upon him the title of Lieutenant Commander of the new rite, and is dated the 21st February, 1802.

Having little hope of being recognized as a Masonic authority in America, this new power sought the recognition of the different Masonic powers established in Europe; and, with this object, it sent to all the Grand Lodges of Europe a circular, dated the 11th of December, 1802, by which it informed them of its installation, and gave them the names of the degrees which it conferred itself, and authorized its Grand Commander to confer in its name.

The Grand Lodge of St. John of Scotland, located in Edinburgh—which was generally regarded, though wrongfully, as the mother lodge of all the Scotch Rites, and which, on this account, had the greatest interest in protesting against this new creation—was indignant upon sight of this circular, and, in the response that it made thereto, declared "that such a number of degrees could not but inspire the most profound surprise in those professing Scottish Masonry; that it could never recognize such a collection, seeing that it had always preserved the Scottish Rite in the simplicity of its primitive institution, and that it would never disarrange its system in this respect."

This Grand Lodge of Scotland, sitting at Edinburgh and directing all the lodges of Scotland, has, in fact, never practiced any other rite but that of the three symbolic de-

---

[1] See *History of Freemasonry*, by Alexander Laurie.

grees;[1] and, upon many occasions, it has disowned, in the most formal manner, the charters and patents which have been attributed to it, and by which it was accused of having authorized the exercise of the high degrees called Scottish. In view of this fact, we believe it to be important and necessary to the better understanding of Freemasonry every-where, and to dissipate the opinion that prevails upon this subject, to here state that the Grand Lodge of St. John of Scotland, sitting at Edinburgh, is an utter stranger to all the systems called Scottish Masonry, practiced as well in France as elsewhere in Europe and America.[2]

---

[1] The regulations that it published in 1836 were entitled "The Laws and Constitutions of the Grand Lodge of the Ancient and Honorable Fraternity of Free and Accepted Masons of Scotland;" while article four contained a passage thus expressed: "The Grand Lodge of Scotland practices no other degree of Freemasonry but those of Apprentice, Fellow-craft, and Master Mason."

[2] It was by a patent of this same Charleston Council—father of all the bastard children of Freemasonry—that the first Supreme Council established in Great Britain was organized, at Dublin, in 1808. The latter was the only Supreme Council that existed on English territory prior to 1846. In that year, however, there were organized one at London and another at Edinburgh. The first was instituted by Dr. Crucifix, editor of the Freemason's Magazine, by authority of a patent obtained by him from a Supreme Council sitting at New York; and the last was instituted by Walter Arnott d'Arlary, who fabricated for himself a constituting power. The title of this council being in consequence disputed, it was reconstituted on the 14th July, and installed on the 17th, by the brother Morrison of Greenfield, a member of the Supreme Council for France, who was invested with powers, called regular, for this purpose.

The most deplorable fact in regard to all these creations, the regular as well as the irregular, is, that they are constantly fighting, criminating, recriminating, and anathematizing each other. Thus, the Supreme Council at Edinburgh (which must not be confounded with the Grand Lodge of Edinburgh, the only regular Masonic authority in Scotland, and which recognizes but the three symbolic degrees,) declared, immediately after its reconstitution in the manner indicated, that it would not recognize the letters or diplomas emanating from the Supreme Council attached to the Grand Orient of France; and also interrupted all commu-

These pretended high degrees, into which have been introduced the reveries of the Templars, the speculations of the mystics, the deceptions of the alchemists, the magii, and many other idealists more or less dreamy, and the greater part of which repose upon legends absurd and contradictory with the truths of history, are, in fact, a mass of informal and undigested matters. Those of the Scottish Rite, in particular, are a monument of folly, and which would have been derided as nonsense long ago but for man's vanity, which is gratified by the titles and decorations of which this rite is the parent.

After this exposition of the origin of the Scottish (33d) Rite, let us cast our eyes over the condition of Masonry in Paris, immediately before this rite was brought to that city by the Count De Grasse-Tilly.

The compromise which took place, in 1799, between the Grand Lodge and the Grand Orient of France had not been joined in by all the brethren, and the intolerance exhibited by the Grand Orient gave occasion to a consider-

---

nication with the Supreme Council of Dublin, until the latter had ceased connection with the Supreme Council established, since 1815, within the Grand Orient of France. We have already stated how this Supreme Council of Edinburgh was healed. Since then it has set itself up to be the most regular of all the Supreme Councils, and has declared schismatic the council in London, which, as we have shown, was established by virtue of a constitution delivered by the Supreme Council existing, in 1813, at New York.

These Supreme Councils established in Great Britain enjoy but little reputation—so little, indeed, that some brethren of merit who have been elected by them honorary members, have refused to accept the distinction.

Unhappily, this mercenary creation, as unmasonic as it is illegal, has, since 1846, been extended into and has established its Supreme Councils in many countries The Supreme Council at Charleston was revived in 1845, after a sleep of nearly forty years. And although in no case are the bodies composing the rite recognized by the Grand Lodges, they are by the Grand Orients, which confer, in common with them, their high degrees.

able number of those members of the Grand Lodge, who did not wish to recognize the Grand Orient, to reject the terms of the compromise. It was more particularly the party called Scottish who exhibited this disposition most bitterly; and their reason was, that as the Grand Orient, by the terms of the compromise, recognized only a rite of but seven degrees—the highest of which was that of Rose Cross—their higher degrees, with their decorations and devices, could not be worn by them or made available in the assemblies or exhibitions of the legislative body.

The Grand Orient acted in this case, as in many others, not as a Masonic authority, but as an oligarchical power, and excluded the Scottish Rite Masons from the lodges of its jurisdiction, by an order dated the 12th November, 1802. This new act of intolerance served no other purpose than to irritate the brethren excluded, and was the principal reason that induced them to propose founding a new Masonic power. Some preparatory meetings were held, and many lodges of Paris, and particularly the Lodge of St. Alexander of Scotland, embraced openly the cause of the dissenters.

Following these inclinations, there was at first formed a new authority, established by virtue of a patent that a brother named Hackett—who had been a notary in St. Domingo—had brought from America, and which had been delivered to him by a Supreme Council sitting at New York, and professing the Rite of Perfection of twenty-five degrees that Stephen Morin had taken to America in 1761. This authority took the title of "Supreme Council of America."

But some months afterward, also from St. Domingo, the brother Count De Grasse-Tilly arrived, bringing with him the patent of the Supreme Council of Charleston, and the history of which we have already given. This patent conferred upon him the right to constitute chapters, councils, and consistories in the leeward and windward islands, that is to say, in St. Domingo and the other French colonies of America; but, in consequence of the political events which, occurring about this time, occasioned the loss of this island to France, he had no opportunity of realizing his projects. He had then returned to France, where, regardless of the conditions of his patent, he announced himself as supreme chief of a new Masonry of thirty-three degrees. Having been informed of the large body of excluded brethren who, since 1802—being prohibited by the Grand Orient from participating in the meetings of the fraternity in consequence of their refusal, for the reasons already given, to sign the compromise of that year—had assembled themselves in a cellar of the Fisherman's Walk, he approached these brethren, and immediately arranged to organize, with these elements and, by virtue of the patent delivered to him on the 21st February, 1802, at Charleston, to constitute a Masonic power, under the pompous title of the "Supreme Council for France of Sovereign Grand Inspectors General of the 33d and last degree of the Ancient and Accepted Scottish Rite." This done, on the 22d of October, 1805, the new authority organized and installed a Scottish Grand Lodge, as we have stated at the beginning of this history.[1]

---

[1] We regret much to find, in a work that we consider as one of the most important among those composing the literature of Freemasonry, styled "*The Philosophical History of Freemasonry*," by the brethren Kauffman and Cherpin, the voluntary omission these authors have made, contrary to the duty of an historian, in not mentioning at this date (1805) the foundation of the Scottish Grand Lodge, nor that of the Supreme Council, and in feigning to be completely ignorant that there existed at this time any Masonic authority in France of the name of Supreme Council. If the brethren K. and C. have believed it their duty to respect the oath that they have taken to the Grand Orient—to recognize it as the sole legislative authority of Freemasonry in France, and to not admit that there can exist any other—we shall not follow their example, first, because we have not taken any such oath; and, second, because that we believe it ever to be the duty of the historian, in his relation of facts, to flinch not, from any cause whatever, in his object of relating the truth.

As our view of Masonry is similar to that of these brethren, and as we find ourself in communion with them, in a more or less degree, in ideas, sentiments, and in nearly every matter connected with the institution, we are truly pained to find in their book, so praiseworthy and meritorious in almost every respect, the omission that we have mentioned; and, in addition thereto, a general partiality very significant in favor of the Grand Orient—a partiality of which we distinctly comprehend the good ntention, but which our conscience will not permit us to imitate. On the contrary, *to seek the truth and to disseminate it with courage,* has always been our motto. We believe that Masonry will be better served by speaking the truth without reserve, though that annunciation may seem to its detriment, than in expressing the accepted views of those who, like the brethren K. and C., may have some reason or weakness for failing to represent facts as they know them.

Remarks in connection with the foregoing History of the Origin of the Ancient and Accepted Scottish Rite.

Brother Rebold, in his preceding history of a rite that during the past fifteen years has gradually increased in importance in America, can not be said to have gratified the brethren who have given their thoughts and time to its dissemination in the United States or elsewhere. He has given us a plain narrative of unvarnished statements of fact; he has proved conclusively that this rite was either created by parties named in Charleston, S. C., or, from the twenty-five degrees of the Rite of Perfection as known in 1761, and which Brother Stephen Morin brought to America, it was, in 1802, there and by those persons extended to the thirty-three degrees of the present Ancient and Accepted Scottish Rite; and he has furnished most conclusive circumstantial evidence to support the belief entertained by at least every learned German Freemason in America and elsewhere, that Frederick the Great never had any knowledge of the rite in its present form, whatever knowledge he might have had of it as the Rite of Perfection of twenty-five degrees.

Under these circumstances, the friends of the Ancient and Accepted Scottish Rite find themselves in the predicament Sir William Drummond describes, in his preface to Origenes, when he says, "In questions unconnected with sacred and important interests, men are rarely very anxious to discriminate exactly between truth and fiction; and *few of us would, probably, be much pleased with the result,* could it now be certainly proved that Troy never existed, and that Thebes, with its hundred gates, was no more than a populous village. It is perhaps still with a secret wish to be convinced against our judgment, that we reject as fables the stories told us of the Grecian Hercules, or of the Persian Rustem; and that we assign to the heroes and giants of early times the strength and stature of ordinary men." So it is with our Ancient and Accepted Scottish Rite. It is proven to be neither an ancient rite nor one accepted by or acceptable to but a very small portion of the Masonic Fraternity, nor is it a Scottish—otherwise Jacobin—rite; and yet we wish to be convinced, even against our judgment, that it comes up to the mark set by these conditions, because our prejudices have long cherished so pleasing an idea.

But, although shorn of what has been considered its brightest attribute, viz., its creation by Frederick the Great; and although deprived of such regal parentage by being proven, instead, to be the progeny of five mercenary Israelites of Charleston, S. C., the rite, so far as it can subserve any useful purpose in connection with Freemasonry, can not lose any of its excellence. If its claims to regal parentage are not well founded, its advocates are maintaining a fallacy in their advancement of such claims, and do constantly find themselves in a dilemma when proofs are demanded which it is impossible for them to produce. And as the case has been candidly stated by Brother Rebold, and with the fewest possible offensive reflections upon the creators of the rite, and none at all upon those who—its present friends and patrons—conscientiously believe that it is calculated to confer dignity upon Freemasonry, no exceptions can be taken to the object I have had in view in the translation and publication of this work, which was to disseminate the truth[1] with regard to every portion of the history of Freemasonry in Europe.

I fear, however, that the patrons as well as the propagators of the rite, in our own day, have given too much significance, in their regards for it, to that remark of Horace, in his "Ars Poetica," beginning with—

"Intererit multum Davusne loquatur an heros"—

and not enough to whatever inherent excellence the rite itself may possess. If this should be the fact, as a S. P. R. S., I have no better proposition to suggest to the chiefs of the rite than the following:

1. Remove all equivocality as to its origin by excising the present statements upon that subject from the work, lectures, and history, wherever they occur; and,

2. Then take the thirty degrees of the rite (all of which are given in America) and *compress* them into twenty-one, which done, fit these twenty-one to the present American system or rite of twelve degrees.

---

[1] Brother Rebold has been officially pronounced by the highest Masonic authority in France, the Grand Orient—through its Deputy Grand Master, the Chevalier Heullant—a careful and impartial Masonic historian.

By this arrangement, all doubt as to the origin of what might then be called the *Reformed and Accepted American Rite of Thirty-three Degrees* will be removed, and such rite will, in a short time, be generally understood and appreciated as a work which, being necessary for the satisfaction and unity of the Fraternity in America, was undertaken by enlightened American Freemasons, and successfully accomplished.

J. F. B.

A CONCISE HISTORY

OF THE

EGYPTIAN RITE OF MISRAIM,[1]

SINCE ITS CREATION, IN 1806, AT MILAN, TO THE PRESENT TIME.

IN a work published in Paris, in 1848, under the title of "*The Masonic Order of Misraim*," the brother Mark Be-

---

[1] REFLECTIONS ON THE RITES OF MISRAIM AND MEMPHIS.—The history of the Rite of Misraim, as also that of the Rite of Memphis, which we are about to record, is calculated to suggest to enlightened Masons reflections of sadness in more than one connection. But it would be impossible for us to pass by in silence these works of feebleness, of error, and of pride, inasmuch as the profane as well as the initiated ought to be informed of the truth.

If the individuals who have created these rites were but few, unhappily those who participated in the result of such aberrations of the human mind may be called a multitude. It is the duty, therefore, of the historian to notice the side-tracks upon which these jugglers have at times drawn our institution, in order that their example may teach us, and preserve us from falling into new errors.

That the Jesuits, that powerful association, aided by a legion of active emissaries, should have been enabled, in the last century, to form associations and knightly orders enveloped in Masonic forms, with the intention of at first turning men aside from the pure Masonry of England, which extended itself rapidly upon the continent, and of which th object was contrary to their desires and operations, and subsequently to extend their dominion, under cover of Masonry, to the re-establishment of the Stuarts, is nothing astonishing. That some impostors, encouraged by their success, should, in their turn, and in a spirit of pecuniary gain, conclude to create rites and orders of chivalry, and, having found

darride, Grand Conservator of this Masonic heresy, commences its history in the following manner:

"Since the first age of the world, the period when our venerable Order was created by the All-Powerful, no Grand Conservator has ever taken the pencil to trace and reunite the perfect plans of his scientific labors, and thus enrich the human race: some for the want of the necessary documents,[1] and others from the fear of perjuring themselves or of impairing in any manner the sublime heritage which they had been delegated to transmit to their disciples in all its purity. But if these celebrated Grand Conservators, [names not given,] our predecessors, have not performed this sacred duty, they have not failed to leave to their successors the traditions of our mysteries, in hieroglyphic characters, in a manner intelligible to none but the initiated, and thus these documents have been preserved from all profane indiscretions."

---

[1] The reader will easily comprehend the cause of this dearth of documents; for, according to the language of our author, Adam, installed by the "All-Powerful" as the first Grand Conservator, could not have bequeathed the manuscript transactions of his direction of affairs of this " venerable Order" to his descendants, seeing that he had not learned the useful accomplishment of writing, hieroglyphically or otherwise, and that he had no one to direct in such transactions but Eve, his wife, and subsequently their children. One thing, however, the author does not explain, and the omission on his part leaves us with a very feeble comprehension of the matter; and it is that Adam, or the "All-Powerful," baptized this order with the name of an Egyptian king who, if we take the commonly received Hebraic Genesis for authority, was born eight hundred years after Adam appeared upon the earth!

---

in France—where a passion for the chivalry of the middle ages favored their projects—a country propitious to this species of speculation, did create such rites and orders, is not difficult to comprehend. But this which appears inexplicable is, that after having recognized the illegitimate source of all these rites and high degrees, of which the fabricators had been unmasked, hunted, and imprisoned in Germany; after having reformed all these rites, (between 1782 and 1790,) and having reduced the numerous scale to three, seven, ten, and, at most, twelve degrees, Freemasons in the present century should have been the dupes of jugglers of a like category, and accept of individuals without character, without legal or any other recognized public distinction, new rites of

Commencing in this manner, the author, M. Bedarride, continues the history of his "venerable Order," traversing, by forced marches, whole series of centuries, and stopping every two or three hundred years to indicate the existence of some Grand Conservators, without designating where, how, or by what means they were initiated. He pursues this romance until the beginning of the present century, when he begins to make a little history; but even of this his recital is so much mutilated that he fails in his search to discover the truth, though he attempts to ascend to the sources of his facts.

We deem it impossible to unite in one book a greater

---

similar value, but much more extravagant, the one counting ninety and the other ninety-five degrees—*this is utterly beyond our comprehension.*

What makes the matter more strange is, that all enlightened Masons of the present time know very well that true Freemasonry—such as is practiced by every Grand Lodge in Great Britain and America, and such as was practiced by the first and last National Grand Lodges of France, and the operative lodges under their jurisdiction—is composed of but three degrees. It is true they do not offer to the initiate, as do the rites of the higher degrees, gilt-lace cords or brilliant decorations.—[The author very suddenly stops here in his reflections. That he does so because he will not believe, or, believing, will not say, that men enlightened and seriously earnest in the business of elevating the condition of the human race by means of Masonry, can be affected by these "gilt-lace cords or brilliant decorations," or that he stops so suddenly to allow his readers the privilege of thus believing and of finishing his abrupt period with such a conclusion, I can not determine. My own opinion, as one of his readers, is well known to those for whom I wrote and published from 1858 to 1861; and, though it may be unacceptable to some for whom I write at present, I will take the liberty of here expressing it. So long as human nature remains constituted as it is, glitter will attract and decorations will incite men to desire their possession; and it is a pleasure taken in the exhibition of the decorations recognized by these rites and orders, as indicative of *higher rank* in confessedly a philosophical institution, and, presumably, a *higher degree of intelligence*, rather than any actual advantage derived from the possession of their degrees, that induces wise and serious men to seek for and obtain them.—Translator.]

mass of absurdities than its author has collected and exhibited in his history of this rite: and we believe we will render our readers good service by not fatiguing them with a refutation of all the inaccuracies with which this book is filled.

It is generally believed in the Masonic world that the brothers Mark and Michael Bedarride, who were the chiefs of this rite, also were its inventors; but it has been recently discovered that they were but its propagators.

Commencing by stating that this rite is composed of an aggregation of monstrous legends, stolen from all the rites, including those taken from the Scottish, Martinist, and Hermitic Rites, we will add that after the sixty-seventh degree, it runs but upon wheels supplied by Bible subjects; and that so purely is it Israelitish in its bearings, that it would with more correctness be called the "Jewish" than the "Egyptian Rite." We also find that this collection of degrees is divided into four series, in manner similar with the rite called Egyptian, created by Joseph Balsamo, surnamed Cagliostro,[1] which had been professed by the mother lodge "Wisdom Triumphant," founded by him at Lyons, in 1782. This Egyptian Rite[2] had but an ephemeral existence; and it is probable enough that some of Cagliostro's rituals have served to complete the deplorable work of the Rite of Misraim, whose author was the brother Lechangeur of Milan, as we shall proceed to demonstrate.

A Grand Orient of Italy had been founded at Milan

---

[1] This extraordinary man, born at Palermo in 1743, acquired a celebrity rarely attained by impostors. Arrested at Rome on the 25th December, 1789, he was condemned to death by the Holy Office on the 21st March, 1791; but Pius VI commuted his punishment to perpetual imprisonment in the castle of St. Angelo, where he died.

[2] Cagliostro, in a voyage that he made to London, bought a manuscript which belonged to a man named G. Coston, in which he found the plan of a Masonry founded upon a system which was part magical, part cabalistic, and part superstitious. From this work he arranged the plan of his Egyptian Rite.

shortly after the organization of that at Naples, and the prince Eugene Beauharnais had been invested with the dignity of Grand Master. Some superior officers, resident at Milan, who had been initiated, in Paris, into the high degrees of the Scottish (33d) Rite, resolved to establish a Supreme Council of that rite, at the suggestion of brethren, in Paris. A person named Lechangeur, an officer or master of an operative lodge in Milan, demanded to become a party in this arrangement, and his demand was complied with. They conferred upon him certain degrees; but having some motive for keeping him out of the organization of their Supreme Council, they refused to give him the superior degrees. Vexed at this refusal, Lechangeur informed the members of this Supreme Council that he would get the better of them, in creating a rite of ninety degrees, into which he should not admit them. He accomplished his threat in fact, and it is to him that is to be attributed the creation of this self-styled oriental rite.

The first thing Lechangeur did, after having elaborated his rite, was to elevate himself to the highest office recognized by it—in this respect imitating all the other fabricators of rites—that of "Superior Grand Conservator of the Order of Misraim," and in this capacity to deliver patents of authority to all who offered to propagate this new rite *to his profit*. These delegates, being thus authorized, were confined in their operations to the organization of chapters in the cities of the Italian peninsula, more particularly to Naples; and those chapters should, in their turn, create delegates, and deliver to them patents of authority, *to their profit*.

We will now explain how and by whom this Rite of Misraim was first introduced into France.

Bro. Michael Bedarride, a native of Cavaillon, in the department of Vaucluse, and belonging to the Jewish religion, was initiated into Freemasonry on the 5th of July,

1802, in the lodge "Candor," at Cezena, in Italy, and affiliated, in the year 1805, with the lodge "Mars and Themis," in Paris, which conferred upon him, as it did also upon his brother, Mark Bedarride, the degree of Master.

Michael Bedarride, who was a merchant in Naples, obtained the position of commissary of subsistence in the service of the Italian army, upon the staff of which army his brother Mark had a position. During their sojourn in Italy, the two brothers had affiliated with several lodges of that country. On the 3d December, 1810, through the intervention of one of the patentees of Lechangeur, Michael Bedarride obtained a similar patent, authorizing him to confer the degrees of the Misraimites up to the 73d degree. Subsequently, at Milan, he received of the brother Lechangeur himself an increase of the degrees, and a patent, dated 25th June, 1811, conferring upon him the degree of "Grand Hazsid," or 77th degree, with the right of conferring all the degrees to that point. A similar patent had already been delivered, on the 3d of January, 1810, by Lechangeur to Mark Bedarride.

It seems that, for some reason not known, the brother Lechangeur did not wish the brothers Bedarride to possess the degree of "Grand Conservator," or 90th degree, of his rite; but, notwithstanding, the possession of this degree became absolutely necessary, to enable them to succeed in their projects. With this object, Michael Bedarride addressed a delegate named Polack, an Israelite—resident at Venice—who, usurping the rights claimed by Lechangeur, had proclaimed himself Superior Grand Conservator, or independent Grand Master—and obtained of this person, on the 1st September, 1812, a patent conferring upon him the title he so greatly desired. This document, however, did not appear to be sufficiently authoritative for his purpose, as it bore but one signature, and consequently lacked evidences of authenticity; for, immediately after the death of Lechangeur he sought at the hands of the brother

Theodore Gerber, of Milan—to whom Lechangeur had bequeathed the powers he had given to himself—another patent. The application was successful, and on the 12th October, 1812, Michael Bedarride procured this new authority, signed by Theodore Gerber, and conferring upon Michael Bedarride the title of Superior Grand Conservator of the Order of Misraim in Italy. Besides the signature of Gerber, this document bore also the signatures of Mark Bedarride, who, as we have shown, had not then obtained but the 77th degree, and seven or eight other brethren who were reputed to compose the "Sovereign Grand Council of the 90th degree of the Grand Masters absolute;" and it is by virtue of the powers that they having arrogated to themselves, in concert with the chief of this rite, that they delegated to Michael Bedarride the same powers and all their supreme rights as therein expressed by this patent, to "*create, form, regulate, dissolve*, whenever desirable, lodges, chapters, colleges, directories, synods, tribunals, consistories, councils, and general councils of the Order of Misraim"—a prerogative that this brother, as therein expressed, has merited "by *the most profound study of the sciences, and the most sublime practice of every virtue that is known to but a very small number of the elect*—inviting all brethren, of every degree and every rite, to assist the *puissant and venerable Grand Conservator*, Michael Bedarride, with their council, their *credit* and their *fortune*, him and the rejected of his race," etc., etc.

It is by virtue of this curious document, which we consider it unnecessary further to explain, that the brother Michael Bedarride, through the organ of his brother Mark Bedarride, announced himself, in Paris, chief of this self-styled Oriental, Ancient, and Sublime Order, which, he says, is the stem of all the Masonic rites in existence, although he must have suspected by whom it had been fabricated. The text of this proclamation affords some idea of the arrogance of these Jewish Masons, and recalls to our mind the five Masons, also Jews, who, at Charleston, fabricated the Scottish Rite of thirty-three degrees; and had it not been for the success of which the Rite of Misraim never would have seen the light, and but for which the obstacles to the unity of Freemasonry in France, as well as in other countries, would have been easily removed.

When the brother Mark Bedarride, then a retired officer of the army of Italy, arrived in Paris in 1813, where he was joined shortly afterward by his brothers Michael and Joseph Bedarride, the latter of whom had also, at Naples, received some patents from a delegate patented by Lechangeur, these three brothers found four others—two of whom were named respectively Joly and Gaborea—who had likewise procured in Italy some patents which conferred upon them also the right of creating lodges, councils, etc., up to the ninetieth degree; while the other two, named respectively Garcia and Decollet, bore patents giving them authority to the seventy-seventh degree. As the brothers Bedarride had decided to fix their residence in Paris for the purpose of working up this new branch of Masonry, the competitors whom we have named incommoded them in the execution of their project. Having arranged matters with them, they next proceeded to obtain the protection of the brother Count Muraire. Succeeding in this as in the other, Michael Bedarride was not long in gaining the consent of several other brethren, nearly all of whom were members of the Supreme Council of the Scottish (33d) Rite, among whom we may name Count Lallemand, Thory, Colonel Martin, Count Chabran, General Monier, Barbier de Finant, the Chevalier Chalon de Collet, Vidal, Perron, General Teste, etc., to receive the highest degrees of the rite, in order to enable him to organize a Supreme Council of the ninetieth degree, necessary for the definite establishment of the Supreme Power of the Order for France. On the 9th of April, 1815, the brothers Bedarride, taking the title of Grand Conservators of the Order, issued their circular, by which they declared "the supreme power constituted in the valley of Paris to govern the Masonic Order of Misraim *upon all the globe*"—and, the reader will carefully observe—"for France by the Supreme Council of Most Wise Grand Masters for life of the 90th and last degree." It will be observed, in passing, that all the decisions of this council could be revoked by the Superior Grand Conservator of the Order, conformably to the constitution that he had given, in his capacity of autocrat, to the future Misraimite people.

To make acceptable a rite with a scale of degrees so numerous, and of which the chiefs had given themselves titles so pompous, certainly no city of the world afforded better facilities than Paris, the center of all folly and extravagance, as well as of much that was really great.

We will here observe that the ninety degrees composing the Rite of Misraim should have comprised every known science, divided into four series, forming seventeen classes. The first series was called *symbolic*, the second *philosophic*, the third *mystic*, and the fourth *cabalistic*. After this classification, the neophytes, upon their initiation into the different degrees, should have received instruction embracing all that was known of the sciences involved in each series. Such a course of instruction would, if faithfully given, have been frightful to any earnest mind, so imposing a task being so much beyond the grasp of an ordinary human life. But, in reality, the neophyte had nothing to fear from this vast vocabulary; it was merely a recital of fables more or less absurd, and embraced not a word of science or philosophy outside of what truths were implied in the first symbolic degrees. How could it be otherwise? The brothers Bedarride, no more than the creator of the rite, Lechangeur—not possessing even the most elementary notions of the sciences enumerated in their four series and seventeen classes of degrees—could not, in consequence, teach to others what they did not know themselves.

After taking possession of this prospectively lucrative field of labor, the brothers Bedarride found the greatest difficulty in organizing a working lodge; for France was then in mourning. However, with great labor, they succeeded in establishing a first lodge, the "Rainbow," which became the mother lodge of the rite; but it did not enter upon active duty until the month of June, 1816.

Then the proselytes quickly augmented. The brethren Baucalin de Laroste, the chevalier Larrey, Auzon, Ragon, Clavet-Gaubert, Redarets, Chasseriau, and Beaurepaire became Misraimites, and immediately constituted themselves into a new lodge, of which the meetings were most brilliant, under the name of "Disciples of Zoroaster." In this assembly the brother Dr. Ganal, who presided, and who understood, much better than the brothers Bedarride, the exigencies of the rite, called to his aid physic and chemistry to render his initiations imposing, and thus succeeded in gathering in many new members.

When they arrived in Paris, the brothers Bedarride had only some incomplete rituals which they had copied from those in the possession of the persons who gave them the degrees, and not one of the ninety lectures which the rite required to explain its degrees; for neither Lechangeur nor Gerber possessed them. To produce these, the brethren Mealet and Joly, erudite and capable men, drew upon their imaginations. So slowly, however, did these lectures appear, that in 1816 they were enabled to exhibit but ten, having borrowed from the lodge "Hope," at Berne, the lectures of the first three degrees, and these alone expressing all of a Masonic spirit which the rite exhibited; and thus, like the Grand Orient and the Supreme Council, they jumped, in their initiations, from the third to the eighteenth, and from the eighteenth to the thirtieth, or twelve degrees at a time. The brothers Bedarride were obliged, for the reasons that we have indicated, to confer a series of degrees at a time, giving it as their reason that such a course was most convenient, and explaining the intermediate degrees as best they could.

From the beginning, grave abuses appeared in the administration as conducted by the brothers Bedarride. The members of the rite, tired with submitting to the caprices of the three Israelitish chiefs, demanded a code of laws. They openly accused the Grand Conservators of making a scandalous traffic in communicating the degrees, and, in fact, of speculating with the rite as a manufacturing property, and seeking to retire the principal part of the profits to their own use, though they had shown a laudable desire to hide such a diversion of the funds. Then a certain number of brethren resolved to create a new power, founded upon the plenary powers which the brother Joly had received at Milan, and, with a number of the dissatisfied, they did form a Supreme Council of ninety degrees, composed of the said Joly, an author, the brethren Auzon, private secretary to His Majesty King Charles IV, Gaborea, a clerk in the Bureau of Finance, Mealet, Secretary of the Academy of Sciences, Ragon, chief of the Staff Bureau of the National Guard, Richard, Lange, Decollet, Amadieu, Pigniere, and Clavet-Gaubert, colonel of artillery.

In September, 1816, this new organization requested permission to rank under the jurisdiction of the Grand Orient, and, to allow them to do so, proposed to abandon the administration of the first two series of the rite, comprising sixty-six degrees, and reserve to themselves but the power to control those from sixty-seven to ninety. Some commissioners were named on the part of each body to arrange the particulars; but the Grand Orient, though at first very well disposed to conclude the arrangement, after a more mature examination of it, rejected the proposition on the 14th January, 1817, and, on the 27th of the following December, addressed to the lodges of its correspondence a circular, by the terms of which it prohibited them from receiving the members of the Rite of Misraim in their assemblies.

Unlike the generality of such documents as issued by the Grand Orient, the motives expressed in this edict were logical. It stated that "the patentees had not furnished the titles required to authenticate the origin and the authenticity of the Rite of Misraim; that the assertion of its introduction into Italy, under the pontificate of Leo X, in the sixteenth century, by Jamblicus, a platonic philosopher who lived in the fourth century, eleven hundred years before Leo X, was destructive in the nature of dates; that this rite was never practiced at Alexandria nor at Cairo, as it pretended to be, etc., etc.; that for these reasons this rite could not be admitted into the Grand Orient."[1] The Grand Orient having thus brought to public notice the irregularity of the powers claimed by the brothers Bedarride, the latter sought, as much as it was possible, to destroy the doubts thus engendered. Michael Bedarride had, on the 3d May, 1816, exhibited a document, signed by seven brethren, which detailed all the Masonic titles he had obtained; that is, the dates of his receipt of them in Italy; but this document, though in it he was named "Superior Grand Conservator," gave him no legal power; and to meet this contingency it was necessary to produce another document. This latter soon appeared, signed by thirteen brethren of the rite, and among them the Count De Grasse-Tilly, founder of the Supreme Council of the Scottish (33d) Rite at Paris, the Count Muraire, the Count Lallemand, the Duke of St. Aignan, the Chevalier Lacoste, etc. These brethren in this patent styled themselves "Sovereign Grand Masters absolute of the Rite of Misraim," a title which had been conferred by Michael Bedarride, after he had or-

---

[1] It is to be regretted that similar cogent reasons did not exclude, in 1862, the Rite of Memphis from admission into that body.

ganized his Grand Council of ninety degrees; and it was by virtue of the powers which this title conferred, and with which they had been invested by Michael Bedarride, that they, in their turn, by means of this patent, bestowed upon him the title and powers of Supreme Grand Conservator of the Order for France.

The new patent which we have just mentioned was dated the 7th of September, 1817; but, unlike the other, it bore no mark of having been produced at Milan, and this fact somewhat invalidated its use at Paris; nevertheless, as the brothers Bedarride had the whole world to operate in, this circumstance merely induced them to change slightly the field of their operations. In 1818, Joseph turned up at Brussels, and Michael in Holland. It would appear, however, that the means which they employed were not the most laudable; for, upon the 18th of November, 1818, the Prince Frederick, Grand Master of the Netherland lodges, addressed a circular to all the lodges of that country, pointing out the brothers Bedarride, who by that time were running about the kingdom, as dishonorable men, who, to attain their objects, had recourse to very reprehensible tricks and means unworthy of true Masons, and which had already brought them into discredit at Paris. This circular wound up its charges with interdicting the exercise of the Rite of Misraim in all the lodges under his authority, and supported this interdiction with the reasons advanced by the Grand Orient of France on the 29th December, 1817, and which we have mentioned.

Notwithstanding these prohibitions; notwithstanding all the difficulties which opposed them, the brothers Bedarride succeeded in establishing in Paris, besides the lodges "Rainbow" and "The Disciples of Zoroaster," four other lodges, namely, "The Twelve Tribes," "The Disciples of Misraim," "The Burning Bush," and "The Children of Apollo," all of which were in active operation toward the close of the year 1818. This increase of lodges permitted them to give, on the 19th January, 1819, a brilliant feast of Adoption, which was presided over by the Count Muraire and the Countess of Fouchecourt. Notwithstanding their seeming success, the brothers Bedarride were constantly at war with their own lodges, which complained of their administration and demanded an account of the funds. The brothers responded to these demands by expelling the most clamorous of the claimants. It was thus that, by the decision of a self-styled Council, which the brothers Bedarride directed as they wished, bearing date the 15th August, the brethren Marie, Richard, Chasseriau, Beaurepaire, Ragon, Mealet, and Joly were expelled from the rite. But this despotism but increased the indignation. The lodge "Disciples of Zoroaster" separated itself from the Rite of Misraim by a unanimous decision, dated the 30th of April, 1819.

In the minutes of this occasion, and which this lodge published at the time, the motive for separation is thus expressed:

1.—They had vainly called for the correction of many articles, contained in the general regulations, in consequence of their despotic and unsatisfactory character; and,

2.—The suppression of the word "absolute" in connection with the title of "Sovereign Grand Master;" as, "in the present century, such a distinction is a usurpation and an offense to free men."

3.—In nearly all of the general regulations the Grand Conservator has arrogated to himself powers as obscure as they are arbitrary.

4.—And, finally, according to a judgment of the tribunal of commerce of the Seine, the firm of Joseph Bedarride & Co., (the brothers Mark and Michael were the associates not named,) living in Moon street, at No. 37, was in a condition of open bankruptcy.

This proceeding was signed by the Worshipful Master

and by all the officers of the lodge, to the number of twenty. The supreme power confined itself to striking the Worshipful Master, and, by an edict dated 11th June, 1819, Dr. Ganal was expelled.

The mother lodge "Rainbow" also revolted against the administration of the Grand Conservators, which its members unanimously declared to be most deplorable, and brought this declaration before the chiefs of the Order, in the hope that they would require the brothers Bedarride to render an account of the receipts and expenses.

In the position in which they found themselves, the brothers Bedarride could not satisfy the demands which were addressed to them in connection with the finances, because the revenues of all kinds which they received through their connection with the rite were necessary to pay their debts and support their personal expenses. They, in consequence, made use of their omnipotence to declare all the members of the lodge "Rainbow," who had taken part in the revolt against them, as disturbers of the peace of the Order; and this done, they dissolved the lodge for the purpose of reconstructing it with more non-dissenting materials, and its president, the Count Lallemand, sharing the fortunes of the opposing members, by an edict of the Grand Council, of 7th July, 1810, was expelled.

It is necessary and proper here to state that the brothers Bedarride based their refusal to render an account of the revenues of the rite upon the statement that they had withdrawn but sufficient to cover the interest of the capital which they pretended to have spent in organizing the rite in Paris,[1] together with what they were properly entitled to for conducting the affairs of the Order.

---

[1] To support this statement the brethren exhibited an account, which was dated the 11th June, 1818, for the sum of $550, incurred by them for engravings, cyphers, diplomas, etc., and indorsed as correct by— among other members of the General Council of the ninetieth degree— the Count Muraire.

The lodges founded, in 1818, in the Low Countries having enjoyed but an ephemeral existence, the brothers Michael and Joseph Bedarride again withdrew from Paris, in 1820, to propagate their rite. They first appeared in England, from whence Michael went to the Low Countries and Joseph to Switzerland. In 1821 and 1822 they made other voyages into the departments of France, and about the close of the latter year they had organized twelve lodges, with several councils, all of which, like the former, lived but a short time.[1]

The progress made by the brothers Bedarride in the propagation of their rite, although slow, nevertheless disquieted the Grand Orient, and that authority labored to interrupt it. The circular edict already mentioned, with another, dated the 21st December, 1821, not having arrested, either in Paris or in the provinces, the creation of Misraimite lodges, the Grand Orient continued to pronounce severely against the brethren who had embraced their cause. Thus, at the solstitial feast, celebrated the 24th June, 1822, the brother Richard, orator of the Grand Orient—who, in 1817, had been advanced to the highest degrees of the Rite of Misraim, and consequently had taken a solemn oath,[2] written by his own hand, of the most absolute fidelity to that Order, but who subsequently had been stricken from the list of members—made a long report against the system of the brothers Bedarride, etc., and concluded by urging the Grand Orient to close the meetings of the Misraimites, as irregular, illicit, and dangerous, and to renew its edict of interdiction, enforcing compliance

---

[1] The author here gives the names and locations of these lodges, etc.; but as they are all extinct, we believe our readers will not miss their omission.—TRANSLATOR.

[2] The author here gives a transcript of this oath; but as the translation of this transcript would be offensive to members of the rite in America, and in nowise beneficial to those who are not, I respectfully suppress it.—TRANSLATOR.

with the same, under most severe penalties. In this report we find, among others equally severe, the following passage:

"* * * But toleration has a limit, the Grand Orient has duties to perform, and longer silence to the call of such duties would render this legislative body amenable to the charge of complicity in the disorders which have distinguished the administrators of the Rite of Misraim. These men, who, investing themselves with functions which they hold to be the most important of an Order that they proclaim superior to all Masonic rites, forgetful of their dignity, run over the departments of this kingdom, armed with their ninety degrees, which they offer to all purchasers at any price and in the most public places, and thus, by their mysterious forms, compromise the state, as also the security, honor, and even peace of our citizens, trouble the repose of the magistrates, awaken the attention of the authorities intrusted with the security of the state, and, above all, provoke such suspicions of their designs as cause them, in their travels from city to city, to be sometimes imprisoned: these are excesses committed by men calling themselves Masons, for which, it is true, they can not be impeached, but for which they should be held up to the indignation of every worthy brother," etc., etc.

We believe that this report exaggerated facts in some of its particulars.

The report of this feast, including the protest of Brother Richard, was sent to all the lodges and even to the public authorities. The latter, desirous of assuring themselves of the truth or falsehood of these accusations of the Grand Orient, ordered the police to investigate the subject; and the latter, for this purpose, made a descent upon the dwelling of the brother Mark Bedarride, on the 7th September, 1822; but a minute examination thereof elicited no charge, except a slight one under the terms of the penal code bearing upon persons assembling themselves together for secret purposes. For this the brother Bedarride and some others held themselves to answer on the 18th January, 1823, and submitted to some small fine. The result, however, of the general dissemination among the lodges of the report of the feast, was to induce the authorities to close the lodges of the rite in Paris and those in the provinces, to the number, in all, of seventeen; and they remained in this condition until 1831.

During this long period the brother Mark Bedarride remained unemployed. After the revolution of 1830, he sought for restoration to the military rank he had in 1814; but he failed in this object. From the Minister of the Interior, however, he obtained permission to reopen the lodges of his rite.

From that auspicious moment the two brothers Mark and Michael Bedarride made strenuous efforts to avail themselves of the advantages of this permission. Their first act was to inform the partisans of the rite of the happy circumstances which once more allowed the lodges to resume their labors, and to demand that all the representatives of the rite assemble the divers classes of the Order, and forward a list of their members, accompanied by a gift of thirty cents for each brother, as a voluntary offering of dues for the years in arrear, or those during which the lodges had been closed.

The primary meetings of the old lodges took place at No. 41 St. Mary street, and the brothers Bedarride succeeded in reconstructing, under their original names, the lodges "Rainbow," "Pyramids," and "Burning Bush." This reconstruction accomplished, the chiefs judged it necessary to prevent the attacks to which their administration had been subjected, and, for this purpose, convoking the brethren composing the General Council, they directed the recognition in their own favor of an account for services, etc., amounting to $20,550.[1]

Thus the account, which in 1818 was but $550, had been increased to $20,550, as well by the interest which had accrued upon the original sum as by the additional grants claimed, to the extent of $12,000, for administration of the affairs of an Order while its lodges were closed and its business totally suspended. As a set-off to this demand, the sums received by the brothers Bedarride for fees and diplomas from 1816 to 1822, while the lodges were in operation, ought to have amounted to a very handsome figure, and they did, as they appeared in the cash-book of the brothers; but the whole of this amount was absorbed, as further appeared by the same, in defraying the rent of lodge-rooms, etc., and all other necessary running expenses, for nineteen years.

To put an end to all further disputes upon the subject, the chiefs of the rite prepared an oath to be administered, *sine qua non*, to the receipt of the higher degrees, by which every member taking such degrees obligated himself in language very enigmatical, but the real meaning of which was to never question in any manner, under penalty of being blotted from the list of honorable mem-

---

[1] This sum of $20,550 was made up in the following manner:

1. Amount of the obligation of 11th June, 1818...... 2,735 fr. 37
   17 years' interest at 5 per cent. per annum......... 2,324 fr. 93—5,060 fr. 30
2. Claim of 2,500 fr. per annum from the 25th
   May, 1816, to 25th May, 1822—6 years......... 15,000 00
   6 years' interest at 5 per cent. per annum......... 4,500 00—19,500 00
3. Claim of 3,500 fr. per annum, from the 27th
   May, 1822, to 27th May, 1828—7 years.......... 24,500 00
   7 years' interest at 5 per cent. per annum......... 6,475 00—30,975 00
4. Claim of 5,000 fr. per annum, from the 27th
   May, 1828, to the 27th May, 1835—7 years..... 35,000 00
   7 years' interest at 5 per cent. per annum......... 12,250 00—47,250 00

Total.. 102,785 fr. 30

bership, the accuracy of this account or the justness of its claims.[1]

When this matter was thus arranged, the Council made it conditional that the brothers Bedarride should render true accounts from that time of all their receipts and expenses, to the end that the excess of the former should be appropriated to the reduction of their account against the Order of Misraim, and the same be liquidated at as early a day as possible.

It is a sacred principle in Freemasonry that, with the exception of the office of Secretary of a lodge, or Grand Secretary of a Grand Lodge, all other offices are filled gratuitously and for the honor they confer upon the incumbent. This being a fact well known, it is not difficult to decide, from what we have shown, that the charges made against the brothers Bedarride, of speculating with their rite, were not devoid of foundation.

Nothwithstanding the activity of the brothers Bedarride, their rite has made but little progress since that time. It has but a sort of vegetating existence in Paris, and it is extinct every-where else in which they succeeded in planting it. A great many eminent men, whose names figure upon the list of membership, have long since withdrawn from it, and others have died. They never did, in fact, take any active part in the labors of the rite, and the majority of them had not even assisted at a single meeting of Misraimites: they had accepted the high degrees offered them simply because their pompous titles tickled their vanity. The brothers Bedarride had never expected to derive any advantage from conferring their degrees upon such men, except that which their names would afford in the propagation of their rite among strangers. When we look over the list of membership, published in 1822, we are

---

[1] Our author gives the text of this oath; but, for the reason already given, I do not translate it.—TRANSLATOR.

astonished to find thereon so great a number of distinguished persons, and occupying the highest social positions. Such of these brethren as belonged to the Supreme Council or the Grand Orient of France never allowed themselves to be initiated into the fearful catalogue of the Rite of Misraim; they confined themselves simply to the acceptance of a diploma conferring upon them the rank of the ninetieth degree.

Many of these brethren, if not all, resigned their position between 1817 and 1822, when the chiefs of the rite were attacked on all sides. After the revival of the rite in 1832—thanks to the political changes which the revolution of 1830 effected in France—its chiefs were unable to enroll the names of important men, such as figured upon their register of 1822; even the meetings of the latter period were few and insignificant. To remedy this failure, the brothers Bedarride resolved to hold a Grand Lodge of Adoption, which took place on the 25th August, 1838. The following passage of the discourse, addressed to the sisters and brethren present, will give our readers some idea of the arrogance of the language of their claims: "The Masonic Order of Misraim has this advantage over all other rites: it furnishes to the initiate scientific compensations which afford him an abstract knowledge of our Order." So far is this from the truth, that, it is believed, the meetings of the Misraimites are more devoid of any thing pertaining to science or philosophy than are those of any other rite. Notwithstanding all the pomp, magnificence, and expense attending this exhibition of a "Grand Lodge of Adoption," it had not the least effect in forwarding the fortunes of the Order.

If any questions were put to the brothers Bedarride upon the condition of the funds, they would reply that the supreme authority had no accounts to render to any person. If changes were desired in the general regulations, they replied that the regulations were unalterable, and all the members had solemnly sworn to be governed by them. Should a brother publicly attempt to decipher the riddle which veiled their power, the chiefs would cry out that their authority was being questioned, and threaten the offender with arrest and trial. In 1839, the brother Ternesien Leserne, advocate at the court of the king, having made some remarks in his lodge—the "Rainbow"—upon the administration of the chiefs of the rite, he was, by order of the supreme power of 3d January, 1840, arraigned for contumacy. In his defense, he published his accusations, under the title of "The Morality of the General Regulations and Administration of the Rite of Misraim." The brothers Bedarride endeavored to refute the charges contained therein, but their response served rather to confirm than to destroy the accusations of the brother Ternesien.

The adversaries of the Rite of Misraim, or, more properly, those of the brothers Bedarride, rapidly increased. In an article in the "Globe," entitled "Archives of Ancient and Modern Initiations," in which the utility of Masonic decorations is questioned, Brother Juge, the senior editor, expresses himself thus: "This poor Rite of Misraim, which so piteously exhibits its distress in its slender report of lodges and members, and so audaciously parades its wealth of degrees—a wealth so excessive that it is not only unknown in all its fullness to the highest dignitaries, but even to its inventor, M. Bedarride, who has not the ability, I do not say to communicate all the degrees without reading from his manuscripts, but who can not recite without this help, and in the order in which they occur, even the names of his frightful vocabulary."—This article brought on, between the brothers Bedarride and the editor of the "Globe," a war which terminated very much to the disadvantage of the former; for the latter applied himself with so much ability to his task, in the last numbers of his paper for 1840, that he demonstrated to the intelligence of all that the Rite of Misraim was but "a miserable parody on Freemasonry, and the creation of a juggler."

The chiefs continued to impose upon their lodges the burden of an honor of $1,000 a year as the price of their administration; and, pretending that the receipts had gradually fallen off, so that now there were not enough to pay even the interest upon the obligation of 1835, they induced their ever-devoted General Council to make them a second letter of credit for the sum of $26,358,[1] dated the 20th of September, 1840, and bearing interest from that date.

After that time a treasurer controlled the receipts and the expenses, and in this manner the lodges were enabled to ascertain the excess of the former and apply it to the liquidation of this letter of credit. Thereafter the lodges assembled peaceably, and submitted to the despotic government of the supreme power; but the members gradually diminished each year.

In the month of April, 1856, the brother Mark Bedarride died. His death effected no change in the situation of the rite, which pursued its unsteady course, affording nothing incidental worthy of note.

A reproach of a very grave character had been addressed to the chiefs of the Rite of Misraim, viz., that no acts of charity had ever been known to be performed by them, and in this respect they had failed to comply with the first duty of Freemasons. In 1851, a fact of this nature occasioned a new schism. A brother, an officer of the empire, possessed of all the high degrees of the rite, died

---

[1] This obligation was made up as follows:

1. Amount of the claim October 1, 1835............		102,785 fr. 30	
2. For the direction of the Order for five years, at 5,000 fr. a year, from 1835 to 1840......... 25,000 fr.			
Five years interest at 5 per cent. per annum 1,250—		26,250	00
3. Interest on the principal of 102,785 fr............		2,757	70
		131,793 fr. 00	

in a hospital. Several brethren, desirous of defraying the expenses of his funeral, and aiding his widow, who was in deep poverty, sought the chief, Michael Bedarride, who responded to their request by saying, coldly, "The Order has no funds. All the receipts are absorbed in defraying necessary expenses, and in paying the interest due upon a etter of credit delivered to me by order of the General Council." The majority of the members, even those who possessed the eighty-seventh degree, had never heard of this obligation of the General Council, although they had signed the oath by which it was recognized. They were surprised, and, after some conference among themselves, they delegated one of their number to wait upon the chief, and propose to him that if he would renounce his claim under this letter of credit, they would pay him four thousand francs a year. This proposition, as might be expected, was rejected with disdain by the Grand Conservator. Then, thirty-three members, led by the brother Boubee, resolved to detach themselves from the Order, and to found another Masonic assembly professing the same rite. With this object they addressed, on the 22d of May, 1851, to the Minister of the Interior, a petition, and supported the same with the following reasons for separating themselves from what they styled "the supreme power of the Order of Misraim:" 1.—The facts we have mentioned. 2.—That the chiefs had prepared an oath guaranteeing the payment of a claim which was unknown to the petitioners, although they, by subscribing to such oath, became responsible for the payment of this claim. 3.—That by virtue of the absolute power with which he pretended that he was invested, the brother Michael Bedarride not only retained all the money received for initiations and degrees; but, contrary to the regulations, conferred at his own residence all kinds of degrees upon whoever would pay him the money demanded for them. 4.—That ashamed to state they had been enslaved so long, they had given in their demission, and formed the design of founding a lodge under the title of "Grand Orient of the Valley of Egypt."

The prayer of the petition having been refused, the thirty-three dissenters conferred with the brother Voury, an officer of the Grand Orient of France and Worshipful Master of the lodge "Jerusalem of Constance," then suspended, and decided to reorganize this lodge, under the title of "Jerusalem of the Valley of Egypt." It was in this manner that the anti-masonic sentiments which animated the chief of the Rite of Misraim detached from that rite its valuable members and diminished the revenues of its jurisdiction.

The Lodge of Adoption, created from the foundation of the rite, very rarely gave any sign of life. It had been organized, we regret to say, with an entirely speculative object, which should have been repugnant to the feelings of the worthy and respectable ladies who, at the order of the brother Bedarride, filled its offices on certain occasions. The ladies who successively filled the office of Grand Mistress of this Lodge of Adoption are the respectable sisters Gabrielle Pernet, Courtois, Breano, Maxime, of the Theater Francais, and Block de Berthier.

The death of the brother Michael Bedarride, which took place on the 10th February, 1856, put an end to the laceration of feelings endured for so long a time by the members who remained faithful to the rite. Feeling his end approaching, Michael Bedarride, by his will, dated the 1st January, 1856, created the brother Hayere[1] Grand Conservator of the Order; but, on the 24th January, he named him his representative, legatee, and successor, and, upon condition that he would pay his debts, placed in his hands the letter of credit of which we have spoken.

By a decree of the new supreme power, dated 27th March, 1856, it was decided that they would not leave, as

---

[1] Brother Hayere, a physician and chemist, was initiated into the Rite of Misraim on the 13th October, 1840, and created Grand Master of the ninetieth degree on the 11th June, 1855.

a charge upon the lodges of the Rite of Misraim, a debt,[1] styled by Brother Hayere as "accursed," and which had caused so much perjury, seeing that, with the actual revenues of thirty years, it had not been extinguished. By the General Council this debt was then declared extinct, while that body, nevertheless, charged itself with the settlement of the debts, amounting to about $1,000, of the deceased chief. This decision, honorable in all its bearings, proves that true Masonic sentiments animated the brethren of the Rite of Misraim.

The lodges of Misraim, thus discharged from a debt amounting to $15,589, and a yearly tax of $1,000, were made easy in their finances, and their receipts enabled them in a few years to pay the debt of their chief, and reimburse gradually Brother Hayere the advances made by him, with a generous disinterestedness upon this debt, to the most pressing creditors.

The new chief strove, as much as possible, to meet all the exigences, abolish the abuses, and introduce reforms. None of the numerous complaints made against the administration of his predecessor were heard, and the loyal character of Brother Hayere guarantee us in believing they will never be renewed so long as he controls the administration of the rite.

But no effort that can be put forth by the new chief can long arrest the certain dissolution of this Order. The germs of its mortality are borne within its bosom; and when it shall descend, like its brother rite of Memphis, to the tomb, nothing but its total regeneration can ever recommend it to the Masonic Fraternity.

---

[1] The debt as recognized by the last letter of credit, amounting, in the month of September, 1840, to $26,358, was found, at the death of Michael Bedarride, by the excess of receipts which had been applied by the treasurer to its liquidation, and credited by M. Bedarride, to be reduced to $15,589.

A CONCISE HISTORY

OF THE

RITE OF MEMPHIS,

SINCE ITS CREATION, IN 1838, TO ITS FUSION WITH THE GRAND ORIENT OF FRANCE, IN 1862.

THE Rite of Memphis, next to that of Misraim, is the most recent creation of Masonry. Its author is the brother Marconis de Negre, who has copied it from the Rite of Misraim, to which it principally belongs.

In a book entitled "The Sanctuary of Memphis," the brother Marconis, who therein discovers himself as the creator of this rite, briefly touches up its history as follows:

"The Rite of Memphis, or Oriental Rite, was carried to Europe by Ormes, seraphic priest of Alexandria and Egyptian sage, who was converted by St. Mark, in the year 46 of Jesus Christ, and who purified the doctrine of the Egyptians according to the principles of Christianity.

"The disciples of Ormes remained until 1118 sole possessors of the ancient wisdom of Egypt, purified by Christianity and the science of Solomon. This science having been communicated to the Templars, they were then known as *Knights of Palestine*, or *Rose-Cross Brothers of the East*. It is the latter who may be recognized as the immediate founders of the Rite of Memphis." * *

"The Masonic Rite of Memphis is the continuation of the mysteries of antiquity. It taught the first men to render homage to the divine principle; its dogmas repose upon the principles of the human race; its mission the study of wisdom, which seeks to discover the secrets of nature. It is the beatific aurora of the development of reason and intelligence; it is the worship of the best qualities of the human heart and suppression of its vices; it is, finally, the echo of religious tolerance, the union of all beliefs, the bond that unites humanity, the symbol of the happy illusions of hope, preaching faith in God, who preserves, and charity, which blesses."

As will be seen, from what we have quoted, this rite has all the pretension possible to be claimed for it, in giving it to us as the continuation of the mysteries of antiquity, and more than was ever claimed for any condition of Freemasonry. Nevertheless, its founder is the first to contradict his preachings by his practice; for one of the principal duties of his adepts consists in being always truthful. His book—which is but a frame-work of absurdities invented by himself with the object of deceiving the credulous—will, in the passages quoted and in the following, prove this:

"The Rite of Memphis is the only depository of high Masonry, the true primitive rite, the rite *par excellence*. It has come down to us without alteration, and, consequently, is the only rite justified by its origin, by its constant exercise of all its rights, and by its constitutions, which it is impossible to revoke or doubt their authenticity. The Rite of Memphis, or Oriental Rite, is the true Masonic tree, and all the Masonic systems, such as they are, are nothing but the branches detached from this respectable and highly antique institution, whose birth took place in Egypt—the real depot of the principles of Masonry, written in Chaldean, and preserved, in the venerated ark of the Rite of Memphis, in the Grand Lodge of Scotland, at Edinburgh, and in the convent of the Maronites, on Mount Lebanon."

To this extract we subjoin the first article of the organic statutes, and by which we may judge the remainder:

"*Brother Marconis de Negre, the Grand Hierophant, is the only sacred depositary of the traditions of this Sublime Order.*"

After that it would be superfluous to ask what are the constitutions "which it is impossible to revoke, or doubt their authenticity;" or what are these precious documents, "written in the Chaldean language, and preserved in the venerated ark of the Rite of Memphis," etc. With those in the Grand Lodge of Scotland and in the convent on Mount Lebanon, it is simply necessary to say that, like those upon which the Supreme Council for France was founded, they never existed.

It is ever thus the same language, the same tactics are employed, by the inventors of rites, wherewith, during the last century and a half, to delude their proselytes.

Concerning the introduction of this rite into France, the brother Marconis de Negre, and, after him, some of his credulous adepts, recounted that the brother Honis, a native of Cairo, had brought it from Egypt in 1814, (but without saying by whom it had been there communicated to him,) and had, with the father of Brother Marconis de Negre, (the brother Gabriel-Mathew Marconis,) Baron Dumas, and the Marquis de la Roque, founded a lodge of this rite at Montauban, on the 30th April, 1815; that this lodge had been closed on the 7th March, 1816, (they did not say why,) and that, in consequence, the archives had been confided to the father of Marconis de Negre, named (they did not say by whom) Grand Hierophant of the Order, or, otherwise, Grand Master.

The incorrectness of these assertions is easily demonstrated. Brother James Stephen Marconis was initiated at Paris into the rite of Memphis on the 21st of April, 1833. He was then twenty-seven years of age. He received on that day thirteen degrees; for the ladder of Misraim is quickly mounted. In consequence of the complaints made against him by some of his brethren, he was expelled on the 27th June, 1833. He shortly afterward quitted Paris and went to Lyons, where, under the name of Negre, he founded a lodge of the Rite of Misraim, under the style of "Good Will," and of which he was the president. While occupying this position, he was elevated to the sixty-sixth degree by the brothers Bedarride, who were not aware that Brother Negre and Brother J. S. Marconis were one and the same person. In consequence of some new complaints addressed to the brothers Bedarride, as chiefs of the rite, by the brethren at Lyons, Brother Marconis was again expelled, under the new name of Negre, on the 27th May, 1838.

After this latter expulsion, having no hope of again being able to play any part either in the Rite of Misraim or any other rite then practiced, and feeling conscious that he possessed much more capacity to direct a lodge, or even a rite, than the brothers Bedarride, he did as was done by Lechangeur of Milan, and by the five Israelites at Charleston—he *created* a Masonic power.

The ladder of Misraim, as fabricated by Lechangeur, and augmented by the addition of a few more rounds, gave him his Rite of Memphis with but little labor. The work finished, he constituted himself its chief. To give his rite an origin and a history was not difficult. In this department he exhibited, however, more respect for the opinions of mankind, and the good sense of the Fraternity, than did the brother Michael Bedarride, who, in his history of the "Order of Misraim," was not content, as Lechangeur had been, with stating that this Order was the work of a king of Egypt named Misraim, but went much further for its origin, even to God himself. Brother Marconis dated his rite from but the commencement of the Christian era. By this exhibition of modesty he probably expected to disarm inquiry, convert the credulous and religiously disposed, and inspire them with faith in the "precious documents written in the Chaldean language," which he announced were to be found in the "venerated ark of the Rite of

Memphis," whenever he would think proper to exhibit those documents to their admiring gaze.

As Brother Marconis was much the superior, both in education and talents, of the fabricator of the Rite of Misraim, he found it very easy to vary the degrees of that rite, change their names, and give them a signification sufficiently different to destroy the identity of their origin.

To give the reader an idea of the extravagance of this creation, we will present here an extract from the constitution of the Rite of Memphis:

"The Rite of Memphis is regulated by five Supreme Councils, viz.: 1. The Sanctuary of the Patriarchs, Grand Conservators of the Order. 2. The Mystic Temple of Sovereign Princes of Memphis. 3. The Sovereign General Grand Council of Grand Regulating Inspectors of the Order. 4. The Grand Liturgical College of Sublime Interpreters of Masonic Sciences and Hieroglyphics. 5. The Supreme Grand Tribunal of Protectors of the Order.

"The Sanctuary is divided into three sections, viz.: 1. The *Mystic* Section, in which reposes the venerated ark of the traditions. 2. The *Emblematic*, *Scientific*, and *Philosophic* Sections; and, 3. The *Governing* Section.

"The Mystic Section, in which are to be found the traditions, rituals, documents, instructions, and general archives, etc., is composed of the Grand Hierophant and his organ.

"The Emblematic, Scientific, and Philosophic Section is composed of seven lights, viz.: 1. The Grand Hierophant, Sublime Master of Light, (Brother Marconis.) 2. The organ of the Grand Hierophant. 3. The Grand Master, President of the Sanctuary, (particular executive of the Order.) 4. The Grand Master, President of the Mystic Temple (general executive.) 5. The Grand Master, President of the Sovereign Grand General Council. 6. The Grand Master, President of the Grand Liturgical College. 7. The Grand Master, President of the Supreme Grand Tribunal.

"This Section exercises no authority in the government of the Order, its action being purely doctrinal and magisterial."

It might be readily believed that such an organization as the above might be sufficient to regulate the affairs of an Asian or African Empire, comprising millions of human beings. Ridicule will, therefore, be pushed to its utmost when it is known that this formidable construction was organized to govern an association of men who are believed to be devoted to the development of their reason and intelligence, and to the study of wisdom.

After having completed the rituals of his rite, in 1838, Brother Marconis presented himself in Belgium as the successor of his father in the high office of Grand Hierophant, and entered into some negotiations to establish his rite. He then returned to Paris, where, under the name of Marconis Letuillart, he succeeded in enrolling some isolated brethren, and, with them, organizing a lodge which he named "Disciples of Memphis;" and, on the 2?d March, 1838, he organized a Grand Lodge, under the title of "Osiris," to which was intrusted the direction of all the operative lodges which he hoped he might establish. On the 23d May, 1839, he organized a chapter of "Philadelphics," and on the 29th February, 1840, the lodge "Sages of Heliopolis."

On the 7th April, 1839, he published his organic statutes, and organized two lodges in Brussels.

Immediately following the organization of his first lodge in Paris, the brothers Bedarride wrote the prefect of police, informing that officer that Brother Marconis had been twice expelled, for malfeasance, from the Rite of Misraim, and requesting that he be prohibited from engaging in Masonic labors thereafter in that city. The prefect not having immediately complied with their demand, on the 2d November they issued a circular, warning their lodges and councils against Brother Marconis, and stating the reasons of his duplicate expulsion. Thereupon the police visited the lodges organized by Brother Marconis; but it was not until the 17th May, 1840, that permission to assemble their membership was refused him; and, without any reason being assigned, those lodges had to suspend their meetings.

From that time Brother Marconis devoted his attention to Masonic literature.[1]

Favored by the political events of 1848, Brother Marconis labored to revive his lodges in Paris, and succeeded in reorganizing, in 1849, three of them, and afterward a council and chapter; but the lodges which he had established in Belgium refused resurrection.[2]

During the short time Brother Marconis de Negre—for it is under this name he is best known—maintained his lodges in activity, he followed the example of the brothers Bedarride, and obtained adherents among the members of the Grand Orient and the Supreme Council, who, although remaining attached to these bodies, accepted of him diplomas conferring upon them the high degrees of Memphis.

Finding that his rite was not obtaining any consistence at Paris, Brother Marconis repaired, in 1850, to London, in the hope there to find some person disposed to accept its distinctions; and, not without considerable effort, he succeeded in establishing a lodge, under the title of "The Sectarians of Menes," which was instituted on the 16th July, 1851, and which was charged with the responsibilities of a Supreme Council for the British isles. Brother

---

[1] The principal works published by Brother Marconis (de Negre) are: "The Sanctuary of Memphis," "The Hierophant," "The Mystic Sun," "The Mystic Temple," and "The Masonic Pantheon." As explanatory of the symbols and principles of Masonry, these works have undisputable value; but as history they are worthless, being principally drawn from the imagination of their author.

[2] In common with all other fabricators of rites, Brother Marconis sold, to all who offered to buy them, his constitutions with which to establish lodges, chapters, councils, grand lodges, etc. It was by these constitutions, and in this manner, that his rite was made known and established at a few points on the continent of Europe, and in New York.

14

J. P. Berjean was nominated Grand Master of it, and representative of the Grand Hierophant.

The accusations which, in 1850, dissolved the new National Grand Lodge of France, equally affected the lodges of the Rite of Memphis, and, for a second time, caused their suspension. Hence, Brother Marconis, finding his Masonic activity completely paralyzed in France, was, in a manner, forced to transmit the government of his rite to the lodge at London, as the principal authority extant; and, on the 30th November, 1853, in accordance with this arrangement, Brother J. P. Berjean was solemnly installed "Grand Master of Light" of the new mystic temple and General Grand Council, and, at the same time, as organ of the Grand Hierophant.

Starting with but thirty members, the labors of these were sufficiently arduous, when devoted to the administration of so extensive a form of government as the rite of Brother Marconis required; but this Grand Lodge soon found its ranks freely recruited from among the political refugees who, about this time, sought England as a place of safety. Such a class, however, possessed few of the elements suitable to harmoniously carry on the work of the rite, and it was soon found necessary to dissolve the lodge: Brother Marconis himself considering it prudent to announce that he had retired from all participation in its labors, and, consequently, that he declined all responsibility for its actions.

These circumstances, so little conducive to the success of the Rite of Memphis, induced Brother Marconis, by the aid of the author of this work, to propose, in 1852, to the Grand Orient, its affiliation of the lodges of Memphis. This proposition being refused, Brother Marconis thereupon ceased all further effort on behalf of the lodges of his rite, and confined his labors to the publication of his many Masonic books.

Having for some time meditated a voyage to America,

Brother Marconis de Negre, in 1860, embarked for that country, and, on the 14th July of that year, organized at Troy, in the State of New York, a lodge, under the title of "Disciples of Memphis," and of which Brother Durand, a professor of languages, was nominated Grand Master.

After the publication of the circular of the 30th April, 1862, addressed by the Grand Master, Marshal Magnan, to the dissenting Masons of France, Brother Marconis solicited, in the name of one of his suspended lodges, (the "Sectarians of Menes,") his affiliation with the Grand Orient of France. This request was complied with, and, on the 18th October, 1862, this lodge was formally installed by commissioners appointed for that purpose by the Grand Orient. On the 30th December following, a similar action took place with the lodge "Disciples of Memphis."

Thus despoiled of its government, its councils, and of all its peculiar attributes, the Rite of Memphis finds itself transformed into, at best, the Scottish Rite, as recognized by the Grand Orient; and yet, by a strange anomaly, the lodges which we have named have been permitted to retain the name of practicing the Rite of Memphis. Otherwise, for the honor of Masonry, we consider the work of Brother Marconis extinct in France, and we trust that wherever else it exists it may shortly be consigned to the tomb of its race.

A CONCISE HISTORY

OF THE

ORIGIN OF ALL THE RITES FOR HIGH DEGREES,

INTRODUCED INTO FREEMASONRY FROM 1736 TO THE PRESENT TIME.

FREEMASONRY, after its transformation at London, in 1717, from a partly mechanical and partly philosophical institution to one purely moral and philosophic, retained the three traditional degrees of *Apprentice, Fellow Craft,* and *Master Mason;* and all the lodges organized since that time, as well by the Grand Lodge of London as by the Grand Lodges of Scotland and Ireland, have been so constituted, and have never conferred any other than the three symbolic degrees above named, and which constitute the Rite of the Ancient Free and Accepted Masons of England— the only true traditional Masonry.

It was not until the partisans of the Stuarts had come to France, in the *suite* of the Pretender, that English Masonry was denaturalized by them, and used as a cloak to cover their revolutionary projects.

The desire to restore the family of the Stuarts to the throne of England, and thus to favor the interests of Roman Catholicism, suggested to the partisans of that family and those interests the idea of forming secret associations, by which to carry out their plans; and it was with this object that they obtained entrance into the Masonic lodges on the continent.

They commenced in France, through the agency of one of their most eminent emissaries, the Doctor, Baron of Ramsay,[1] to spread a rite of five degrees which they had vainly endeavored to make acceptable in London. This Doctor or Baron of Ramsay, between the years 1736 and 1738, augmented this rite by the addition of two degrees, and then called it "Scottish," because, as he maintained, it proceeded from a powerful Masonic authority in Scotland. He delivered to the proselytes, whom he had known himself to have made in France, personal constitutions or patents, emanating from a self-styled chapter of Masons sitting at Edinburgh. This chapter was composed of partisans of the Stuarts, who had constituted themselves into a Masonic authority before the Grand Lodge of Scotland existed, with the sole object of forwarding the projects of the uncrowned princes. According to the Baron of Ramsay, and other emissaries, this chapter alone possessed the true science of Masonry, which science, as

---

[1] Baron Ramsay was converted to the Roman Catholic religion by Fenelon, and afterward became preceptor at Rome to the son of the dethroned king, James III. He came to France in 1728. After having failed in London in his attempt to organize, in the interests of the Stuarts, a new Masonry calculated to annihilate the influence of the Grand Lodge of London, he addressed himself to a like work in France, and presented himself in Paris, furnished with powers from a Masonic authority represented to be sitting at Edinburgh. It was not until about 1736 that he appears to have succeeded in establishing in some lodges his political system.

It is true that Lord Derwentwater, and also Lord Harnwester, who succeeded each other as the first Grand Masters of the Provincial Grand Lodge of France, were also partisans of the Stuarts; but they do not appear to have been initiated into the revolutionary projects of the Jesuits, as was Doctor Ramsay; for it was not until after their departur for England—where both perished on the scaffold, victims of their attachment to the Pretender—that Baron Ramsay introduced his system among the lodges. While Lord Derwentwater was Grand Master of the Provincial Grand Lodge of France, in 1729, Baron Ramsay filled the office of orator. He died in 1743, aged fifty-seven, at St. Germain-en-Laye.

was apparent from the history of it which they had established, had been created by Godfrey de Bouillon. We have no account of any of the chapters founded by Baron Ramsay, and they do not appear to have been of much importance; but, in 1743, another partisan of the Stuarts founded at Marseilles a lodge of "St. John of Scotland," with eighteen degrees, which subsequently took the title of *Scottish Mother Lodge of France*, and constituted many lodges in Provence, and even some in the Levant. Another system, probably Ramsay's, was established at Lyons by a partisan of the Stuarts, and afterwards worked by the Jesuits.

It was not, however, until after Charles Edward Stuart, born at Rome, the son of the Pretender, had been initiated, and had founded, by a charter granted by himself, as patron, a chapter of high degrees at Arras, in 1747, under the title of "Scottish Jacobite Masonry," that the lodges to which were attached high degrees increased in France. At Toulouse, in 1748, an *attaché* of the Pretender, named Lockhart, organized a chapter which practiced a rite of nine degrees, under the name of "Faithful Scots." In 1766 another adherent constituted the mother lodge of the county Venaissin, in Avignon, which, in its turn, in 1776, organized the "Grand Lodge of the Philosophic Rite in Paris," and then united itself with that Grand Lodge.

Another partisan of the Stuarts, the Chevalier Bonneville, one of the most zealous emissaries of the Jesuits— under the patronage of the Chapter of Clermont, which was, in 1754, created by the Jesuits of the College (Convent) of Clermont[1]—organized several chapters, and which, for the purpose of more fully working this system of Masonry, they installed in a magnificent locality, outside the walls of Paris, called New France. In 1756, these chap-

---

[1] It was in this college that the Pretender lived for many years.

ters elaborated a new Masonic system, which they styled "Strict Observance"—an arrangement which has been wrongly attributed to the Chevalier Bonneville, he being, with others, nothing more than one of its most zealous propagators in France, while a person named Stark acted in a like capacity in Germany, between 1756 and 1758.

An extravagant and ambitious man named Pirlet, the presiding officer of a lodge in Paris, and who had recognized the true authorship of these new Masonic systems, sought their injury, if not destruction, by the creation of an opposing system. For this purpose, in 1757, by the aid of some Masons to whom he imparted his knowledge, he created a chapter of "Knights of the East." Not meeting with the success he had expected, he concluded to accept the office of propagator of a new rite elaborated by the Jesuits at Lyons, with a scale of twenty-five degrees, and to which was given the pompous title of "Emperors of the East and West, Sovereign Prince Masons." The propagators of this rite announced to their proselytes that it was the most elevated of all Masonry practiced in the East, and from whence it had been imported to France. This was the rite subsequently called "Perfection, or Harodom." Pirlet, directed secretly by the Jesuits, who were not seen in the management, gave, like all the propagators, inventors, and importers of rites, who make of them a species of property, a fabulous origin to this new rite; and several officers and members of the Grand Lodge of France were initiated, though bound by an oath, under its constitution, not to recognize any degrees as Masonic except those of their Grand Lodge, which consisted of the three symbolic degrees alone. These initiates became officers of the "Council of Emperors of the East and West, Sovereign Prince Masons;" and it was this council that, in 1761, delivered to Stephen Morin a patent wherewith to enable him to propagate the rite in America. This Rite of Perfection, of twenty-five degrees, was propagated in Germany by the officers of the army of Broglie. but more particularly by the Marquis of Berny, a French gentleman, and his deputy Rosa, a Lutheran priest, who in a short time organized seventeen lodges of the rite in the States-general, or parliament of the country. This rite infiltrated itself, in this manner, into the Grand Lodge at the Three Globes in Berlin; and when the king, Frederick the Great, who had been Grand Master of this lodge from 1744 to 1747, was advised of this fact by one of the officers of the lodge, his minister of war, he was so enraged that he manifested his discontent by a great oath. Many of the Grand Lodges of Germany, and those of Hamburg and Switzerland more particularly, who for a long time resisted the admission of these innovations, closed and became dissolved after the high degrees had insinuated themselves among and into their constituent lodges. But these degrees were not always so successful in their object to destroy primitive Masonry; for as soon as, by pushing inquiry, it was found from whence they had emanated, and their source discovered to be impure, they fell into disrepute and contempt.

It was thus that this Rite of Perfection became unpopular in Paris in 1780, and unable to sustain itself, and its membership obliged to unite their scattered fragments into a chapter of "Knights of the East"—the rite created by Pirlet. Notwithstanding this union, however, so low had the reputation of the possessors of these degrees fallen, that they were forced to recruit their ranks and the membership of this chapter from among any persons who could pay them the price of their degrees. Such action, persisted in, caused the death of this chapter, but not without leaving some unhappy traces of its labors; for while some of its members endeavored to organize a General Grand Chapter of the Rite of Perfection for France, others became discontented, discordant, and, in this condition of mind, became willing assistants of De Grasse-Tilly, who, in 1804, arrived in Paris from St. Domingo, bearing a patent from a Supreme Council sitting at Charleston, empowering him to organize a council of a rite of thirty-three degrees, and, by the aid of such malcontents, he did organize the "Supreme Council for France of Sovereign Grand Inspectors General of the 33d and last degree of the Ancient and Accepted Scottish Rite."

It will be easily perceived that, at an early stage of its popularity, the Jesuits found Freemasonry an institution they would have to use or destroy. Finding it impossible to use it, they concluded to destroy it; and to do so, they adopted the plan of inventing and propagating rites and high degrees calculated to confuse a correct knowledge of its history, and create discords and dissatisfaction among its members. As creators of these rites and degrees, they freely, through their partisans and emissaries, disposed of patents and constitutions which empowered the holders not only to organize bodies of men whom they might initiate into these degrees, but to sell to any person so initiated other patents and constitutions empowering them to do the same. In this manner the very object desired by these Jesuitical inventors was attained in a multiplied result; for a rivalry sprang up between these opposite authorities, who soon found that the best recommendation for their wares was an increase in their variety; and to give such variety it was necessary to fabricate additional degrees and additional rites, which they might offer, as something entirely new, to satisfy the eager appetite exhibited, and which they appeased in restaurants and taverns, and wherever they could find a purchaser. By reference to our history of Freemasonry in France about this time, (1736 to 1772,) the reader will perceive how completely the object desired by the Jesuits was effected. "Confusion worse confounded" reigned among the Fraternity—false titles, antedated constitutions, charges of fraud well sustained, and even exhibitions of violence, characterized the Masonic institution, and the civil government had to interfere to prevent worse results. It was during this period that there might be seen systems called Masonic and new degrees bursting almost daily into the light—systems incoherent, crude, and unfledged, having nothing to recommend them save their very dreamy or mystical tendency—the work of fabricators, who cared for no vow or obligation, but sought only to dispose of their trumpery and valueless commodities.

These combinations, the work of such impostors and political hucksters, produced, in about twenty years, such a result of doubt and uncertainty, that scarcely any one could determine which of the numerous pretending bodies was the true or legitimate Masonic authority in France. Yet, notwithstanding the confusion they had thus created, the Jesuits had accomplished but one of their designs, viz., denaturalizing and bringing into disrepute the Masonic institution. Having succeeded, as they believed, in destroying it in one form, they were determined to use it in another.

With this determination they arranged the system styled "Clerkship of the Templars," an amalgamation of the different histories, events, and characteristics of the crusades, mixed with the reveries of the alchemists. In this combination Catholicism governed all, and the whole fabrication moved upon wheels representing the great object for which the "Society of Jesus" was organized. The emissaries, De Bonneville, in France, and Professor Harck, in Germany, were immediately engaged in the dissemination of this system; but, in consequence of the very condition of disrepute then enjoyed by Masonry in that country, the emissary for France had little if any success.

With their knowledge of the human heart, the Jesuits brought into this system a series of inferior degrees proper to engage the curiosity of the neophyte, and assure themselves of his unlimited obedience. Beyond all else, this condition of unlimited obedience was always exacted before the advancement promised to the new revelations of yet higher degrees was accorded. In this manner were the brethren decoyed away from the pure and simple doctrine of English Freemasonry, to throw their aid and influence into the object of enlarging Jesuitical influence, by the hope of gaining ten degrees of exaltation above their fellows. In order further to assure themselves of the faith of their adepts, and to strike deeper the roots of that faith into the soil of their spirits, *the doctrine of obedience to unknown superiors* was advanced, and the chiefs directed to communicate the real plans to none but those whom they should initiate into the last and highest degree of the system.

As the monastic institution and ecclesiastic tendency of this false Masonry could not adapt itself to the feelings of all whom they desired to influence, they next resolved to create another association, much more extended, and which would be susceptible of establishment in Protestant countries. The project succeeded better than any or all the others. It was this system styled "Strict Observance" that, originating, like all the others created by the Jesuits, in their College of Clermont at Paris, was transported to Germany, and there propagated by the Baron of Hund, and other emissaries, instruments of the Jesuits, but ignorant of being such. The fundamental belief connected with this system, as entertained by those propagators, was, that "the Masonic fraternity is nothing but a continuation of the Order of Knights Templar, propagated by members of this Order while sheltered from persecution in the fastnesses of Scotland." Otherwise the propagators of this system held forth to and indulged their proselytes in the dangerous hope of gaining possession of the riches and property of the Order of Knights Templar, confiscated by

Philip the Fair and his abettors, after the execution of Jacques de Molay.

To have the system correspond, as much as possible, with its hierarchical object, the country over which they expected their Order to reign was divided into nine provinces, viz.: 1. Lower Germany, consisting of Poland and Prussia; 2. Auvergne; 3. Western France; 4. Italy and Greece; 5. Burgundy and Switzerland; 6. Upper Germany; 7. Austria and Lombardy; 8. Russia; and 9. Sweden.

The governing Grand Lodge of the system was established at Brunswick, and was to be ostensibly directed by the Duke of Brunswick, but who really was but the mouth-piece of the "unknown superiors." Each province had its *heermeister*, or general, a provincial chapter, many priories, *prefectures*, and commanderies—names and establishments belonging to the Ancient Order of Knights Templar; while the three degrees of St. John uniformly comprised the Freemasonry, properly so called, of the lodges governed by a *Meister vom Stuhl*, or Worshipful Master, and six officers.

The system of "Strict Observance" was so called because of the severe monastic subordination which it enjoined, in contradistinction with the liberal system of English origin, styled "Observance at Large;" and, under the notorious nonsense of alchemy, mysticism, and the mysteries of the Rose Cross, which were by its members professed, this "Strict Observance" system for a long time hid the secret intentions and objects of its unknown chiefs. In Germany, however, both clerical and secular systems remained under secret direction until 1772, when dissatisfaction and dissensions having taken place, the King of Prussia ordered the union of the two systems, and, after 1767, the clerical system had place but in the seventh province, viz., Austria and Lombardy.

The excessive extravagance of enthusiasm with which

the Templar system was regarded speedily abated, as soon as the unknown superiors were identified. Suspicion engendered investigation, and investigation elicited the fact that these "unknown superiors" were no other than leading Jesuits and partisans of the Stuart interest. Up to this time the Baron of Hund himself seems to have been a victim of the general deception.

Thereafter the Jesuits, unmasked in the persons of their chiefs, and deceived in their hopes, appear to have retired from the field; for we hear no more about the "unknown superiors." It was then that the investigation began to be seriously directed to the consideration of how far this "Strict Observance" system departed from the spirit and principles of the lodges working under the system of the Grand Lodge of England, and which latter had been contemptuously represented by the Jesuits as the bastard offspring of the working corporations of the middle ages. This investigation was not confined to Germany, but extended throughout the country occupied by the Templar systems. The general inquiry seemed to be whether these systems were charged with any abstract science, or any doctrines of a purely moral or secret character, relating to art, history, or to the sciences generally. The French Templar lodges met at Lyons, in 1778, in a convent, and undertook the total revision of their system, from which resulted a new plan of constitution. This advance movement gave an impulse to the German lodges, and induced them, in their turn, to examine the entire Templar system, and to manifest a disposition to return to the Masonry of England, in case their investigation should develop the improper tendencies of which this hierarchical system had been accused.

The Duke Ferdinand of Brunswick, who, in 1772, was chosen General Grand Master of all the "Strict Observance" lodges, seriously occupied himself with this investigation; and, for this purpose, having called, in 1772, the

Congress of Kohlo, and, in 1775, that at Brunswick, without eliciting any satisfactory result, he yielded to the views expressed by many German lodges, and, in 1782, convoked a third congress at Wilhelmsbad, to which he invited all the Freemasons of Europe.

The first assembly of this congress took place on the 16th July, 1782. All the Grand officers of all the provinces of the Templar system, and delegates from all their lodges were present, as also many delegates of other rites then extant in Germany and France. After thirty sittings, none of the questions upon the origin, doctrines, etc.,[1] had been resolved in a satisfactory manner; when, finally, upon the proposition of the French delegates of the Templar system from the province of Burgundy, the views of the congress were thus expressed:

"Modern Freemasons are not only *not* the true successors of the Knights Templar, but, as worthy recipients of the three symbolic degrees, they *can not be.*"

Notwithstanding this decision, however, the assembly decided that a lecture, giving a synopsis of the history of the Templar Order, should be added to, and incorporated with, the last degree of symbolic Freemasonry.

We should have remarked that the exterior organization of the Templar system, which established union and harmony among the parts of this system, was worked with care, and conformably to a vast plan. The interior ties, founded upon the position of the employés and the prerogatives of the chapters, composed a powerful band. The whole might be assimilated to a system of nerves extending from a central organ of life—which, in this case, was the convent of Clermont—to the most distant periphery of the organism, to communicate movement to all parts of the body, and to bring up to a general and common conscience, as it were, the impressions received, and the ob-

---

[1] See these questions in the historical notice of Masonic conventions.

servations made, by each part, wherever situated, outside of the great center.

After the congress of Wilhelmsbad had changed the Templar system, they baptized their modification of it with the name of "Refined Scottish Rite," a name as improper, however, as that which it displaced. At first, this new rite was not adopted but by the lodges of the province of Burgundy, and it was not until after the lapse of some years that it extended elsewhere. Many of the German operative lodges, and even several grand lodges, abandoned completely the system of high degrees, and returned, in great part, to the simple forms of English Masonry. The Provincial Grand Lodges of Frankfort and of Wetzlar, who created the Eclectic Rite, of three degrees, were the only Grand Lodges which radically adopted the reform, all the other Grand Lodges having retained some fragments of the high degrees. In this manner, the system of "Strict of Observance" or "Templar System," transformed to the "Refined Scottish Rite," existed for a long time in Germany and France, under the name of Scottish Masonry, with a more or less number of degrees constituting the rite, and there may be found at the present day some lodges in Belgium still practicing it.

In France, neither the National Grand Lodge nor the Grand Orient were successful in striving with the high degrees, which they had both anathematized, seeing that neither of these grand bodies practiced but the three symbolic degrees. The Grand Lodge always remained faithful to its principles; but the Grand Orient, on the contrary, sought connection with the lodges professing the high degrees, and finally, in 1786, arranged a rite of seven degrees, which it called the French Rite, and by means of which it hoped, but in vain, to suppress the other high degree systems.

Thus, as we have shown, it resulted that, apart from the two Templar systems created by the Jesuits for their own purposes, an infinite number of rites were produced, for quite as unworthy purposes, the names of many of which will be found at the close of this chapter.

These rites, it is true, had but a short existence. Most of them were changed after the congress of Welhelmsbad, or disappeared during the revolution; but they, neverthe-ess, largely contributed to the disrepute into which Freemasonry had fallen in the latter part of the eighteenth century, and the results of which condition remain to be contended with to the present day.

It is, however, but just to mention here one exception among the crowd of extravagant and anti-masonic rites, that of the "Philalètes," created in 1773, in the lodge of "United Friends," at Paris, by the brethren Savalette of Langes, Court of Gibelin, and the archeologist Lenoir, who, to approach nearer to the English Rite, had abolished all distinctions of degrees,[1] and proposed as their object the perfection of man, and his nearest approach to the Great Being from whom he emanated. It was by these "Philalètes" that there were convoked at Paris the two conventions of 1785 and 1787, and at which the founders just named exhibited so remarkably the true philosophy of Masonry.

Wherever Masonry was introduced prior to 1750, whether in Germany, Sweden, Denmark, Russia, Prussia, Poland, Turkey, Italy, Switzerland, Spain, Portugal, or America, there was not produced the slightest collision, nor could there be so long as the three degrees of the English Rite alone were practiced, and a unity of purpose in the Masonic system by such practice preserved. But as soon as this unity was destroyed in France, in the manner we have

---

[1] In that celebrated lodge the Nine Sisters, founded in 1776, and in which had been initiated Voltaire, Helvetius, Lalande, Court of Gibelin, Benjamin Franklin, etc., no desire has ever been expressed for the attainment of any degree above that of Master Mason. (*See Masonic Oxthodoxy*, by *Ragon*, p. 111.)

ORIGIN OF ALL THE RITES FOR HIGH DEGREES.   225

shown, by the introduction of high degrees, and political objects as well as mercenary tendencies began to characterize our beautiful institution, the suspicions of the governments were aroused, and inquiry provoked prohibitions the most severe, even under pain of death, against assemblies of Freemasons.[1]

Since the beginning of the present century, the principal rites created have been the Ancient and Accepted Scottish Rite, the Rite of Misraim, and the Rite of Memphis. The origin and history of these rites having been given in previous chapters of this work devoted thereto, it is unnecessary to say any thing further about them in this one. Regarding some two or three others, however, as worthy of notice, we will mention them:

1. The Order of Modern Templars, constituted the 4th of November, 1804, by virtue of an old constitution [2] found in the possession of a brother, and according to which the founders afterward pretended to be the legitimate successors of the Knights of the Temple. This association at-

---

[1] It is in great part, if not entirely, to the introduction of the high degrees, whose history so far we have just recorded, that the numerous literary attacks, from which Freemasonry has so greatly suffered during the latter half of the last century, are due. The works of Luchet, of Robison, the Abbé Barruel, Payard, Cadet-Gassecourt the Abbé Lefranc, and many others, would probably have never seen the light, had not Masonry become adulterated with objects as improper as they were unsuited to mix with its principles, while preserved in the fervor and faith of their primitive simplicity. The writers named, not being able to distinguish the true from the false, endeavored to involve all in a common ruin, and for a time they were successful. "*Resurgam,*" however, is written upon every page of truth immortal; and no more fitting front for the emblazonment of this glorious motto has ever been afforded than that presented to-day by English Freemasonry.

[2] This constitution was written in Latin, and its object is thus expressed: "To reëstablish the Order of the true successors of the Knights of the Temple, in its primitive purity, as it had been instituted by Hugh de Payen, in 1118, and in accordance with the laws of 1605, under the Grand Mastership of Montmorency, etc."

15

tained in France some degree of stability. The brother Fabre-Palaprat, a distinguished physician, became, under the assumed name of "Bernard Raymond," the first Grand Master. After his death, which occurred on the 18th of February 1838, the "Order of the Temple" met, at a convent, in general assembly, and voted itself a new constitution and laws; and, on the 13th of January, 1841, the members united in the election of Sir Sidney Smith to the office of Grand Master. He subsequently took the title of Regent of the Order; and this, so far as we are aware, was the last manifestation of this last parody on the Order of Knights of the Temple, as in 1843 no trace of it could be found in France.[1]

2. The "Rite of Rigid Observers," created in 1819, by seven officers of the Grand Orient of France,[2] with the object of bringing Freemasonry back to its primitive purity and simplicity, by re-establishing the modern English

---

[1] It was by members of this "association" that Knight Templarism, as known in America—comprising the three degrees, viz: Knight of the Red Cross, Knight Templar, and Knight of Malta—was introduced into the United States in 1808, and which degrees now compose the highest grades of the American Masonic system. Delegates from seven Encampments of Knights Templar, and one Council of Red Cross—none of which were located south or west of New York—organized in New York city, on the 20th of June, 1816, a General Grand Encampment for the United States. At this assembly, Hon. De Witt Clinton, of New York, was elected General Grand Master, and Thomas Smith Webb, Esq., of Boston, his Deputy. On account of the conservative stand then taken by the few brethren representing this Order at that time in America, it has, during the half a century now drawing to its close, kept suitable pace with the other divisions of the American Masonic system, and attained to a degree of popularity it would not, probably, if left to stand alone, or to stumble against those other divisions. This, and the additional reason that the American mind is notably Christian and spiritual in its tendencies and aspirations, will continue to accord to the Order of Knights Templar, as a Christian attachment to the Masonic Institution, the full meed of value to which it may be entitled.—TRANSLATOR.

[2] Renon, Borie, Caille, Delaroche, Geneux, Pages, and Vassal.

Rite. Notwithstanding their position and their talents, these brethren failed in their project, for no other reason, we believe, than that they had neither decorations nor pompous titles to offer to their adepts.

3. The "Rite of Unitarian Masonry," adopted by the National Grand Lodge of France, after its organization, in 1848. This lodge, not to wound the susceptibility of its membership, by this title denominated the symbolic rite of three degrees. Notwithstanding its tenderness in this respect, however, it had no better fortune than the preceding rite, as the National Grand Lodge of France expired in 1851.

After this succinct exposition of the history of the principal systems for high degrees, we hope that the good sense of the brethren, who are yet partisans of these high degrees, will induce them to regard them as useless and embarrassing baggage, borne along in opposition to the spirit of true Freemasonry, and only calculated to excite discord and impede the march of our humanitarian institution. We hope that they will abandon these works of a foolish and ambitious imagination, and degrading and mercenary spirit of speculation, and return or confine themselves to the practice of the true Masonic rite, that of three symbolic degrees, the only primitive rite of the Ancient Free and Accepted Masons of England.

We shall add, in closing this chapter, that Brother Ragon has published, in his *"Manual of Initiations"*—we presume to exhibit the tendency to aberration of the human mind—the names of seventy-five different styles of Masonry, fifty-two rites and thirty-four orders called Masonic, twenty-six androgynous orders, six Masonic colleges, and more than fourteen hundred degrees, while, in reality, there has never existed any other rite entitled to the name of Freemasonry than the modern English rite of three symbolic degrees. Upon this rite, as the stock of Freemasonry, the Jesuits and partisans of the Stuarts grafted their clerical and secular orders of chivalry, which we have described; and it is this stock upon which has been grafted every other species of jugglery assuming to be Masonry which has had place within the last century.

NAMES OF MASONIC RITES EXTANT, AND WHERE PRACTICED.

Rite of Ancient Free and Accepted Masons, practiced by nine-tenths of all the lodges of the globe, the same being the Modern English Rite of three symbolic degrees, as arranged by the Grand Lodge of London in............ 1717
Rite of Zinendorf, practiced by the National Grand Lodge of Germany, at Berlin, comprising seven degrees, arranged in 1767
Rite practiced by the Grand Lodge of Stockholm, commonly called the Swedish Rite, or System of Swedenborg, comprising eight degrees, and arranged in............ 1773
Rite practiced by some lodges in Belgium, called the Scotch Philosophic Rite of eighteen degrees, arranged in...... 1776
Rite known as the Royal Arch or York Rite of seven degrees, practiced in the United States of America, and the higher degrees of which are believed to have been arranged, by Lawrence Dermott, in........................... 1777
Rite practiced by some lodges in Belgium, known as the Refined Scottish or Reformed Ancient Rite, arranged as the successor of the Rite of Perfection, after the Congress of Wilhelmsbad, in................................ 1782
Rite practiced by the Grand Lodge of Frankfort and Hamburg, known as the Eclectic Rite, comprising three degrees, arranged, in conformity with the opinion expressed by the Congress at Wilhelmsbad, in 1782, by Baron Knigge, in 1783
Rite practiced by the Grand Orient of France, commonly called the Modern French Rite, comprising seven degrees, and which was arranged by a commission of that body as a basis of compromise between it and the "General Grand Chapter of the Rite of Perfection," organized, in 1783, as the successors of the "Grand Council of Emperors of the East and West, Sovereign Prince Masons," and adopted in 1786

Rite practiced by the Grand Royal York Lodge of Berlin, known as Fessler's Rite, comprising three degrees and a chapter, arranged in.................................. 1796
Rite of the Grand Lodge at the Three Globes, in Berlin, comprising twenty-five degrees, as arranged to admit, in 1760, the high degrees then prevalent, but which was reduced to ten degrees in........................... 1798
Rite known as the Ancient and Accepted Scottish, practiced in various countries and by all Supreme Councils, comprising thirty-three degrees. It is believed to have been extended from the Rite of Perfection of twenty-five degrees to its present number, in Charleston, S. C., in 1802, and mainly arranged, as it now exists in France and elsewhere, in.. 1804
Rite known as the Order of Modern Templars, or Knights Templar, comprising three degrees, practiced in the United States of America and Great Britain. As the successor of the secular Templars of the Jesuit system of Strict Observance, this rite was arranged in France in......... 1804
Rite of Misraim, practiced in Paris, comprising ninety degrees, invented by Lechangeur, of Milan, in 1806, and introduced into France by Mark and Michael Bedarride, in.. 1815
Rite of Memphis, now practiced only in the United States of America, comprising ninety-five degrees, the same being an extension and improvement of the last-named rite, made by Marconis de Negre, in...................... 1838

RITES, CALLED MASONIC, WHICH HAVE BECOME EXTINCT, OR WHICH HAVE BECOME ABSORBED INTO SOME EXISTING RITE.

Rite of Noah, arranged as the Order of the Noahchites in 1735
Scottish or Jacobin Rite of Ramsay, first known in....... 1736
Rite of Herodom of Kilwinning, first practiced in........ 1740
Rite or Order of Fidelity, by Chambonet 1742
Rite or Order of the Anchor.......................... 1744
Rite of the Areopagists............................. 1746
Scottish Jacobin Rite, created by the Pretender, in........ 1747
Rite of the Elect of Truth, at Rennes, in............... 1748

Rite of the Old Daughter-in-law, by Lockhart, an emissary
  of the Jesuits, in........................... 1749 or 1750
Rite of the Illuminati of Stockholm, founded in 1621, and
  resuscitated in France, under Masonic forms, in........ 1750
Rite or Order of Prussian Knights..................... 1756
Rite of the Clerks of Strict Observance, or clerical Templar
  system, founded by the Jesuits, and united, in 1776, with
  the Secular Templars, also a creation of the Jesuits..... 1756
Rite of Knights of the East, by Pirlet.................. 1757
Rite of the Emperors of the East and West, Sovereign Prince
  Masons. This was the Rite of Herodom extended to the
  Rite of Perfection of twenty-five degrees, by the Jesuits,
  and propagated by Pirlet about..................... 1758
Rite of Strict Observance, or modified Templar system of
  seven degrees, known as the Secular Templars......... 1760
Rite of the African Architects........................ 1762
    Between 1762 and 1766 there were introduced five rites,
  named respectively the Asiatics, the Patients, the Seekers,
  the Princes of Death, and the Reformed of Dresden.
Rite of the Flaming Star, founded by Baron Schudy, an
  emissary of the Jesuits, in......................... 1766
Rite of the Rose Cross, founded by Valentine Andrea in
  1616, and resuscitated, under Masonic forms, in......... 1767
Rite of the Knights of the Holy City, by an emissary of the
  Jesuits, in..................................... 1768
Rite of the Elected Cowans, by Martinez Paschalis........ 1768
Rite of the Black Brethren........................... 1770
Scandinavian Rite, and the Hermitic Rite, in............ 1772
Rite of the Philalethes, founded in Paris by Lavalette de
  Langes, Court de Gebelin, the Prince of Hesse, etc..... 1773
Rite of the Illuminati of Bavaria, by Professor Weisshaupt. 1776
Rite of the Independents, and Rite of the Perfect Initiates
  of Egypt....................................... 1776
Rite of the Illuminati of Avignon, being the system of Swe-
  denborg, in.................................... 1779
Rite of the Philadelphians of Narbonne, a rite of ten degrees,
  founded by some pretended superior officers, major and
  minor, of "the Order of Free and Accepted Masons".... 1780
Rite of the Martinists, founded by St. Martin............ 1780

Rite of the Sublime Masters of the Circle of Light......... 1780
Rite of Knights and Nymphs of the Rose (one degree).... 1781
Rite of the Masons of the Desert...................... 1781
Egyptian Rite, by Cagliostro.......................... 1781
Rite of Universal Harmony, by Dr. Mesmer............. 1782
Rite of the Illuminati of the Zodiac................... 1783
Rite of Zoroaster..................................... 1783
Rite of High Egyptian Masonry (adoptive), by Cagliostro.. 1784
Rite of Adonhiramite Masonry......................... 1787
Rite of the Holy Order of the Sophists, by Cuvelier of Treves... 1801
Rite or Order of Modern Templars, founded by Drs. Ledru and Fabre-Palaprat[1].............................. 1804
Rite or Order of Mercy................................ 1807
Rite or Order of Knights of Christ, founded by E. de Nunez. 1809
Rite or Order of French Noachides, or Napoleonic Masonry. 1816
Rite of Rigid Observers, founded by some officers of the Grand Orient in................................... 1819
Persian Philosophic Rite, created in Erzrum in 1818, and introduced in France in............................ 1819

---

[1] This rite is not extinct in Great Britain and United States of America, it being, in those countries, fitted on to the York Rite, as high degrees.

DOCUMENTARY AND HISTORICAL EVIDENCE

BEARING DIRECTLY UPON THE

ORIGIN AND GENERAL HISTORY OF FREEMASONRY,

TOGETHER WITH

INDICATIONS OF THE CAUSES FOR THE DIVERSITY OF OPINIONS WHICH EXIST AS TO SUCH ORIGIN.

I.—DOCUMENTARY EVIDENCE.

FOR all which relates to the foundation of the Roman Colleges of Builders, (*collegia fabrorum,*) created by Numa Pompilius, in the year 715 B. C., their constitution and the modifications made in their privileges after the fall of the Roman Republic—particularly in the second century of the Christian era, under the emperors Trajan and Adrian—consult the following works, viz. :

1.—The Laws of the Twelve Tables, instituted in the year 451 B. C. The eighth of these tables refers particularly to those colleges.

2.—The Body of Roman Rights.

3.—First and second Epistles of Cicero to his brother Quintus.

4.—Architecture by Vitruvius. This work has been often translated.[1]

---

[1] In the edition of Anderson's Constitution for 1725, Vitruvius is stated to be, in the year 29 B. C., the representative of Cesar Augustus in the corporations of Builders.

5.—History of Architecture. By Schoell. Vols. 1 and 2.
6.—Pollion. By De Bugny.

As containing the text of many historic documents, as also the history and doctrines of the Masonic institution, consult the following works, viz.:

7.—The Book of Constitutions. By Dr. James Anderson. First published in 1723, and subsequently to the extent of five separate editions.

8.—The History of Freemasonry, Drawn from Authentic Sources of Information. By Alexander Laurie. London: 1804.

9.—Illustrations of Freemasonry. By William Preston. London: 1772 and 1812.

10.—The Three Oldest Documents of the Fraternity of Freemasons. By K. C. F. Krause.

11.—The Three Oldest Historical Documents of the Fraternity of Freemasons of Germany. By Professor Heldmann.

12.—History of Freemasonry. By Professor Bobrick. Zurich.

13.—The Actual Condition of Freemasonry Discovered. By De Hammer.

14.—Encyclopedia of Freemasonry. By Lenning. Leipsic.

15.—Memoirs of the Architecture of the Middle Ages. By Widdekind.

16.—The German Colonies and Division of Lands in the Western Roman Provinces. By Gaup. 1844.

17.—Handbook of the Different Masonic Symbols. By Dr. Schauberg. Zurich: 1861.

18.—History of Freemasonry. By Kloss. Frankfort: 1861.

19.—Freemasonry, its Origin, Development, etc. By Hanau. 1862.

20.—History of Freemasonry, from its Origin to the Present Day. Leipsic: 1862.

21.—History of Freemasonry. By J. G. Findel. Leipsic: 1863.[1]

In addition to the works named, we find some valuable teachings in the following books, the productions of authors who, as they have themselves informed us, are not Freemasons, and whose opinions, on that account, should be of more weight, as they must be disinterested writers upon the subject of Freemasonry:

22.—The Monumental Art. By Baptissier. Paris. (See pp. 466, 469.)

23.—History of the Cathedral of Cologne. By J. Boisserré. Paris.

24.—General History of Architecture. By Daniel Ramee. Paris: 1843. (See vol. 2, p. 234.)

These three authors, who are architects, unite in recognizing the fact that it is to the Freemasons of the middle ages we are indebted for all the monuments erected during that period.

II.—Historical Evidence.—(*Chronologically arranged.*)

A. D. 52.—The corporations of Constructors are established at this time in Great Britain. This fact is proven by the inscription upon a tubular stone found at Chichester in 1725, and whereon was chronicled the erection at that place of a temple to Neptune, and another to Minerva. (See the London Freemason's Magazine for 1862.)

A. D. 290.—The constitution or ancient privileges accorded by Numa Pompilius to the colleges of Constructors, and which were considerably restricted and diminished since their primitive concession, were this year renewed, fully and without any restriction, by Carausius, commander of the Roman fleet, who, after possessing himself of Great

---

[1] From No. 10 to No. 21, inclusive, the works named are in the German language.

Britain, and declaring his independence of Rome, in 287, had taken the title of emperor. By this favor, accorded to the Builders, he sought to assure himself of the assistance of that association, then the most powerful in the country.

The architect Albanus, originally a pagan, but converted to Christianity, was named by Carausius, Inspector of the Masonic Corporations of Great Britain. Two years afterward he was beheaded by his protector for having preached the doctrine of Christ. He was the first martyr in Britain, and he is, according to authentic documents, ranked first on the historical list of the inspectors of Freemasonry in Britain. It was to these inspectors that subsequently was given the name of Grand Masters.

A. D. 296.—After the death of Carausius, which took place in 295, Constantius Chlorus, who succeeded him, chose for the place of his residence the city of York, (*Eboracum*,) where he found the most important lodges or colleges of Builders in Britain.

From A. D. 350 to 430.—During this period the first corporations of Artists and Operatives were instituted, with particular rules and regulations, out of the remains of the general association, dissolved after the retreat of the Romans in 426. These statutes, of which many libraries in France possess manuscript copies, evince, with more or less distinctness, the marks of the old association, as well in the connection of their humanitarian principles as in their secrets of art.

A. D. 557.—In this year Austin, an architect and Benedictine priest, was nominated to the dignity of Grand Inspector of the Masonic Fraternities. It was by this priest that the Anglo-Saxon kings were converted to Christianity. He died in 610, and was canonized under the name of St. Augustine.

A. D. 614.—Pope Boniface IV conferred, by diploma, upon the Masonic corporations the exclusive privilege of erecting all religious buildings and monuments, and, by the same document, made them free from all local, royal, or municipal statutes, taxes, etc.

A. D. 620.—During the international and civil wars, which had paralyzed their development, the Masonic corporations sought refuge in the monasteries, which thus became the schools of architecture, and from which subsequently went out the most celebrated architects, among whom may be named St. Aloysius, bishop of Noyen (659), St. Ferol, of Limoges, Dalmac, bishop of Rhodes, Agricola of Chalons (680 and 700).

A. D. 680.—In this year the King of Mersey nominated Bennet, Abbot of Wirral, to the dignity of Inspector General and Superintendent of Freemasonry.

From A. D. 700 to 900.—The Anglo-Saxon documents, emanating directly from the Masonic Fraternity, during this period, owing to the continual wars and pillagings, in great part disappeared or were destroyed. A large portion of what were saved became, possibly, the property of the lodges in London, and, in 1720, were nearly all burned by brethren of these lodges, in the belief that it was improper to have the information they contained disseminated by publication in the work of Dr. Anderson. In some of the Anglo-Saxon documents which exist in the libraries of England, the Masonic fraternities are sometimes designated as "Freemasons."

A. D. 850.—The Saxon king, Ethelwolf, promotes the priest-architect, St. Swithin, to the directorship of the Freemasons, the assemblies of whom were much interrupted during this century.

A. D. 900.—The successor of Alfred Edward, King of Mersey, named, as grand inspectors of the Fraternity, his son Ethelward and his brother-in-law Ethred, both having become, through attendance in the schools of the Freemasons, practical architects.

A. D. 925.—All the Masonic lodges of Great Britain

were this year convoked in a congress by the king, Athelstan, grandson of Alfred the Great, who had been prompted thereto by some priest-architects. The object of this assembly was to reconstitute the Fraternity, according to the laws and written documents saved in the convents from destruction during the wars, and afterward disseminated through the country, divided, as it had been during five hundred years, into seven kingdoms. This assembly discussed and accepted the constitution submitted to it by Edwin, son of King Athelstan, and the city of York was chosen for the future seat of the Grand Mastership.

A. D. 926.—In this year the charter of York, adopted at the assembly of 925, was promulgated, and this charter from this time became the basis of all Masonic constitutions. Prince Edwin is nominated to the dignity of Grand Master. (See the text of this charter, *suppeto*.)

A. D. 960.—The Archbishop of Canterbury, St. Dunstan, is named Grand Master of the Fraternity.

A. D. 1040.—Edward the Confessor, King of England, declares himself the protector of Freemasons, and names Leofrick, Count of Coventry, as his substitute, and, by his intervention, reëstablishes the Abbey of Westminster.

A. D. 1066.—Nomination of the Count of Arundel, Roger of Montgomery, to the Grand Mastership.

A. D. 1100.—King Henry IV, of England, accepts the Grand Mastership of the Fraternity.

A. D. 1145.—The Archbishop of Rouen publicly blesses the Freemasons assembled at Rouen, who came from upper Normandy at the call of those who were engaged in the construction of the cathedral of Chartres, and who desired their help to more speedily complete that work. These brethren made a triumphal entry into the city, accompanied by the brethren of neighboring corporations, particularly those of Caen and Bayeux. (See History of France. By Henry Martin. Vol. 2.)

A. D. 1155.—Richard Cœur de Leon, Grand Master of the Knights of the Temple, is nominated to the Grand Mastership of the Masonic Fraternity of Great Britain.

A. D. 1185.—Gilbert of Clare, Marquis of Pembroke, is nominated Grand Master.

A. D. 1199.—It was under the Grand Mastership and direction of Colechurch, Chaplain to King John, that the work on the first London bridge was begun, and finished under the direction of his successor, William Allemain, in 1212.

A. D. 1250.—The Grand Lodge of Cologne is instituted. The master of this lodge, and director of the work on the cathedral of this city, is regarded and obeyed as the master of all the Freemasons of Germany.

A. D. 1275.—A Masonic congress is convoked by Erwin of Steinbach, with the object of concerting measures to continue the work, which for a long time was interrupted, on the cathedral of Strasburg. This assembly organized itself into a Grand Lodge, (*Haupt-hütte,*) and nominated Erwin architect-in-chief of the work, and chair-master, (*Meister vom Stuhl.*)

A. D. 1277.—Pope Nicholas III confirms, by diplomas in favor of the Masonic corporations, the monopoly accorded to them by Pope Boniface IV, in the year 614.

A. D. 1314.—Documents, the genuineness of which has not been established, assert that in this year Robert Bruce, King of Scotland, founded the Order of Harodom of Kilwinning, and also elevated to the rank of a Grand Lodge of Harodom of Kilwinning the lodge founded in 1150, at the time of the erection of the Abbey of Kilwinning.

A. D. 1334.—Pope Benedict II confirms, by diploma, to the corporations their exclusive privileges for the construction of religious edifices.

A. D. 1358.—Under Edward III the charter of York of 926 is submitted to revision. In an appendix to this charter, which contains only some new regulations relating to the rights and emoluments accruing to Grand Masters, there is prescribed that, in future, at the reception of a brother, the constitution and old instructions shall be read to him by the master of the lodge. A charter in verse, written upon parchment, and bearing the title, "*Hic incipiunt constitutiones artis geometriæ secundum Euclidem*"—(Here begin the constitutions of the art of Geometry, according to Euclid)—has been found in the British Museum by an antiquary named J. O. Halliwell, and published by him in 1810, under the title of "The Early History of Freemasonry in England," and translated into German by Brother Afher, of Hamburg, in 1842. This document, submitted to the examination of experts, has been recognized, from its favorable comparison with the statutes of the parliament of 1425, as having been produced in the latter part of the fourteenth century, and, consequently, may be considered as based upon the charter of Edward III.

A. D. 1360.—At this time Germany had five grand lodges: Cologne, Strasburg, Berne, Vienna, and Madgeburg, upon which were dependent the local lodges of France, Belgium, Hesse, Swabia, Thuringia, Switzerland, Franconia, Bavaria, Austria, Hungary, and Styria.

A. D. 1425.—The English Parliament passed a bill this year suppressing the assemblies of Freemasons. The General Assembly which, notwithstanding, took place at York in 1427, protested against this bill, and annulled its effect. The manuscript register in the Latin language, containing all the names of the Master Masons who signed this protest, is to be found in the library of Oxford, and is dated with the year 1429.

A. D. 1438.—James II, King of Scotland, accords jurisdiction to the Grand Masters of the lodges of his kingdom, and authorizes them to establish special tribunals in the principal cities, by which are to be recognized the privileges of Freemasons. For this privilege the Grand Master is charged with the payment into the state treasury of a tax of four pounds, to be collected from each Mason passing to the degree of Master; and such Grand Master is further authorized to impose upon each new member a right of reception (fee). These two documents are to be found in the Law Library in Edinburgh.

A. D. 1439.—James II, King of Scotland, nominated William Sinclair (St. Clair) to the dignity of Grand Master adjunct for the lodges of Scotland.

A. D. 1442.—Initiation of Henry VI, King of England, into the Masonic Fraternity—an example followed by nearly all the gentlemen of his court, admitted as "Accepted Masons." The number of these latter-named had already increased so as to exceed the "Freemasons."

A. D. 1459.—A Masonic congress is held at Ratisbonne (the seat of the German Diet), devoted principally to the discussion of the new constitution compiled at Strasburg in 1452, which was based upon the laws of the English and Italian corporations, and which constitution was styled "Statutes and Regulations of the Fraternity of Stonecutters of Strasburg." The text of this constitution is to be found in many German works.

A. D. 1464.—Second congress of Freemasons assembles at Ratisbonne.

A. D. 1469.—A congress of Freemasons assembles at Spire. (The object of this congress will be found in our Historical Summary of Masonic Conventions, *suppeto*.)

A. D. 1498.—The Emperor Maximilian sanctions the Masonic constitution of Strasburg, and renews the ancient privileges accorded to the Freemasons.

A. D. 1502.—A Grand Lodge of Master Masons is held at London on the 24th June of this year. It is presided over by Henry VII of England, who lays the corner-stone of Westminster Chapel, or chapel of Henry VII.

A. D. 1522.—By a decree of the Helvetian Diet, the Grand Lodge of Zurich is dissolved. This Grand Lodge had been transferred to Zurich from Berne in 1502, after the cathedral of the latter city was finished.

A. D. 1539.—By an edict, Francis I dissolves the ancient corporations of Freemasons, because they had vindicated their ancient rights and privileges, and, by meeting in secret, gave offense to the clergy.

A. D. 1540.—Thomas Cromwell, Count of Essex, beheaded for political offenses, is succeeded, in the Grand Mastership of Freemasons, by Lord Audley.

A. D. 1550.—The Duke of Somerset, who succeeded Lord Audley as Grand Master, is decapitated—a victim of his attachment to the Stuarts.

A. D. 1561.—Queen Elizabeth, indignant that the Freemasons had not offered the Grand Mastership to her consort during his life, on the 27th of December of this year, ordered the dissolution of the Masonic assembly which on that day commenced its semi-annual meeting, and ordered the execution of her edict to be enforced by a detachment of armed men; but, upon a report having been made to her by the commanding officer of the detachment expressive of the politically harmless character of the assembly, the Queen revoked her order. Subsequently Queen Elizabeth became the protectress of the Freemasons of her kingdom, and confirmed their choice of Thomas Sackville for Grand Master.

A. D. 1563.—Congress of Swiss and German Masons takes place at Basle.

A. D. 1564.—Congress of Masons at Strasburg.

A. D. 1590.—Charter of James IV, King of Scotland, granted, on the 25th November of this year, to Patrick Copland of Urdaught, and which conferred upon him the right of filling the office of senior warden of Freemasons in the districts of Aberdeen, Banff, and Kinkardine.

A. D. 1598.—Acceptance of the new statutes for all the lodges of Scotland in a general assembly, which took place at Edinburgh, on the 29th December.

A. D. 1607.—James I, King of Great Britain, having proclaimed himself the protector of Freemasonry in his kingdom, affords much brilliancy and importance to the institution; and the high consideration which it enjoys at this time is greatly augmented by the election of the celebrated architect Inigo Jones to the dignity of Grand Master. The new direction that he initiated in the English lodges developed a spiritual movement in their Masonic life that compared favorably with that of the art academies of Italy. From this time, also, the Accepted Masons greatly preponderated over the Freemasons.

A. D. 1630.—A document is signed by all the representatives of Scottish lodges, by which are confirmed to the successor of William St. Clair, Baron of Roslin, the dignity and hereditary rights of Grand Master of the lodges of Scotland, and which were conferred upon the head of that family by James II of Scotland, in 1439. This document may be found in the law library of Edinburgh.

A. D. 1650.—This was the year of mourning for all true Freemasons, it being signalized by the political tendencies into which many of the lodges were precipitated by the decapitation of Charles I. The Masons of England, and particularly those of Scotland, partisans of the Stuarts, labored in secret to reëstablish the throne overturned by Cromwell. Not being able to induce all the Masons to become adherents of their propositions, they invented two superior degrees, viz.: Templar and Scottish Master, into the secrets of which they initiated those who were favorable to their secret plans.

A. D. 1663.—A general assembly of the Masons of England takes place at York, and which is presided over by King Charles II. At this assembly the king confirmed the Grand Master, Henry Germain, Count of St. Albans, in the dignity of his office, and decorated him with the ribbon of the Order of the Bath. This assembly passed a series of regulations, conceived entirely with reference to passing and past political events, and confirmed the continuance of the two superior degrees of Scottish Master and Templar.

A. D. 1666.—The great fire of London destroys forty thousand dwellings and eighty-six churches. As there did not exist at this time but seven lodges in London, nine-tenths of the members of which were "Accepted Masons," it became necessary to invite the Freemasons of Europe generally to England to reconstruct the city. All the Freemasons, as also the Masons and architects which did not belong to the Masonic association, put themselves under the direction of a central lodge, governed by Christopher Wren, the Grand Master, and architect of St. Paul's Cathedral, and in accordance with whose plans the city was rebuilt.

A. D. 1685.—James III reëstablished the Order of Knights of St. Andrew, which, established by Robert Bruce, King of Scotland, in 1314, in favor of the Freemasons who fought for him, had been suppressed, and the property of the Order confiscated, during the Reformation. This order, according to the intention of the king, should be conferred as a sign of distinction and recompense awarded to the Freemasons who had stood by his house; and it is probable, had fortune favored James III, he would have reinstated this Order in its possessions.

A. D. 1703.—At this time there existed but four lodges of Freemasons in London; and, notwithstanding the zeal exhibited by the aged Grand Master, Christopher Wren, the members of these lodges gradually decreased. The annual feasts were completely neglected and the lodges deserted. Under these circumstances, the Lodge of St. Paul, (known at the present time as the Lodge of Antiquity,) with the object of retarding the continually decreasing number of its membership, as also to give some importance to its existence, passed a resolution that entirely changed the face of the society. (This resolution will be found on page 56, *ante*.)

. A. D. 1717.—This memorable year, from which it is necessary to date the era of modern Freemasonry, was marked by the death of Christopher Wren. (The Masonic events of this year will be found first given at pages 51 and 57, *ante*, and subsequently often referred to in this work.)

III.—Indications of the Causes for the Diversity of Opinions which exist as to the Origin of Freemasonry.

The opinion that has generally prevailed, as well in Europe as in America, that Freemasonry is indebted for its origin to the religious mysteries of the Jews, or to the initiations of India, Persia, or Egypt, is owing, to a great extent, to the numerous writings of an eccentric character which have been published, principally in France, by designing persons, for political purposes, during the last century.

This opinion, however, has never had supporters among such English Masonic writers as have produced histories of Freemasonry, of whom the number, however, has been few. These writers remain faithful to their ancient traditions and documents in their possession, and, according to which, Freemasonry existed under this name since the occupation of Great Britain by the Roman legions; and, therefore, they very logically determine that the institution was brought to that country by the Romans.

Within the present century, two works have appeared which have helped to strengthen French Masons in the errors into which they have fallen upon the subject of the origin of Freemasonry. The first is the work of Brother Lenoir, a distinguished antiquary, published at Paris in 1814, and bearing the title, "Freemasonry Restored to its True Origin, or the Antiquity of Freemasonry proven by the Explanation of its Ancient and Modern Mysteries;"[1] and the second is the work of Brother Reghelini de Chio, entitled "Freemasonry in its Connection with the Religions of the Egyptians." The first of these works has displayed a rare quality of research for proofs to support the opinions of its author, while the second exhibits less care in establishing, by the aid of science and history, the connections which its author believes he has discovered between the religions of the Egyptians and Freemasonry. It is but doing justice to both authors, however, to believe that they earnestly desired to seek the truth. But while, in the forms, symbols, doctrines, and principles of Freemasonry they have discovered the true secrets of the philosophic schools of Greece, Egypt, and India, introduced, during many centuries which have preceded our era, into the Roman colleges of constructors, and which latter were, from their foundation, the theater of all initiations, and open to all mysterious doctrines, it may not be concluded that Freemasonry sprang by direct issue from these schools of antiquity. If these doctrines have been religiously preserved by the corporations, as we have stated, and by them as religiously transmitted, with little alteration, to those which succeeded them in Gaul and Britain, these corporations alone should not monopolize the merit of such transmission; for the Greeks and Jews, and particularly the primitive Christians, have equally propagated these doctrines. Now, notwithstanding the connection that Freemasonry presents, in its forms of initiation, with the

---

[1] In the work of Brother J. G. Findel of Leipsic, entitled "History of Freemasonry from its Origin to the Present Day"—one of the best German works of its kind—in speaking of the diversity of opinion prevalent, particularly in France, upon the origin of Freemasonry, the author remarks that all the French Masonic writers have accepted and followed the opinion of Alex. Lenoir, with the exception of Brother Rebold and Brother Moreau. These brethren, he continues, coincide in the opinion of all our (German) earnest and thorough historians, such as Krause, Boberich, Heldmann, and others.

ancient mysteries—a connection that has induced error among most writers—it can not be considered more than a feeble imitation, instead of a continuation, of these mysteries; because, from the beginning, initiation into the mysteries of the ancient Egyptians, Greeks, and Hindoos was the teachings of the worship, philosophy, philanthropy, and morality, as well as art, science, and legislation of these peoples, while Freemasonry should be considered as a purely philosophic school of perfection, having for its leading object universal fraternity.

We will refrain from quoting much that has been published upon this subject by writers more or less convinced, and which has contributed greatly to mislead the minds of brethren, even the most enlightened.[1]

Can it be wondered that among Masons, such as Brother Garon, who would bid historians look into their own hearts for authentic materials with which to construct a *history* of any human institution, there will be found to-day—notwithstanding the consistent, straightforward, and authentic productions on this subject which have been given to the brethren during the past ten years—orators of lodges in France, and probably elsewhere, misleading the minds of young Masons and disgusting those of the old with their Masonic romances and absurd histories, as gathered from their favorite Masonic authors?

To discover the cradle of the institution, it should suffice to seek it in the history of England, and at the time

---

[1] In the report that Brother Garon, president of the Chamber of Correspondence, made to the Grand Orient of France, upon the General History of Freemasonry—the earlier production of the author of the present work—he says, in closing: "All Masons who may read the learned work of this historian will find therein much valuable information and historical instruction; but they will also be convinced, as I am, that if Brother Rebold had sought the History of Freemasonry *in his heart*, in place of taking it from books, he would not have landed this almost divine institution from among an association of workmen constructors."

when are first mentioned the corporations known by the name of *Free Masons*. Then, after having consulted all the documents of this period, go back still further, by the aid of such marks as can be found, to the place or first appearance of the persons among whom the society appears; then follow it down through the wars and invasions to which that country has been subject. If, after this process of investigation, and notwithstanding the changes of its primitive name, the identity of the affiliation is established, or successively developed, it is not necessary then to have recourse to hypothesis to indicate with certainty its origin. It is by proceeding thus that we have found that Freemasonry is the issue of an ancient and celebrated corporation of artists and mechanics, united for the prosecution of civil, religious, naval, and military architecture, founded at Rome in the year 715 B. C., by the celebrated legislator, Numa Pompilius; and which, during the eleven hundred years which elapsed subsequent to its foundation, had been known, in all the countries subject to Roman rule, under the designation of *Corporations* or *Fraternities of Roman Builders;* but, after the retreat of the Roman legions of the Gauls, and being no longer sustained by the Roman powers, these associations were forced to dissolve and divide themselves into separate corporations, (between A. D. 486 and 500,) from which sprang the artists and mechanics of the middle ages, as the new corporations of mason builders, and preserving only their ancient laws and the artistic and philosophic secrets of their art.

The members of these corporations, remaining in Britain after their transformation, were called *Free Masons*, to distinguish them from the masons and stone-cutters who were not in the enjoyment of the privileges extended to them by written constitutions and diplomas. These Freemasons have had, since that time, an immense political and scientific influence; they communicated their secrets but to those whom, according to traditional forms, they initiated into their mysteries; they had a liberal organization, and a philosophic code of laws which had governed them from ancient times. This association, dissolved in the sixteenth century in consequence of the peculiar circumstances of the Protestant Reformation in the countries where it then principally subsisted, is subsequently maintained without interruption in England, under its traditional forms, even after having abandoned its material object. Numerous fractions of it, called lodges, continue to exist until the beginning of the eighteenth century, disseminated throughout the country, and meeting only once a year, at the feast of St. John, to distribute aid among the brethren, and elect their officers; while, beyond the control of any state laws, they conserved the privilege unabated of uniting in public processions and laying the corner-stones of all public buildings and monuments. This corporation of Freemasons, finally transformed at London in 1717, declares its wish to continue and to propagate the philosophical principles which, from all time, have been the basis of the society; and, renouncing forever material architecture, to thenceforth employ itself wholly with moral architecture and philosophy. Such is the origin of Modern or Philosophical Freemasonry.

And why should not such an origin be acceptable to all Freemasons? Because, simply, it is repugnant to their self-love to acknowledge the descent of their society from an association of practical masons, or, in the language of Brother Garon, from "an association of workmen-constructors;" and this, too, notwithstanding the very name *Freemason* indicates no other source or origin.

Examine more closely this association of which they are ashamed.

By its antiquity alone—an antiquity which they at all times desire most heartily to endorse and extend beyond all reasonable limit—is it not respectable?

By its having been based upon the laws of the Dionysian priest-architects, admitted by Solon in his legislation, and subsequently inscribed by him upon the Roman tables—is it not respectable?

By its having been composed, from the beginning, of the most eminent men of the most eminent nations—of Greeks, of Egyptians, of Phenicians—initiates into the mysteries of their respective countries, and experts in all branches of human knowledge—is it not respectable?

Did not these corporations collect and adopt all the philosophic and humanitarian truths taught and implied in the doctrines of the greatest thinkers of antiquity; and, by having, long before the birth of Christ, practiced those principles pointing to the emancipation and elevation of woman, as the fountain of our existence, and to the abolishment of human slavery—are they not respectable?

Can we point to any other association which for twenty-five centuries has preserved in their primitive simplicity and purity, and written, as it were, with a pen of steel in the rock forever, those humanitarian principles of love to God and to our neighbor?

Was it an association of no importance which erected those thousands of majestic temples, those superb monuments whose very ruins to-day involuntarily excite our admiration?

Were they simple associations of workmen-constructors who, possessing all the art, science, and knowledge of any value acquired at that time, exercised so great an influence upon Roman civilization, that it may be considered indebted to them for all of art and civil law disseminated wherever the legions fixed themselves, and who thus became the forerunners of Christian teaching and civilization?

Was it a simple association of practical masons who, during the middle ages, constructed those numerous and sublime religious edifices, which shall be forever the admiration of posterity—those master-pieces of Christian genius, those grand, gigantic conceptions of religious faith and zeal—the cathedrals of Strasburg, Cologne, Rouen, Paris, etc.? Could such monuments be the work of ordinary masons and stone-cutters? If so, where shall we find their like to-day?

These sanctuaries of the Great Architect of the Universe, as they are avowed to be by the most distinguished architects—strangers to the Masonic institution—are due to the Freemasonry of the middle ages: to "these philosophic, learned, modest, pious, and truly Christian Freemasons," as they are called by the author of one of the best and most recent works upon architecture.[1]

Was it a simple association of workmen-constructors who by their protest annulled an act of the Parliament of England of 1425?

Is that an association of no importance which, since the sixth century, can count as its presidents, thirteen bishops and archbishops, twelve dukes of the kingdom, and fourteen princes and kings?

And should we, as Freemasons, blush to descend from those corporations of mason philosophers, because they wrought, in their time, as workmen-constructors?

No associations of any period of the world's history have produced works so remarkable as those which are due to these corporations; and no society that ever had place on the world's surface can be compared to them either as to length of years or value of principles.

Far from contemning so respectable an origin, we should seek glory in acknowledging it, at all times and in all places; and endeavor to render ourselves worthy of it by continuing, in our own persons, that sublime work of which the Roman constructors, in the spiritual darkness of twenty-five hundred years ago, laid the foundation stone.

---

[1] See "General History of Architecture," by Daniel Ramee, p. 234.

HISTORICAL ENUMERATION

OF THE

PRINCIPAL MASONIC CONGRESSES AND CONVENTIONS

WHICH HAVE HAD PLACE IN EUROPE SINCE THAT OF YORK, A. D. 926, TO THAT OF PARIS, A. D. 1856.

YORK, IN 926.

CONVOKED by Edwin, son of King Athelstan, for the reconstitution of the Masonic corporations. A new constitution, based upon the ancient laws, is at this time promulgated.

STRASBURG, IN 1275.

Convoked by Erwin of Steinbach for the continuation of the work on the cathedral of Strasburg. A great number of architects and workmen from Germany, England, and Lombardy are assembled at this congress. At the instance of the lodges of England, they constituted themselves under the rule of the Freemasons, and each took the oath to faithfully observe the ancient laws and regulations of the Fraternity of Freemasons.

RATISBONNE, IN 1459.

Convoked by Job Dotzinger, working master of the cathedral of Strasburg, to discuss the affairs of the Fraternity generally, and sanction the new laws and regulations prepared at a meeting that took place at Strasburg in 1452.

Ratisbonne, in 1464.

Convoked by the Grand Lodge of Strasburg with the following objects: 1. General affairs, and to receive reports concerning the edifices then in course of construction, with the intention of overcoming or removing the difficulties which prevented their completion. 2. To define more precisely the rights and attributes of the four Grand Lodges, viz.: those of Cologne, Strasburg, Berne, and Vienna. 3. The nomination of Conrad Kuyn, working master, to the Grand Mastership of the Grand Lodge of Cologne, etc.

Spire, in 1469.

Convoked by the Grand Lodge of Strasburg, with the following objects, viz.: 1. To receive and act upon communications concerning all the religious edifices finished, as well as in course of construction, and also as to those the work upon which has been arrested. 2. To hear reports upon the situation and condition of the Fraternity in England, Gaul, Lombardy, and Germany.

Cologne, in 1535.

Convoked by Hermann, bishop of Cologne, to take measures to meet the accusations and dangers which menaced the Freemasons. The "charter of Cologne" is stated to be the offspring of this congress; but the authenticity of this statement is not believed by those who have critically examined that document.

Basle, in 1563.

Convoked by the Grand Lodge of Strasburg, with the following objects, viz.: 1. To receive and act upon a general report of the condition of architecture and that of the Fraternity. 2. To discuss and amicably terminate the differences which had arisen concerning the rights of some of the twenty-two lodges subordinate to the Grand Lodge of Strasburg. 3. To sanction the revised statutes prepared by a commission of the Grand Lodge of Strasburg, to date from the feast of St. Michael, 1563.

Strasburg, in 1564.

Convoked as an extraordinary convention by the Grand Lodge of Strasburg, with the objects, viz.: 1. To explain definitely all the subjects in dispute among the lodges, and to decide that the difficulties which should hereafter arise among them should be submitted directly to the Grand Lodge of Strasburg, and adjudged (decided) by that body without appeal. 2. To continue the customary reports, etc.

London, in 1717.

Convoked by the four lodges which at this time existed in London, at the head of which was the old lodge of St. Paul. Approving and ratifying a resolution adopted by this lodge in 1703, viz.: "That the privileges of Masonry shall no longer be confined to operative Masons, but be free to men of all professions, provided that they are regularly approved and initiated into the Fraternity," they constituted themselves, in accordance with this decision, a Grand Lodge of England of Free and Accepted Masons, with a rite consisting of three primitive degrees, called symbolic.

Dublin, in 1729.

Convoked by the lodges of Dublin, with the object of organizing Freemasonry upon the basis adopted in England in 1717, and to institute a Grand Lodge for Ireland. At this convention the viscount Lord Kingston was elected Grand Master.

Edinburgh, in 1736.

Convoked by the baron Sinclair of Roslyn, Grand Master of the Masons of Scotland by appointment of King James II in 1439, with the object of abdicating his dignity of hereditary Grand Master, and organize Masonry upon the new basis recognized and sanctioned by the Grand Lodge of England and Ireland. There were present at this convention the members of thirty-two lodges, who instituted the Grand Lodge of Scotland, and elected Baron Sinclair Grand Master for the year 1737.

The Hague, in 1756.

Convoked by the mother lodge "Royal Union," of the Hague, with the object of instituting a national Grand Lodge for the United Provinces, under the auspices of the Grand Lodge of England. The object of this convention was consummated by the thirteen lodges assembled, and the baron of Aersen-Beyeren was elected Grand Master.

Jena and Altenburg, in 1763, 1764, and 1765.

In the first of these conventions, Johnson, the self-styled plenipotentiary of the "Unknown Superiors" resident in Scotland, assembled at Jena, on the 25th October, the lodges established under the system of Strict Observance, for the purpose of recognizing him in his office of Superior. A second convention was convoked by him at Jena to establish his system. To this was invited Baron Hund, and the lodges of the same rite founded by him; but Hund, who had at first believed in the mission of Johnson, discovered and declared him to be an impostor. At the third convention, held at Altenburg, near Jena, the following year, Baron Hund was proclaimed Grand Master of all the lodges of this system.

Kohlo, in 1772.

Convoked by some lodges of the system of Strict Observance, with the object of opposing a new rite established by Zinnendorf. At this convention the duke Ferdinand of Brunswick was elected Grand Master of Strict Observance lodges.

Brunswick, in 1775.

Convoked by Ferdinand, Duke of Brunswick, with the object of ascertaining which, if any, of the rites pretending to the possession of the true Masonic science, really possessed it. Baron Hund, and twenty-three lodges of the system he had instituted in the convention of Altenburg, assisted at this convention, in which the discussions took place daily, from the 22d May to the 6th July, without any decision having resulted.

Leipsic, in 1777.

Convoked by the lodges of the system of Strict Observance located in Berlin, with the object of putting into operation the resolutions passed at a meeting, or succession of meetings, which took place at Hamburg, from the 4th to the 16th June, relative to the establishment of a compact of union among all the lodges of the system, both in Sweden and Germany, and to nominate a new Grand Master, for which office they proposed the Duke of Sudermanie. This convention lasted from the 16th to the 22d of October, and then dissolved without having decided on any thing.

Lyons, in 1778.

Convoked by the lodge of the "Benevolent Knights" at Lyons, under the pretext of reforming Freemasonry, throwing light upon all obscurity, and correcting the rituals; but the real object of which was to establish the Martinist rite over that of the Templars. Only one of their objects was accomplished: they changed the rituals. The convention remained in session from the 23d November to the 27th of December.

WOLFENBUTTEL, IN 1778.

Convoked by Frederick, Duke of Brunswick, with the like object of the convention at Brunswick in 1775. It lasted from the 15th July to the 22d August; and the assembly not seeing any clearer on the last of those days than they did on the first through the chaos into which the mystical systems had plunged Freemasonry, decided that they should make a general appeal to all the Masonic bodies, and convoke at Wilhelmsbad a convention of all the Masons of Europe.

WILHELMSBAD, IN 1782.

(This convention was at first fixed for the 15th October, 1781, afterward for Easter week, 1782, and finally for the 16th July, 1782.)

Convoked by Ferdinand, Duke of Brunswick, agreeably to the decision of the convention at Wolfenbuttel, in 1778, with the following objects, viz.: 1. The general reformation of Freemasonry; 2. To discuss, with the object of obtaining light as to the origin of the different systems and doctrines; and, above all, 3. To solve the following questions: Is Freemasonry a modern society? Is it, on the contrary, derived from an ancient society? If so, from what ancient society is it derived? Has Freemasonry Superior Generals? Who are they? What are their attributes? Do these attributes enable them to command or to instruct?

All these questions, submitted to the assembly during its thirty meetings, were unanswered. The congress succeeded, however, in exposing a number of mystical systems, and in remodeling the system of Strict Observance. It also caused the creation of the Eclectic Rite.

Paris, in 1785.

Convoked by the Philalètes of the Lodge of United Friends of Paris, for the purpose of assembling all the learned Masons in France to clear up the fog produced by the numerous systems introduced into Freemasonry; to discuss and arrange the essential points of Masonic doctrine, origin, and historical affiliation, and determine the actual condition of Masonic science. This congress continued in session from the 15th February to the 26th May, without determining any thing.

Paris, in 1787.

Also convoked by the Philalètes, to continue the discussions opened at the previous congress upon many dogmatic and historic points already settled by the congress of Wilnelmsbad; but none of the questions which induced the assembly of this congress were at this time determined, and the origin, nature, and object of perpetuating Masonry continued to remain an insoluble problem to the greatest number of the Masons of the continent.

Switzerland, in 1836 to 1842.

The first of these conventions was held at Zurich in 1836, the second at Berne in 1838, the third at Basle in 1840, and the fourth at Locle in 1842. Their object was the fusion of the Masonic powers of Switzerland, the abolishing of high degrees, and the organization of one Masonic authority, to be called the Alpine Grand Lodge. The constitution of union was signed at Locle in 1842, ratified in 1843, and became the law of the Fraternity in 1844.

Paris in 1848.

Convoked, after the revolution in February 1848, by a few members of the "Supreme Council for France" calling all the lodges of France to constitute a new power, to elaborate a constitution based upon the broadest democratic principles, and to adopt exclusively the modern English rite. The result of this congress was the organization of The National Grand Lodge of France.

Paris, in 1855.

Convoked by Prince Lucien Murat, Grand Master of the Grand Orient of France, who had extended an invitation to all the Grand Orients and Grand Lodges of the world to unite in a Universal Masonic Congress, the object of which would be to cement more closely the bonds of union among all the Masonic powers wherever dispersed. A very small number of those powers responded to this call; and the propositions discussed and adopted were of so feeble a nature that they are not worth mentioning. The result of this congress has been nothing.

CHRONOLOGICAL ARRANGEMENT

OF THE

HISTORY OF FREEMASONRY,

BASED UPON THE ANCIENT DOCUMENTS, AND UPON THE PRINCIPAL MONUMENTS ERECTED BY FREEMASONS: DIVIDED INTO THREE EPOCHS.

First Epoch.
From the year 715 B. C. to the year 1000 A. D.

715 B. C.

FOUNDATION of the colleges of Roman Constructors (*collegia fabrorum*), composed of all the arts and trades necessary for the execution of religious and civil, naval and hydraulic architecture, with their own laws and lawgivers—laws at this time based upon those of the priest architects of Greece, whose mysteries, under the name of Dyonisian, had spread among the principal peoples of the East. Numa Pompilius, in organizing these colleges, constituted them at the time as a civil and religious society, with the exclusive privilege of erecting the public temples and monuments in Rome. Their connection with the State and the priesthood was determined by the laws with precision;[1] they had

---

[1] Consult on the subject of these associations the *Body of Roman Rights;* Cicero's *Second Epistle to his Brother Quintus; The Pollion* of De Bugny; Schœll's *History of Architecture, vol.* 1; De Hammer's *Discovery of the Actual State of Freemasonry;* Lenning's *Encyclopedia of Freemasonry;* C. Krauser's *Three Oldest Landmarks of Freemasonry;* De Widdekind's *Memoir upon the State of Architecture in the Middle Ages;* and Heldmann's *History of Freemasonry.*

their own jurisdiction, their own worship: at their head were to be found presiding officers called *magistri* (masters), wardens, censors, treasurers, keepers of the seals, archivists secretaries, etc.; they had special physicians, serving brothers, and they paid into their treasury monthly collections. The number of members of each college was fixed, and determined by law. Composed principally of Greek artists, they, surrounding the secrets of their art and of their doctrines with the mysteries of the worship of their country, enveloped them in the symbols borrowed from these same mysteries, and of which one of the characteristic traits was the employment, in a symbolical sense, of the tools of their profession.[1]

710 B. C.

Numa, the wise lawgiver, who founded the colleges, immediately assigned to them their work: at first the enlargement of the Capitol; next the completion of the temples dedicated to the Sun, to the Moon, to Saturn, Rhea, and Vesta, to Mars, and the other pagan divinities, which were begun under Romulus and the king of the Sabines. These monuments finished, Numa ordered them to erect temples to Faith, to Fidelity, to Romulus, and to Janus the god of Peace, whom Numa particularly adored. He ordered them to fortify the city and surround it with walls; and this work accomplished, he directed them to continue the construction of that famous temple that Romulus erected to Jupiter Stator, upon the spot where his army, when nearly vanquished, recovered their strength and courage, after Romulus had addressed a prayer to Jupiter.[2]

---

[1] By virtue of these privileges, all the public monuments which were constructed from the organization of these colleges until the reign of Constantine the Great, (330 years after Christ,) in Rome and the provinces, were exclusively erected by them, or under their direction; but of which nothing exists to-day but ruins of more or less importance.

[2] The great number of temples which were subsequently erected in Rome are due to the practice which was thus originated by Romulus—that the commander in chief should erect a temple to the god whom he invoked dur-

650 B. C.

The population increases much under Ancus Martius, who fortifies the city anew and surrounds it with new walls; and a considerable aqueduct, that takes his name, is constructed by his orders. He orders the colleges of constructors to erect at Ostia a port of entry, or harbor, to encourage maritime commerce; and they there constructed some ships.

610 B. C.

Under the reign of Tarquin the Elder, some temples were erected; upon the Capitoline Hill one to Jupiter, one to Juno, and one to Minerva. He had constructed within the city a wall of cut stone, a subterranean canal (the *cloaca maxima*) for the drainage of the city, and a great many other public monuments. Under his orders the first circus was constructed.

580 B. C.

Rome is further aggrandized under the reign of Servius Tullius, and increased in size by taking within its limits the Virinal, Quirinal, and Esquiline Hills, which, by his orders, are surrounded with walls. He erected a temple to the idea Manly Fortune, and another to the goddess Diana.

530 B. C.

The monuments and temples begun under Tarquin the Elder are completed under Tarquin the Superb, who also continues the famous *cloaca maxima*, in which a person might row a boat. He finishes the temple of Jupiter Capitoline, and the circus begun by his predecessor; while another circus, dedicated to the exercises of the Roman youth, is constructed by his orders.

---

ing the progress of a battle won. This custom explains the great number of monuments erected to the same divinity.

500 B. C.

The temples of Vesta and Hercules are erected upon the Aventine Hill, and the temples of Pallas and Minerva Medica are erected under Junius Drusus.

490 B. C.

The Consuls Sempronius and M. Minucius order the erection, by the colleges of constructors, of two temples; the one dedicated to Saturn, the other to Mercury. They also establish the Saturnalian feasts.

480 B. C.

The temples of Castor and Pollux are erected under the dictator Posthumius, who, after his victory over the Latins, also ordered the erection of two other temples—the one in honor of Ceres, the other of Bacchus. The most remarkable of all that he had erected, however, was the temple to the idea Better Fortune.

451 B. C.

Creation of the laws of the Twelve Tables, the eighth of which is confined to provisions concerning the colleges of builders.

396 B. C.

Furius Camillus, during his consulate, orders the erection of temples; one to Queen Juno, after a victory; also, one to Jupiter, and one to Concord.

390 B. C.

Destruction of a part of the public monuments at the sacking of Rome by the Gauls.

385 B. C.

Re-erection of the destroyed monuments under Flavius Quintus, who also orders the erection of new temples, which he dedicates; one to Mars, another to Juno Moneta; while two others are consecrated to Salus (health) and Concord.

312 B. C.

The first stone road is constructed by the colleges, under the orders of Appius Claudius, who directed that it be continued to Capua. The first great aqueduct was constructed at this time.

290 B. C.

The temple of Romulus, who was, by order of the Senate of Pompilius, deified, under the title of Quirinus, is erected, and in it is placed the first solar dial. The consul, Spur. Carvilius, also ordered the erection of a temple to *Fortis Fortuna*, to contain the spoils taken from the Etruscans. He also ordered the construction of a temple in honor of Æsculapius, to be situate upon the island of the Tiber.

285 B. C.

The Fraternities of Constructors, as they are called at this time, attached to the Roman legions, locate themselves in that portion of Cisalpine Gaul known to-day as Venice and Lombardy, whither they had followed the conquest of the Roman arms. To these fraternities—of whom a brigade was attached to each legion, and which they accompanied every-where—was entrusted the designing of the plans of all the military constructions, such as intrenched camps, strategic routes, bridges, aqueducts, and dwellings. They directed the labors of soldiers and the more ignorant workmen in the mechanical execution of these works; and it was them who also manufactured the implements of war. They were submissive to the generals or chiefs of the legions in such matters as related directly to the movements of the army, but in all else they remained in the enjoyment of their privileges. Composed of artists and learned men, these fraternities spread the ideas of Roman taste, and the knowledge of Roman manners, literature and art, wherever the Roman nation carried its victorious arms; while, at the same time, they insured the vanquished in the possession of the pacific element of Roman favor, her arts and civil laws.

280 B. C.

Under the consulate of Caius Duilius new temples are erected, one of which, after having vanquished the Carthaginians at sea, he dedicated to Janus. Another temple, erected by order of Actilius, he dedicated to Hope.

275 B. C.

The conquest of nearly all of Cisalpine Gaul— now known as the Sardinian States—was followed by this country being at once taken possession of by the fraternities of constructors, who, never remaining inactive, re-erected every-where, and always in better manner, those monuments which the legions had destroyed.

250 B. C.

While Cisalpine Gaul was covered over with military colonies, surrounded with fortifications executed by the fraternities of constructors, who likewise erected in their midst habitations and palaces for the principal commanders, other legions carried their conquering arms beyond the Alps into Transalpine Gaul and Spain. The first great highway is constructed about this time across Gaul, and leading from Rome to the valley of Ostia.

225 B. C.

The fraternities of constructors, who followed the legions into Gaul and Spain, completed their mission. In Spain they founded *Cordova;* in Gaul, *Empodorum.* Those of Rome there constructed the famous Flaminian Circus, to which the Consul, C. Flaminius, attached his name.

220 B. C.

The Romans, attacked by Hannibal, erected after his retreat, in commemoration of that event, a temple to the god (idea) Ridicule. Under the direction of the colleges, and by order of the censor Flaminius, the Roman soldiers construct a great strategic route. Flaminius also orders the erection of a circus in Rome.

210 B. C.

During the second Punic War the colleges had no employment at Rome, there being nothing for them to construct; they, therefore, went into the conquered provinces. Subsequently they returned, and under the orders of Marcellus, they constructed two temples, bearing the titles respectively, of *Virtus* and *Juno Hospita*.

200 B. C.

The Roman people having decided, in the year 202, to erect a temple to the god Mars, and another to the founders of Rome, Romulus and his brother Remus, both of these temples are completed during this year.

148 B. C.

The first temple in marble is ordered to be erected by the general Metellus, who, after his victory over the king of Macedonia, dedicated it to Jupiter Stator. Afterward he ordered the erection of another temple at his own expense, which he dedicated to Juno; also, a remarkable sepulcher, that bears his name.

125 B. C

The legions, become masters of Helvetia, there fortified themselves, and gradually enriched the country with camps and the cities *Augusta Basilia* and *Aventicum*, the latter of which became of some importance.

121 B. C.

A Roman colony, commanded by Marsius, founded *Narbo Marsius*, (*Narbonne*,) which became the principal head-quarters of the Roman armies until the time of Augustus. The consul Opinius ordered the construction at Rome of the first court of justice or city hall. He also ordered the erection of a temple, which he dedicated to Concord.

101 B. C.

After the victory over the Cimbrians and the Teutons, vanquished by Marius, he ordered the erection in Rome, under the special direction of the architect C. Musius, a temple in honor of the divinities Honor and Virtue.[1]

79 B. C.

The ancient city of *Herculaneum*, in which were erected by the fraternities of constructors numerous monuments of art, is overthrown and buried in the lava of an eruption of Mount Vesuvius. The magnificent monuments with which Pompeii, no less celebrated than Herculaneum, had been ornamented by the Roman constructors, crumbled and disappeared, in great part, in consequence of the earthquake that accompanied the eruption which destroyed the latter city, and all that remains is covered with the ashes and lava thrown out by the eruption mentioned.

75 B. C.

A great number of towns are erected in Gaul in the district of Narbonne. Military colonies are every-where established to maintain the conquered country against the

---

[1] Up to this time architecture partook of the Etruscan style, and the attempts made to embellish the public temples and edifices consisted but in the ornamentation of statues and other objects erected in conquered countries, particularly in Greece; but from this time the predilection of the Romans for Greek art and architecture became dominant, and the Etruscan style of architecture was abandoned, as being too severely simple.

neighboring peoples, and principally in the neighborhood of the ancient *Massilia* (Marseilles) founded by the Phonecians in 549, and of *Arelate* (Arles), of which the origin goes back to 2000 years before Christ. Among those are *Aqua Sextia* (Aix) and *Nemausus* (Nimes), which became important cities. *Arelate*, before mentioned, subsequently became the capital of the kingdom of Arles, and attained the rank of a powerful city, wherein the Masonic fraternities constructed some sumptuous monuments. The ruins of an amphitheater, an obelisk, a temple, an arch of triumph, and an aqueduct, reveal to us the ancient importance of the residence of Constantine in this city.

60 B. C.

After ten years of almost continual war, during which, according to Plutarch, 800 villages were devastated, Julius Cæsar made himself master of all Transalpine Gaul. He at once put the numerous fraternities of constructors attached to his legions at work, and ordered the attendance of many others scattered throughout the provinces, to re-erect, with the aid of his soldiers, the towns and cities destroyed, and to render more beautiful and ornamental the monuments of the people. By his orders and those of his successors, the following named cities became important, viz.: *Treviri* (Treves), *Remi* (Rheims), *Rothomagus* (Rouen), *Cesarodunum* (Tours), *Avaricum* (Bourges), *Senones* (Sens), *Burdigala* (Bordeaux), *Vesontio* (Besançon), *Lugdunum* (Lyons), Vienna, *Tolosa* (Toulouse), and *Lutetia* or *Parisie* (Paris). A great many other cities are erected by the colleges, such as *Geryobia*, *Xelodunum*, *Avaricum*, etc., but none of them attained the importance of the above. Treves was subsequently chosen as the residence of the prefect or governor of the Gauls.

55 B. C.

Britain, conquered in part at this time, some reinforcements of constructors were sent there to establish more extended fortifications. Under the command of Julius Cæsar, one of his legions pushed further into the country, and, to hold its ground, there constructed an intrenched camp, with walls, inside of which the constructors immediately erected, as elsewhere, habitations, temples, aqueducts, etc., and in this manner gave birth to *Eboracum* (York), a city celebrated in the history of Freemasonry.

50 B. C.

While Julius Cæsar pushed his conquests, and destroyed druid altars and celtic monuments, Pompey erected in Rome numerous temples and the famous amphitheater, built of white marble, capable of containing thirty thousand persons. He also, under the direction of the fraternities of architects, constructed the not less famous road which led from Rome through Italy across the Alps into Gaul. Julius Cæsar, upon his return to Rome, also ordered the construction of many temples, of which he dedicated one each to Mars, Venus Genitrix, and Apollo. All the colleges located in the cities of Cisalpine Gaul (actual Italy) are called together by him and sent to Carthage and Corinth to reërect those ruined cities.

45 B. C.

The Roman senate, after the civil war, ordered to be erected, by the colleges of constructors, many monuments of different kinds, in honor of Julius Cæsar, among which were four temples, dedicated respectively to Liberty, Concord, Happiness, and Mercy. In the year 42 the triumvirs of Rome erected a temple to Isis and another to Serapis.

41 B. C.

A military colony is established on the site of a Gallic village, at the confluence of the Rhone and Saone, and there is founded *Lugdunum* (Lyons.) [It was burnt, re-erected by Nero, and beautifully embellished by Trajan. Lugdunum became afterward the capital of Gaul, the seat of government, and the imperial residence during the voyages of the emperor Augustus and the majority of his successors.]

37 B. C.

The Roman legions, stationed along the Rhine to protect Gaul against the continual aggressions of the German peoples, formed at many points intrenched camps, which became strong colonies. *Colonia Agrippina* (Cologne) had its origin in this manner. It was enlarged at this time, and invested with the rights of a Roman city, under the emperor Claudius.

35 B. C.

The Pantheon, at Rome, is finished under Marcus Agrippa, who also constructed some superb hot baths, which bore his own name. The great road from Rome, crossing Cisalpine Gaul and the valley of Ostia to Lyons, is continued by his orders, under the direction of the fraternities of constructors, in four main directions, viz.: First, to Aquitaine, by Auvergne; second, to the Rhine; third, to Laon, by Burgundy and Picardy; fourth, to Marseilles, by Narbonne.

32 B. C.

The Roman legions who located themselves at *Lutetia*, (Paris,) under Julius Cæsar, there, side by side with the Gallic altars erected to Teuton gods, erected temples to Isis and Mithra.

30 B. C.

The reign of Augustus is fruitful in great constructions. The fraternities of architects are greatly increased, and a certain number form themselves into special colleges for the branches which occupy their attention more particularly, viz.: naval and hydraulic architecture. The extensive knowledge of these men, initiated into the mysteries of every art, the humanitarian principles which they profess, their tolerance and their mysterious oganization, surround them with such consideration, that all the distinguished men seek admittance into their association.

The most considerable monuments at this time erected by them, at Rome, are the temple of Jupiter Tonans, the theater commenced under the consulate of Claudius Marcellus, the mausoleum that bore the name of Augustus, two arches of triumph, also named after him, and two Egyptian obelisks. In the Roman provinces we are unable to mention others among the monuments erected by them at this time, beyond the temple of Clitum at Foligui, that of Jupiter at Pouzzoli, of Sibyl at Tivoli, and the arch of triumph at Suza. In Gaul a great number of somewhat less sumptuous constructions ornament the cities erected and founded by the Romans. A great many roads, and particularly that of Emporium, situate near the Pyrenees, to the crossing of the Rhone, are due to the orders of Augustus. The friends of this emperor rivaled him in the construction of magnificent monuments. Statitius Taurus constructed an amphitheater; Marcus Phillippus a temple to Hercules Musagètes; Munatius Plancus one to Saturn; Lucius Carnifucius one to Diana; and Lucius Cornelius Balbus finished his great theater in stone.

A. D. 1.

Augustus erected at Nimes, in the first year of the Christian era, a temple in honor of his friends Caius and Lucius.[1]

---

[1] The remains of this temple are now known under the name of the Square House.

A. D. 5.

The Jewish architects are protected at Rome, where they have been authorized, under Julius Cæsar, to establish synagogues. Admitted into the colleges of constructors, which, at this time, were the theater of all foreign initiations, they instructed them in the knowledge of the Hebrew mysteries—a type of the Egyptian.

D. 10.

The celebrated architect Vitruvius Pollio establishes in his writings upon architecture—works translated into all languages—the flourishing condition in which this art existed at this time at Rome. He depicts the humanitarian doctrines which go hand in hand with the material objects of the Fraternity, and which, enveloped in allegories and illustrated by symbols, formed the basis of the teachings of these colleges.

A. D. 14.

The palace of the Cæsars is commenced during the reign of Tiberius. It was continued under that of Caligula, and finished under Domitian. Tiberius erected an arch of triumph in honor of his brother Claudius Drusus, and another in honor of Augustus. That consecrated to Castor is also due to his orders.

The cities of Pergamus, Nicomedia, Mylassa, Cesarea, Pouzzolea, and Pola, brought architects and companions from Rome to erect in their midst temples in honor of Augustus.

A. D. 25.

The bridge of Rimini, commenced by Augustus, is finished under Tiberius, who also ordered the erection of temples in honor of Proserpine, Juno, and the goddess Concord.

A. D. 41.

A superb aqueduct, which bears his name, is constructed under the reign of Claudius.

A. D. 43.

Some brigades of constructors are detached from the fraternities which are stationed on the banks of the Rhine, and led by the emperor Claudius to Britain, where the legions experience difficulty in maintaining their ground against the incursions of the Scots. The better to enable them to hold their position, these brigades of constructors erect a line of fortified camps and a certain number of strong castles.

A. D. 50.

Architecture at Rome has attained, at this time, its culminating point. The colleges of constructors, deprived of encouragement under the despotism of the Emperors, who by turns gradually took from them their privileges, seem to have lost their powers of architectural conception. The monuments of this time are greatly inferior in the elevation of their character to those which placed them at the summit of human intelligence. The same decadence is observed in the monuments of Greece, of which the Romans had borrowed their most beautiful models. What contributed to bring about this fall in the architecture of Rome was the absence from that city of all the principal men of talent that the colleges of constructors had produced, and who had become celebrated in some branch of the art. Those men had been sent by Julius Cæsar and Augustus into the conquered provinces, there to erect temples; and, in fact, to give to those conquered peoples an elevated idea of the science and art of their conquerors, and to inspire them with admiration for the latter. The colleges of constructors, who concentrated within their membership a great amount of the knowledge acquired at this period, thus contributed, by their science and the magnificence of their constructions, as much as did the arms of Rome to the consolidation and glory of the Roman power.

Among the architects or *magistri*, as they are called—such as Cossutius, Caius, Marcus Stallius, Menallippus, Cyrus, Clautius, Chrysippus, Corumbus—who belonged to those times, there were a certain number who especially occupied themselves with making known, by their writings, the theory and rules of their art. In this manner was the time of Vitruvius Pollio, Tulfitius, Varron, Publius, and Septimus occupied; and they were thus enabled to communicate with the brethren situated at a distance from the principal center of their schools of architecture. Of these writings those of Vitruvius Pollio alone have come down to us.

A. D. 54.

The temple of Bellona; that of Roman Charity; also, some baths and aqueducts are constructed at Rome by the orders of Nero, and bear his name. This emperor, after having set fire to the capital, by which the most beautiful monuments were destroyed, ordered the construction of his famous palace, called the palace of gold, upon which the two masters, Severus and Celler, directed the work. Under the preceding reign—of the emperor Claudius—Rome was greatly increased; an arch of triumph was dedicated to the Tiber, and a beautiful aqueduct, which bore the name of Claudius, was begun.

A. D. 70.

At this time were constructed, under the reign of F. Vespasian, the famous temple of Peace, and the Colosseum, or Flavian amphitheater, capable of containing one hundred and ten thousand persons, and upon which were forced to labor twelve thousand Jews, carried captive to Rome after the overthrow of Jerusalem.

This amphitheater was not finished until the year 80, when, under Titus, it was completed.

A. D. 80.

Under the emperor Titus public baths, which bear his name, are completed; he also constructed a palace. The houses and public edifices, destroyed by fire the preceding year, are not rebuilt until the reign of his brother Domitian.

A. D. 85.

The emperor Domitian greatly enlarged and embellished the palace of the Cæsars; a new theater and many temples are erected by his orders at Rome, and a number of temples in Gaul. He finished the famous military road that crosses Savoy and Provence.

A. D. 90.

The fraternities of constructors in Britain, by order of the general Agricola, constructed fortifications which extended from the Gulf of Solway to where he had penetrated in repulsing the Scots, and there, with his legions, he fixed his residence to hold the country.

A. D. 98.

Of numerous celebrated temples, among others those of Faunus and Diana, that of Quirinus, with its sixty-six columns, is, under the reign of Trajan, constructed at Rome, and many others in the Roman provinces. At Amonias is erected to his honor an arch of triumph, while he himself orders the erection of one in honor of Vespasian Augustus, and another to Pautanus. He also built hot baths, and the famous circus, capable of containing two hundred and sixty thousand persons.

A. D. 120.

New temples are erected at Rome, under the reign of

Adrian—that of Venus, among others. He orders the erection of the Trajan column, in honor of that emperor, and also constructs a mausoleum, known to-day as the castle of St. Angelo. The celebrated architect Apollodorus, to whom were due the plans of that building, is banished for having spoken the truth. This emperor, with indefatigable ability, visited the most distant provinces of his vast empire. In Britain he ordered the construction, by the fraternities of architects, of an immense wall, which, extending from the Tyne to the Gulf of Solway, thus crossed the country from east to west, to protect the military colonies from the continual invasion of the Scots. In Spain he finished temples begun by Augustus; and it is to his orders are due several temples erected in Africa, particularly those which to-day are to be seen in Algiers and Tunis. Asia is equally indebted to him for numerous public monuments; but it was Greece that was particularly favored by his constructive genius, and in which country he ordered the erection of the most celebrated of her temples, such as the Pantheon and the temples to Jupiter Panhellenes, and that to Jupiter Olympus, with its one hundred and twenty-two columns.

A. D. 130.

After the fall of the Roman Republic, all the other corporations founded at the same time as the colleges of constructors by Numa Pompilius, have lost their ancient privileges, in consequence of the distrust entertained for them by the despotic emperors. The colleges of constructors are also restrained by Trajan and Adrian, but their love of glory and luxury made it necessary that these colleges should be allowed to retain their privileges nearly intact; for, without the aid of the artist constructors, all hope of transmitting to posterity the grandeur of their names and actions would have been vain.

A. D. 140.

Under Antoninus the temples of Mars, of Faustinus and Antoninus Pius are erected at Rome, besides many others already begun are finished. He orders the construction of another wall in Britain, where the legions are unceasingly menaced by the Scots. This immense wall, which extended from the Forth to the Clyde, required the aid of the natives for its completion, many of whom became incorporated in the fraternities of the Romans, and learned their art. But that which, above all, distinguished the reign of Antoninus are the magnificent edifices of colossal dimensions which he constructed at Balbec, (Heliopolis,) of which the two principal temples, dedicated to the sun, are inexplicable marvels of masonry. It was by the Masonic fraternities, remains of the ancient Roman colleges, who, in the time of the Christian persecutions ordered by Nero, Domitian, and Trajan, sought refuge in those provinces the most distant from Rome, and which were governed by men more humane than the emperors, that those masterpieces of architectural grandeur were erected.

A. D. 166.

The famous road which, leading from Civita Vecchia, —at the Aurelian *Forum*—to Arles, is commenced by the colleges of constructors, under the orders of Marcus Aurelius, and finished during his reign. Most of the members of the colleges of constructors embrace Christianity. At this time their number had greatly increased, as well in Rome as in the provinces. The emperor Marcus Aurelius, greatly irritated in view of the astonishing progress made by the new doctrine, and wishing to destroy it by force, followed the example of his predecessors, and this year ordained new persecutions against the Christians. In consequence many took refuge in Gaul and Britain— particularly within the latter country—where they found, among the Masonic corporations, that protection they sought for in vain elsewhere.

Numbers of Christian Masons, finding themselves unable to leave Rome, sought in the catacombs a secret asylum, in which to sustain themselves against the bloody edicts launched at them, and to escape the punishment to which they are condemned. It is in the dark bosom of these subterranean caverns that they often met in fraternal embrace with their fellow religionists, with whom they found refuge. During the ten years of continued persecution against the Christians, under Marcus Aurelius, these catacombs are transformed by those Christian artists into churches, ornamented with sarcophagi, paintings, and encaustic adornment—the faith that inspired them inducing them to there erect chapels over the graves of martyred fellow-Christians, and thus the tombs which covered their precious remains became altars for sacrifice and prayer. The number of the martyrs augmenting, these chapels were subsequently replaced by sarcophagi, which, in later times marked the places in which their remains reposed.

A. D. 180.

Some temples and hot baths are constructed by order of the emperor Titus. He also ordered the erection of pillars in honor of Antonius and Marcus Aurelius. The members of the corporations of constructors are atrociously persecuted anew for their doctrine, and of them those who escaped fled to the east. In this manner the constructors were driven from the city of their birth, and none remained but the few who had not been converted to Christianity.

A. D. 193.

A temple to Minerva, an arch of triumph to Rome, and another to Valabro, in honor of Septimus Severus, are the only important monuments erected at Rome under the reign of this emperor. In Britain, in the year 207, he commenced a third wall, further north, with the old object of protecting the legions; but the fraternities, finding themselves unequal in numbers to the task of undertaking a work so gigantic, accorded to the Britons, who had learned their art, to assure themselves of their assistance, the same advantages and the same privileges which they enjoyed themselves.[1]

A. D. 211.

The construction of many temples, baths, and a circus, marked the reign of Caraçalla.

A. D. 222.

Under the reign of Alexander Severus, who openly protected architecture, and secretly Christianity, some new monuments are erected at Rome. He ordered the restoration of many ancient edifices, and the erection of a city hall and magnificent baths. He desired also to consecrate a temple to Christ, but was restrained in so doing by the representations made to him that, were he to do so, the other temples would go to ruin.

A. D. 235.

Numerous new temples are erected at Rome and in the provinces, under Maximin and Gordian. By the former, amphitheaters were erected in various cities in Italy, and, by the latter, baths at Rome, that bore his name.

A. D. 250.

No construction of any importance signalized the reigns of Decius or Valerian, except the baths which were constructed by order of the former. The new persecutions directed by them against the Christians greatly diminished

---

[1] The most important of the military colonies at this time in Britain was *Eboracum*—the city of York—which became celebrated in the history of Freemasonry.

the colleges of constructors, and dispersed such of their members—a great number—as had embraced the tenets of that faith which inculcated the doctrine of fraternity. Flying from Rome, they sought refuge in that country wherein they would be least persecuted, viz., Britain, where the new doctrine had already numerous partisans. Those who could not leave the city took refuge in the catacombs, the asylum of the Christians.

A. D. 260.

Reformation of the colleges or fraternities of constructors in Gaul and Britain. The new doctrine, notwithstanding its affinity with that professed by the artists, produced, however, some schisms among them—a portion of those who belonged to different professions separating themselves from the general association, as it had existed until that time, to form separate associations, composed of one art or one trade.[1]

A. D. 270.

The Masonic fraternities in Gaul, as in Britain—whose members had generally adopted the Christian doctrine, devoting themselves, particularly in Gaul, to the construction of religious edifices—undertook to build the new churches that the apostles, who came from Rome in the year 257, desired to erect at Amiens, Beauvais, Soissons, Rheims, and Paris, where these apostles have established themselves in the capacity of bishops.

A. D. 275.

This epoch is marked in the history of architecture by

---

[1] It is these associations that we subsequently find organized under the name of corporations of arts and trades, the laws of which exhibit more or less traces of the ancient constitution of the Roman colleges, from which they have descended. The Masonic Fraternity preserved only its antique organization, together with 'ts humanitarian and artistic secrets, and its privileges, all of which, however, were very much modified.

one of the most sublime conceptions of the artistic genius of the philosopher constructors, executed under the reign and by the orders of the emperor Aurelian. They are the two temples of the sun at Palmyra, which surpass in beauty and grandeur those of Heliopolis. The principal one of these temples has four hundred and sixty-four columns, many of which are composed of a single block of marble. The whole number of columns which ornament the two temples and the galleries attached to them is fourteen hundred and fifty. Aurelian employed the last two years of his short reign to, among other peaceful measures, the revival of architecture at Rome, and in this project was ably assisted by the Byzantine architects, Cleodamus and Athenacus.

A. D. 280.

Architects who have acquired great celebrity in Britain are called by Diocletian to construct the monuments he has designed to erect in Gaul.

A. D. 287–290.

Carausius, commanding the Roman navy, takes possession of Britain and proclaims himself emperor. To conciliate the Masonic fraternities, then wielding an immense influence in the country, he confirmed to them at Verulam, (Saint Albans,) the place of his residence, in the year 290, all their ancient privileges, as they had been established by Numa Pompilius, in the year 715 B. C.; and it is from this time that the Freemasons began to be distinguished from those who were not free, or upon whom these privileges had not been bestowed.

A. D. 293.

Albanus, architect and first grand inspector of the Freemasons in Briton, who represented the Masonic societies in their negotiations with Carausius, originally a pagan, is converted to Christianity; and, at the risk of his life, he preaches the doctrines of the new faith to the emperor, and is consequently beheaded. In this manner a grand master of Freemasons became the first Christian martyr in Britain.

A. D. 296.

The city of York, in which are found the most important lodges of Freemasons in the country, is chosen as his residence by the under-emperor, Constantius Chlorus, who, upon the death of Carausius, came to Britain by order of Maximin, to assume the government of that country.

A. D. 300.

At this epoch Rome counted within its walls more than five hundred temples, thirty-seven gates and arches of triumph, six bridges, seventeen amphitheaters and theaters, fourteen aqueducts, five obelisks, and of monumental columns a great number, such as military, warlike, statuary, honorary, legal, (upon which were engraved the laws,) and lactary, (at the base of which were laid children found astray,) and, finally, palaces, mausoleums, baths, and sepulchers in proportionate number. All of these monuments, without exception, were erected by the fraternities or colleges of architects and builders.

A. D. 303.

The emperor Diocletian—under whose reign were erected, in many of the Roman provinces, temples, aqueducts, and baths—distinguished himself particularly by the most atrocious persecution of the Christians, and whom were executed with cruelty in the more distant provinces. Notwithstanding the humanity of the (at this time) governor of Britain, the Christians, of whom a great number were members of the Masonic fraternities, found it necessary to seek refuge in Scotland and the Orkney Islands, and there they carried Christianity and architecture. It was by them that those strong and admirably-constructed castles—built in a style so peculiarly appropriate to the character of the country and the people—were erected for the clans of the Scots. The artist constructors attached to the colleges established at Rome also fled to the east, or buried themselves within the catacombs—their usual refuge in times of religious and social persecution—where many of them perished.

The last monuments of any importance which were erected at Rome were due to Diocletian—the baths which he built surpassing, for grandeur and magnificence, even those of Alexander Severus; but the most remarkable monument of the times of this emperor was the palace he had erected for himself at Salona, in Dalmatia, and wherein he passed the remainder of his life after he had resigned his government of the empire.

A. D. 313.

This year closed the persecutions of the Christians, and by the edict of Milan, rendered by Constantine the Great, Christianity was declared the religion of the State. Subsequently, (A. D. 325,) by the Council of Nice, in Bythnia, the forms and doctrines of the Christian religion were arranged, and thereupon, with the advent of peace, the Masonic corporations awoke to new life.

A. D. 325.

The fraternities, no more persecuted in the persons of their membership, multiplied in Rome with extraordinary activity, and displayed great ability and alacrity in the construction of the Christian churches ordered by Constantine. In the year 323 the first Christian church was built upon the Lateran Hill, and thereafter are erected, upon the ground occupied and in great part with the materials afforded by the pagan temples and halls, the cathedrals of Saint Lawrence of Sessomanca, of Saint Marcellus, of

Saint Agnes, and of Saint Constance. Constantine ordered the erection of an obelisk to Saint John of Lateran, and also the erection, upon the Vatican, of a church, which was by him dedicated to Saint Paul. This church was built in the form of a cross, in commemoration of that cross[1] which had been seen by him in the heavens, and to which he attributed his victory over Maxentius. The people subsequently erected an arch of triumph, which they dedicated to Constantine the Great.

A. D. 330.

Constantine the Great changes the name of Byzantia to Constantinople, and raises it to the rank of capital city of the Eastern Roman Empire. At this place the building brethren concentrate, to engage in the immense constructions which he projects there. The church of St. Sophia, begun in the year 326, was the first Christian church Byzantia saw erected within her walls. The foundations of many others are laid. A new style of architecture is

---

[1] The Greek cross, which was copied by Christian architects as the model upon which to erect all edifices devoted to Christian worship, was chosen by them, not because Constantine had prescribed this form, but because this cross mysteriously attached itself to the worship of every people, and made part of the symbolism of their art, and a knowledge of which formed a portion of the secret teachings of the colleges. This cross exhibits, in its proportions what are known as the sacred numbers, and which numbers are the basis of geometry. It was also the form and base of the Holy of Holies, in the temple of Solomon; and, in a word, it represents the unity and the trinity. For the other dispositions, proportions, and details of the religious edifices, the temple at Jerusalem—of which the holy books of the Hebrews contained precise details—served always as a model; that temple being recognized as the great masterpiece of architecture, as it was also the first temple erected and consecrated to an only God. It is this temple which even yet, and in our own day, is considered the most significant symbol of Freemasonry. The plans of Christian churches, from the fourth century to the present time, following those which have preceded them, are derived from a mixture of Jewish and pagan elements. The form of the cross was subsequently adopted for the foundation of nearly all the religious edifices of the Christian world.

formed—the Latin and Greek intermixing with the Arab, and giving birth to what was subsequently known as the Byzantine, which was not distinctly developed until the eighth century.

The emperor Constantine, who had proclaimed that the sign of the cross should ornament the imperial standard, continued, nevertheless, to sacrifice to the gods of paganism. He despoiled Rome, Athens, Rhodes, Chios, Cyprus, and Sicily of their riches and their monuments of past-time art; and thus the cities of Italy, Greece, and Asia Minor furnished him with works of art wherewith to adorn the new capital of his empire.

The Masonic fraternities, who, during the persecutions of the Christians, had taken refuge in Syria and in Palestine, are now, by the orders of Constantine, occupied in those provinces in the erection of churches. Heliopolis, Jerusalem, and the village of Bethlehem are the places wherein the first of these churches were constructed; and subsequently he ordered the erection of the church of the Holy Sepulcher, at Jerusalem. In Syria and Palestine the Masonic corporations greatly increased, and extended into the borders of Arabia and countries beyond the Roman empire.

A. D. 340.

The Masonic fraternities continued to increase in Byzantia. All those who had acquired celebrity in religious architecture, such as constructors, sculptors, and painters, sought occupation within this great city, and therein helped to complete the twenty-three churches which, in ten years, were erected inside its walls.

A. D. 355–360.

The emperor Julian, who at this time commanded in Gaul, ordered the construction at Paris, which had become the capital of the Parisians, a magnificent temple, with vast baths, the ruins of which may be seen in the *Rue de la*

Harpe at the present day. After his victory over the Franks, he arranged to reside at Paris, and therein ordered the construction of churches upon the ruins of pagan temples.

A. D. 380.

During the incessant invasions of the Germans, Saxons, and Burgundians, followed by the Alans and Huns, who pillaged and devastated the country, the Masonic fraternities were dispersed, while art of all kinds, and more particularly architecture, took refuge within the monasteries, where the ecclesiastics, who had affiliated with the fraternities of architects, studied and preserved the artistic and humanitarian doctrines of their art.

A. D. 410.

The Scots and the Picts, continuing to disturb the peace of the Romans in Britain, and to destroy their walls and fortifications, the latter are rebuilt by the great concourse of Masons from all parts of the island of Britain. Even the new constructions not proving adequate, however, to defend them from the constant inroads of these barbarous tribes, and the Romans being attacked upon all sides, and their legions being enfeebled by the withdrawal of numbers of their forces from Britain to the continent, they judged it prudent to abandon the island of Britain entirely, a decision which they carried out, according to some authorities, in the year 411, and according to others in the year 426. After their retreat, the fraternities, who found themselves composed of various elements—that of native Britons not being the least—took refuge where they might be protected by the Romans, upon the continent, in Gaul, and in Scotland. Here, as in the time of the first Christian persecutions, they propagated Chrstianity and architecture, and, above all, religiously preserved the antique organization of their lodges.

A. D. 430.

The Masonic fraternities, dispersed and dissolved since the beginning of barbarian invasions, which devastated Gaul, Italy, and even Rome, experience great difficulty, notwithstanding the encouragement offered them by the clergy, led by the Popes, to reëstablish themselves in the latter city. They commenced, however, to repair and reconstruct some churches, and for this purpose freely helped themselves with the materials composing pagan temples.

A. D. 455.

Under Genseric new invasions of the barbarians everywhere destroyed the public monuments, and for a long time arrested, in Rome and Italy, all new constructions.

A. D. 476.

Rome is invaded for the sixth time within the fifth century. During these invasions—those of Alaric in 410, of Genseric in 455, and, at this time, of Odoacre—the cities were sacked and burnt, and their temples and monuments destroyed, the greater number of them never to be replaced, and the masterpieces of art buried beneath their ruins. The fraternities of builders, finding themselves, in these times of war, without occupation, and unprotected in the west by the Roman power, dispersed into Greece and Egypt, and many of them took up their residence permanently in Syria. All the masterpieces of art, which were at this time buried beneath the ruins of temples overthrown or destroyed, subsequently served to ornament Christian churches, and the palaces and museums of the affluent in various parts of the continent.

A. D. 500.

The remains of ancient fraternities, who had sought refuge in other countries, appear in Rome, and endeavor to revive the colleges of builders. Architecture revives, and some of the churches are repaired and reconstructed.

A. D. 525.

The example of Rome is imitated in Gaul; and everywhere such beautiful temples as were erected to the gods of the Romans, and which hitherto have escaped the destructive tendency of the international invasions, are destroyed to give place to and with the remains of which churches are built and consecrated to the saints. Under the reign of Childeric (460–481), of Clovis (481–511), of Clothaire (511–561), who have protected the Masonic corporations and encouraged their labors, there are erected many churches. The fraternities of Roman architects, as well as those of Gaul, who remained in the country after the retreat of the Romans (486), are recognized and confirmed in their ancient privileges.

A. D. 530.

Some fragments of the Roman colleges, which had taken up their residence in Syria, are called, at different times, by the kings of Persia to erect monuments of a public character, bearing the characteristics of the Persian taste. Latin, Greek, and Byzantine styles here enter into a new intermarriage, with the pomp and display of Persian magnificence.

A. D. 550.

By order of Justinian I, the great church of St. Sophia, at Constantinople, is constructed by a fraternity of Greek architects, over the remains of that erected by Constantine the Great, which had been destroyed by fire.

This monument, converted by the Turks into an imperial mosque, is the most magnificent conception of our time, as it was of that most flourishing period—when art received its most powerful impulse.[1] The Masonic fraternities of Byzantia and other provinces of the empire, spreading themselves at this time into Italy, Sardinia, Corsica, and a part of Africa, submitted once more to be swayed by the scepter of their ancient masters. These countries, relieved of the rule of the Goths and Vandals, encouraged the erection of religious monuments, for which the great church of St. Sophia served as the model. Subsequently (726) all these monuments were destroyed during the revolutions which prevailed under the iconoclastic emperors.

A. D. 557.

Austin, a Benedictine monk and architect, arrived in England for the purpose of converting the Anglo-Saxons to Christianity. He placed himself at the head of the Masonic fraternities, and lifted them out of the many difficulties into which they had fallen during the last wars.

A. D. 580.

At this time the Freemasons became fully recognized in Britain, by the fact that their numbers were insufficient to execute the immense constructions projected by the

---

[1] Justinian I, in reconstructing the great church of St. Sophia, confided the general direction to two Greek architects. These were assisted by one hundred master workmen, who had each one hundred workmen to execute their orders, and each of whom had ten laborers under their direction. Five thousand men were, in this manner, employed on each side of the building; and in the sixteenth year from the commencement of its construction it was finished, and inaugurated by the slaughter of one thousand oxen, ten thousand sheep, six hundred stags, one thousand hogs, ten thousand hens and ten thousand pullets, which, with thirty thousand measures of grain, were distributed to the people. Justinian, having expended enormous sums for the erection of this construction, was forced to order taxes to be levied for its completion. It is said that before the walls had risen three feet above the ground, he had expended four hundred and fifty-two hundred weight of golden coin

new apostles of Christianity. In their voyages to Rome, whither they went to collect statues and pictures wherewith to adorn the churches in Britain, these apostles always returned bringing with them workmen, sculptors, and painters; and the bishop of Weymouth imported from Gaul into Britain men of like professions in great number.

A. D. 600–602.

During these years the cathedrals of Canterbury and Rochester were erected.

A. D. 607.

The cathedral of St. Paul, at London, begun in 604, is finished, and that of St. John, at Winchester, begun in 605.

A. D. 610.

Death of Austin, grand inspector of the Freemasons. He is subsequently canonized under the name of St. Augustine.

A. D. 620.

The Masonic corporations at this time, although governed by the same laws and characterized by the same principles, partook not every-where of the same qualifications, or rather they were known by different names in different countries. For instance, in Italy they were known as the Colleges of Architects or Builders, and oftentimes simply as the Masonic Fraternities; while in Gaul they were called Brother Masons, Brother Bridgers, (bridge-builders,) or Free Corporations; and in Britain, by reason of their well-known privileges, they were called Freemasons. At this time they are all employed exclusively by the religious orders, directed by them, and even quartered in the monasteries. The abbot, or such other ecclesiastic as may be sufficiently acquainted with the rules and practice of architecture, upon this account, presides over the meetings of the lodges—general assembly of all the artists and workmen—and, consequently, is addressed in such assembly as *Worshipful Master*. [To the present time does this title attach to the presiding officer in a lodge of Freemasons.]

A. D. 660.

The arts and architecture take refuge within the monasteries, whenever their progress is arrested or paralyzed by international wars. There they are cultivated with success by the most distinguished ecclesiastics, who are admitted as members of the Masonic fraternities. It was also, in great part, according to the designs and plans drawn by these ecclesiastics that the corporations executed the religious monuments of this time. The monastic schools of architecture not only produced some ecclesiastics celebrated as architects, such as St. Eloi, bishop of Noyon (659); St. Ferol, bishop of Limoges; Dalmac, bishop of Rhodes; Agricola, bishop of Chalons (680–700); but they also gave to the profession of architecture laymen not less distinguished, and under whose direction numerous public monuments were erected in Gaul and Britain.

A. D. 680.

The Freemasons of Britain, having remained without a chief since the death of Austin, the king of Mercy, grand protector of the Fraternity, appointed Bennet, abbot of Wirral, inspector-general and superintendent of Masonry. Nevertheless, the labors of the Fraternity were conducted with but little spirit during a century.

A. D. 685.

The Masonic fraternities of Roman origin, who had been ordered into the East, and many of whom had remained in Constantinople, acquired great reputation, and were successively sought for by Persian, Arabian, and

Syrian potentates. Among others, the caliphs of Damascus and Medina intrusted to them the erection of the mosques of those cities.

A. D. 700.

Architecture has attained at this time a high degree of perfection in England,[1] the style and expression of the edifices presenting exclusively the characteristics of what was then known as Scottish architecture, which, at this time, was considered among the Fraternity the most perfect in outlines and details, and the masters of it the most learned of any of the brethren. On this account they were called Scottish Masters.

A. D. 720.

The progress that architecture had made in Gaul, in the course of the last century and the early part of the present, was arrested by the incursion of the Arabs, in the year 718, and remained in a paralytic condition for many years.

A. D. 740.

Upon the demand of the Anglo-Saxon kings, Charles Martel, who had at this time governed Gaul as "Mayor of the Palace," sent to Britain many architects and Masons.

A. D. 750.

Under the reign of the caliph of Bagdad, architecture

---

[1] When Honorius abandoned Britain, in 426, in consequence of his inability to hold the country against the invasions of the Picts and Scots, the Britons called to their aid, for that purpose, the Angles and the Saxons. After making themselves masters of the country, the latter founded within it four kingdoms, and the former founded three, which in 827 were united, under the general name of *Angle-land*, with the Saxon king Egbert as ruler. In 835 the Danes and Normans desolated the country, but between 871 and 900 Alfred the Great forced them to terms of peace. Shortly afterward, however, they invaded the country anew, and nearly all the public monuments, churches, and monasteries became a prey to fire and pillage.

and the arts generally attained to a high degree of perfection. Arabia, at this time, exhibited a degree of civilization far in advance of that known in Asia or Africa. The fraternities of architects who, after the fall of the Roman Empire of the West, remained in Syria and Arabia, contributed in a great degree, by their knowledge of art, to the splendor and reputation Bagdad at this time enjoyed.

A. D. 775.

Arabian architecture is introduced into Spain, under the rule of the caliphs of the East, and directed, as it was every-where, by the Masonic associations. These corporations, called from Bagdad by the viceroys of the caliphs to Cordova—a city founded by the Romans 252 years before the birth of Christ—there successively erected a series of marvelous monuments, inspired by Byzantine art. The organization of these corporations is unknown, and they were, no doubt, subjected—in contradistinction to those of the Roman colleges, from which they descended—to modifications according with the manners and character of the people among whom these associations had place; but it is not probable that there was any essential difference. The Mussulmans were, at this time, more advanced in the scale of art and civilization than the Christians, and consequently they exercised very considerable influence in the various provinces of the Peninsula.

Abderam I, viceroy of Cordova under the caliph of Damascus, having declared his independence of the Damascene, enriched his caliphate, the city of Cordova, with so great a degree of splendor that the character of the architecture therein exhibited created a school of architecture, whose reputation was only equaled by the magnificence of its monuments. From this time that city became the center of Moorish art.

A. D. 780.

Under the reign of Charlemagne architecture flourished anew in France, that monarch having invited from Lombardy numbers of architects and workmen, who were then generally called stone-cutters.

A. D. 850.

Many religious edifices, burnt or destroyed by the Danes, are reconstructed by the corporations under the Saxon king Ethelwolf, and the immediate direction of the priest and architect St. Swithin. At this time were renewed the meetings of the brethren, which were much interrupted during the previous century.

A. D. 875.

Under the reign of that most illustrious of Saxon kings, Alfred the Great, the arts, and particularly architecture, flourished. The fraternities rebuilt the towns, castles, monasteries, and churches, which were destroyed during the Danish wars.

A. D. 900.

The successor of Alfred, Edward king of Mersey, appointed, as grand inspectors of the fraternities, his brother Ethelward, and his brother-in-law, Ethred, who had become practical architects in the school of the Freemasons.

A. D. 925.

At this time all the more important towns in England had their lodge of Freemasons; but, notwithstanding the general conformity of their laws and principles, but little connection existed between them. The cause of this is explained by the fact that, for the five centuries in which existed the heptarchy, or seven Anglo-Saxon kingdoms, there was little connection between those brethren scattered throughout the kingdoms; and, following the union of the government, the wars of the Danes kept the country in a condition into which the arts of peace entered but in the smallest proportion. During these wars the monasteries being burnt, the fraternities suffered an irreparable loss in the destruction of all their documents, written in various languages and at various times, brought into the country by the Romans, Greeks, Syrians, Lombards, and Gauls. Athelstan, the grandson of Alfred the Great, who at this time governed England, with his palace at York, having been elected as their chief by the priest architects—himself an architect before he ascended the throne—had also inducted his younger son (Edwin) into the mysteries of art, and appointed him chief or grand master of the Fraternity. In this position the latter convoked all the lodges scattered throughout the country to a general assembly, to be held at York, and there to present all the documents and deeds which they had saved from the fire of the invaders, to the end that the Fraternity be regularly constituted anew, according to the forms of those written laws. It was at this assembly that a constitution, prepared and submitted by the king, was discussed and accepted by the representatives of the lodges, and thenceforth proclaimed as the law. Promulgated the following year, this constitution, styled the *Charter of York*, formed the basis of all subsequent Masonic constitutions. Thenceforth York became the seat of the grand mastership of English Masonry.

A. D. 930.

Henry I (the Fowler) invites from England to Germany the corporations of Freemasons, for the purpose of constructing edifices projected by him, such as the cathedrals of Madgeburg, etc. These edifices were not erected, however, until the subsequent reign—that of his son, Otho the Great.

A. D. 936.

The Arabian fraternities of Masons and artists, of Roman origin, commence this year the construction of that famous royal castle Alcazar, that was built for the caliph Abderam at Zara, near Seville, and ornamented with four thousand three hundred columns of purest marble. This prince invited the most skillful and learned architects of Bagdad and Constantinople to direct and aid the fraternities of the country in their labors upon this important and magnificent edifice.

A. D. 940.

The queen—Bertha of Burgundy—wishing to renew the prosperity of her country, which had been devastated and demoralized by the wars, sent to England for masters and workmen, who, under the direction of a Scottish master named Mackenbrey, undertook a series of constructions to be consecrated as churches and convents, which they executed with astonishing rapidity, and consummate skill. The abbot, Majolus of Cluny, had the superior direction of these great erections, which were commenced in the year 930. The grandest and most magnificent of these constructions were the abbey and the church of the Benedictines at Payerne. From this time the Masonic corporations of England spread themselves upon the continent, under the name of St. John Brothers.

A. D. 960.

The death of king Athelstan again disperses the Freemasons of England. Some of the most important constructions are, however, undertaken during the reign of Edgar, under the grand mastership of Dunstan, (St. Dunstan,) archbishop of Canterbury. Many of the brethren pass over to Germany, and there permanently locate themselves, under the name of St. John Brothers, and Brothers of St. John.

Second Epoch.

From the year 1001 to the year 1717.

A. D. 1001.

In the course of the tenth century the Christian population of the west found themselves under the influence of an unhappy discouragement, which had seized upon their spirits, in consequence of the predictions that the end of the world might be expected at this time, and the result of which was their abandonment of all works of art. The artists, and principally the fraternities of Masons, condemned to inaction, fall into the miseries and unhappiness of the times. The schools of architecture of Lombardy, at Padua, and at Como, are not, however, entirely deserted. The learned architects of these schools, initiated—as had been those of Egypt—into the secrets of nature and the study of astronomy, happily did not partake of this general terror, which was invented by the priests, for selfish purposes; and such schools continued to teach, as in times past.

A. D. 1003.

No unnatural movement having thrust our planet from its course, the people welcomed with joy the aurora of a new world; and it is from this epoch it is proper to date modern civilization. The terror of the Christian world had continued to the close of this year, as the reign of Antichrist, it was believed, would continue for two years and a half subsequent to the year 1000; and now art and society in general awoke from their long trance, to **renewed** life and usefulness.

A. D. 1005.

It was necessary that nearly all the religious edifices of the Christian world should be renewed. Up to this time such buildings were principally composed of wood and plaster; but now these are razed to the ground, and rebuilt in more enduring material.

A. D. 1010.

A great number of ecclesiastics repair to Lombardy, there to study religious architecture, and to form an Italian school. Lombardy is, at this time, an active center of civilization, where the fragments of the ancient colleges of constructors reside, having lived through the ordeal of international wars, and maintained their ancient organization and their privileges, under the name of Free Corporations. The most celebrated of these was that of Como, which had acquired such superiority that the title of *magistri comacini* (Masters of Como) had become the generic name of all the members of the architect corporations. Always teaching in secret, they had their mysteries, their judiciary and jurisdiction. The architects from distant countries, from Spain, Greece, and Asia, at this time were accustomed to repair to their school at Como for instruction, to attain a knowledge of the new combinations of the Latin and Greek styles of architecture, which had been modified by intermixing with that style which was developed during the ninth century at Constantinople, and which was considered the most suitable for religious buildings. It was this combination that gave birth to the style called "Roman."[1]

---

[1] It was in this style that were erected the religious edifices of the 11th century and part of those of the 12th, and following which succeeded the newer style, called Roman ogee, which latter prevailed but from the year 1150 to the year 1200, or thereabouts.

A. D. 1040.

The Masonic corporations covered Italy, and more particularly Lombardy, with religious edifices, and to such an extent did the membership of the corporations increase that the country could no longer offer occupation to all. Then they formed particular corporations, which traveled into foreign countries; and a large number of them united in forming a general association, and constituting themselves into a great fraternity that should travel into all Christian countries wherein the necessary churches and monasteries had not yet been erected, and demanding for this object authority from the pope, and the confirmation to them by him of all the ancient immunities which had at any time attached to the building corporations, as also the protection necessary to so grand an enterprise. The pope, without delay, seconded this design, and conferred upon them the exclusive monopoly of erecting all religious monuments, as also making them free of all local laws, all royal edicts and municipal regulations concerning statute labor, together with immunity from every other obligation imposed upon the inhabitants of whatever country, city, or town they might be employed in. These monopolies are respected and sanctioned by all the kings and all the governments.

A. D. 1060.

The Masonic fraternities of Lombardy extend themselves into Germany, into France, and into Brittany and Normandy. William the Conqueror, king of England (1054,) sent from Normandy a crowd of prelates and architects, graduates of the school of the Lombards, such as Mauserius, Le Franc, Robert of Blois, Remy of Fecamp, and many others, to plan and construct the most magnificent cathedrals in England. Every-where, in all Christian countries, the same passion for religious edifices seemed to prevail at this time. and, in consequence, religious architecture made great progress.

A. D. 1080.

Some Masonic corporations fixed themselves in the Low Country, and there erected churches and monasteries. The bishop of Utrecht, desirous of constructing a great cathedral, sought the aid of the leading architect of that city, a man named Plebel, and obtained from him the necessary plans for the proposed construction. Having obtained possession of these papers, the bishop dismissed Plebel, and, desirous of passing himself as the author of the plans, and engage in directing the labors of the workmen without having been initiated into the secrets of the art, sought, by all sorts of menaces and promises, to wring from the son of the architect Plebel, a young master mason, the secrets and manner (*arcanum magisterium*) of laying the foundations. These rules, applied to the construction of religious edifices, were held in the most inviolable secrecy by all members of the association of Freemasons—a secret solemnly imposed upon them by their oath. The architect, indignant at a perfidy so base on the part of one whom the people regarded as their supreme spiritual adviser, on learning of the perjury of his son, determined to prevent the divulging the secret of his art, and thereupon, having obtained an opportunity, killed the bishop.

A. D. 1100.

During the century just closed, the Masonic corporations completed the construction of more than one hundred cathedrals, churches, monasteries, abbeys, and castles, scattered over the five principal European countries of that time, viz.: England, France, Germany, Italy, and Switzerland.

A. D. 1125.

The Masonic corporations, under the style and name of Brothers of St. John, extend themselves over civilized

Europe anew, and give their assemblies the name of Lodges of St. John. This qualification, which was first known in England, goes back to the sixth century, and originated as follows: In those days the Freemasons' feasts, following the ancient usage of the Roman colleges, were held upon the return of the yearly solstices, particularly upon that of summer. Christianity having taken the place of paganism, induced them to invest the occasion of their feasts with another sign, more in keeping with the wishes of the clergy. They, therefore, chose St. John for their patron, because it was the ancient Janus, a god of the Romans, whose feast fell upon the 24th of June, which was also the epoch of the solstice of summer, and which anniversary they could thus continue to celebrate under the name of St. John's day. From the importance they attached to these party assemblies, they came to be called St. John Brothers—a name under which they were universally known upon the continent during the twelfth century.

A. D. 1150.

A fraternity of Masons, called from Lombardy direct to England, in the reign of Alexander III, erect, under this prince and his successors, a great many beautiful monuments of their art, the major part of which are apparent but as ruins. Among the others, the town and abbey of Kilwinning, where subsequently were held the general assemblies of this fraternity, were constructed by them.

A. D. 1155.

The grand master of the Templars, Richard, king of England, surnamed the Lion Heart, is elected by the lodges of English Freemasons to the like position over them; and he governs the two fraternities until his death. A Masonic fraternity, of Syrian origin, detained in Europe by the immense constructions which were then erected, in this year construct for the Templars their church in Fleet

Street, London. This fraternity had preserved intact the ancient initiation practiced among the Romans.

A. D. 1175.

A Masonic fraternity, to which was given the name of Brother Bridgers, and which occupied itself particularly with the construction of bridges and roads, located itself in the midst of France, where, at Avignon, in 1180, it constructed the bridge of that name, and, subsequently, all the bridges of Provence, of Lorraine, and of Lyons.

A. D. 1200.

During the century which this year closed, the fraternities of builders have added to the numerous magnificent erections of the preceding period some of the finest constructions of the middle ages. In England, France, Germany, Italy, and Spain such of the oldest ecclesiastic and monastic erections as have survived the decaying touch of time, were completed during the twelfth century.

A. D. 1225.

Lombardy has attained its preëminence as the principal European school of architecture. Thither, from all countries, the master masons repair for new ideas and new knowledge. The Scottish artists, the Byzantine, and also those of Cordova, who affected more of pomp, and what was known as the style Arabesque, in their details of decoration, there modified their art; while, in their turn, the Lombards, recognizing the beauties of these different forms, intermix them with the more severe simplicity of their Roman ogival, from which intermixture there results a new combination, inappropriately styled Gothic,[1] which is

---

[1] We find in that most remarkable work, published in 1843, and of which the architect Daniel Ramée is the author, some passages bearing upon this fact, one of which we will take the liberty to quote. After having enumerated the different opinions upon the origin of the ogival style, the author, in

distinguished by the most harmonious reunion of opposite elements, by hardihood of conception and solidity of execution. This style is immediately adopted in all Christian countries, and totally changes nearly all the established plans which, up to this period, prevailed in the construction of religious edifices.

A. D. 1250.

The changes which have been introduced within the past twenty-five years in the outlines and details of Christian architecture, stamp this period as the most remarkable of any preceding time. The striking analogy which the monuments of this time afford when contrasted with those of the fifteenth century, is explained by the tie of the Fraternity which, uniting the Masonic brethren of every nation, afforded them identity of progress and knowledge in their art. Lombardy, that central school of art, had its prototype in the fifteenth century at Strasburg and Cologne; while, ever obedient during the past three hundred years to the lessons taught in those central schools of their art, the knowledge of one became the property of the whole, and individual promptings of beauty in ornament or decoration were not admissible, as none were free from that obedience which involved the use of a similar style of ornament. The symbolic and satirical markings which distinguished the architectural monuments of the fifteenth from those of the twelfth century are indicative of the gradual change that had been wrought by the abuses of the clergy, and by those attempts to enslave the popular mind in ignorance and

---

his turn, although very desirous of claiming the credit of the invention for France, is compelled by his regard for truth to say: "There is no doubt that the employment of the ogee, or pointed arch, and the style which resulted therefrom, was first practiced among the learned, modest, pious, and truly Christian Freemasons of foreign countries, and the knowledge of which they communicated to their brethren in Germany, England, France, Spain, and Italy.'

superstition, which subsequently culminated in the Protestant Reformation.

A. D. 1251.

Louis IX, called St. Louis, directs the architect Endes, of Montreuil, to fortify the harbor and town of Joppa, and he is accompanied thither by a certain number of Freemasons.

A. D. 1272.

The construction of Westminster Abbey is completed this year, under the direction of the grand master Giffard, archbishop of York.

A. D. 1275.

Erwin of Steinbach[1] evoked at Strasburg a Masonic congress, for the purpose of adopting measures to continue the labors which for a long time had been interrupted, upon the cathedral of that city, and to enlarge the dimensions of that structure to a plan more extended than that by which the foundations had been laid in the year 1015, and upon which latter plan a part of the church was erected. The architects from all countries of Europe repaired to Strasburg, and there, according to their usage, organized a general assembly, or grand lodge, at which each representative renewed the oath to observe the laws and rules of the Fraternity. Near the foundations of the cathedral is constructed a wooden building, wherein are held the meetings of the assembled brethren, and the objects of that assembly discussed and adopted. Erwin of Steinbach is elected, by the architects and directors of the

---

[1] Since the thirteenth century the names of some of the most celebrated architects who conducted the labors upon the most remarkable cathedrals of the middle ages are known to us; but, for the chief part, their names remain unknown, and this is easily explained: these monuments were the creation of a general association, and it was not necessary that the proper names of persons comprising its membership, no matter how important, should be publicly mentioned.

edifice, president (chair master); and, as a sign of the judicial character delegated to him by these brethren, he is seated under a canopy, with a sword in his hand. Signs and tokens which enable the workmen upon the cathedral to distinguish themselves from others not so engaged are adopted, and made known to all the brethren assembled, some of which words and signs being those in use among the brethren in England. Apprentices, fellow-crafts, and masters are initiated with particular symbolic ceremonies, under which are indicated the most profound secrets of architecture.

A. D. 1300.

The number of monuments commenced or finished within the thirteenth century, just closed, far exceed any previous similar period. Among the most remarkable were, in England, Westminster Abbey, at London, and the cathedral of Litchfield, at Exeter. In France, the cathedrals of Paris,[1] of Rheims, of Chartres, of Rouen, of Amicus, Bruges, Beauvais, and Strasburg; the holy chapel at Paris, and the church and abbey of St. Denis. In Germany, the cathedrals of Cologne, Friburg and Breslau; the domes of Madgeburg and Halberstadt; the churches of Notre Dame of Cologne and St. Elizabeth, at Marburg, and of St. Catharine, at Oppenheim. In Belgium, the churches of St. John at Tournay, those of the Dominicans

---

[1] This cathedral was built, according to undisputed authority, with the money that Maurice, bishop of Paris, obtained from the sale of indulgences, and of which he had sufficient to also erect four abbies. The French bishops, following the example set in 1016 by the pontifical bishop of Arles, who was the first to preach this matter, established this principle, viz.: that whoever consecrated a small sum of money to the erection or restoration of a church or a chapel, received, in the name of the Lord, remission of the third to the fourth part of the penitential punishment awarded them in the confessional. When Pope Julius II wished to build St. Peter's church at Rome, he followed the example set by the French bishops, and promulgated his order for the sale of indulgences. The Protestant Reformation was the result.

at Gand and at Louvain; of St. Paul and of Sante Croix at Liege; of St. Gudule and Our Lady of the chapel, at Brussels. In Italy, the cathedral of Venice, the dome of Arezzo, and the churches of St. Francis of Padua, and those of Campo Santo and St. Marie della Pina; of St. Margaret at Crotona, of St. Mary the New, of St. Croix, and of St. Mary of the Flowers, at Florence; of St. John and of St. Paul, at Venice; of St. Francis, at Bologna; the lodge of the public palace at Padua; the old palace at Florence; and the ducal palace at Venice. In Spain, the cathedrals of Burgos and Toledo; the monastery of Pobelt, and the churches of St. Thomas and St. Maria Blanca, at Toledo.

A. D. 1310.

The construction of the magnificent cathedral of Cologne, commenced in 1248, elevates the fraternity engaged in this work to a high degree of superiority—in fact, raises it to the rank of a school to which repair brethren from all countries for the purpose of studying this masterpiece of architectural genius. The lodges of Germany, recognizing this superiority, regard the master of this work as the master of all the German masons, and the brethren engaged upon it as the Grand Lodge, (*Haupthütte.*)

A. D. 1312.

During the persecutions directed by Philip the Fair, king of France, and Pope Clement V, against the Knights Templar, many of the latter sought refuge in the fastnesses of Scotland, where, until after the death of their grand master, Jaques de Molay, they found security for their persons in the bosom of the Masonic lodges.

A. D.

At this time nearly every city in Germany had its lodges, for wherever religious edifices were being constructed, there the fraternities of builders were congregated. These lodges had accorded to and recognized a superiority as existing among some of their numbers, and, in consequence, characterized them, as in England, by the title of grand lodges. That at Cologne was from at first the most important of all, and continued to be the central lodge for a long time after that at Strasburg was elevated to the same rank; and the master of the work was equally recognized as chief of the Masons of upper Germany, as him of Cologne was of those of the lower country.

A. D. 1380.

The fortress and palace of the Alhambra at Grenada, the capital of the kingdom of this name, which was founded by the Moors, under Mahomet I, creator of the dynasty of the Alhamarides, in 1235, and the construction of which fortress and palace was begun in 1248, is finished during this year.

This marvelous monument is the most beautiful that Moorish architecture has produced in Spain. If we examine this edifice in all its details, we will find that it is unsurpassed in luxury and taste by any construction of modern times. The palace of the Alhambra is the work of a happy congregation of artists of every kind, such as composed the Roman colleges until after the third century of our era; and this fact allows us to believe that this monument of human genius, like others in Grenada, was equally the work of Masonic and artistic associations, organized and directed in manner similar to those of other countries at the same period, of whom, however, history has failed to furnish us with any record.

A. D. 1400.

The monuments the most remarkable which have been erected, begun, or finished by the Masonic fraternities within the century just closed, are, in England, the cathedrals of York and Exeter, and the King's College at Cambridge. In France, the cathedrals of Perpignan, Meaux, Auxerre, Toul, Tours, and Metz; the churches of St. Ouen at Rouen, and of St. James at Dieppe. In Belgium, the belfry, the cloth hall, the city hall, and academy of fine arts at Tournay; the church of the Dominicans, and the cloth hall at Louvain; the city hall at Brussels, and the cathedral of Malines. In Germany, the dome of Gefurth, as also those of Prague and of Ulm; the church of Notre Dame at Nüremberg, and that of St. Nicholas at Stralsund. In Italy, the cathedrals of Como and Milan; the dome of Orvita; the churches of Anastasia and St. Peter at Verona, of St. Mary at Rome, and of St. Stephen at Venice; the ducal palace at Venice, and those of Florence and of Bologna. In Spain, the cathedrals of Seville and Barcelona; and the church of St. Mary at Toledo. In Switzerland, the cathedrals of Berne, of Lausanne, of Friburg, and of Zurich.[1]

A. D. 1480.

The astonishing sacrifices which the people had made to erect so many magnificent churches, joined to the crying abuses of the clergy and of the popes at this time, have relaxed the religious ardor and weakened the popular faith to such an extent as not only to preclude the idea of erecting new church edifices, but also to stop operations upon many of those which were yet unfinished for want of funds. In consequence of this condition, and notwithstanding the renewal, in 1459, by the emperor Maximilian, of their ancient privileges, and his sanction to their constitution, the number of the Masonic corporations established in every continental country declined, and their privileges became of little value; so that, having no more religious edifices to construct, they disperse

---

[1] For the years 1425, '37, '42, '59, '64, and '69, see those dates at pp. 239 and 240, *ante*.

and seek employment at such places and of such kind as hitherto had been occupied and executed by men not connected with the fraternities of builders. More particularly was this the case in France; while in Germany they still preserved some consistence and connection among themselves—the fortune of their French brethren not having overtaken them until later; and in England they continued to flourish with unabated prosperity.[1]

A. D. 1500.

During the century just closed, the Masonic fraternities may be said to have finished their labors in church architecture, and dispersed to find occupation in their individual capacities as constructors of public buildings for civic and municipal purposes.

A. D. 1575.

Since the beginning of this century, when the greater part of the fraternities found it necessary to dissolve their associations, the more wealthy architects undertook the erection of public buildings, and employed the others to construct the same, in the capacity of hired workmen. The tie of brotherhood which, up to this time, had closely united master and workmen, was gradually dissolved, and they assumed such relationship toward each other as was habitual with other bodies of tradesmen since the fourth century. In this manner, and at this time, the trades unions appear to have had their origin.

A. D. 1600.

With the close of the sixteenth century, the Masonic corporations had entirely disappeared in continental Eu-

---

[1] It was not until the middle of the seventeenth century that the Masonic corporations in England abandoned, to some extent, the material object of their organization, and admitted to honorary membership many persons not artists as *accepted Masons*. It was this element that subsequently caused their entire dissolution as operative Masonic bodies.

rope, as long before that time all religious constructions had been abandoned. After this date no traces of any regular Masonic organization can be found outside of the kingdom of England.

A. D. 1646.

The Masonic corporations in England are found to be composed for some time and in great part by learned persons, artists, and men eminent for their knowledge of science and art, as well as their influential positions in society, who had been received into the corporations as honorary members, under the designation of Accepted Masons. It was at this time that the association, no more occupied with the material object of its organization, initiated as an accepted Mason the celebrated antiquary Elias Ashmole, who founded the museum at Oxford, and who re-arranged and composed the forms of the society of the Rose Cross Brothers, which had been organized in London, after the model of the new Atlantis of Lord Bacon, and held its assemblies in the hall which had been hitherto used by the Freemasons. To the rituals of reception of the Rose Cross Brethren, which consisted of some ceremonies having a historical foundation, and the communication of the signs of recognition, and which, to some extent, resembled those used among the Freemasons, Ashmole added some others. This labor inspired him with the idea of arranging also a new ritual for the Freemasons, and he therefore composed and substituted for the ritual then in use another mode of initiation, copied in part from the ancient manuscripts and the Anglo-Saxon and Syrian rituals, and in part from the mysteries of Egypt, and otherwise, as he supposed, most resembled the initiation ceremony, as it was conducted in the colleges of Roman architects and builders. These rituals were at once adopted by the lodges in London, and subsequently by those every-where in England.

A. D. 1670.

The progress of Masonry having been suspended by the civil wars which during the previous twenty years had been desolating England, Charles II sought its revival by assuming its protectorship; and the fire of London, which took place four years previous, gives employment to the lodges, of which, at present, seven exist in the city of London.

A. D. 1685.

When James II ascended the throne in 1683, his leaning toward Roman Catholicism greatly agitated a number of his subjects; but in this year, having accorded freedom of conscience in religious matters the most complete to all within the bounds of his kingdom, the Freemasons divided into two camps, which, arrayed against each other, threw their whole influence into the political rather than the architectural or philosophical arena. The Scottish Masons, having at its head the knights of St. Andrew, adhered to James II, or the Catholic party, while the English Masons ranged themselves among the ranks of that party which decided to remove the Catholic king. This latter party succeeding; James was forced into exile, and, accompanied by many of the nobles of his court and the leading Jesuits, took up his residence in Paris, in the convent of Clermont. [The revival of the order of St. Andrew[1] engendered the Templar system, subsequently called Strict Observance, which gave birth to various fashions of exclusive Christian Freemasonry during the last century, with the hierarchical forms of the Knights of the Temple, and the ancient titles of grand commander, etc.[2]]

A. D. 1695.

The revolutions in England which succeeded the exile

---

[1] See pages 238 and 243, (A. D. 1314 and 1685.)
[2] See History of all the Rites for High Degrees, p. 212.

of James II having completely suspended the labors of the Masonic institution, king William III afforded it some protection and character by being himself initiated, and often presiding in the lodge he assembled at Hampton Court.

A. D. 1700.

At this time, except in England, the Masonic corporations were every-where dissolved. The close of the seventeenth century, in consequence of the active part taken by the fraternity in politics, wars, and revolution, saw them scattered, their lodges dissolved, and the operative members of the Masonic lodges exerting no influence upon architecture, and had no rank or importance in the land. Having ceased their labors as operative Masons, the vast crowd of operatives, the protectors, the friends of art and of humanity, who, during fourteen centuries, had contributed, through the organization of the Masonic fraternity, so much to the increase of civilization in Europe, are to-day represented by a few persons, who resolve to perpetuate the name of their ancient organization by remodeling it as a purely philosophic institution; and at a meeting of the lodge of St. Paul, held on St. John's day,

A. D. 1703,

Resolve, "That the privileges of Masonry shall no longer be confined to operative Masons, but be free to men of all professions, provided they are regularly approved and initiated into the Fraternity." At this time Christopher Wren, Knt., was grand master of Freemasonry, nearly all the operative Masons in England being employed under him upon the construction of St. Paul's cathedral. He opposed the execution of this famous resolution while he lived; so that it was not until after his death, which occurred in 1716, that the brethren were at liberty to enforce their new regulation.

Third Epoch,

From the year 1717 to the present time.

A. D. 1717.

After the death of the grand master, Christopher Wren, the four lodges of London resolve to elect a new grand master, detach themselves from their connection with the brethren at York, of whom they held their constitution, for the purpose of forming a new grand lodge, and thus be at liberty to put into execution the resolution of 1703. The four lodges, with these objects in view, invoked in general assembly all the Masons of London and vicinity, and constituted a central authority, under the title of the Grand Lodge of England, and recognizing in the three symbolic degrees alone all the principles of Masonry.

It is from this time we must date the era of modern or philosophic Freemasonry.

A. D. 1720.

The Grand Lodge of England has, since its installation, organized a certain number of lodges, in which many persons of distinction have been initiated. The Grand Lodge of York, suddenly excited with sentiments of jealousy at the growing prosperity of its young rival, the Grand Lodge of England, and in defiance of the principles of the Fraternity, proscribes those members as illegitimately made. An irreparable loss has been perpetrated by some too jealous brethren of the lodge of St. Paul, who, fearing that improper use may be made of them, burn all the ancient manuscripts, charters, rituals, and documents of all kinds.

A. D. 1721.

Freemasonry begins to extend upon the continent. The grand lodge organize a lodge at Dunkirk, and another at Mons, and the rules and regulations of the Fraternity are revised. George Payne, being reëlected grand master, compiled from the ancient charter documents a series of "charges" and "regulations" more suited to the present condition and objects of the Society, and, prefaced by a history of the Fraternity as an association of architects, he submitted the same to the grand lodge. This work being submitted by that body to the examination of a committee composed of fourteen of its members, was intrusted to the critical revision of Dr. James Anderson, with directions to prepare the same for publication, as a body of law and doctrine, for the use of the lodges of England.

A. D. 1722.

The manuscript, with the revision of which he was intrusted, is presented by Dr. Anderson to the grand lodge, and upon reception of the report of the commission of fourteen, it is adopted and ordered to be printed under the title of "The Constitutions of the Freemasons, containing the History, Charges, Regulations, etc., of that Most Ancient and Right Worshipful Fraternity."

From this time the organization of the new Freemasonry was established in prosperity. In accordance with the constitution—which is, in fact, but an adaptation of that of York of 926, more suited to the people and present time—the new grand lodge of England took up its position as the only legitimate Masonic authority in England, and thus excited the ill-will of such scattered bodies as assumed to be invested with inherent rights, because antedating the grand lodge in authority. This constitution, in fact, deprived Freemasons in their lodge capacities of their ancient privileges, in prohibiting, among other restrictions, the formation of any lodge without being authorized in such act by this grand lodge. The consequence of this assumption of authority on the part of the grand lodge promptly occasioned the protest and denial of such rights by the grand lodges of York and Edinburgh.

A. D. 1725.

This year the new Freemasonry is introduced into Paris, where many lodges are organized within a few years.

A. D. 1728.

Baron Ramsay, a Scotchman, and a partisan of the Stuarts, sought to introduce in London a new style of Masonry, created in the interest of "the Pretender," and which he asserted had descended from the crusades, as it was created by Godfrey of Bouillon, and of which the lodge of St. Andrew, at Edinburgh, was the principal modern authority. The political character of this Masonry caused it to be very promptly rejected, and he returned to France without meeting with any success.

A. D. 1729.

The activity displayed by the lodges holding under the Grand Lodge of England, and the brilliancy which attached to their labors, stimulated the zeal of the Masons of Ireland and Scotland, who previously had assembled themselves together, but at irregular and uncertain periods. The Masonic temples are opened in all parts of the kingdom, and the initiations greatly multiplied. A convocation of Irish Freemasons resolve to organize a grand lodge upon the basis and constitution of that of London; and thus a central power is constituted under the title of the Grand Lodge of Ireland.

A. D. 1730.

The lodges greatly increase as well in England as upon the continent—the latest being those at Hamburg and the Hague. A provincial grand master, named Pemfrees, is employed to go to India, and in a short time he organized in Bengal eleven lodges. A central committee of charity is instituted in London to succor brethren in distress, and the funds for this institution are raised by a voluntary annual contribution of four shillings from each member of a lodge in London, and two shillings from each member of a lodge elsewhere in England.

A. D. 1732.

The Grand Lodge of York, representing the ancient system of operative Masonry, and of which the regulations conform more readily to the free system of the ancient Masonic corporations, recognized the necessity of changing this system to correspond in greater degree with the object of the new Freemasonry.

A. D. 1733.

The first provincial grand lodge in America is instituted at Boston. During this year lodges have been organized in Italy, at Rome and Florence; in Spain, at Gibraltar and Malta; in Russia, at St. Petersburg. The lodges in Bengal have sent abundant aid to the charity fund in London.

A. D. 1734.

A general assembly of the Masons of Holland is convoked at the Hague, for the purpose of organizing a provincial grand lodge, which being done, the same is chartered regularly by the Grand Lodge of England, in 1735.

A. D. 1735.

The Grand Lodge of England nominate provincial grand masters for South America and Africa. Lodges are organized at Madrid and at Lisbon. This year is rendered memorable by the commencement of persecutions directed against the Fraternity by the general government of Holland, which interests the Masonic assemblies.

A. D. 1736.

The Grand Lodge of Scotland, at Edinburgh, believing the great prosperity of the new English lodges to be consequent upon the more liberal constitution of the new grand lodge, is desirous to introduce similar changes into its own system; but the hereditary charge of patron that James I had, in 1430, conceded to the family of Roslin prevented. The baron Sinclair of Roslin, the grand master, being approached by the grand lodge upon the subject, acceded readily to the request; and, in an assembly convoked by the four oldest lodges of Scotland, at Edinburgh, after reading his renunciation to the rights and privileges of patron, George Sinclair, baron of Roslin, was duly elected grand master of the Grand Lodge of Scotland for 1737, and the same was properly organized under a constitution, charges, and regulations similar to those of the Grand Lodge of England.

In this year, also, a provincial grand lodge of England was organized as the governing body of the lodges in Paris.

The Grand Lodge of England named the count Scheffer provincial grand master for the lodges of Sweden.

A. D. 1737.

During this year the English provincial grand lodges of Switzerland and Saxony are founded, respectively at Geneva and Hamburg; and the Grand Lodge of England nominates William, king of Prussia, provincial grand master for the lodges of Lower Saxony.

A. D. 1738.

Pope Clement XII promulgates his bull of excommunication against the Freemasons; and it is followed by the edict of the emperor Charles VI, who interdicts the assemblies of Freemasons in the Low Country. Prince Frederick subsequently, as Frederick II, king of Prussia, is initiated, at Brunswick, on the night of August 15 of this year.

A. D. 1739.

The Grand Lodge of England is accused, by many of the brethren, with having suppressed some of the ceremonies, altered the ritual, and introduced innovations; also of having appointed provincial grand masters to organize lodges in towns under the jurisdiction of the Grand Lodge of York—a measure that of itself was considered sufficiently offensive. From these charges there resulted some new divisions among the lodges of the north and south of England. Many of the discontented separated themselves from the grand lodge at London, and declared themselves adherents of the grand lodge at York, and then formed a new grand lodge, neither of England nor York, which they styled the Grand Lodge of "Ancient and Accepted Masons." The grand lodges of Ireland and Scotland, having recognized this body as truly representatives of the *ancient* rite, refused to correspond with the elder jurisdiction, contemptuously styled by this new body as *modern*. Nevertheless, the so-called *modern* grand lodge augmented in importance and consideration, while the latter organization, though styling itself *ancient*, remained in obscurity, and was but little known outside of London city.

A. D. 1739.

The cardinal Ferraro, in his edict, published on the 14th January, wishing to remove all doubt and equivocation in the interpretation of the bull of excommunication of his holiness the pope, launched against the Freemasons on the

27th of April of the preceding year, explained that document in the following manner: "That no persons should assemble or meet in any place in the capacity of a society, nor be found present at such assemblies, under the *penalty of death* and confiscation of all their goods, and also incur *damnation without hope of grace.*" By the same edict it is expressly directed that "all house-holders are prohibited from allowing meetings of Freemasons to take place within their houses, under penalty of having the same demolished, and themselves mulcted in a fine of one thousand crowns of gold, and being condemned to the galleys."

A. D. 1740.

The Grand Lodge of England named a provincial master for the lodges founded in Russia. At this time France had two hundred lodges, twenty-two of which were located in Paris. The provincial grand lodges instituted, to the present time, in different countries, by the Grand Lodge of England, in their turn now began to organize themselves into independent grand lodges.

A. D. 1741.

Foundation of the provincial grand lodge of Hanover, at Hanover; and the provincial grand lodge of Saxony, at Dresden, by the Count Rutowski, who is elected grand master, and which became an independent grand lodge in 1755.

A. D. 1742.

Founding of the provincial grand lodge of the Sun at Beyreuth, and a provincial grand lodge at Antigua, for the English West Indies.

A. D. 1744.

The grand lodge at the Three Globes, in Berlin, which was organized in 1640 by Baron Bielfeld is this year elevated to the rank of a grand lodge by Frederick the Great, king of Prussia, and he is elected its permanent grand master, a position which he filled until 1747. (In 1849 this grand lodge had organized fourteen operative lodges.)

A. D. 1746.

Lord Derwentwater, the first grand master of the provincial grand lodge of France, perishes upon the scaffold, a victim of his attachment to the Pretender, Charles Edward Stuart.

A. D. 1747.

The Grand Lodge of Scotland institutes, at Copenhagen, a provincial grand lodge for Denmark, which, shortly afterward, proclaimed its independence of the Grand Lodge of Scotland. In this year Charles Edward Stuart, known as "the Pretender," son of James II, deposed king of England, institutes the chapter of Arras, and delivers to the Masons who are attached to his person a bull of institution, or letters patent, for a governing chapter of what he named the Scottish Jacobite Rite.

A. D. 1751.

Freemasonry, as constituted in London thirty years ago, has now extended into nearly every civilized country. Its humanitarian doctrines and the civilizing principles it manifested, together with its radical leaning toward the dogma of "Liberty, Equality, Fraternity," had, by this time, intimidated kings, popes, and princes to such an extent that they seek to arrest its progress. As early as 1731 edicts had been promulgated against it in Russia, while in 1735, in Holland, and in 1737–'38–'44–'45, at Paris, similar interdictions had been ordered. At Rome and in Florence, the meetings of Freemasons were prohibited, as also in Sweden, Hamburg, and Geneva the bull of Pope Clement was enforced. The Holy Inquisition, as the court accusative in those countries wherein it existed, caused the brethren to be imprisoned, and their books and papers to be burned by the hands of the public executioner. But to crown all these persecutions, King Charles of Naples, as also Ferdinand VII, king of Spain, wishing to interdict Masonry within their States, rendered edicts prohibiting the assemblage of Freemasons, under pain of death; and the pope, Benedict XIV, renewed this year the bull of excommunication of Clement XII, in 1738, against the Freemasons, whose assemblies he interdicted under penalty of death. But all these violent measures had but slight effect in stopping the progress of Masonry, which finds itself propagated upon the civilized globe with a rapidity that nothing can arrest. Notwithstanding the bull of Benedict XIV, Freemasonry is practiced at this time openly in Tuscany, at Naples, and in many other parts of the Italian peninsula. At Rome, even, there are lodges which adopt but feeble measures to keep themselves hidden.

A. D. 1753.

The Masonic Orphan Asylum is established at Stockholm. Its fund is the accumulation of special collections taken up in the Swedish lodges. (At the present time this institution is very rich.)

A. D. 1754.

Under a patent or charter from the Grand Lodge of Scotland, the provincial grand lodge of Sweden is organized. The Grand Lodge of England transmits charters to organize lodges in South Carolina, Guadaloupe, and Gibraltar, and in this year many new lodges are instituted in England. The Templar system, created by the partisans of the Stuarts, is revived at Paris by the institution of the chapter of Clermont, in the convent of that name, under the direction of the Chevalier de Bonneville.

A. D. 1753.

The Grand Lodge of England, in consequence of the

schism that has taken place in its ranks, establishes the custom of granting diplomas to the brethren under its jurisdiction, to distinguish them from those initiated by the seceders.

A. D. 1756.

The English grand lodge in France, instituted in 1736, and which took the title in 1743, detaches itself from the Grand Lodge of London, and proclaims itself the Grand Lodge of France. The confusion manifested under the grand mastership of the Duke of Clermont, however, does not abate, but rather increases. By constitutions delivered to masters of lodges, securing them in the enjoyment of such office for life, Masonic authorities never contemplated are established in France. The practice, begun with a political motive by the lodge of St. Andrew of Scotland, situate at Edinburgh, was continued by the English provincial grand lodge of France, and the confusion thus engendered the new Masonic authority, into which that body has resolved itself, now finds it impossible to correct. Those masters of lodges, for the sake of gain, vend the privileges accorded to themselves; and, to do this the more easily, they fabricate false titles, and antedate charters and diplomas. In shaking off the control of the Grand Lodge of England, and in proclaiming itself the grand lodge of the kingdom of France, that body declared in its constitution to sacredly continue the custom of granting personal titles to these lodge masters *ad vitam* and, by so doing, increased the existing confusion; for the result was that these masters governed their lodges not more by the forms laid down by the grand lodge than by their individual caprices, and this, taken with the vending of authorities to open lodges, which lodges, in their turn, felt at liberty to organize grand lodges, (or bodies in authority amounting thereto,) chapters, councils, and tribunals embracing the objects and practice of all the degrees then known, created, at this time, so chaotic a condition that it was apparently impossible to determine the legal governing Masonic authority in France.

A. D. 1756.

In this year the national grand lodge of Italy was organized at Naples. (In 1790 this body was dissolved.) At the Hague the representatives of thirty lodges in the Netherlands constitute a grand lodge of the United Provinces, and elect the Baron of Aerssen-Beyeren first grand master.

A. D. 1758.

The Grand Lodge of Scotland, at Edinburgh, in adopting and conferring the high degrees, and establishing rituals for each of these degrees, renders herself liable to the same charges of unmasonic conduct which she had but a short time before directed against the Grand Lodge of England, viz.: of changing the basis of Freemasonry and altering the rituals. These high degrees give her, however, an influence not before enjoyed, and creates a corresponding energy in the work of the Scotch lodges. Perceiving the increasing prosperity of her sister grand lodge at London, occasioned mainly by the custom, originated by the latter, of establishing, every-where, provincial grand lodges, the Grand Lodge of Scotland, for the purpose of initiating a like proceeding, authorized a Colonel Young as provincial grand master of such lodges as he might organize, as well as those already existing and holding their charters from the Grand Lodge of Scotland in North America and the British West Indies, with plenary powers to introduce the high degrees then known to Scottish Masonry into those countries.

A. D. 1760.

At Avignon, the mother lodge of the Rite of Swedenborg is instituted by the Benedictine monk Dom Pernetti, and a Pole named Grabianca. The philosopher Swedenborg, one of the most learned and illustrious Freemasons of his time, in instituting this rite, had in view a desire to reform the Roman Catholic religion. The dogmas of the reform of Swedenborg are adopted by a good many influential persons in Sweden, England, and Germany, where societies which practice his religious system have been formed by these persons.

A. D. 1760.

In this year Freemasonry in Germany was greatly confused and injured by the introduction of the high degrees of every kind known to and having their inception in France. Chapters of Emperors of the East and West, with a rite of twenty-five degrees, (subsequently known as the Rite of Perfection,) founded in Paris in 1758 by the establishment of the Chapter of Clermont, are the children of this parent, and they are introduced by the Marquis of Berny, a French gentleman, into the lodge at the Three Globes, in Berlin. This lodge propagates this right by the aid of its deputy Rosa, a Lutheran priest, who in a short time has organized seventeen lodges. Subsequently the army of Broglie introduced the other rites, such as Templarism, Rosecrucianism, etc., until, in a few years, the brethren in Germany are in as great confusion, as to what is and what is not Freemasonry, as they are in France.

A. D. 1762.

At this time Freemasonry had attained great progress, the different grand lodges of Europe having instituted lodges in nearly every part of the world. The baron of Hund introduces into Germany the Templar system known as "Strict Observance," which he has studied at Paris, where he was initiated into the high degrees of the chapter of Clermont.

A. D. 1763.

The two parties into which the Grand Lodge of France had been divided, in consequence of the maladministration of the grand master, the duke of Clermont, reunited in 1762, after having, during their separation, injured the Masonic institution almost beyond repair, by their creations of moveable lodges and immoveable matters. Notwithstanding the union, confusion, consequent upon their previous misconduct, continued, and the effects of the high degrees are as apparent for evil as they are lamentable, not only in France, but wherever they have been introduced.

A. D. 1764.

A man named Johnson, a secret agent of the Jesuits, who styled himself Envoy and Plenipotentiary of the unknown superiors of Strict Observance, establishes at Jena some chapters of this system. He announced, in an assembly that he convoked at this place on the 25th December, 1763, that he alone had the power of conferring the degrees of the system and organizing chapters, by virtue of the documents, patents, and briefs granted to him by the unknown superiors of his system in Scotland. At a second convention, assembled on the 14th of June of this year (1764), he invited the presence of Baron Hund, who had been engaged in similar duty elsewhere in Germany since 1762. At this convention the baron, who had never heard of unknown superiors, requested the privilege of inspecting the documents, patents, etc., possessed by Johnson, which request being refused, the baron denounced this self-styled plenipotentiary as an arrant imposter.

A. D. 1765.

The baron of Hund is elected at Jena, grand master of the Templar System of Germany, styled " Strict Observance."

A. D. 1766.

By an edict of the Grand Lodge of France, all charters granted by chapters, councils, colleges, and tribunals of the high degrees are declared void and of no effect. The attempt to enforce this decree causes greater confusion than ever among the Masons in France. The Grand Lodge of England organizes a provincial grand lodge for the country of the Lower Rhine.

A. D. 1770.

At Avignon is organized the grand Scottish lodge of the county Venaissin, which adopts the Hermetic Rite of Swedenborg. The Grand Lodge of the United Provinces, sitting at the Hague, proclaims itself the National Grand Lodge of Holland, in accordance with an agreement entered into with the Grand Lodge of England, and notifies all the grand lodges of Europe of this fact.

A. D. 1772.

Under the grand mastership of Louis Philippe Joseph D'Orleans, duke of Chartres, the National Grand Lodge of France is dissolved, and the Grand Orient of France organized.[1] Ferdinand, duke of Brunswick, is elected grand master of the lodges organized under the Templar system of Strict Observance.

A. D. 1773.

Under letters patent from the Grand Lodge of England is organized the National Grand Lodge of Germany. This grand lodge had been in course of organization since 1770, and this year, representing twelve operative lodges, its first act was to adopt the ritual of Ziennendorf, its most intelligent and able friend and chief officer.

A. D. 1775.

A grand lodge is organized at Basle, under the name of

---

[1] The Grand Orient at first adopted the modern English rite of three symbolic degrees, and called it the French Rite. Five years afterward, in its circular of the 3d of August, 1777, it exhibited all that was dangerous and anti-masonic in the rituals of the high degrees, and refused to recognize them; and yet, ten years afterward, it is obliged, perhaps unwillingly to constitute chapters of those very high degrees!

the Scottish Helvetian Directory. The grand master, Ferdinand of Brunswick, convoked in that city a congress, to consider the idea of uniting all the rites. The baron of Hund, and the representatives of twenty-two lodges of the system propagated by him, were present at this assembly. The discussions began on the 23d of May, and closed on the 6th of July, with no result.

A. D. 1775.

A mother lodge of the Scotch Philosophic Rite, under the name of "Social Contract," is constituted by the grand lodge of the county Venaissin.

A. D. 1778.

Under the pretext to reform Masonry, and throw light upon many obscure points in the rituals, the lodge styled Benevolent Knights of the Templars (Strict Observance) System, convoke a congress at Lyons; but as there was nothing discussed but a proposed change of rituals, it was evident that the real object of the assembly was to substitute the Martinist for the Templar ritual, which was so done.

The congress of Wolfenbuttel, convoked by Ferdinand, duke of Brunswick, grand master of the Templar system in Germany, assembled at Brunswick for the same object that had been discussed at the previous meeting, called by him in 1775. The congress remained in session from the 15th July to the 27th August; and the assembly, finding it impossible to work their way through the chaos of mysticism into which the numerous systems of high degrees had plunged Freemasonry, decided that there should be convened, the following year, at Wiesbaden, a general congress of all the most intelligent Masons in Germany.

In this year is instituted a grand lodge at St. Petersburg, Russia.

A. D. 1779.

This year the Masonic Benevolent School is instituted at London, by some members of the Grand Lodge of England. The object of the society is to help and support the infirm, the aged, and those in prison; also to protect the wives, children, or orphans of deceased members.

A. D. 1780.

A council of the high degrees, called the Emperors of the East and West, take the title of Sublime Scottish Mother Lodge of the great globe of France, and Sovereign Grand Lodge. This authority sets itself up as the rival of the National Grand Lodge, and the Grand Orient disgraces itself by a shameful commerce of the Masonic degrees.

A. D. 1782.

The congress of Wilhelmsbad, convoked by Ferdinand, duke of Brunswick, agreeably with the decision of the congress of 1778, invites all the grand lodges of Europe to participate. Proposed to convene, at first, on the 15th of October, 1781, it was postponed until Easter week, 1782, and finally assembled on the 16th July of this year. In this congress, the way for which was opened by those of Wolfenbuttel and Lyons, where a general reform of Freemasonry, as practiced generally upon the continent, was urgently recommended, a great many questions were proposed for discussion and decision, among which were the following:

Is Freemasonry a modern society? Is it, on the contrary, derived from an ancient society? If so, what society is it the descendant of? Has the present society *unknown superiors?* If so, what are their privileges and attributes?

These questions, and others of minor importance, submitted, during a session of thirty daily meetings, though freely discussed, elicited no satisfactory solution. The congress, however, succeeded in extinguishing a number of so-called Masonic systems, and altering others.

It was in this year that Joseph Balsamo, better known as Count Cagliastro, succeeded in organizing at Lyons the mother lodge of his rite, styled Egyptian, under the title of "Wisdom Triumphant."

A. D. 1783.

A grand lodge of the Eclectic Rite, composed of the provincial grand lodges of Frankfort and Wetzlar, is organized at Frankfort. This rite was the creation of members of this grand lodge, who, selecting from all the rites and systems, as exhibited at the congress of Wilhelmsbad, such points and parts as seemed to them most rational, styled their creation the "Eclectic Rite." In the circular addressed by this grand lodge to the Masonic authorities of Europe, announcing the reform they had instituted, it was distinctly declared that all speculation in magic, cabalistics, Templarism, and other follies of the day, were by this grand lodge renounced and forbidden to its jurisdiction, and that Freemasonry, in the purity of its institution, according to the regulations of the Grand Lodge of England, as promulgated in 1723, was the only style of Freemasonry it would thereafter recognize.

A. D. 1784.

A new grand orient of Poland is organized at Varsovia. A grand lodge of Austria is organized at Vienna. A mother lodge of adoption of the Egyptian masonry of Count Cagliastro is instituted by him, of which the prince of Montmorenci Luxembourg accepts the grand mastership.

A. D. 1785.

The congress of the Philalètes is convoked at Paris to disentangle Freemasonry from the mass of high degrees and mystic systems; but though in session from the 15th February to the 26th May, it failed in its object.

A. D. 1786.

A Grand Orient of Geneva is organized by the seven lodges in that city. (This grand lodge was dissolved in 1790 by the incorporation of this city into the territory of France.) A provincial grand lodge is instituted at Rouen, by the Grand Lodge of St. John, at Edinburgh, with a chapter of the order of Harodim, of Kilwinning.

A. D. 1787.

The second congress of the Philalètes is convoked at Paris, to continue the discussions begun at that of 1785, upon such dogmatic and historical points as had been submitted to the congress of Wilhelmsbad. None of the questions, however, were satisfactorily decided, and the origin, nature, and object of Freemasonry continued to be an insoluble problem to the greater number of the Freemasons of the continent.

A. D. 1800.

During the past century the modern or philosophic Freemasonry, as instituted by the Grand Lodge of London in 1717-'23, was introduced at the dates given in the various countries and states named below:

EUROPE.

England............1717.	Tuscany............1732.	Poland............1739.
Ireland............1720.	Russia............1732.	Malta............1741.
Scotland............1721.	Florence............1733.	Denmark............1742.
France............1721.	Portugal............1733.	Rome............1742.
Belgium............1721.	Switzerland............1736.	Bohemia............1744.
Holland............1725.	Sardinia............1737.	Hungary............1744.
Gibraltar............1726.	Saxony............1738.	Norway............1744.
Spain............1728.	Bavaria............1738.	Guernsey............1753.
Hamburg............1736.	Prussia............1738.	Jersey............1753.
Sweden............1731.	Austria............1738.	Hanover............1754.
Naples............1732.	Turkey............1738.	

Asia.

Benga............1727.	Surinam..........1771.	Prince of Wales
Bombay..........1728.	Ceylon............1771.	Islands..........1780.
Madras...........1752.		Persia............1789.

Oceanica.

Java...............1730. Sumatra............1772.

Africa.

Cape of Good Hope, 1733.	Senegambia........1736.	Isle of France......1778.
Cape Coast..........1736.	Mauritius..........1744.	St. Helena..........1798.

America.

Canada............1721.	Jamaica............1743.	Grenada..........1764.
Massachusetts......1733.	St. Vincent........1745.	Newfoundland....1765.
Georgia............1734.	Porto Rico.........1746.	Dutch Guiana.....1770.
South Carolina....1736.	St. Domingo.......1746.	Vermont..........1770.
New York..........1737.	Barbadoes.........1750.	Bermuda..........1771.
St. Christopher....1738.	Guadaloupe.......1751.	Louisiana........1780.
Martinique........1738.	Pennsylvania.....1753.	Maryland.........1781.
Antigua...........1742.	Trinidad..........1760.	Nova Scotia......1762.
	North Carolina...1788.	

Freemasonry was interdicted or prohibited during the past century in the countries and cities named, and at the different dates given below, viz.:

Russia...............1731, '94, '97.	Vienna...............1743.
Holland..............1735, '37.	Canton of Berne....1743, '70, 82.
Paris.................1737, '38, '44.	Austrian States.....1742, '64.
Sweden..............1738.	Turkey...............1748
Hamburg............1738.	Spain................1751.
Geneva..............1738.	Naples...............1752, '75.
Roman States.......1739, '51.	Dantzic..............1763.
Portugal............1739, '42, '76, '92.	Aix-la-Chapelle....1779.
Florence............1739.	Morocco............1784.
Marseilles..........1742.	Basle................1785.

A. D. 1804.

The Count De Grasse Tilly organizes a central grand odge of France, with a supreme council, at Paris.

A. D. 1805.

The Grand Orient of Lusitania is organized at Lisbon; also the Grand Orient of Italy at Milan.

A. D. 1806.

The Grand Lodge of Scotland organizes at Xeres a grand lodge for all Spain. The Grand Orient of Baden is organized at Mannheim.

A. D. 1807.

The Grand Lodge of Harodim of Kilwinning, acknowledged to have existed as Canongate Kilwinning lodge of Freemasons since the construction of the abbey of Kilwinning, in 1150, surrenders its independence as a self-constituted grand lodge, and takes rank with the lodges of its creation, under the Grand Lodge of Scotland, as Canongate Kilwinning, No. 2.

A. D. 1809.

A grand orient of Naples is organized under the direction of Prince Joachim, duke of Berg. Also a grand orient of Spain is organized at Madrid.

A. D. 1811.

A grand orient of Westphalia is organized at Cassel. Charles XIII, king of Sweden, institutes a civil order, which he confers upon deserving Freemasons.

A. D. 1813.

The two grand lodges of England—that of York, the legitimate successor of the organization of 926, and which in 1755 merged into the schismatic grand lodge, under the title of the "Grand Lodge of Ancient York Masons," and that of London, founded in 1717, under the title of the "Grand Lodge of Free and Accepted Masons"—are this year united. By this union are terminated all the differences which had caused so much bitterness during the past fifty or sixty years. In the act of union, dated December 1, 1813, the ancient laws, as well written as traditional, are explicitly recognized, and taken for the basis of this act, and it is drawn up in that spirit of fraternity which dictated the charter of York, A. D. 926. It also recognized and proclaimed that the ancient and true Freemasonry is composed of but three degrees, viz.: those of apprentice, fellow-craft, and master mason.

A. D. 1814.

On the 15th of August of this year Pope Pius VII publishes his edict against the Masonic society, in which he pronounces corporal punishment, even to death, and the confiscation of all his property, upon any person who should join or be known by the authorities to belong to this society. This edict is immediately followed with like prohibitions by the regent of Milan, Henry IV of Venice, Maximien Joseph, king of Bavaria, the emperor of Austria, the king of Spain, the grand duke of Baden, and finally by the duke of Parma. All these edicts repeat, in their turn, accusations similar to those contained in the bull of Pius VII, and interdicted, in their several States, all Masonic assemblies, under whatever name they might be held. All the lodges existing in these countries are immediately closed.

The famous edict of Pius VII is a document as curious as it is incomprehensible for the time at which it was published; for the accusations it contains against the Fraternity are without a shadow of foundation. The tendency of the Masonic society being continually toward the amelioration of the moral and intellectual condition of the people, it is a natural but free auxiliary of an enlightened government desiring progress, and desiring it gradually. This same pope reëstablished the order of the Jesuits, which had been abolished by Clement XIV.

A. D. 1816.

Foundation, in Paris, of the mother lodge of the Rite of Misraim, under the title of the "Rainbow."

A. D. 1817.

The Fraternity in Holland mark the bounds of their grand lodge jurisdiction by the organization of two grand lodges independent of the grand orient situate at the Hague. One of these is located at the Hague; the other at Brussels.

A. D. 1818.

Prince Frederick, grand master of the lodges of the Low Countries, interdicts the exercise of the Rite of Misraim.

A. D. 1822.

The emperor of Russia publishes a ukase which interdicts the meetings of Freemasons within the empire.

A. D. 1824.

The king of Portugal interdicts Freemasonry in his kingdom.

A. D. 1825.

General Lafayette is welcomed to Boston, is feasted by the brethren and citizens, and attends at the laying of the corner-stone of the monument subsequently erected near that city to perpetuate the remembrance of the defense of the rights and liberties of America.

A. D. 1827.

Renewal by the pope of the edict of Pius VII against the Freemasons.

A. D. 1827.

The Mexican Congress, provoked by the calumnies of the clergy, take measures to retain the Freemasons of that country from increasing their meetings, which were believed to be devoted more to political discussions than to any other business.

In the United States some circumstances take place, in the State of New York, calculated to fix the public mind upon the Fraternity, and, for the first time, public notice is taken of the society in the Congress of that country.

A. D. 1828.

The king of Spain renews his edict against the Freemasons.

A. D. 1832.

The Grand Orient of Belgium is instituted at Brussels, and a Masonic authority, styled the Supreme Council for Belgium, is also organized. At Frankfort, a Jewish lodge, styled the "Frankfort Eagle," is instituted, under the authority of the Grand Orient of France. In Germany, obedient to the injunctions of the authorities which instituted them, the operative lodges refused to acknowledge the members of the Jewish lodge, and, contrary to the principles of Masonry, they close their doors against them.

A. D. 1836.

Some disputes spring up among the lodges of Germany, principally in Berlin, with regard to the admission of Israelites into the lodges. The refusal of many of the lodges to affiliate, or to admit them to seats in their assemblies, notwithstanding they have been regularly initiated, produced numerous controversies. In a sort of congress of Jewish Masons, held at Berlin, they prepare an address to the mother lodges of Berlin, and adjure them, in the name of Masonic principles, in the name of justice and reason, to withdraw the restrictions against them. This important question, introduced and discussed at divers meetings of grand lodges of Berlin, Dresden, and Frankfort, can not be decided satisfactorily. To the assertion of those lodges which refused to admit the Israelites, upon the principle that Masonry is essentially a Christian institution, with the Holy Bible its greatest symbol, and upon which no Jew can be sworn, was opposed by the counter assertion that Masonry is not a Christian but a universal institution, having for its object to rally under one banner and unite under one bond all religionists; that, following the standard of no prophet, neither Moses, Christ, nor Mahomet, it adopts the sublime doctrine of the second of these lawgivers, seeing that such doctrine embodies more nearly than any other the universal spirit of charity and brotherly love which Freemasonry would inculcate, to the end that by opening her temples to men of every worship she may therein free them from the prejudices of their country and the errors of their religious education, and teach them to regard each other but as brethren all united in the bonds of peace, science, and labor.[1]

A. D. 1841.

The three grand lodges of Berlin adopt measures to exclude Jews from their assemblies, and the benefit and privileges of Freemasonry.

A. D. 1844.

Formation of the Alpine Grand Lodge at Zurich, by the union of the two Swiss Masonic authorities, viz.: the Scottish Helvetian Directory, at Zurich, and the National Grand Lodge, at Berne. The new grand lodge is constituted in conformity with a charter signed and accepted by fourteen lodges at Zurich, on the 22d June, 1844.

A. D. 1845.

On the 30th of August, of this year, agreeably to the invitation extended by the lodge "United Brothers," of Strasburg, there assembled at Steinbach, the birth-place of Erwin, architect of the cathedral of Strasburg, Masons from many parts, to inaugurate a statue to his memory, as the first grand master of the Masons of Germany and France.

---

[1] The true principles of Freemasonry, as herein set forth, have not, however, even to the present time, removed those absurd gothic prejudices; for to this hour Jewish Masons are excluded from many German lodges.

Before the dedication of the statue, it was decreed, at a general assembly which had taken place in the town hall, which was wreathed and adorned for the occasion as a Masonic temple, that a Masonic congress should thereafter take place, in succession, in the village, town, or city represented by every brother assenting to this proposition.

A. D. 1847.

The law of exclusion of 1841, by which the three grand lodges of Berlin had prohibited certain brethren from participation in the privileges of intercommunion with the lodges of their jurisdiction, is at this time again brought up in those grand lodges. The formal declaration of the Grand Lodge of England to cease all correspondence and relations with them, if the paragraph relating to the exclusion of the Israelites was not effaced from their statutes, produced this result.

A. D. 1848.

In conformity with the constitution discussed and agreed to in December of this year, in a congress to which had been invited all the lodges of France, a National Grand Lodge for France is organized. Based upon the democratic system in its largest conception, this grand lodge adopted the modern English rite, and gave it the name of Unitary Rite. It notified all the lodges of Europe of its organization and decision as to a rite.

A. D. 1849.

After the political discussions of the preceding year, which shook a great part of Europe, the necessity for reforms in the Masonic institutions was felt more than ever. Already at different periods, since 1820 more particularly, views had been expressed by a great many lodges and submitted to their grand lodges, for the purpose of obtaining changes in the laws, and particularly in the exceedingly aristocratic organization of the mother lodges; and also demanding to be represented near these governing bodies in a manner more in harmony with the ancient Masonic device of "Liberty, Equality, and Fraternity." These views, however, were provocative of little response and no result.

The political events, joined to the symptoms of discontent which generally became manifest, and which appeared likely to lead to complete revolution, determined some grand lodges to undertake some degrees of reform.

A. D. 1850.

At this time Freemasonry has extended into all parts of the civilized world. In EUROPE it is in a most flourishing condition, protected and respected. England, Scotland, Ireland, Sweden, Denmark, Holland, Prussia, Saxony, and the German States, France, Switzerland, and the Protestant part of Bavaria, number nearly three thousand lodges, governed by twenty-one grand lodges.

In Russia, Austria, and their dependent States, it is, on the contrary, prohibited; also, in the kingdoms of Naples, Sardinia, Rome, Tuscany, Spain, and Portugal.

In AFRICA we find lodges in Algiers, at Alexandria, Senegal, Senegambia, Guinea, the Cape of Good Hope, Mozambique, Canaries, and St. Helena, Bourbon, and Mauritius; while there are no lodges in Tunis, Morocco, or the Barbary States.

In AMERICA it is every-where prosperous, there being few, if any, of the States of the American Union which has not its grand lodge. Freemasonry has penetrated into every portion of this vast continent. The British possessions of Nova Scotia, New Brunswick, Canada, and Newfoundland have each their provincial grand or independent grand and operative Masonic lodges; while all the more southern and western States which latterly have been received into the Union have each their grand and operative lodges. The West India islands, Cuba, Porto Rico, have their lodges, and that of Hayti its grand and operative lodges. In Central America it is to be found in the French, Dutch, and British Guianas, and also in the republics of Venezuela, Guatemala, Columbia, Bolivia, and Peru, and the united provinces of La Plata, Uruguay and Paraguay; while in Rio Janiero, capital of the empire of Brazil, there is a grand lodge with twenty-five operative lodges under its jurisdiction.

In ASIA, Freemasonry has existed for more than a century in Hindostan. Lodges are to be found in Bombay, Pondicherry, Alahabad, Bejapoor, Chazepoor, Carnute, Darrely, Concan, Futteghur, etc. At Agrah is to be found the Grand Lodge of Bengal; while in China, at Canton, and the islands of Ceylon and Prince of Wales, in Persia and in Turkey, lodges exist. There is no lodge in Japan.

In OCEANICA, Freemasonry was introduced in 1730, into the island of Java. At the present time, Sumatra, New Holland, New South Wales, New Zealand, and Van Dieman's Land have all their Masonic lodges.

The number of lodges upon the globe, at present, has been variously estimated as high as five thousand; of this number, three thousand are in Europe, fifteen hundred in America, and five hundred in Asia, Africa, and Oceanica.

Thus, within a century and a half, the modern or Philosophic Freemasonry has been propagated over the whole surface of the earth, and in its progress always spreading seeds of civilization and friendly intercourse. From habits practiced in the lodges, have gone out principles of peace, fraternity, freedom, and equality, which have softened the asperities of social intercourse, given birth to a greater breadth of charity for the prejudices of mankind, and expanded the human mind beyond the exclusiveness of caste, origin, national education, and religion. Is it, then, astonishing that the Roman Catholic clergy, who are notorious as partisans of the stationary order of things, and bitter opponents of all progressive views in human affairs, should be opposed to an institution that operates so insensibly in transforming and enlightening man to a knowledge of his true manhood; and that they should, from so early a period in its history, have perceived the true tendency of the Masonic institution, and opposed, with all their power, its establishment? On the contrary, the wonder is that they have not carried its persecution more fully to the bitter end, as it was and has been the only institution of a non-clerical or lay character which has stood between them and unlimited power; but, fortunately for it, and unfortunately for them, it had assumed shape and consistence in a country where, and at a time when, their power was not in the ascendant. Upon the continent, however, whither the institution rapidly extended, the clergy, being very powerful, had more success; yet here, finding it impossible, from the peculiar nature of its constitution, to use Freemasonry, they resolved to abuse it, ban it, and excommunicate its adherents from religious privileges here and hope of heaven hereafter. This failing, they finally resolved to introduce into its lodges a number of rites with their degrees, appealing to the weaker points in the human character, and thus they succeeded in denaturalizing the institution to such an extent that its original constitution became, in a great measure, lost sight of. So intense, however, did Jesuitism labor in this regard, that it overdid itself; for this very denaturalization led to inquiry and investigation which, in evolving the true condition, unmasked the perpetrators of these wrongs inflicted on the institution, and restored it, in a great degree, to its primitive simplicity and usefulness.

EDICT

of

POPE PIUS VII AGAINST THE FREEMASONS.

EDICT.

If the ancient legislation of the Roman States has interdicted, under penalties the most rigorous, all secret and hidden assemblies, by reason that their jealous clandestineship induced the belief that, in such assemblies, the well-being of the state and public tranquillity were endangered, and that therein were formed schools of depravity, the sovereign pontiffs, in like manner, are equally bound to entertain a similar opinion as to the object of those assemblies of Freemasons, Illuminati, Egyptians and others, who, surrounding their hidden operations with forms, ceremonies, and oaths to guard secrets which they must believe are, at least, liable to be suspected; and as their assemblies are particularly composed of persons of divers nations and conditions, worships and degrees of morality, admitted without distinction, they can not free themselves from the suspicion that their assemblies are gotten up to arrange the destruction of not only thrones and governments, but even religion itself, and particularly the only true religion of our Lord Jesus Christ, of which the Roman pontiff was constituted chief, master, and guardian by its divine founder and legislator himself.

Informed as to these facts, and animated by their evangelical zeal—although then they had not foreseen, as has been since generally remarked, the murderous development and hidden designs of these secret assemblies and infernal conventicles—the pontiffs Clement XII and Benedict XIV, of glorious memory, who have since appeared at the bar of God, opposed all their force and their apostolic ministry to the debauchery which these assemblies every-where threatened. The first, by his decree, which, commencing "*In eminenti apostolatus specula,*" published the 27th April, 1738, not only forbade, but condemned in all their extent, the meetings or assemblies of these so-styled Freemasons, or other similar societies, of whatever denomination or by whatever designation they might be known; and, subsequently, by *the thunders of excommunication, to be incurred by the act,* without regard to any declaration made by the accused, and from the effects of which none other than the Roman pontiff could absolve him, except at the point of death, promulgated against all individuals proscribed, whether such accusation proceeded from their being initiated into any of the degrees of these societies or from being accessory to the initiation of others. His immediate successor, Benedict XIV, knowing the great interests involved and the necessity for this disposition, particularly as regarded the well-being of the Catholic religion and the public security, did, by a new decree, which, commencing in these words, "*Providias Romanorum Pontificum,*" published on the 18th of May, 1751, confirmed in its fullest extent the decree of his predecessor, not only in the insertion of it, word for word, in his own decree, but in explaining and expounding with his usual wisdom (§7) the motives which determined all the powers of the earth to prohibit Freemasonry, which motives it would be here unnecessary to enumerate, but of which the justness is demonstrated by experience, as they are well known to most enlightened people.

The foresight of these two pontiffs was not confined to this measure. They were not ignorant that the horror of crime and the thunders of the Church were ordinarily sufficient to convince and advantageously secure the consciences of the good, but that these means must, when directed toward the wicked, be aided by afflictive penalties. Hence the pontiff, Clement XII, by his edict, published by the cardinal Joseph Ferraro, his secretary of state, on the 14th January, 1739, inflicted the most severe temporal punishments against the contumacious, and ordered even, among other dispositions, their effective execution; and to which His Holiness, Benedict XIV, by his published decree, gave a new and additional force, charging all magistrates for the prosecution under these decrees to employ their most active and energetic assistants to fully execute the penalties therein prescribed.

However, in the general overthrow of the order of things which has been accomplished during the unhappiness of the Holy See and of the Church, these dispositions have been treated with impunity, notwithstanding their justness, wholesomeness, and indispensability; and the meetings and assemblies interdicted by them have had all sorts of facilities of communication, not only at Rome, but also in all parts of the pontifical states.

His Holiness, Pope Pius VII, wishing to administer a prompt and efficacious remedy to an evil which it is necessary to extirpate immediately, and opposing himself to the spread of this pernicious cancer ere it takes root throughout the state, does enjoin and ordain, and by this present edict makes known, to all his supreme wish, which should have the force of law, and should so serve in the tribunals of justice both civil and spiritual, in all countries, cities, lands, and provinces which appertain or n any wise recognize allegiance to the temporal dominion of the Holy Apostolic See.

By these dispositions it is intended to say that, for those who regard the pains and penalties to be incurred by these unhappy persons who, during the lapse of time which they have had wherein to have allowed their tendency to favor these assemblies to subside, (God forbid that this be not a question with our well-beloved subjects,) or at the present or in the future shall have the unhappiness to become, in any manner, a party to or connected with the Masonic or other similar assemblies, His Holiness relinquishes them entirely and without exception to the penalties and dispositions pronounced by the aforesaid decrees of his predecessors of glorious memory; hereby recalling and maintaining the same in their fullest force and tenor, as his special care.

The Holy Father, moved by the energetic sentiments of his pontifical zeal, and by the affections of his paternal heart, warns all the faithful who shall fall into this deplorable error to seriously consider the state of damnation into which they have plunged their souls, by incurring the penalty of major excommunication with which they are afflicted, as also of being deprived of all the advantages of communion in the Church, and to pass away in this condition to that awful tribunal where nothing is hidden, and before which vanish the vain supports which they may find to lean upon in this world. That they humble themselves, therefore, by a sincere repentance, and be taken once more into the arms of the holy Church, that compassionate mother who calls them, and who would receive them tenderly, to the end that she may reconcile them with the Father of all mercy, whom they have abandoned with ingratitude.

With regard to the outside world and the feelings which, under these imperious circumstances, should animate the general police of a well-ordered state, His Holiness wishes also to be understood as to the measures of clemency which may have been adopted for those times of disorder and impiety which preceded his happy return to the holy city, and the promulgation of this edict. Now this detestable pest has but to little if any extent infected the territory and the subjects of the pontifical state, but many individuals have allowed themselves to be entrapped by circumstances. The Holy Father deplores their unhappy blindness, and would remove them from its influence forever; it is for them, however, to render themselves worthy, by a return prompt and permanent, at least so far as concerns their outward conduct, for which every citizen is responsible to society. Otherwise, that they hold themselves in readiness to inform and not seek to hide from the knowledge of the government officers, the places wherein they may be assembled at any time, that the same may be watched; and that, to prevent the return of similar offenses, the names of the principal persons among them should be communicated to the chiefs of the tribunals, in order that, in case of relapse, the old offenses should be aggregated with the new. Nobody, then, at the present or any future time, can allege, for a pretext, that he has found no evil in this following of preparatory scenes, sometimes indifferent and sometimes ridiculous, but by which is artificially held in suspense the curiosity of the initiate, the better to dispose and enlist him in mysteries of greater atrocity. In consequence we decree, as follows, the measures which we believe necessary and just to prevent such offenses in the future:

1. In conformity with the dispositions of the edict of the 14th January, 1739, it is forbidden, in the first place, to all persons, as well in Rome as in the other parts of the pontifical domain, to continue, extend, renew or establish the said assemblies of Freemasons, or any similar society, whether instituted under ancient or modern denominations, or under the newly-imagined title of *Carbonari*, the latter of which have exhibited a pretended pontifical letter of approbation which bears upon its face evidence of its own falsity. It is also forbidden to all persons to act in the capacity of clerk or scrivener to these societies, or to assist in such capacity one single time, from any reason or pretext whatever; or to invite or solicit any body within the room wherein such assemblies may take place, or to

receive into his house, or any other place, any member of such societies, or bail or loan money to, or favor such persons in any manner whatever.

2. The dispositions of the present edict bear also upon those persons who may transgress its requirements, in entering into any relations direct or indirect, immediate or remote, with the aforesaid associations which are now established, or which may at any future time be established, outside of the pontifical state.

3. It is forbidden to all persons to have in possession or under their charge or care, within their dwelling or elsewhere, instruments, weapons, emblems, laws, records, patents, or any other thing used by or in any manner appertaining to the societies aforesaid.

4. Whoever shall know of the existence of such secret and clandestine meetings, or shall have been engaged therein, either as assistant or scrivener, shall be held as a witness against such assembly—for that which concerns the capital to the governor of Rome, and, for the other parts of the state, to the commandants of provinces or to the apostolic delegates. Those who, in view of the requirements of this article, shall be obliged to inform against and denounce such assemblies may be certain that they shall be held entirely blameless and unknown to the accused; that they shall be free from all penalty which they would otherwise incur as accessories or accomplices, and that they shall receive, at the expense of the delinquent, a recompense corresponding to the value of the information conveyed by them tending to convict the accused. And, upon this subject, His Holiness desires to be fully understood to announce and decide, that nothing improper or dishonorable can attach to a revelation to the proper authorities of that which may prevent to the government and to the state the consequences of a conspiracy menacing good order and religion itself; and that all oaths, in opposition to this principle, become a bond of iniquity, in

no degree binding, and leaving the obligated as free as if he had never taken such oath or obligation.

5. The penalties to be undergone by all who may contravene the dispositions of the present edict *shall be corporeal and afflictive,* and even *very serious,* according to the importance or malignity of the circumstances attending the transgression; and, in addition thereto, there shall attach *partial or entire confiscation of the property of the condemned, or fine, to be paid in money,* of which the judges and agents of the tribunals shall receive a part, in proportion to the extent of their labors and exercise of care in discovering and establishing the guilt of the delinquent, who shall be convicted according to law.

6. His Holiness especially orders and decrees that all edifices, such as palaces, public and private residences, or any other description of inclosed building, wherein an assembly of any of the societies aforesaid, under whatever name, may have taken place, shall be immediately, and without any delay being incurred to prove the offense, *declared confiscated,* and put in charge of the Government treasurer; and if the fact of offense can not be proved satisfactorily, then a fine may be levied and collected from the owner of the property.

7. Finally, it is enjoined upon all the chiefs of tribunals, as well as all local judicial authorities, to use every care in the execution of the dispositions of this edict; and should they, upon any point, entertain doubt as to the proper understanding of such dispositions, they shall address, without delay, the Cardinal Consalvi, Secretary of State, who will communicate to them the decision of the Sovereign Pontiff.

Done at the Secretariat of State, this 15th day of August, 1814

P. Card. Pacca,
Chamberlain of the Holy Church,
and Assistant Secretary of State.

PRIMITIVE
MASONIC LAWS AND CHARTERS.

In examining the basis of the charter of York, the text of which follows these observations—and which charter, although presented to the Masonic lodges as emanating from the king, could not be other than the production of the chiefs of the lodges—we find it imbued with the spirit of the first Christian communities, whose members, having separated themselves from those who were animated by totally different feelings, had surrendered themselves to such apostolic teaching as might present to them the pure doctrines of the new faith. The fraternal and uniformly equable principles of the ancient laws of the Roman colleges were very intimately known to those who preached the primitive doctrine of Christ. The teachings of the Hermit schools, the most prominent instructors at that time in the doctrines of the new faith in Britain, were found by the assembly of Freemasons convened at York so identical with the principles professed by them and their predecessors, for nearly five hundred years, that they did not believe it necessary to envelope such teachings in new forms, and the more so as already there existed great divergence among the various creeds of the new church, consequent upon the spirit of investigation which even at that early day had place. The assembly, therefore, adopted, as the basis of its new constitution, its ancient humanitarian principles, which were in entire harmony with universal morality, and in entire conformity with the early Christian doctrine.

The freedom from Roman Catholic influence of the Masonic lodges at this time exhibits itself in this charter in a very striking manner, in the prayer or invocation which begins thus: "All powerful and eternal God, Father and Creator of heaven and earth," etc. In this prayer we perceive no mention made of a Trinity, the Deity invoked being none other than the great Architect of the Universe, that great first cause recognized by the Noachidean doctrine, and the belief in the eternal existence of which can readily be concurred in by men of every confession.

The third and fourth articles of this constitution suppose, in fact, and with a degree of tolerance very humane, that the true religion, inborn in the hearts and consciences of all men, can not fail to harmonize characters the most diverse, seeing that it is to the conscience of every man, and to that alone, that the religion of justice strictly appeals. The other articles of this constitution or charter are confined to the consideration of the state of art, and to the simple and dignified oversight and arrangement of Masonic affairs proper, but always imbued with this same spirit, embracing humanity as an entire whole.

The constitution or charter of York is not only the basis of the British Masonic corporations, from the time of its promulgation to the separation of the lodges of Freemasons from the companionship of ordinary stone dressers and masons, (which virtually took place, as we have shown, in 1717,) and as the different ordinances, published under the reigns of different kings, relating to the affairs of these corporations, distinctly prove; but it became the model of the Masonic corporations, which, subsequent to its promulgation, were gradually organized upon the continent. The ancient corporations of Lombardy, of which the principal branches were at Como and at Pavia, and which should have conserved the laws as they were known to the ancient Roman colleges, adopted this charter immediately, as did also those of Germany and France; for we find it the basis of that printed constitution of the Freemasons of Strasburg which was adopted in 1459, and into which it is copied in all its extent, except the opening prayer, which, in accordance with the Roman Catholic influence of that period, is changed to read: "In the name of the Father, and of the Son, and of the Holy Ghost, and the Worthy Mother Mary," etc. This influence was inevitable; for the German Masons at this time were organized, and in great measure controlled, by the ecclesiastic architects of the convents and monasteries; and it was not until the latter part of the fifteenth century they obtained from the popes the confirmation of the exclusive privileges accorded at the beginning to the corporations of Lombardy. More favored than the latter, however, they were in receipt of special diplomas which made them free of royal edicts, and conceded to them the right of communicating directly with the popes in all matters connected with operations of any magnitude. This clerical influence, however, did not protect the clergy from complaint, rendered in a manner at once spirited and daring, against their tendency to vice and immorality; and this fact has come to us in the shape of numerous marks which figure upon the religious edifices of the period, sometimes symbolic, sometimes satiric, expressive of their criticism of the abuses of the clergy, as contrasted with their own religious belief and doctrine.

The charter of York also served as the basis of that constitution of modern Freemasonry which was adopted at London in 1717, and altered but in those points necessary to make that constitution correspond with the new object of the society, and the changes and developments wrought by the lapse of eight centuries in the condition of British law, customs, and usages. This constitution of the Grand Lodge of London has, in its turn, served as the model for the constitutions of all the grand lodges which have been formed since 1717 upon our globe; and it is only to be regretted that, among this great number of lodges, there should be found so few who have had the courage and the Masonic spirit to reform that part of the constitution of the Grand Lodge of England which provides for the predomination of that body, and replace it by a form in harmony with the fundamental principles of the Masonic institution.

The small number of documents which the Masonic society possess besides its charters, of which the most ancient have been destroyed, is easily accounted for by the fact that absolute silence had been imposed by oath upon every member of the society, solemnly binding them not to communicate in any manner except verbally, and in that way only to each other, any of the secrets confided to them; while, as an association, the society imposed upon itself similar restrictions. Its existence is engraved upon the fronts of the monuments of its art, in the ornaments and symbols reproduced upon the stones which have entered into their construction. True Freemasonry has never had any secrets other than those which have been connected with its art, its humanitarian doctrines, and its signs of recognition.

CHARTER OF YORK.

A. D. 926.

Fundamental laws of the Fraternity of Masons, based upon the ancient writings concerning the laws and privileges of the ancient corporations of Roman builders, as they were confirmed to Albanus, in the year 290, by the emperor Carausius, at his residence at Verulam (St. Albans), received, discussed, and accepted by the lodges of England, convoked for this object in a general assembly at York, in the year 926, by prince Edwin, son of king Athelstan.

The omnipotence of the Eternal God, of the Father and Creator of heaven and earth, the wisdom of his Divine Word, and the coöperation of his Spirit sent among us, may be with our commencement, and grant us grace so to govern ourselves in this life, as to obtain his approbation now, and, after our death, life eternal.[1]

* * * * * * *

Finally, peace is restored, and the bishop of Rome converts the Angles and the Saxons to the Christian faith, among which are found to be many native craftsmen in Britain who had been instructed by those vigilant old masters who remained in this country. Then they erected the churches of Canterbury (600) and of Rochester (602), and they repaired the ancient houses of God. Subsequently, the king, Charles Martel, sent masons from beyond the sea, upon the demand of the Saxon kings, and it was then that architecture flourished anew, *under the direction of the ancient master masons of Britain*. It is to be regretted that many Roman edifices should have been devastated upon the occasion of the incursions of the Danes, and that many documents and records of lodges, which in those times were held and preserved in the convents, should have been burnt, under like circumstances. But the pious king Athelstan (925), who has much esteem for the art, and who has established many superb edifices since the peace concluded with the Danes, has desired to make up this deficiency. He has ordained that the institution founded in the time of the Romans by St. Alban should be reëstablished and confirmed anew. It is in this intention that he has remitted

---

[1] After this introduction, or prayer, follows a long history, in two parts, of architecture in Great Britain and other countries; a historic abridgement of the art of building from the most ancient mythical times to that of Athelstan; and, after that, the particular rules which served as fundamental laws to the Masonic corporations. To convey an idea of the manner in which this history is written, we submit its closing passages. Its similarity of style to that which is given by Dr. Anderson, in his "Constitutions," etc., of 1723, will doubtless be remarked by the reader, and convince him of the truth of our statement, that the charter of York was the model as it was the basis of these "Constitutions," etc.

to his son Edwin (member of the association) an edict by which *the Masons can have their own government, and establish all proper rules to render their art prosperous.* He has also invited Masons from Gaul, and appointed some chiefs. Finally, he has examined the Greek, Roman, and Gallic institutions which these last have brought in writing with them, and compared them with those of St. Alban, and it is after such that all the Masonic corporations ought to be organized.

Behold, then, in the pious prince Edwin, your protector, who will execute the orders of the king, and who would encourage and exhort you no more to fall into past faults.

Thus, each year, the masters and the chiefs of all the lodges shall assemble themselves together, and make a report of all the constructions and ameliorations which they have produced, and such assembly shall be convoked here at York, and the chiefs shall proclaim the laws which are to be found in the ancient writings, and which they have found good, and useful to observe. The following are the obligations which you are to accept, and which, when you shall have accepted, you must promise to observe by placing your hand upon the holy book of the Gospel, which the chief shall present to you. Each master, also, must cause the same to be read in his lodge, and he must likewise cause the same to be read at the reception of a new brother, as he must require him, upon the authority of the Gospel, to observe the same.

Fundamental Laws of the Brother Masons.

Article I.

Your first duty is that you reverence God with sincerity, and submit to the laws of the Noachides, because these are the divine laws to which all the world should submit. For this reason you should also avoid following false doctrine and offending against God.

Article II.

You should be faithful to your king, without treason, and obedient to constituted authority, without deception, wherever you may find yourself, to the end that high treason should be unknown to you; but if you should be apprised of it, you must immediately inform the king.

Article III.

You should be serviceable to all men, and a faithful friend, to the extent of your ability, without disquieting yourself as to what religion or opinion they shall hold or belong to.

Article IV.

You should be, above all, faithful among yourselves, instructing each other and aiding each other, not calumniating one another, but doing to each other as you would have done to yourself; so that, according as a brother shall have failed in his engagement with his fellow, you ought to help him to repair his fault, in order that he may reform.

Article V.

You should assist assiduously at the discussions and labors of your brethren in the lodge, and keep the secret of the signs from all who are not brethren.

Article VI.

Each should guard himself against infidelity, seeing that without fidelity and probity the fraternity can not exist, and a good reputation is a valuable property. Also constantly hold to the interests of the master whom you may serve, and honestly finish your labor.

Article VII.

You should always pay honorably that which you owe, and, in general, do nothing that will injure the good reputation of the Fraternity.

Article VIII.

Furthermore, no master ought to undertake a work which he may be unable to perform, for, by doing so, he puts his fellows to shame. Masters, however, ought to demand that a sufficient salary be paid them, so that they can live and pay their fellow-workmen.

Article IX.

Furthermore, no master ought to supplant another, but leave him to finish the work that he has found to do; at least to the extent of his ability.

Article X.

Furthermore, no master ought to accept an apprentice for less than seven years, and not until after the expiration of that time ought he to be made a Mason, after the advice and consent of his fellows.

Article XI.

Furthermore, no master or fellow-craftsman should accept indemnity for admitting any person as a Mason if he be not free-born, of good reputation, of good capacity, and sound of limbs.

Article XII.

Furthermore, no fellow-craftsman ought to blame another if he does not know better than him whom he may reprimand.

Article XIII.

Furthermore, each master, when he is reprimanded by the architect (chief of the lodge), or each fellow-craftsman, when he is reprimanded by the master, should listen respectfully, correct his work, and conform to instructions.

Article XIV.

Furthermore, all Masons should be obedient to their

chiefs, and execute with good will that which may be ordered.

Article XV.

Furthermore, all Masons should receive their fellows coming from abroad, and who will give the signs; but they ought to be careful, and as they have been taught. They also ought to come to the relief of brethren who may need assistance, as soon as they shall learn, in manner as they have been taught, that such assistance is necessary, and the distance be within half a league.

Article XVI.

Furthermore, no master or fellow-craftsman shall admit into a lodge another who has not been received a Mason, to learn the art of dressing stones, or allow him to dress; neither shall he show him how to use square or compass.

These are the duties which he well and truly ought to observe. Those which shall yet be found good and useful in the future ought always to be written and published by the chiefs of the lodges; for all the brothers to learn the same, and to be sworn to their performance.

SUMMARY
OF
ANCIENT MASONIC CHARTERS.

ROMAN CHARTER, 715 B. C.

Containing the laws relating to and governing the Colleges of Builders, founded by Numa Pompilius. These laws are to be found on the 8th of the Twelve Tables of the Roman Laws, created in the year 451 B. C.

Charter of St. Alban, A. D. 290.

Based upon the ancient laws of the Roman colleges, as collected by Albanus, an architect, and sanctioned by the emperor Carausius.

Charter of York, A. D. 926.[1]

The original of this charter, preserved during many centuries in the archives of the grand lodge at York, was probably destroyed during the wars of the Roses, of which York was the theater. Its contents have come to us through the constitution of Edward III, which is simply a copy of it, with some additional articles concerning the rights and privileges of the grand masters, and their duties in connection with the government of the country. Authentic copies of this charter were to be found in the beginning of the 18th century, in the lodges of London and York, and one of them served the grand master, George Paine, as the basis of that collection which he had been charged to present to the new grand lodge, and which collection, as subsequently arranged and compiled by Dr. Anderson, was printed in 1723. In 1720, it is believed, members of the lodge of St. Paul, alarmed at the publicity that promised to be made of papers which they believed very private, burnt many documents, and, among the number, such copies of the charter of Edward III as they could discover.

Charter of Edward III, A. D. 1350.

Fundamental laws of the charter of York revised, with some slight changes, and the addition of some articles concerning the rights of grand masters, and the emoluments appertaining to their office.

---

[1] See preceding article.

Charter of Scotland, A. D. 1439.

This document, which is rather a diploma than a charter proper, recounts the privileges and the duties which attach to the position of grand master, that James II conceded, in 1430, to William Sinclair, baron of Roslin, and to his heirs—a position that the lodges of Scotland, through the representatives whose signatures it bears, recognize, under the terms of this instrument, to attach to the said Sinclair and his descendants. This document, as contained in a manuscript of the year 1700, may be seen in the Advocates' Library at Edinburgh.

The Charters of Strasburg, of 1459 and 1563.

These are entitled "Statutes and Rules of the Fraternity of Stone Cutters, founded upon those of the year 1275, revised, and their publication ordered by the Masonic Congress of Ratisbonne in 1464, and by that of Basle in 1563." The charter of York formed the basis of these charters. Many lodges in Germany are in possession of copies of the 1464 edition.

Charter of Cologne, A. D. 1535.

Laws and Doctrines of Philosophic Freemasonry, or a profession of their principles, rendered by a number of Masons assembled at Cologne in the year 1535. The Grand Lodge of Holland, at the Hague, is in possession of the original of this charter. It is upon parchment, written in Masonic characters rendered into the Latin of the middle ages. The authenticity of this document is disputed. Experts in the examination of ancient documents are divided, some believing it an original, and others a spurious production, written at a much later date than that which it bears. [See pp. 51 and 127 for further details as to this charter.]

Charter of Scotland, A. D. 1630.

This charter contains nothing beyond the confirmation of the privileges, etc., enumerated in that of 1439, granted to William Sinclair, baron of Roslin, by the lodges of Scotland. This confirmation was rendered necessary in consequence of the document of 1439 having been destroyed by fire in the conflagration of Roslin Castle, and the privileges acceded thereby having been subsequently denied to the heirs of "St. Clair of Roslin." The original of this charter or diploma is to be found in the Law Library at Edinburgh, with the copy of that which was burned.

Charter of London, A. D. 1717.

This charter, the basis of modern Freemasonry, is contained, as revised by George Paine, in 1717, from the charter of Edward III, in the work first published by order of the Grand Lodge of England in 1723, and which is generally known as Anderson's "Constitutions," etc.

EPITOME

OF THE

WORSHIPS AND THE MYSTERIES[1] OF THE ANCIENT EASTERN WORLD.

"The wise man brings all to the tribunal of reason—even reason itself."—*Kant.*

INTRODUCTION.

From amidst the thick darkness which covers their nature, we propose to deduce the origin and the history of the opinions which have been taught us by the instructors of the peoples, and which, imposed by the force of authority—inculcated by education and example—have been perpetuated from age to age, and their empire established by habit and inattention. But when man, enlightened by reflection and experience, turns to a close examination of these prejudices of his infancy, he immediately finds a crowd of disparities and contradictions which challenge his sagacity and provoke his reason.

Remarking the diversity and opposition of the beliefs which distinguish different peoples, he naturally doubts that infallibility each of them arrogate to themselves; and, falling back upon his own *sense* and *reason*, which must have emanated immediately from God, he conceives that the result of such a combination, when brought to bear upon this, as upon all other subjects, can not be a law less holy or a guide less certain than the mediatorial codes and contradictions of priests and prophets. For,

---

[1] See *Notes*, 1 to 38, illustrative of this text, commencing at page 384.

when he examines the fabric of these codes, he perceives that these laws, pretended to be divine—that is to say, immutable and eternal—are but begotten by circumstances of time, of place, and of person; and that they are derived from each other in a special order of genealogy, since that there is imprinted upon their derivation a resemblance of ideas modified by the taste of each people to more fully satisfy its own intelligence.

If we mount to the source of these ideas, we find they are lost in the night of time, in the very infancy of the human race, and that to reach them we must approach almost the origin of the world itself; and there, in the obscurity of chaos and the fabulous empire of tradition, they are presented to us, accompanied by a condition of things so superhuman that they interdict all approach to judgment or reason. But even this very superhuman condition resuscitates a train of reasoning which resolves the difficulty; for, if the prodigious existences which are presented to us in the theological systems of the world have really existed—if, for example, the metamorphoses, the apparitions, the conversations held by one or by several gods with man, traced in the sacred books of the Hindoos, the Persians, and the Hebrews, are historical events—it necessarily follows that the nature of these gods of the two former, or the one god of the latter, at that time differed entirely from that which now exists; that the men of our day have nothing in common with those of that period; and that such men as then existed exist no longer, nor have they existed for ages of time. If, on the contrary, these prodigious occurrences and existences have not really had place in physical order, we will naturally believe that they existed only in and were the creations of the imagination of those who penned them; and our own natures, capable as they are to-day of executing fantastic compositions, immediately recognize a reason for such monstrosities to appear in a history of the world.

No longer, then, does the student agitate himself with efforts to explain the why and the wherefore of the subjects of these pictures, or in analyzing the ideas they combine and associate; but, putting together all the circumstances that they allege, he thinks he ought to discover a solution conformable to the laws of nature. Yet he does not arrive at such a solution. He perceives that these recitals of a fabulous character have a figurative sense other than the sense apparent; that these pretended marvels are physical facts, simple as the elements of nature, but which, ill conceived and badly painted, have been denaturalized by accidental causes independent of the human spirit: by the confusion of the signs which were employed to represent the objects, by the equivocality of the words which described them, the degeneracy of language, and the imperfection of writing. He finds that these gods, for example, who play such singular parts in all the theological systems of the eastern world, are no other than the physical powers and play of the elements of nature, which, by the necessary mechanism of language, have been personified; that their lives, their manners, and their actions are nothing but the play of their operations, and that all their pretended history is nothing but the description of their phenomena, traced by such of their first observers as were competent to do so, and these descriptions taken in a literal sense by the ignorant and vulgar who understood not the spiritual or real sense, and which sense, in consequence, was by subsequent generations forgotten and lost; in fine, he will observe that all the theological dogmas about the origin of the world, the nature of God, the revelation of his laws, the apparition of his person, are nothing but the recitals of astronomical facts—nothing but figurative narratives of the movements of the solar system. It is by such a course of reasoning that one becomes convinced that the idea of the Divinity, which even at present is with us so obscure, was not, in its primitive state, but that of the physical powers of the universe, considered sometimes as multiples, by reason of their agents and their phenomena, and sometimes as a single being, by the complete connection of all their parts; in short, that the being called God has been sometimes the sun, sometimes the stars, the planets and their influences; sometimes the matter of the visible world—the universe as a whole; sometimes the abstract and metaphysical qualities of the universe, such as time, space, movement, and intelligence; and always with this result, that the idea of the Divinity has not been a miraculous revelation of invisible beings, but a natural production of the reasoning faculty, an operation of the human spirit, in which it has followed the progress and been influenced by the revolutions which have taken place in our knowledge of the physical world and of its agents.

Thus, then, the ideas of God and religion—ideas which absorb all others—have their origin in physical objects, and have been, in the mind of man, the product of his sensations, his cares, the circumstances of his life, and the progressive state of his knowledge.

Now, as the ideas of a Divinity had for their earliest models physical beings, it resulted that the Divinity was at first varied and multiplinary, as were the forms under which he appeared to act. Each being was a power, a genius; and in the eyes of the first men the universe was filled with innumerable gods. Then, as the affections of the human heart and its passions became enlisted, there was superinduced an order of division of these gods, based upon pleasure and pain, love and hate: the natural powers, the gods, or geni, were separated into benefactors and malefactors—workers of good and workers of evil; and hence the uniformity with which these opposite characters appear in all systems of religion.

SABEISM, OR SUN WORSHIP, AND ITS LEGENDS.

And first, among these systems may be found *Sabeism*, or the worship of the Sun.

From what has been already stated, it necessarily resulted that the theologies[2] of all the peoples, after those of the Hindoos and the Persians, down to those of the Egyptians and the Greeks, as we find them in their sacred books[3]—their cosmogonies[4]—were nothing but a system of physics—a tabular arrangement of the operations of nature, enveloped in mysterious allegories and enigmatic symbols.[5] Thus we find the worship of the Sun to be the primordial basis of all the worships and mysteries of antiquity. The Sun is, in fact, to every living thing upon the earth, the most attractive and interesting of all the heavenly bodies. He constantly directs our attention and attracts our admiration to the magnificence of the solar system. As the innate fire of the body, the fire of nature, author of light, heat, and ignition, he is the efficient cause of all generation; for without him there can be no movement, no existence, no formation. He is immense, indivisible, imperishable, and ever-existing. It is this want of light—it is his creative energy which has been felt by all mankind, who see nothing more frightful than his continued absence. Thus he becomes their divinity. His presence is the happy influence that revives every thing, and thus has he become the basis of all worship, whether ancient or modern—then directly, now indirectly—under symbolic forms; and the Brahma of the Hindoos, the Mithra of the Persians, the Osiris of the Egyptians, the Adonai of the Phenicians, the Adonis and Apollo of the Greeks are but representatives of the Sun, the principles of beauty, generation, and perfection—the images of that principle of reproduction which perpetuates and rejuvenates the world. The Sun is likewise the physical representative of that Supreme Being that the

Hindoos named *Baghaven*, the Persians *Zerouane-Akerene*, the Hebrews *Jehovah*, the Egyptians *Ammon* and *Youpiter*, the Greeks *Zeus*, the Mohammedans *Allah*, and the Christians *Lord* and *God*.

The legends upon which repose the worships of the ancients, like that of Hiram among the Freemasons,[6] are founded upon the apparent progress of the Sun, which, to speak figuratively, having ceased to ascend when he attains his highest point in the southern horizon, begins to descend, and finally is vanquished and put to death by darkness, which is represented in the same language as the spirit of evil; but, returning toward our hemisphere, he appears as the revived conqueror. This death and this resurrection thus prefigure the succession of day and night—of that death which is a necessity of life—of that life which is the child of death—in fact, of the combat of those two principles, directly the antagonists of each other, and which may be discovered every-where—in Typhon, in opposition to Osiris, of the Egyptians; in Juno, in opposition to Hercules, among the Greeks; in the Titans against Jupiter, in Ohromaze against Ahrimane, among the Persians; and in Satan, among the Christians, against God[7]—do we perceive the types of evil as opposed to good exhibited among the peoples of every clime and worship, whether they be more or less advanced in the scale of civilization.

THE MYSTERIES OF INDIA.
Bhuddist Priests, Brahmins, or Gymnosophists.

It is in India, the cradle of the human race, that the history of the world began; to that vast and fruitful country are we indebted for the first families of man; for no other portion of the world offered to him a dwelling-place so rich and so delicious. In these regions, the most elevated of the globe, may be found vegetation the most luxuriant, and the products of the soil the most useful and varied. All science, then, as well as all history, indicate the fact that it was in the highest lands of India man first appeared upon our earth.

The Hindoos adored in Bhagavan, the eternal being who, in his own person, fills all worlds, comprises all the forms and all the principles of living creatures, and who acted through Brahma, Vishnu, and Shiva the triple manifestation of himself. Menou, a Hindoo legislator, is the founder of the doctrine of the three principles or gods; the first of whom, named Brahma, being the creator (the sun of spring-time); the second, named Shiva, being the destroyer (sun of winter); and the third, named Vishnu, being the preserver (the sun of autumn, middle, or ripening sun); all three powers being distinct, but forming the representatives of an only god or power.

The doctrines of the immortality of the soul, of future rewards and punishments, and transmigration of souls after death, composed the secret teachings of the priests; and it was from them that the neighboring peoples borrowed these doctrines and the idea of an only all-powerful and eternal God. After Menou, the most anicent reformer of the religion of the Hindoos (sun worship) whose name has been transmitted to us, came Bhudda-Shaucasam, who announced himself as the mediator and expiator of the crimes of man (3600 B. C.), to whom succeeded, about 1000 years apart, three others of the like name, and of whom Bhudda-Guatama was the most celebrated (557 B. C.) These four moral reformers differently modified the principles of Menou, and deduced therefrom some mystic doctrines. Men of rare genius, without doubt, these four reformers were regarded by the Hindoos as incarnations of the Supreme intelligence, and, in this quality, divine. Following this example, the other nations elevated their great citizens and reformers to the rank of gods.

In India, as subsequently in Persia, Ethiopia, and Egypt, the priests were the sole depositaries of scripture knowledge, and exercised power without bounds; for every thing was founded upon religion. The great monuments of India[8] are immeasurably ancient. The immense grottoes, believed to be the most ancient Hindoo temples, the caverns of Elephanta, of Elora, of Salcette and of Carli, the temple of Kailaca—a most prodigious monument, cut in the bosom of a rock mountain, an open and roofless pantheon of Indian divinities—presuppose in the people who have produced them a knowledge of art and a degree of civilization far in advance of that of the Egyptians, as evinced in their works, and exhibit the magnificence of a highly enlightened people. All that mind could invent and heart appreciate of the grand and the beautiful, the noble and the elevated in conception, the elegant in design, and the perfect in execution, are found united in these groups of sanctuaries. These works recall far distant periods, going back to the night of time, and since which immense intellectual development has wrought a gradual change in the history of the Hindoo people. The *bas-reliefs* the figures, and the thousands of columns which ornament those Hindoo temples, scooped out and graven in the solid rock, indicate at least three thousand years of consecutive labor, and their present appearance indicates the lapse of a like number of years since they were finished.

The doctrine of Bhudda,[9] or Brahma, passed into Asia Minor and became the basis of the Persian worship, and subsequently that of the Ethiopian. Bhuddism penetrated into China; in that country Bhudda was called *Fot* (Bood), and his priests *bonzes*. His worship spread over all Thibet, where it was known as Lamaism, from the title of *Dalai-Lama* given to the supreme pontiff of the worship, who resided at Lahsa. The higher classes of the Chinese have generally adopted the doctrine of Confucius (Kong-Tseu), the reformer of the degenerate Bhuddism, or Lamaism, which, in our day, fills a part of China and Japan with the most ridiculous and revolting superstitions.

MYSTERIES OF THE PERSIANS.

Worship of Fire; worship of the Magi; worship of Mithra; worship of Zoroaster. (Assyria, Babylon, and Chaldea.)

The ancient Persians adored a being unrevealed, and who, self-consuming, self-absorbing, lost his individuality under the name of Zerouane-akerene. The worship of fire, among the Persians, preceded the worship of the sun. Hom, their first prophet, was its founder. After him came Djemschid, who brought them the worship of the Hindoos, founded upon the three principles or gods personified by Brahma, Vishnu, and Shiva, manifested by the principles of generation, preservation, and destruction. But the astrological doctrine of the magi was developed by time, and after they had acquired a general knowledge of the use of the globes, they observed vegetable and animal nature from a single point of view. Afterward, perceiving that this nature was susceptible of division, composed, as it was, of a principle of life which was the presence of the sun, causing heat and light, and a principle of death, caused by his absence, and consequent cold and darkness, they divided it. Then the priests, abandoning the system of the Hindoos, and admiring nothing but the principles of good and bad, or the struggle between light and darkness, life and death, supplied with their imagination a personification of each of these principles. The good principle received the name of Ohromaze and the bad that of Ahrimane. The priests of this worship, called *magi*,[10] were celebrated for their mathematical and astrological knowledge, which they had imbibed from their neighbors the Hindoos; all the occult sciences were practiced by them, and by the exercise of which they attained the name of being possessed of supernatural power, and, indeed, among the people and their kings, they were all-powerful. The most ancient and the most celebrated of their temples was that consecrated to Belus, god of light, at Babylon. This temple, called the Tower of Babel,[11] was erected by them, with a great number of other monuments, at Persepolis, at Ecbatane, and at Babylon,[12] and to-day is buried under a vigorous vegetation; but their mausoleums, cut into the everlasting rock, yet exist, to remind present generations of their science, their morals, and respect for their dead.

A reformer, named Mithra (2250 B. C.), born in Midia, overthrew among the Medes the system of the magi, and founded a worship more austere. Deified, Mithra was regarded by the Medes as the personification of Ohromaze and Ahrimane, the divine duality of the Persians, and consequently became himself the object of a special worship. The mysteries of this worship were celebrated in subterranean temples, as among the ancient Hindoos, and were called "Retreats of Mithra."[13] The aspirants for the privileges of these mysteries submitted to proofs so terrible that many became insensible. In the initiation there were seven distinct degrees. Mithra, regarded as the sun-god, is represented in Persian art under the form of a young man with a Phrygian bonnet, armed with a sword, which he is in the act of plunging into the throat of a bull.[14]

Another religious legislator, named Zoroaster, (1220 to 1200 B. C.) who came after Mithra, renewed his worship. Zoroaster[15] having found it necessary to quit his country, then subjugated, retired with some disciples into a cavern of the neighboring mountains in Persia, which he thereupon consecrated to Mithra (the sun), creator of all things. This retreat he partitioned into geometrical divisions, which represented the climates, the elements, the plants, and, in fact, imitated the universe. There he studied, with his disciples, the movements of the heavenly bodies and the mechanism of the world. His theology was that of the Hindoos—the study of nature and its original contriver in the movements of the celestial and terrestrial bodies.

Zoroaster, after having passed twenty years in this retreat, returned to his country, and began to promulgate his doctrine at Bactria, the capital of the kingdom of the Bactrians. There he became their prophet, and the grand master of the priest magicians, who were then more powerful than ever. He reassembled the remains of the ancient laws of the magi, which dated back to the highest antiquity, and formed with his own theology a new body of doctrines, contained in the Zendavesta,[16] of which he is the author, and which became the religious code of the Medes and the Bactrians, and, subsequently, that of the Persians, Chaldeans, and Parthians.

The great institutions of the primitive races—those learned corporations in which they took so much pride—have disappeared; and we are pained to recognize, in the unhappy Parsees of to-day, disgraced and persecuted, the scattered remains of an ancient enlightened people, and the last inheritors of much that was glorious. Nevertheless, by the practice of some simple symbolic ceremonies, to which the Parsees themselves are no less attached than their opponents are zealous to proscribe, we are assured that they are the successors of the ancient Mithraiques. Their meetings—imitations of those of the retreat of Mithra—have caused them to be accused, according to modern custom, of the most atrocious crimes, and to receive the epithet of *Guebers*—a term that, from all time, designates that moral turpitude attributed by the ignorant to the members of all secret societies.

MYSTERIES OF ISIS AND OSIRIS.

Ethiopia and Egypt.

The worship of the ancient Ethiopians and Egyptians is a sort of *pantheism*, in which all the forces of nature are personified and deified. Superior to all the gods, however, is placed a God eternal and infinite, who is the source of all things.

The most ancient trinity of the Ethiopians and the people of that part of Abyssinia adjoining Arabia, the blest, and of Chaldea, was *Cneph-Ammon* (Youpiter), god creator, of which the emblem was a ram; *Ptha* (Brama-Theos), god of matter, primitive earth, the emblem of which was an egg or sphere; *Neith*, god of thought, the emblem of which was light, which germinates all things. Thus was comprised a triple manifestation of an only God (Iehov), considered under three connections, the creative power, goodness, and wisdom—merely the Hindoo trinity, with other names.

The number of super-celestial gods augment by following those of *Fta*, the god of fire and of life, representing the generative principle; of *Pan-Mendes*, the male principle, and *Athor*, the female principle, which are the auxiliaries of *Fta*, generator; of Frea or Osiris, the sun; of Pijoh or Isis, the moon. But, besides these which we have mentioned, they had twelve other celestial and three terrestrial gods. Of these the celestial gods were called respectively Zeous, Rempha, Artes, Surot, Pi-Hermes, Imuthes, corresponding to the mythological Jupiter, Saturn, Mars, Venus, Mercury, and one other known but to the Ethiopians, viz.: Starry Heavens. These were all male gods; and after them came six females, viz.: Rhea, or the Earth, the Moon, Ether, Fire, Air, and Water. Then, in the third rank, were placed the terrestrial gods, viz.: Osiris, genius of good, whose brother, Typhon, was genius of evil; Isis, the wife of Osiris, and Horus, their son, and genius of labor. This trinity subsequently became the principal object of the Egyptian worship. Isis, as the generative divinity, was sister and wife of Osiris, the sun-god, and figured as the earth, which latter, in fact, is simply rendered productive by the action of the former; and hence that worship which, at a later day, merged, in the eyes of other nations, into bestiality, though held very sacred among the Egyptians.

The gymnosophist priests who came from the banks of the Euphrates in Ethiopia brought with them their science and doctrines, and cultivated the knowledge of them among this people. They formed colleges known as the colleges of the priests, the principal one of which was at Meroë, the capital of Ethiopia, and the mysteries of their worship were celebrated in the temple of Ammon [17] (You-piter), renowned for its oracle. Ethiopia, then a powerful State,[18] and which had preceded Egypt in civilization,[19] had a theocratic government. The priest was more powerful than the king, and could put him to death in the name of the divinity. The magnificence of the ruins of Axom, with its obelisks, hieroglyphics, temples, tombs, and pyramids which surround ancient Meroë, with a hundred other pyramids in Ethiopia, are evidently of a period prior to that of the eight pyramids of Ghizze,[20] near ancient Memphis, and which date from the sixth to the twelfth centuries before Christ. It then becomes certain that the Theban priests went forth from the colleges of Ethiopia. Hermes,[21] priest king, the deified author of the castes, and who, bound by the legends of Isis and Osiris, taught to the Egyptian priests the occult sciences. The priests committed to the only books which at this early time were to be found among them the sciences called to-day hermetic, and to them added their own discoveries and the relations which were made to them by their sybils.[22] They occupied themselves particularly with the more abstract sciences, by which they discovered those famous geometric theorems which Pythagoras subsequently obtained a knowledge of from them, and by which they calculated the eclipses three hundred years before Cæsar, and regulated the year that we call Julian. Sometimes they would descend to engage in some practical researches upon the cares of life, and read to their associates the fruits of their investigations; and sometimes they would, in the cultivation of the fine arts, inspire the enthusiasm of the people who constructed the avenues of Thebes,[21] and the Labyrinth, the admirable temples of Karnak, of Dendorah, of Edfou, and of Philae; those people who sat up so many monolythic obelisks, who hollowed, under the name of lake Moeris, an ocean, to guarantee fertility to the country; who constructed subterranean cities,[24] the wonders of which equaled those of any sunlit city; who, prodigal of their labor, and caring for the residence of the dead as much as for that of the living, hid under ground the colors of the most beautiful paintings in the tombs of their ancestors; to this people, finally, whose monuments delight in colossal proportions only because the ideas which inspired them were grand.

The wisdom of the initiates, the high degree of morality and science which they taught excited the emulation of the most eminent men, irrespective of rank or fortune, and induced them, notwithstanding the terrible proofs to which they had to submit, to seek admission into the mysteries of Isis and Osiris.

The worship and the mysteries of the Egyptians at first passing through Moses among the Hebrews, where the primitive god of the Ethiopians, *Youpiter* or *Jupiter*, received the name of *You* or *Jehova*,[25] and Typhon, the genius of evil, was called Satan, and represented under the form of a serpent, passed subsequently into Phenicia, where they were celebrated at Tyre.[26] There the name of Osiris was changed to Adonai or Dyonisius, which also meant the sun

Then these mysteries were successively introduced into Assyria, Babylonia, Persia, Greece, Sicily, and Italy. In Greece and in Sicily Osirus took the name of Bacchus, and Isis that of Ceres, of Cybele, of Rhea, and of Venus; while at Rome she was called the good goddess.

MYSTERIES OF THE HEBREWS.

This worship was founded by Moses, a son of the tribe of Levi, educated in Egypt and initiated at Heliopolis into the mysteries of Isis and Osiris, of which he became a priest. Informed of his origin, he forsook the court of Pharaoh at the age of forty years, and, it is said, passed the subsequent forty years of his life in exile, after which he abode with the Hebrews. Driven from Egypt,[27] under the reign of Amenophis, because they were infected with the leprosy, this people elected Moses as their chief. He became their legislator and adapted to the ideas of his people the science and philosophy which he had obtained in the Egyptian mysteries; proofs of this are to be found in the symbols, in the initiation, and in his precepts and commandments. Moses passes for the author of the first five books of the Old Testament of our Bible, or the Pentateuch.[28] The wonders which Moses narrates as having taken place upon the mountain of Sinai, upon the occasion of his reception of the tables of the law, are, in part, a disguised account of the initiation of the Hebrews. Moses formed with his priests a separate caste or class, who were alone possessed of scientific knowledge, and who stole the knowledge of their sacred books from the "gentiles;" who forbade their own people to enter their dwellings, and punished with death the Levites who, being placed in charge of the sanctuary, neglected that charge night or day, as also the timorous person, unknown to their order, who should dare to approach the entrance to the tabernacle. Moses wished to separate the Hebrew nation from every other, and to form of it an empire isolated and distinct; and, for this purpose, he conceived the design of fixing its foundation upon the religious prejudices of his people, and erecting around them a sacred rampart of opinions and rites. But in vain did he prescribe the worship of symbols; the dogma of an only God,[30] which he taught, was equally the Egyptian god, the invention of the priests of whom he had been a disciple. In the construction of the tabernacle, likewise, Moses observed the manner of the Egyptian priests, and its proportions and measurements were an imitation of their system of the world. This tabernacle was divided into three parts: the holy of holies, the sanctuary, or court of the priests, and the court of the people. Within the holy of holies none but the high priest was admitted, and he but once a year; within the sanctuary, or court of the priests, none but the Levites and the priests; and the people were confined to the outer court of the people. Moses, who had, not only in the construction of the tabernacle, but in many other matters, imitated the symbolism of the Egyptian priests, sought, however, to efface from his religion all that recalled the worship of the stars,[31] but in vain; for a crowd of its characteristics remained. The twelve signs of the zodiac were but repeated on the banners of the twelve tribes, and on the twelve jewels in the urim of the high priest; the Pleiades, or seven stars, in the seven lights of the sacred candlesticks; the feast of the two equinoxes, openings and closings of the two hemispheres, the ceremony of the lamb or celestial ram; finally, the name of Osiris, preserved in his canticles, and the ark or coffer, imitated from the tomb within which this god was inclosed, all served as witnesses of the birth-place of these ideas and to their extraction from an Egyptian source. Subsequently we find in the construction of the temple at Jerusalem but a repetition, on a grander scale, of the same proportions and measurements which characterize the tabernacle of the fugitive Israelites in the wilderness.

All the doctrines of the Hebrews were not written; they had oral traditions which were known to but a few among them. These traditions were preserved in the *arcanæ* of divers secret Hebrew associations—among the *Kasedeens*, the *Therapeutes*, and the *Essenians*.[32] It was in this latter sect that Jesus Christ, the founder of Christianity,[33] was educated, and wherein he imbibed the sublime doctrine which he revealed to the world. In the beginning, the initiation into the mysteries of Christianity,[34] which was composed of three degrees, was similar to that of the pagans, and the connection between the Christian legend and all those by which the priests allegorically represented the annual revolution of the sun are very striking, as they can not fail to excite the thought that the disciples of Christ had prefigured his birth, his life, and his death under solar appearances.

Among the secret societies who best resisted the universal tendency, and transmitted an uninterrupted succession of the mysteries, after the fall of Jerusalem, should be placed, after the Essenians, those called the *Cabbalists*, who have never ceased to exist, and of whom there are to-day numerous branches among the Jews of the eastern world, in Germany and Poland.

MYSTERIES OF ELEUSIS.

The worship of Ceres, the goddess of agriculture, (the Isis of the Egyptians,) was established at Eleusis, after its initiation in Egypt, toward the fifteenth century before Christ. This worship was founded upon that of Isis and Osiris and the Egyptian gods, and subsequently became, among the Greeks, so fertile in imagination, the beginning of the errors of Polytheism. By the abuse of the figurative language, the phenomena of the heavens and the earth became, in this system, a record of human events, births, marriages, adulteries, combats, flights, and murders—in a word, fables and myths, in the representation of which their original meaning was lost.

The initiation into the mysteries of Ceres was divided into greater and lesser mysteries; the latter were celebrated at the time of the vernal equinox, and the former at that of autumn. The lesser mysteries were a preparation for the greater mysteries by the young, of purifications and expiations, to be followed by a historic interpretation of the fables. In submitting to them, the youths were purged of the polytheism of their principal fancies and immoralities. In the greater mysteries was begun the allegorical explanations of the most abstruse mysteries. By the initiation into these greater mysteries, polytheism was destroyed at its root, and the doctrine of the unity of God and the immortality of the soul was taught, together with a revelation of philosophical truths more extended, more profound, and more mysterious than those of any other known worship. In lapse of time these mysteries were altered and corrupted, like all the others.

MYSTERIES OF SAMOTHRACIA.

The worship and the mysteries of the Cabires (Egyptian gods), established in the island of Samothracia, by Orpheus (1330 B. C.), were originally from Egypt, having passed through Phenicia and there taken other names. The four principal gods of this worship were called, in Samothracia, Axieros, Axiokersa, Axiokersos, and Cadmillus. The initiation was based upon a solar legend, like that of Osiris and Typhon, Adonis and Venus. Subsequently the names of the Cabires was again changed to that of Ceres, Proserpine, Pluto, and Mercury (Hermes).

MYSTERIES OF THE PHRYGIANS AND PHENICIANS

The mysterious worship of the Phrygians in honor of Cybele (the goddess of nature or reproduction), and of her son Atys, had two temples, the one upon Mount Ida, and the other in the city of Pessinuntus. Atys was a deified priest, who taught the Phrygians the mysteries of nature. He represents the sun, and in the legend which forms the basis of the initiation, he is subjected to the same fortune as Osiris and Adonis—always the fictitious death of the sun and his resurrection.

The worship and the mysteries of Adonaï, among the Phenicians and the Syrians, is identically the same. Cybele there takes the name of Adonaï, (of which the Greek was Adonis,) always indicative of the goddess Nature, who, as widow of him in whom she had her joy and her fruitfulness, renews with haste her vows at that moment when, conqueror of darkness, he has again assumed the heat and brilliancy which he had lost.

The feasts which were celebrated among the Phrygians and Phenicians took place at the time of the equinoxes. Their most celebrated temples are to be found at Balbek[36] and at Tadmor, known to-day as Palmyra.[37]

MYSTERIES OF THE ROMANS.

The most ancient god of Latium—brought from the East, however, and not aboriginal with the Latins—was Janus[38] or Saturn, who took many names and many attributes, without ceasing to be recognizable. He presided over revolutions in nature, and particularly that principal and most remarkable of all revolutions, the year or circle of the months. He is sometimes regarded as *time*, sometimes as *astronomy*, and often the *sun* himself, the great regulator of the seasons and the cycles. Janus, with his double face, with the keys which also served him as a more distinctive mark, represented the end and the beginning of a period: he opened and closed the year, which commenced with the equinox of spring-time and ended with the shortest day in December. The eagle, given as a companion to Janus (the St. John of the Freemasons), is the famous cock of the Guebers.

The myth upon which reposed the worship of Janus or Saturn was very mysterious, and was explained but to the highest initiates. The saturnalian feasts were the celebration of the winter solstice.

The worship of the good goddess, which followed that of Janus, was brought to Italy by a colony of Phrygians. The mysteries of Eleusis were imported by Roman initiates from Greece. This worship, adopted and propagated by the great legislator Numa Pompilius, became the basis of the religious ceremonies and the initiation of the colleges of builders founded by him.

The mysteries of Mithra and of Isis, which, under the reign of the emperors, were established at Rome, were polluted with corruption from the beginning, and at many times their abuse caused them to be proscribed. They were a bad resemblance of the old Egyptian or Persian ceremonies from which they were borrowed, and like them only in name.

Rome, which had received from the East gods, legends, and religious customs, having become the conqueror of that vast country, returned to it more than one new divinity and new forms of worship.

SYBILS AND ORACLES

The Clairvoyants and Ecstatic Somnambulists of Our Day.

The name of sybils was given by the Egyptians to those priestesses who were endowed with the gift of *clairvoyance*, whether acquired naturally or by means of magnetism, and who revealed to the priests a portion of the secrets of nature; while the name of oracles was given to those who, plunged into an ecstatic state, predicted future events. There were generally reckoned ten of the first, viz.: the Cumean, the Lybian, the Chaldean, the Delphic, the Erythrean, the Samnian, the Lucanian, the Phrygian, the Hellespontine, and the Tiburtine. The most famous oracles were those of Fta at Memphis, of Frea at Heliopolis, of Isis at Bubaste, of Trephonius at Boetia, of Amphiarus at Oropus, of Fortune at Atium, of Serapis at Alexandria, of Hercules at Athens, of Æsculapius at Epidorus and Rome, of Pan at Arcadia, of Diana at Ephesus, of Minerva at Mycenus, of Venus at Paphos, of Mercury at Patras, of Mars in Thrace, of Apollo at Delphos, at Claros, and at Miletus, and of Minerva at Saos. The Jews also had their sybils, of whom Huldah, in the time of the king Jesias, was the most celebrated.

THE
LEGISLATORS, REFORMERS AND FOUNDERS
OF
WORSHIPS AND MYSTERIES

INDIA.

Bhudda (celestial man), the three most ancient reformers to whom this name is given by the Hindoos, and whose memory they venerate, belong to that period when, according to the hieroglyphic accounts, the stars were personified. The Hindoos had arrived at a high degree of civilization a long time before the advent of Menou, as is proven by their monuments; and centuries before his coming they communicated their science and their astronomical knowledge to the Persians and the Egyptians, seeing that the establishment of the Hindoo zodiac belongs to the century that elapsed between 4700 and 4600 B. C. The three first Bhuddas should then be classed at from 5500 to 5000 B. C.

Menou, Hindoo legislator, founder of the doctrine of the three principles or God, (the sun of spring-time, the sun of summer, and the sun of winter,) all three distinct and yet forming an only god, which were subsequently personified by Brahma, Vishnu, and Shiva (the sun in its three forms of action as the source of all triune systems). The doctrine of Menou is contained in the book, the Manava-Dharma-Shastra, of which a second Menou was the author. He disappeared between 4000 and 3800 B. C.

Bhudda-Shaucasam, reformer and founder of the doctrine contained in the Bhagavat-Ghita, the most ancient book of the Hindoos, which goes back to from 3400 to 3100 B. C. This reformer is considered as the first incarnation of the Supreme Being, and at the same time the mediator and expiator of the crimes of men. He disappeared between 3600 and 3500 B. C.

Bhudda-Gonagom, a reformer, who was also deified as the second incarnation of the Supreme Being. He disappeared about the year 2366 B. C.

Bhudda-Gaspa, a reformer, who was also deified as the third incarnation of the Supreme Being, and who disappeared about the year 1027 B. C.

Bhudda-Somana-Guatama, a profound philosopher, author of the Guadsour (Khghiour), which contained his doctrines and precepts. He was deified as the fourth incarnation of the Supreme Being. Born in the year 607, he died in the year 557 B. C.

PERSIA.

Hom, founder of the worship of fire, between 3800 and 4000 B. C.

Djemschid, founder of the worship of the sun, between 3700 and 3600 B. C.

The Magi Priests, reformers of the worship of the sun, about 3600 B. C.

Mithra, reformer of the degenerate worship of Media, deified as the representative of the sun, about the year 2550 B. C.

Zoroaster, prophet of the Persians, grand master of the Magi priests, and founder of an austere worship, between 1400 and 1300 B. C.

ETHIOPIA.

Osiris, warrior and civilizer, reformer of the worship of Cneph-Ammon, of Fta and Neith, the most ancient trinity of the Abyssinians, above which was placed an eternal and infinite god (Ichov), who is the source of all things. Osiris appeared about 5000 B. C.

Priests of Meroë, founders of the worship of the twelve celestial gods, the same being the powers of nature, the planets, and the elements personified. The celestial bull, which opened the equinox of spring-time (from between the years 4580 and 2428), was the object of a special worship. The temple of Meroë was erected between the years 4700 and 4600 B. C., and the zodiac of the temple of Esneh was erected between 4600 and 4500 B. C.

EGYPT.

Priests of Egypt, reformers of the worship of the twelve celestial gods of the subordinates—You-piter, supreme god—to the trinity of Osiris (god of the sun), of Isis (the moon), and Horus their son (the earth), which became the principal worship of the Egyptians. Besides the worship of the bull (Aphis), they also celebrated that of the celestial ram, which, in its turn, and by the precession of the equinoxes, opened the equinox of spring-time, from the years 2540 to 323 B. C. These priests ruled in Egypt between the years 4200 and 4000 B. C.

Hermes, priest-king, reformer, author of charts and occult sciences, who taught and introduced them into the mysteries. His doctrine and science are contained in the books which bear his name. He disappeared in the year 3370 B. C.

Moses, a priest of Heliopolis, chief and legislator of the Hebrews, founder of their worship, and the doctrines of which are contained in the first five books of the Old Testament; born in 1725 B. C.

GREECE.

Orpheus, philosopher and legislator, initiated in Egypt, founded the mysteries in the island of Samothracia in the year 1530 B. C.

Triptoleme, son of the king Eleusis, initiated in Egypt, founded the mysteries of Eleusis in the year 1500 B. C.

Pythagoras, a celebrated philosopher, initiated into the mysteries of Egypt and Persia, founded at Crotona his mysterious school in which were united the characteristics of worship and initiation. His doctrine embraced all the sciences known in his time.

ROME.

Numa Pompilius, the great legislator and civilizer, introduced into Rome the mysteries of Greece. He founded the colleges of architects and builders (the cradle of Freemasonry) in the year 715 B. C.

CHINA.

Confucius (Kong-Tseu), a celebrated philosopher and reformer of the ancient degenerated worship. His philosophical religious doctrine is contained in the Chou-King, the morals of which are among the most beautiful. Born in 600, he died in the year 550 B. C.

Lao-Tseu, a reformer, who preached a mystical doctrine which is to be found in the Tao-te-King (primitive reason), was considered by the Chinese as an incarnation of the Supreme Being. He lived in the sixth century B. C.

JUDEA.

Jesus Christ, founder of Christianity, and author of evangelical morality, breathing peace and charity, the most simple and the most sublime which has ever been taught to man. It is to be found contained in the books of the New Testament. His birth gives us a new era, and his death took place A. D. 33.

NOTES.[1]

1.—*Worships and Mysteries.*

Mystery properly signifies that portion of the doctrines of any form of religion for which reason is unable to account, and which, consequently, is dependent upon faith. Thus the life of Christ presents, as we find it in the Evangelists, many mysteries, as the incarnation, the nativity, his passion, his resurrection; and, in the earlier days of Christianity, baptism, the eucharist, and the other sacraments, were all called holy mysteries. In the mysteries of Egypt and that of some other nations, the exterior worship, the processions, etc., all that took place outside of the temples, and in the courts of the temples, constituted the feasts. In these every body, even the slaves, could participate and assist; but the initiated alone were admitted to the mysteries.

2.—*Theology of the Ancients.*

All the ancient peoples having their colleges of priests and astronomical and astrological books cotemporaneously, were alike affected by the discoveries, disputes, errors, or perfections that in all times have agitated the students of nature and philosophy. The more we have penetrated, during the past thirty or forty years, into the secret sciences, and especially into the astronomy and cosmogony of the modern Asiatics, the Chinese and Burmese, the more we are convinced of the affinity of their doctrine with those of the ancient peoples from whom they have descended.

Indeed, in certain particulars it has been transmitted more pure than with us, because it has not been altered by those anthropomorphical innovations which has denaturalized every thing else. This comparison of ancient and modern theology is a fruitful mine, which, if entered in the right spirit and with the mind divested of prejudice, will afford a crowd of ideas equally new and historically correct; but to appreciate and welcome them, it is necessary that the reader should also be free from prejudice.

When the Chaldean priests were seeking a general knowledge of the earth's phenomena, as appears by researches in the books of the Hindoos, they studied from a single point of view the

---

[1] Serving to illustrate and authorize sundry passages of the text of the *Worship and the Mysteries of the Ancient Eastern World.*

operations of vegetable and animal nature, and, concluding upon the hypothesis that the sun represented the principles of heat and life, and darkness those of cold and death, from this basis, true as it most assuredly is, have been built up the innumerable fictions which disfigure all ancient theology.

3.—*Sacred Books of all the Peoples.*

The Vedas or Vedams are the sacred books of the Hindoos, as the Bible is ours. They are three in number, the Rig-Veda, the Yadjour-Veda, and the Sama-Veda. These books are very rare, being written in the most ancient known language of the Brahmins. Those who count four Vedas have added the Attar-Veda, which treats of the ceremonies. In addition to these books there are a collection of commentaries upon them which is called the Oupanashada, of which a French translation has been published by Anquetil Duperron, under the title of Oupen akhat—a curious book in this, that it gives an idea of all the others. The date of the Vedas, twenty-five to thirty centuries before our era, and their contents, show that all the reveries of the Greek metaphysicians came from India. After the Vedas come the Shasters, to the number of six. They treat of theology and science. Then, to the number of eight, come the Pouranas, which treat of mythology and history. The book entitled Manava-Dharma-Shastra contains the laws of the first reformer Menou.

After the sacred books of the Hindoos come those of the Persians, the Sadder and the Zend-Avesta, the religious code of the Bactrians, Assyrians, Chaldeans, and Medes. They contain the doctrine of Zoroaster. The Boun-Dehesch, the book of Genesis of the Parsees, successors of the ancient Persians, is a compilation of the ancient laws of the Magi. After these come the five books of Hermes, the priest-king of Egypt, founder of the castes, who lived about 3370 B. C. Then the *Taote-King* and *Chou-King* of the Chinese, the first of which contains the metaphysical doctrines of Lao-Tseu, and the second the sublimely moral doctrines of Kong-Tseu (Confucius.) Then, in point of time, may be ranked our Bible, the Old Testament of which contains the cosmogony of the Jews and Christians, and the laws of Moses, with a history of the Hebrew people, and the New Testament of which contains the Gospels of evangelical morality, peace, and charity of Jesus Christ, the founder of Christianity. The Koran of Mahomet, containing the precepts and doctrine transmitted by him to his followers, would necessarily follow, to make the list complete.

Egypt is the only country which possessed a complete code of doctrines of great antiquity. Clement of Alexandria has transmitted to us a curious detail of forty-two volumes which were carried in the processions of Isis. "The chief, or singer," says he, "carries an instrument symbolical of music, and two books of Mercury (Hermes), one of them containing the hymns of the gods, and the other the list of the kings. After him comes the horoscopist, observer of the seasons, carrying a palm-branch and a time-piece symbolic of astrology. He has to know by heart the four books of Mercury (Hermes), which treat of astrology: the first of which treats of the order of the planets, the second of the ising and setting of the sun and moon, and the third and fourth, of their movements in their orbits, and the aspects of the stars. Then comes the *sacred writer*, having some feathers stuck into his hair, and in his hand a book, an ink-bottle, and a reed for writing, according to the manners of the Arabs. This officer has to understand the language of the hieroglyphics, the description of the universe, the courses of the sun, moon, and planets, the division of Egypt into thirty-six districts, the course of the Nile, the sacred ornaments, the holy places, etc. Then comes the stole bearer, who carries the gauge of justice, or measure of the Nile, and a chalice for libations, together with ten volumes containing the sacrifices, the hymns, the prayers, the offerings, and ceremonies of the feasts. Finally appears the *prophet*, carrying in his bosom, but exposed, a pitcher. He is followed by those who carry the bread, as at the marriage feast of Cana. This prophet, in his position as keeper of the mysteries, must know by heart the ten volumes which treat of the laws, of the gods, and of all the discipline of the priests, etc., which are outside of the forty-two volumes. Thirty-six are known by these persons, and the other six, treating of medicine, of the construction of the human frame, of sickness, of medicaments, and of surgical instruments, belong to the *pastophores*.

4.—*Cosmogonies.*

The recital of the creation of the world, as it is expressed in Genesis, is to be found almost literally in the ancient cosmogonies, and more particularly in those of the Chaldeans and Persians, proving that the Jews but borrowed it from these people. That our readers may judge for themselves, we here give a faithful translation—much more faithful than that which we have from the Greek and Latin:

"In the beginning, the gods (Elohim) created (*bara*) the heavens and the earth. And the earth was confused and desert, and darkness was upon its face. And the wind (or the spirit) of the gods acted upon the face of the waters. And the gods said: Let the light be! and the light was; and he saw that the light was good, and he *separated* it from the darkness. And he called the light *day* and the darkness *night;* and the night and the morning were a first day.

"And the gods said: Let the void (*ragia*) be (made) in the middle of the waters, and let it separate the waters from the waters; and the gods made the void, separating the waters which are under the void, and he gave to the void the name of heavens; and the night and the morning were a second day.

"And the gods said: Let the waters under the heavens collect themselves into one place, and let the dry earth appear. That was so, and he gave the name of earth to the shallows and the name of sea to the body of waters; and he said: Let the earth produce vegetables with their seeds; and the night and the morning were a third day, etc.

"And the fourth day he made the bodies of light (the sun and the moon) for to *separate the day from the night*, and to serve as signs to the times, to the days and to the years. At the fifth day he made the reptiles of the water, the birds and the fishes. At the sixth day the gods made the reptiles of the earth, the four-footed and wild animals, and he said: *make man to our image* and to *our* likeness; and he created (*bara*) man to his image, and he it created to his image, and he them created (*bara*) male and female; and he rested himself at the seventh day.

"Now, it rained not upon the earth, but an abundant moisture arose from the earth, and sprinkled all its surface.

"And he had planted the garden of Eden (anteriorly or to the East); he there placed man. At the middle of the garden was the *tree of life* and the tree of the *science of good and evil*. And from the garden of Eden went forth a river which divided into four streams, called Phison, Gihon, Tigris, and Euphrates.

"And *Jehouh the gods* said: It is not good that man should be alone, and he sent him a sleep, during which he withdrew from him a rib, of which he built the woman," etc.

If such a recital as this was presented to us by the Brahmins or the Lamas, it would be curious to hear our doctors censure these anomalies. What a strange condition of physics, they would say, to suppose that light existed before the sun was created, before the stars, and independently of them, and, what is more offensive to reason, to say that there was a night and a morning, when the night and the morning were nothing but the appearance or disappearance of that body of light which makes the day.

We quite agree with our doctors on this subject, and can no more than they control these anomalies; but because the account resists the laws of sober reason, we must turn to the consideration of the allegorical explanation of it. The reader is, no doubt, surprised with this translation of the *creative gods;* nevertheless, such is the value of the text, in the view of all grammarians. But why this plural governing the singular? Because the Jew translator, pressed by two contradictory authorities, had no other way of relieving his embarrassment. The law of Moses prescribed but an only God, while the cosmogonies, not alone of the Chaldeans, but of nearly all known nations, attributed to the secondary gods, and not to the one great God, the creation of the world. The Jewish translator had not courage enough to reject a word sacred to law and usage. Among the Egyptians these Elohim were the deacons, and, among the Persians and Chaldeans, the geni of the months and the planets, as we are informed by the Phenecian author Sanchoniathon.

Now observe how the Vedas, the sacred books of the Hindoos, account for the creation of the world.

"In the beginning there was an only God, self-created and self-sustaining. After having passed an eternity in the contemplation of his own being, he desired to exhibit his perfections beyond himself, and created the matter of the world. The four elements having been produced, but, as yet, in a confused condition, he blew upon the waters and they became inflated like an immense bubble in the form of an egg, and which, developing, became the vault and orb of heaven which surround the world. Then, having made the earth and the bodies of living beings, this God, essence of movement, to animate these bodies, distributed among them a portion of his own being, and this portion, as the soul of all that respire, being a fraction of the universal soul, *can not perish*, but must pass successively into divers bodies. Of all the forms of living beings, that which pleased the Divine Being most was the form of man, as approaching the nearest to his own perfections; so that when a man, by an absolute abnegation of sense (reason) becomes absorbed in the contemplation of himself, he attains to the discovery of the deity, and actually becomes divine. Among the incarnation of this species which God has already clothed, the most solemn and holy was him who appeared in the twenty-eighth century in Kachemire, under the name of Bhudda, to teach the doctrine of the new birth and the renunciation of self." And the book, retracing the subsequent history of Bhudda, continues to say:

"That he was born from the right side of a virgin of the blood royal, who, in becoming a mother, did not cease to be a virgin. That the king of the country, disquieted by his birth, wished to destroy him, and therefore massacred all the male children born at that time; but that he, saved by shepherds, took refuge in the desert, where he remained until he had attained his thirtieth year, when he commenced his career of enlightening man and casting out devils. That he performed a number of the most astonishing miracles; spent himself by fasting and self-denial the most severe; and that, in dying, he left to his disciples a book which contained his doctrine"— a doctrine which is summed up in the following passages:

"He who abandons his father and mother to follow me, says Bhudda, becomes a perfect Samaneen (celestial man).

"He who practices my precepts to the fourth degree of perfection acquires the faculty of flying through the air, of moving heaven and earth, and of prolonging or shortening his life.

"The Samaneen despises riches; he uses but the most simple necessaries; he mortifies the body; his passions are mute; he desires nothing, is attached to nothing; he meditates my doctrine; he patiently suffers injuries; he bears no hate toward his neighbor.

"Heaven and earth shall perish, says Bhudda; despising, then, your body, composed as it is of four perishable elements, think of nothing but your immortal soul.

"Hearken not to the promptings of the flesh; the passions produce fear and vexation. Subdue the passions, and you will annihilate fear and vexation.

"He who dies without embracing my religion, says Bhudda, returns among men until he does practice it."

The Vedas of the Hindoos which contain these accounts of the creation, and the incarnation and doctrine of a deified man, are believed to have existed at least three thousand years before the Christian era; and this doctrine, presenting, as it does, the most striking analogy to that of Christ, as we find the latter in the gospels, was spread throughout the eastern world more than a thousand years before Jesus Christ appeared upon the earth. In reading these passages does it not seem more probable that the teachings of Christ have come to us rather through Hindoo than Hebrew writings?

5.—*Symbols.*

From that moment when the eyes of the people who cultivated the earth were directed toward the heavens, the necessity of observing the stars, of distinguishing them singly or in groups, and of naming them properly, in order to designate them clearly, became apparent. Now this object, seemingly so simple, was really very difficult; for the celestial bodies, being nearly identical in form, offered no special characteristic whereby to distinguish them by name; this on the one hand, while, on the other, the language of these people, from its very poverty of words, had no expressions for new and metaphysical ideas. But the ordinary spring to genius, *necessity*, surmounted these difficulties. Having remarked that, in the annual revolution of the earth, the periodical appearance and renewal of terrestrial products became constantly associated with the rising and setting of certain stars, and their position relatively with the sun, a fundamental form of comparison was established, which, by a purely natural mechanism, connected in thought those terrestrial and celestial objects which were connected in fact; and, applying to represent them the like signs, they gave to the stars singly, and to the groups which they formed, the names of the terrestrial objects to which they responded.

Thus, the Ethiopian of Thebes, called the constellation of *inundation*, or water-flow, that under which the Nile began to rise; the constellation of the ox or *bull*, that under which he began to till the earth; the constellation of the *lion*, that under which that animal, driven from the desert by thirst, showed himself upon the banks of the river; the constellation of ripe corn, the *virgin harvester*, which brought the return of the harvest; the constellation of flocks and herds, or the *ram*, that under which these precious animals gave birth to their young; and, in this manner, the first part of the difficulty was removed.

As to the other part, man had remarked in the beings around him qualities distinct and peculiar to each species. By a primary operation he selected the name of this quality to designate the being it distinguished; and, by a secondary operation, he found an ingenious means of generalizing these characteristics, in applying the name thus invented to all things which presented similar traits or actions, and thus he enriched his language with an enduring metaphor.

Thus the same Ethiopian, having observed that the return of the inundation, or overflow of the Nile constantly corresponded with the appearance of a very beautiful star, which at this time was always to be seen in the direction of the head-waters of that river, and which seemed to warn the laborer to prepare for its overflow, he likened this action to that animal which, by its timely barking, warns of approaching danger, and he called this constellation the dog, the barker (Sirius). In like manner he named, from the movement of the crab, the constellation *cancer*, which marks that point in the heavens when the sun, having attained the tropical limit of his course, returns by a backward and sideward movement similar to the motion of that animal. By the title of wild goat he distinguished the constellation *capricornus*, which marks the point at which the sun, having attained the greatest altitude in his course, pauses, and, as it were, grips the height, as the wild goat grips the surface of the giddy height to prevent his fall. By the title of the balance, he distinguished the constellation *libra*, which marks the period when, as to time, day and night are equally divided or balanced; and by the name of *the scorpion*, he distinguished that constellation which marks the period when certain winds carry the burning sand across the plain, and cause it to strike with a stinging pain, resembling the stroke of a scorpion. And in this manner, also, was applied the name of rings, rounds, or serpents to that form by which was expressed an orbit, circle, or complete revolution of the planets, whether taken singly or in groups, according to their connection with the operations of the field and cultivation of the earth, and the analogies that each nation found presented by their agricultural labors, and the peculiarities of their soil and climate.

From this process, it resulted that the inferior and terrestrial beings became intimately associated with the superior and celestial; and this association each day gained strength from similar constitution of language and mechanism of mind. Using this natural metaphor, they said: The *bull* scatters upon the earth at his coming (spring-time) the seeds of fertility; he returns with abundance and the creation of plants. The *ram* delivers the heavens from the evils of winter; he saves the world from the serpent (emblem of the rainy season), and he brings back the reign of good (the joyful summer-time). The scorpion cast his venom upon the earth, and scattered sickness and death, etc., and thus of all similar appearances.

This language, then understood by all the world, presented nothing inconvenient; but, by the lapse of time, when the calendar had been regulated, and it became no longer necessary for the people to observe the heavens, the motive that prompted these expressions was lost, and their allegorical sense being suppressed, their use became a stumbling-block to the understanding of the people. Habituated to join symbols to their models, this misunderstanding caused them to confound them. Then these same animals, which in thought had been placed in the heavens, in fact returned to earth, but clothed in the livery of the stars, and imposed themselves upon the people, as possessing the influences attributed to them by their sponsors; and the people, believing themselves within sight and hearing now of their gods, readily addressed to them their prayers. They demanded of the animal ram an abundance of the influences which attended the appearance of the celestial ram; they prayed the scorpion no more to scatter his venom, entailing sickness and death, upon the earth; they reverenced the crab of the sea, the scarabæus of the mud, the fishes of the river; and, by a series of enchanting but vicious analogies, they lost themselves in a labyrinth of consequent absurdities.

Here we behold the origin of that antique and fanciful worship of animals, and how, by the progress of ideas, the characteristics of divinity passing to the most vile brutes, was fashioned that vast, complicated, and learned theological system which, beginning on the banks of the Nile, was carried from country to country by commerce, war, and conquest, and invaded all the ancient world and which, modified by time, circumstances and prejudices, yet exhibits itself among hundreds of peoples, and exists as the intimate and secret basis of the theology of even those who scornfully reject it.

In the projection of the celestial sphere, as traced by the astronomer priests of that time, the zodiac and the constellations, disposed circularly, presented their halves in diametrical opposition.

The hemisphere of winter is the antipodes of that of summer—adverse, opposed, contrary they stood toward each other. From a metaphorical and necessary, this position passed into a moral sense; and to angels were opposed adverse angels, who, having revolted, were cast out, and became their enemies. In this manner, from being simply an astronomical history, the account and representation of the constellations came to be a political history. Heaven was a country subject to and wherein events transpired s upon the earth. And as at that period monarchy was the prevailing style of government upon the earth, a similar style must obtain in the heavens; and of the hemisphere of summer, empire of light, and heat, and joy, and peopled with white angels, it was apparent the sun was king—a brilliant, intelligent, and good creator; so, opposed to summer was the hemisphere of winter, that underground empire of darkness, cold, and sadness, peopled with black angels, giants, and demons, and having for ruler the prince of darkness, who was recognized by the different peoples by the name of that sign whose appearance was attended with most of evil among them. In Egypt this was from at first the *scorpion*, being the first sign of the zodiac after the *balance*, and, for a long time, chief of the signs of winter. Afterward it was the *bear*, or the polar ass, called Typhon, otherwise Deluge, by reason of the cold rains which inundated the earth during the rule of this constellation. In Persia, at a later time, it was the *serpent*, who, under the name of Ahrimane, formed the basis of the system of Zoroaster; and it is this same serpent who, among the Jews and the Christians, tempted Eve, the celestial virgin, and brought sin into the world, as also the serpent of the cross, and which, in both cases, is the emblem of Satan.

6.—*Hiram of the Freemasons.*

The long history of Hiram, the architect of Solomon's temple, which forms the basis of the degree of master mason, is represented by most authors, and in all the lectures which prevail in the lodges in France and elsewhere, as a fact, and not as an allegorical fiction, while in all the higher degrees it is positively recognized as the former. A very limited knowledge of the history of primitive worships and mysteries is necessary to enable any person to recognize in the master mason Hiram, the Osiris of the Egyptians, the Mithras of the Persians, the Bacchus of the Greeks, the Atys of the Phrygians, of which these people celebrated the passion, death and resurrection, as Christians celebrate to-day that of Jesus Christ. Otherwise this is the eternal and unvarying type of all the religions which have succeeded each other upon the earth. In an astronomical connection, Hiram is the representative of the sun, the symbol of his apparent progress, which, appearing at the south gate, so to speak, is smote downward and more down ward as he advances toward the west, which passing. he is immediately vanquished and put to death by darkness, represented, in following the same allegory, by the spirits of evil; but, returning, he rises again, conqueror and resurrected.

7.—*The Angels.*

The names of the angels and of the months, such as Gabriel and Michael, Yar and Nisan (March and April), etc., as we are informed by the Talmud, were brought from Babylon by the Jews. Beausobre. in his *History of the Manicheans*, (vol. 2, p. 624,) proves that the saints of the calendar are imitations of the three hundred and sixty-five angels of the Persians; and Jamblicus, in his *Egyptian Mysteries*, (sec. 2, chap. 3,) speaks of the angels, archangels, and seraphims, etc., like a true Christian Catholic.

8.—*The majestic Monuments of the Hindoos.*

The most celebrated Hindoo temples, cut in the bosom of the solid rocks, are to be seen in the vicinity of Bombay and in the island of Ceylon. That of Elora is considered the most curious. No one can regard without astonishment a whole mountain of porphyry, covering nearly six miles of superficial measurement, converted into a mysterious succession of halls, chambers, antichambers, vestibules, courts, saloons, etc. In the midst of these apartments is the great temple of Elora, a single apartment of five hundred feet in circumference, hollowed out of the solid granite. Its side galleries are supported by sculptured pillars; its walls are polished, and cut into which are forty-four niches extending from floor to dome, and in which stand forty-four gigantic statues of Hindoo divinities. But the monument of all others the most prodigious in Hindostan is the temple of Kailaca, cut in the solid rock, and without roof or dome, cut open to the heavens. In the vicinity of this temple there are ten or a dozen similar but much smaller sanctuaries. At Dhoumar, in the province of Malva, may be counted seventy of these temples, the circuit of which compose what may be called a troglodyte city. Upon the coast of Coromandel, not far from Madras, there are a series of labors of the same kind not less remarkable.

9.—*Bhudda, (Bood, Boudd.)*

This is the name that the Hindoos have given to the seven religious legislators who have successively revived and reformed the laws and doctrines of their first civilizer of this name, and of whose existence there remains no account, except in the traditions of fabulous time. Of these seven reformers the four last alone are known by their doctrines, which are contained in the sacred books of the Brahmins, called Vedas, or Vedam. These are Bhudda-Shaucasam, whose doctrine is found in the Bhagavat-Ghita, and who lived between the years 3200 and 3100 B. C. Bhudda Gonagom, who appeared 1366 years B. C. Bhudda-Gaspa, who appeared 1027 years B. C.; and Bhudda-Somana-Gautama, who lived 557 years B. C. A final Bhudda is to appear five thousand years after the death of the last named.

All these reformers are considered by the Brahmins to have been incarnations of the Supreme Being, and as such they are adored by eastern people under different names. Among the Chinese, for example, Bhudda becomes Fot and Fota. that people having neither *b* nor *d* in their language.

10.—*The Magi.*

The Asiatic rendering of this word signifies *consecrated man*, a man devoted to the worship of God, exactly as the Hebrew Nazarene or Hindoo Samaneen; consequently the word *magic* originally signified the practice of worship, and *magi* those who devoted themselves to science and worship.

11.—*Temple of Bel, or Tower of Babel.*

By consent of the best authors and the geography of Strabo and Berose, there existed a Babel or Babylon—that is to say, a palace or temple—consecrated to (the sun) Bel, titulary god of this country, from whom it received its name of Babylonia, and whose temple, according to ancient Asiatic usage, was the rallying point, the goal of pilgrimage, the metropolis of all the people who submitted to his laws; and, at the same time, this temple was the asylum, the fortress of the priests, the astronomical studio of this astrological judiciary, who were celebrated and who rendered famous the name of Chaldean in far-distant ages of the past.

According to Philo, the Phenician, as cited by Josephus, the foundation of this temple, or tower of Babel (Belus), was laid between the years 3195 and 3190 B. C. The oriental name of Babel for Babylonia signifies a court; and there existed from that time a primitive court or palace, which that wonderful woman, Semiramis, surrounded with her vast constructions when she conceived the project of building a great commercial and military city, even that Babylon which she surrounded with immense walls and fortifications, and which she ornamented with castles, palaces, temples, and bridges, and in the midst of which caused to be erected for the priests that famous tower or pyramid called the Tower of Babel.

This opinion is supported by Ktesias, who, in speaking on this subject, says: "When Ninus attacked Babylonia, the city of Babylon, which at present exists, was not then built." The same historian states "that Semiramis, inspired by her love of grandeur, and desirous of surpassing the glory of the kings who preceded her, conceived, between the years 1195 and 1180 B. C., the project of building in Babylonia an extraordinary city. For this purpose she gathered from all parts a multitude of architects and artists of all kinds, and she provided great sums of money and all the necessary materials; then, having made in the extent of her empire a levy of two millions of men, she employed them to form the surroundings of the city by constructing a wall of three hundred and sixty *stadia* (about twenty miles) in length, flanked with many towers, and leaving the river Euphrates to flow through the midst of the inclosure.

This assemblage of men, levied under the laws of statute labor, of divers colors, clothing, habits, worships, and language, presented a strange spectacle. More than eighty dialects were spoken in the vast empire of Semiramis; and the assembling of bodies of men, each of whom spoke one of these dialects, naturally engendered that confusion which, when these men came to close quarters in the building of the tower, naturally might and probably did increase to a degree most inconvenient, and hence the real source of the vicious origin the Jews have given to the word Babel, or Babylon.

In the account which Herodotus gives of the war of Kyrus against Babylon, he says: "But after the subversion of Nineveh she became the capital of Assyria." And then, from ocular evidence, he describes this immense city, the extent and dimensions of its walls and fortifications, the direction of its streets, the palace of the king, and the great temple of Bel; and, in describing the latter, he says: "The center of the city is remarkable for the temple of Jupiter Belus, which actually yet exists. (Herodotus wrote 480 years B. C.) It is square, regularly built, and its court is fastened by gates of brass. Each square of the inclosure is two stadia in length (about two hundred yards). In the middle of this inclosure is to be seen a massive tower, one stadium on each square of its base, and one stadium in height." Thus, then, the temple of Belus in Babylon was a strong place, a sort of citadel, resembling the temple of the sun at Balbek, and most of the other temples of the ancients, who, for the better security of the priests and the sacred treasures which had been gathered within their temples, protected them by high and strong outer walls. "Upon this tower," continues Herodotus, "there is erected a second, upon the second a third, and others above that to the number in all of eight, each being proportionately smaller in its dimensions than the other, and giving to all the appearance, when viewed from a distance, of a pyramid. In the highest of these towers is a chapel;

in this chapel a great bed, well furnished; and near this bed a table, the surface of which is gold." What was the object of this singular edifice? What could it be but an astronomical observatory? This chapel, in the highest tower, elevated to a height of nearly fifteen hundred feet above the surface of the earth, served the astronomer priests as a look-out from which to observe the solar system, and to learn exactly the movements of the heavenly bodies. The golden table, upon which was no doubt traced a map of the solar system, enabled them to direct their studies, and the well-furnished bed served for repose when wearied by observation and close application of mind. No other furniture was necessary, and no other was there. Astronomy was the important mystery which they guarded with jealous care. since it was the basis of that theocratic, religious, and political power which enabled the priests, by predictions of eclipses and other solar actions, to astonish both kings and people, and lead them to believe that they held immediate communication with the gods.

Behold, then, what was the object of that famous tower of Babel, the hearthstone of that Chaldean science vaunted by the most ancient Greeks as being, even in their time, very ancient. And yet this grand and simple monument, as described by the perverted historians of the Jews, has given birth in modern times, as well as in what we call ancient, to the most singular, extraordinary, and grossly-stupid accounts of its origin and of its object.

12.—*Ecbatana, Babylon, Persepolis.*

Of the immense citadel of the palace of the king of the Medes, Ecbatana, which was seven hundred yards in outer extent, nothing remains but rubbish, in vast quantities, to indicate palace, citadel, or capital of the Median people; while an enormous quantity of ruins, heaped about in the most frightful confusion, mark to-day the spot where Babylon, the city of palaces, once stood. Ranks of columns, separated by ravines, mark the streets; while masses of rubbish show where once stood the grandest edifices. In the plain where once stood the city of Persepolis, and which extended behind Tschil-Minar, nothing remain to mark the greatest architectural conceptions of any age, but ruins of column and wall, pillar and porch, heaped in undistinguishable confusion. The most important ruins are upon the terraces of the mountain of Rachmed, upon the locality where stood the palace of the kings of Persia, and upon the flank of that mountain there appear many funereal monuments of the Persian kings, such as that of Darius, son of Hystaspe, and of Xerxes. Under the terraces which support the palace of Persepolis, there extend vast subterranean passages, of which it is impossible to verify the destination, purpose, or extent, but which, in the opinion of the Arabs, conducted to the mountain of sepulture, nearly six leagues distant, and in which may be found the four royal tombs, cut in the rock to the height of one hundred feet, and which are believed to be those of Darius Nothus, Artaxerxes I, Ochus, and Artaxerxes II, or Memnon.

13.—*The Caves or Retreats of Mithra.*

Zoroaster, according to Justinius, composed in the cave or grotto of Mithra, which he inhabited for twenty years, a great armillary sphere to aid him in the study of the heavenly bodies. According to Celsus, it was after this model that the Persians, in the ceremonies of Mithra, represented the double movement of the fixed stars and the planets, with the passage of the soul in the celestial circles or spheres. To describe the properties or attributes of the planets, they exhibited a scale or ladder composed of seven steps, or stages, with an eighth at the upper extremity. The first step was composed of lead, and indicated Saturn; the second, of tin, denoted Venus; the third, of copper, denoted Jupiter; the fourth, of iron, denoted Mars; the fifth, of divers metals, denoted Mercury; the sixth, of silver, denoted the moon; the seventh, of gold, denoted the sun, then the highest heaven. Without doubt this was the ladder of Jacob's dream, and upon which he saw angels ascending and descending; and yet all these Egyptian and Chaldean ideas and allegories existed centuries before Abraham, Isaac, or Jacob. From thence comes the custom of consecrating caves to the celebration of the mysteries, a custom that we find among the Christians of the first centuries; and from thence have Plato and Pythagoras designated the world as a cave or cavern.

In the mysteries of the ceremonies of Mithra, as they subsequently became developed, we find all the principal ceremonies observed in administering the rites and sacraments of the Christian church, even to the slap on the ear given by the bishop in "confirmation." The priests of Mithra promised their initiates, through confession and baptism, remission of their sins, and a life of happiness and delight instead of pain and torment. They also celebrated the oblation of bread, the image of the resurrection; and, finally, their baptism of infants, application of extreme unction, confession of sins, celebration of the mass (the mysteries), and many other practices analogous to those of the Christian religion, all proving that what we have to-day as religious ceremonies are but the modified prolongation of religious opinions and practices which prevailed centuries before our era.

14.—*In the throat of a Bull.*

This is the bull of the zodiac, which sometimes, by the precession of the equinoxes, has occupied the place of the ram. This is the bull that we find represented in India as opening an egg with his horn, and who already had opened the age of creation, that is, the vernal equinox. This is the bull Apis, adored by the Egyptians, as subsequently the Israelites adored the golden calf. The bull or ox of the Apocalypse, with his wings, symbolic of his celestial nature, has a similar origin; while the lamb of God, immolated as the bull of Mithra, for the salvation of the world, is nothing more than an emblem of the sun in the sign of the celestial ram, which in an after age opened, in his turn, the vernal equinox, and was moved to deliver the world from the reign of evil enjoyed by the serpent or great adder, mother of winter and emblem of Ahrimane, the evil spirit or Satan of the Persians. It will be observed that the contemporaneous worship of the sign *Taurus* by the Egyptians, Persians and Japanese, indicates a communion of ideas among these peoples at this time; and of this worship there has descended to us nothing but the May festival of the fat ox, crowned with flowers.

15.—*Zoroaster.*

The religious legislator called Zoroaster by the Greeks, and Zerdast or Zerdust by the Orientals, was born, according to Herodotus, about 1250, and according to other authors between 1400 and 1300 B. C., in Aderbijan (ancient Media). He commenced to promulgate his doctrine at Bactria, the capital of the kingdom of the Bactrians, about the year 1220 B. C., after a "retreat," according to Pliny, of twenty years' duration. He propagated a new system of theology, which he pretended, according to the custom of the time among men of his profession, to be the only true theology, and revealed of God. Zoroaster, according to the recital of the Parsees, perished with many of the magi, in the last battle fought at Ninus by the king Keshtasy, one of his numerous disciples, who wished to convert his subjects and the neighboring kings.

According to Anquetil Duperron, the principal collection of the traditions of the Parsees concerning Zoroaster is the book entitled Zerdust-Narnah, which, they say, was translated from the ancient Pehlevic idiom into the modern Persian by Zerdust-Behram, scribe and Persian priest, about the year 1176 of our era.

Theodore of Mopsuestus, in his work concerning the magi of Persia, explains the doctrine of Zoroaster in the following remarkable passage: "He is one of those who believes in the existence of two gods—one good, the other evil. He names them Oromaze and Ahrimane, and has said that one is best represented by *light*, and the other by *darkness*. The Persians maintained that Oromaze was formed from light the most pure, and Ahrimane from darkness the most obscure Oromaze made six other good gods like himself, and Ahrimane six wicked ones like himself. Oromaze then made twenty-four gods, which he placed in an egg; but Ahrimane, after making twenty-four evil gods, broke the egg, and thus caused that blending of good and evil which exists in the world.

Theopompus believes, in accordance with the magii books, that one of these gods ruled three thousand years, during which the other is deposed; the succeeding three thousand years they fight and reign equally; but finally the evil one has to succumb, and is forever destroyed.

In reducing these allegories to their natural and simple sense, it is apparent that Zoroaster, after his physico-astronomical meditations, considered the world, or the universe, governed by two principles or powers—the one of production, the other of destruction; that the first governed during the six thousand parts, or six months of summer, or from the vernal equinox to that of *Libra*, and the second during the six thousand parts or six months of winter, or from *Libra* to *Aries*. This division of each sign of the zodiac into a thousand parts is found among the Chaldeans; and Anquetil, who has happily explained the allegory, speaks, in more than one place, of the twelve thousand of Zoroaster as of the twelve months of the year.

The egg is, as is well known, the emblem of the world among the Egyptians; the twenty-four gods are the twelve months divided into *quinzaines*, or fortnights—the one of increase, the other of decrease—a usage that is found among the Hindoos as also among the Romans, and the result is that the whole system of Zoroaster was nothing but a system of astronomy and astrology, like all other ancient systems; and that its disciples, notwithstanding this fact, received and applied this system, especially among the Jews, for moral and political purposes, and this application led to the most singular consequences, and resulted in a system entirely new.

16.—*Zend-Avesta.*

This sacred book of the Persians was mostly written in immense and very complicated characters, and covered twelve thousand skins of parchment, manufactured from the hides of oxen.

17.—*The Temple of Ammon.*

The construction of this celebrated temple, according to Herodotus, took place between the years 2400 and 2300 B. C., and its ruins may be found in the oasis of the Lybian desert. Alexander the Great visited this temple, and caused himself to be proclaimed, by its oracle, son of Jupiter Memnon.

18.—*Ethiopia, then a powerful State.*

During many centuries Egypt was governed by the Ethiopian sacerdotal caste, of Arab origin, which was replaced by the caste of warriors. This revolution was brought about by Menes I, king of the first Pharaonic dynasty, and took place, according to some authors, nearly 6000 years B. C. Menes is said to have built ancient Thebes, then the capital of the country.

In the earliest known times Egypt consisted but of the Theban country. At that time Middle Egypt and the Delta composed a part of the Mediterranean gulf. The Nile, carrying in its overflows an enormous quantity of mud, in time filled up that portion of the gulf into which it emptied, and eventually created an immense tract of swampy land, which, by the aid of man, seconded by nature, was drained, and formed what then became known as Middle Egypt, or Heptanomis, and Lower Egypt or the Delta.

19.—*Egypt in Civilization.*

The chronology of Egyptian history, according to Diodorus, Manethon, and Herodotus, the last of whom visited Egypt 460 years B. C., is as follows:

B. C. 13300.—From this date until the year 4600 B. C., when the zodiac was constructed and set up in the temple of Esneh, there occurred four periods, to the first of which is ascribed the reign of the gods, to the second the first historic period, during which Egypt was inhabited by a barbarous people, and was confined to the Theban country, or Upper Egypt; to the third, the second historic period, during which began to be formed the states and kingdoms, of which there were thirty, forty, or more, and the colleges of the priests were established; and to the fourth, the third historic period, when the different states were consolidated into three large kingdoms, comprising Upper Egypt, or the Theban country, Middle Egypt, or Heptanomis, and Lower Egypt, or the Delta. To this latter period belongs the construction of the temple of Esneh, and the establishment of the worship of the bull Aphis, symbolical of *Taurus* or the sun, which at this time began to mark the vernal equinox. Subsequent to this period there reigned a series of unknown kings, eighteen of them being Egyptians.

B. C. 3360.—Hermes, priest king, observes the star Aldebaran.

B. C. 2454.—The sun enters the ram,[1] and from this date *Aries*

---

[1] By the precession of the equinoxes, allowing 71 years for each degree and 50 seconds for each year, it is estimated that 2130 years are required for the sun to pass through a zodiacal sign. Thus, in the year 4586 B. C., that body having entered *Taurus*, it was not until the year 2455 that he passed through that sign, and entered *Aries* in 2454. From that time until the year 323 B. C., the latter sign marked the vernal equinox.

becomes the constellation of the vernal equinox, and the worship of the ram begins.

B. C. 2400.—Foundation of the temple of Ammon in the desert of Lybia.

B. C. 2400 to 2300.—Construction of the monuments of Karnak and the avenue of the Rams.

B. C. 2056.—Construction of the zodiac of Denderah.

B. C. 1810.—Invasion of the kingdom of Memphis (Middle Egypt) by the pastoral Arabs, presumed to be the tribes of Tamoud, Madian, Amalek, etc.

B. C. 1800.—The pastoral Arabs found Heliopolis.

B. C. 1556.—Tethmos expels the Arabs.

B. C. 1500.—Foundation of the new Memphis.

B. C. 1450.—Re-union of all Egypt under one monarchy.

B. C. 1430.—Construction of Lake Moeris.

B. C. 1420.—Construction of the cities of Ramasses and Heroöpolis, by the Hebrews.

B. C. 1410.—Under the king Amenophis the Hebrews are driven out of Egypt, and, under the direction of Moses, whom they elect as their chief, they are organized into a nation.

B. C. 1390 to 1350.—Reign and conquests of Sesostris.

B. C. 1080.—Ramsinite orders the construction of the great obelisk at Heliopolis.

B. C. 974.—Sesach, king of Egypt, ransoms Jerusalem.

B. C. 790.—During the past two hundred years a succession of obscure kings governed Egypt, and their reign ends with the capture of Thebes by the Carthaginians.

B. C. 750.—Seva, the Kushite, or Ethiopian, invaded Egypt, and reigned with justice and wisdom for nearly twenty-five years.

B. C. 722.—Sethon, priest of the temple of Vulcan, governs Egypt, now fallen into anarchy.

Between Menes and Sethon three hundred and forty-one kings in succession governed Egypt. After him a series of kings ruled whose names are all known.

20.—*Pyramids of Ghizza.*

"During twenty years," says Herodotus, "one hundred thousand men worked daily to build the great pyramid or tomb of the king Cheops, who, like all Egyptians, attached much importance to the construction of his eternal home." The eight pyramids which surround ancient Memphis, the principal seat of the mysteries of Isis and Osiris, communicated with the twelve temples which are found in this vast city. Of this group of pyramids, three are particularly distinguished, which are the largest in Egypt as they were the last which were constructed. At Meroë, the ancient seat of the priests of Egypt, are to be seen a group of twenty-four pyramids, the magnificence and imposing simplicity of which exhibit a degree of elegance very superior to the pyramids of Ghizza. In Ethiopia, at Nouri, may be seen a group of thirty-five pyramids; at Dhibbel-el-Barkal, capital of Ethiopia, another group of seventeen · and at Dhel-Bellal, the remains of a group of forty pyramids.

21.—*Hermes.*

The Egyptian priests inform us that Hermes, in dying, said: 'Until now I have been exiled from my true country, to which I am about to return. Shed no tears for me. I return to that celestial country whither all must repair in their turn. There is God. This life is but a death." (See Chalcidius in Timæum.) Now this doctrine is precisely that of the ancient Bhuddists or Samaneens, who believed that at certain periods impersonations of deity would be sent to earth to reform man, withdraw him from vice, and teach him the way of salvation. With such a dogma spread over India, Egypt, Persia, and Judea, we can easily perceive how readily its believers could accredit the appearance of such an impersonation did he appear at the proper time.

22.—*Sybils.*

This was the ancient name signifying prophetess, given by the Greeks and Romans to those women to whom were attributed knowledge of the future and divine inspiration. Many temples had their sybil or oracle; for, wherever the priests had established their colleges, they found it necessary to engage these persons, to strengthen their power and augment their influence among the people. The vital or physical force to which we give the name of animal magnetism was better known to the magi priests of Chaldea and Egypt than it is at present among us. It was to the study and application of this occult science to which the priests owed much of their great reputation; for they enriched their astronomical knowledge with the addition of botanical, medical, chemical, and anatomical knowledge, from the revelations made to them by their sybils.

The Essenian priests, who were intimately connected with another sect, called Therapeutes, resident in Egypt, and who formed the connecting link between the Egyptians and the Hebrews, as the Essenians continued the affiliation between the Jews and the Christians, without doubt initiated Jesus Christ, who was educated by them, into this sublime science, and thus can we explain how he wrought many of the miracles attributed to him in the Scriptures.

The sybils of antiquity who were most celebrated were those of Ionia and Italy. It is said that this last, to whom are given different names, came to Rome in the reign of Tarquin the elder, and sold him the books (Sybilline leaves), in which were written the future of Rome and that he deposited them in the capitol, confiding their care to two priests named *Duumvirs*, whose number was subsequently increased to fifteen. Therein were found, it is said, some very useful revelations. The Sybilline leaves were destroyed at the burning of the capitol, which took place in the time of Scylla. The senate, immediately upon the loss becoming known, sent into the cities of Italy and Greece to gather up such of the predictions of the Sybils as could be found, for the purpose of making a new collection; but this afforded an opportunity to fabricate many, and from that cause the Sybilline books fell into disrepute. The last collection was burnt in the year 399, by Stilicon, general of the Arcadians.

23.—*The Avenues of Thebes.*

At Karnak, a village that is built upon the west bank of the Nile, may be seen the most imposing monuments at present extant, where once stood ancient Thebes. The approach to these monuments, in coming from Luxor, is announced by the remains of a flagstone pavement which unite the edifices of Karnak with those of Luxor. This avenue, more than a mile long, was once decorated, on the right hand and on the left, with one thousand two hundred sphinxes and six hundred rams, cut in granite, and conducted to a magnificent temple, from which two other ranks of sphinxes reached to the greater and lesser temples at the south, the ceilings of which were supported by some hundreds of columns, seventy feet in height.

24.—*Subterranean Cities.*

In ancient Egypt there were entire cities under ground which have been discovered during the past centuries, and accounts of them imparted to us. A chain of limestone which borders the Nile, protected the works of these subterranean cities, and the tumulary marvels hidden in the necropoli of Thebes and Memphis equal the sunlit masterpieces of Egyptian art which rest upon the banks of that river.

The underground passage of the great pyramid, not far from Memphis, communicates with immense inclosures, wherein may be found delicious gardens, where priests and priestesses reside with their families, including all the population necessary for the service of the mysteries. These subterranean residences and their surroundings, which are nearly six miles in circumference, communicate with the seven other pyramids and the twelve temples which environ the city.

25.—*Jehovah.*

This word, as here spelled, is unknown to any Asiatic Jew or aboriginal Arab. Its origin even among Europeans, who have sanctified it, is neither clear nor authentic. When transcribed into the letters of the Arab alphabet, the sound of the four letters which express the name is *iahouah*, or ya-ho-wa-hoh. Doctor Robert Walton, one of the most learned and rational biblists who has written upon this matter, expressly objects to the pronunciation Jehovah, as unknown to the ancients. He states that "the editors of the Bible have had the audacity to falsify even the manuscripts in this particular; as, for instance, in the eighth Psalm, when Jeremiah says that he will read the name of the Lord in a certain manner, the editors have put the word *Jehovah*, when the manuscript obliges Frobenius to give the word *Jao*."

It appears that it was the German theologians, the first disciples of the Rabbins, who gave involuntary place to this reading, by their *j* and *u*.

The Greek, Philo, translator of the Phenician, Sanchoniathon, concurs with Diodorus of Sicily, Strabo, and other authorities, when he says that the god of the Hebrews was called *Jeuo*, as we learn from Eusebius, in his "Evangelical Preparation." It is evident, then, that the Hebrews never knew this pretended name, so emphatically styled Jehovah by our poets and theologians; and they have to pronounce it as the Arabs of to day, *iehouh*, signifying *to be*, the essence, existence, the principle of life. Their word *jehouh*, therefore, is equivalent to our paraphrase *Him who is himself*, the *Existing Being*.

If the word *jehouh* had been deprived, according to the genius of the Greek language, of the two *h* letters, it would have remained *jou*, base of *you-piter*, or *jou-pater* (jou, generator, essence of life). You-piter (*Jupiter*) was regarded by the Egyptians, according to Manethon, a priest of Memphis, as the father, the generator of living beings. The god of Moses, Jehouh or Jehovah, and whom he called *the soul of the world*, is no other than the You-piter of the Egyptians.

26.—*Tyre.*

According to the chronology of Herodotus, there was a temple founded to the Phenician Hercules (the sun) in the year 2760 B. C., at ancient Tyre, upon the rock facing the island upon which the city stood some thirteen hundred years afterward. The ancient city destroyed by Nebuchadnezzar in the year 572 B. C., was rebuilt a few years after by the remnant of the Tyrian people.

27.—*The Jews Driven from Egypt.*

According to Manethon, the Egyptian priest previously quoted, "the ancestors of the Jewish people were a mixture of divers classes of men, among which were even Egyptian priests, who, from causes of impurity, canonical defilement, and especially for leprosy, were by command of an oracle, expelled from Egypt by a king named Amenophis."

In Exodus it is stated that many strangers followed Israel out of Egypt.

28.—*The Pentateuch.*

A crowd of circumstances tend to prove that Moses was not the author of the Pentateuch, as these books have come to us. Helkiah, the high priest, who, under the reign of the young king Josiah, made this king of eight years old, and also the Jewish people, believe that he had found the book of the law in the temple of the Lord, is, in the sense that he collected and arranged these books and prefaced them with a cosmogony, the real author of them as they were presented to the Jewish king, priests, and people. About this time, it will be noticed, the Jews had generally abandoned the worship of the true God for the worship of Baal (the Belus or sun of the Chaldeans), and the high priest conceived the project of re-animating the national spirit by resuscitating the laws of Moses, comprised in the four books containing the precepts, commandments, prohibitions, rites, and ordinances which constitute that law. It was the mode then to have cosmogonies explanatory of the origin of all things, as well of nations as of the world itself, and each people had their sacred books, commencing with a cosmogony. The Greeks had that of Hesiod, the Persians that of Zoroaster, the Phenicians that of Sanchoniathon, the Hindoos had their Vedas and Pouranas, and the Egyptians had the five books of Hermes. Helkiah desired to give to the Jewish people a book that would serve as their standard, and, so to speak, to promote national concord, he believed it necessary to arrange a cosmogony. Both by nature and education Helkiah was peculiarly fitted for this work; his people, originally Chaldean, had preserved many traditions, and, like his agent, Jeremiah, he had a political preference for Chaldean tradition. He therefore adopted, with modifications, the Babylonish cosmogony. Here we observe the true source of the remarkable resemblance which the historian Josephus, as also all the ancient Christian fathers, have noticed between the first twelve chapters of Genesis and the Chaldean antiquities of Berose.

There is another portion of the Jewish history no more worthy of credence, as it is given in subsequent books; this is what is called the Book of Judges, covering from 1551 to 1080 B. C., and the Book of Joshua, which afford us so vague a record of the history of this time, when contrasted with the exact details of the Books of Kings, that we can not determine but that, previous to the appearance of the high priest, or prophet, Elias, the history of the Jews is broken, dissolved; that all is uncertain and confused, and that their annals really go back no further than 1131 B. C. So much is this the case that it is impossible to determine within twenty or thirty years when Moses died, and that it is only permitted by a reasonable calculation of probabilities to fix the date of that event at from 1450 to 1420 B. C.

From this condition of their history, it naturally results that if the Jews had no exact notions of the time which elapsed between Moses and Elias, nor of the time of the sojourn in Egypt—for nothing is clear in this regard—how could they pretend to have better knowledge of the time previous to their existence as a people in Egypt, or, more anterior far, the time when no nation existed, or about the time man was created, of which no testimony existed, but of which their Genesis give us the recital of events as if the writer had the process passing before him? The Jews say that this was a revelation made by God direct to their prophet Moses. We reply that many nations have held to like language—the Egyptian, the Phenician, the Chaldean, and the Persian peoples all have equally had the history of the creation revealed to their prophets. In our day the Hindoos have presented to our missionaries their Vedas and Pouranas, with some pretensions to an antiquity more remote than Genesis or any other of the books attributed to Moses. It is true that our learned biblists reject, or at least contest the authenticity of these books; but the Brahmins, retorting, use our own arguments, and contest the authenticity of our Bible.

The most convincing proof that the author of the Hebrew Genesis drew his cosmogony from that of the Chaldeans is afforded us by the recital of the details that we therein find of the deluge, in comparing it with the text of two fragments, the one of Alexander Polyhistor, a learned compiler of the time of Scylla, and the other that of Abydene, another compiler, who, Eusebius has informed us, consulted the monuments of the Medes and the Assyrians. That which the Hebrew Genesis recounts of Noah, or Noe, these authors recount of Zisuthrus; and it is plain that the history, from the beginning of the deluge to the account of the rainbow, is purely Chaldean; that is to say, that chapters 6 to 11, inclusive, are taken from the legends of the priests of that nation, of an infinitely remote period of time.

These texts upon the deluge would afford matter for a volume of commentaries, but we will confine our remarks to what will be necessary for sensible men. The three recitals mentioned are a tissue of moral and physical impossibilities; but here simple good sense does not suffice; it is necessary to be initiated into the astrological doctrine of the ancients to interpret the language employed, and to know that the deluges of the Hebrews, Chaldeans, Greeks, Persians and Hindoos, as having destroyed the world under Noah, Ogyzes, Inachus, Zisuthrus, or Satyavrata, are one and the same physico-astronomical event which is repeated every year, and concerning which the principal wonder is the metaphorical language in which it is expressed.

In that language the great circle of the heavens is called *mundus*, of which the analogue *mondola* also signifies, in the Sanscrit, a circle, and of which the *orbis* of the Latins is the synonym. The revolution by the sun of this circle composed the year of twelve months, and was called *orbis*, the *world*, the celestial circle. Consequently, every twelve months the world was finished and the world was begun, the world was destroyed and the world was renewed. The time of this remarkable event varied, according to the usage of the peoples in commencing their year with the solstices or the equinoxes. In Egypt the year began with the solstice of summer. At this time the Nile exhibited the first symptoms of its annual overflow, and in forty days thereafter the water covers all the land of Egypt to the depth of five cubits. This was then, as it is now, for that low-lying country, an ocean, a deluge most destructive in the early times, and before the people, becoming numerous and more intelligent, had drained the swamps, and with dykes defended themselves from the effects of this overflow. Experience proved to them that a group of stars occupied the heavens coincident with the first symptoms of the rise, and this group they called the ship or bark, as it indicated that now they must be ready to embark; another group was called the dog, and the appearance of which indicated that the flow had attained its greatest height; a third was called the crow, a fourth the dove, a fifth the laborer, and, not far from him, was the virgin harvester. All these persons who figured in the deluge of Noah and Zisuthrus are also in the celestial sphere, which was a true table or calendar, of which the two texts from which we have quoted furnish a description more or less faithful.

The most remarkable difference between the Chaldean and the Hebrew recital is, that the one preserves the astrologico-mythological character, while the other is turned into a sense and toward an object exclusively moral. In fact, according to the Hebrew version—of which there are in the text more than a hundred verses, and so well known that it is not necessary here to quote them—the human race, having become perverted, "giants," the progeny of the "sons of God" and "daughters of men," exercised all sorts of violence. Then God repents having made man. He speaks; he deliberates upon this subject, and finally he concludes to exterminate the whole race, not only of man, but, by the manner of their destruction, necessarily of every living thing upon the earth. One man, however, he is content to save, because he is a just man and worthy of preservation. To this man God makes known his design; he announces the coming deluge; he directs him how to build a ship, etc. When the deluge has destroyed all else, this man, being saved, offers up a sacrifice of clean animals, *according to the law of Moses*, as announced by him to the Hebrews in the wilderness God is so greatly propitiated by this that he promises to make no more deluges; he imparts to Noah his blessing, some precepts, and an abridgment of *the law of Moses;* he enters into an alliance with all living beings, and, as a sign of this alliance, he invents the rainbow, etc. All this is represented in other parts of the text with some contradictions, viz.: *it rained forty days*—the waters remained *one hundred and fifty days*, when the winds blew and the rain ceased. On the first day of the *tenth* month the tops of the mountains are visible, and, forty days afterward, a dove was sent forth, but returns, having found no place whereon to rest her foot, etc.

What is this recital but a moral drama; such a lesson in conduct as might be given to the people by a religious legislator—a priest?

29.—*The Prodigies of Moses.*

Moses, or rather Moushah, according to the true pronunciation, conceived the project of becoming ruler of and legislator for the Hebrew people, and this design he executed with means appropriate to the circumstances and a force of character very remarkable. His people, ignorant and superstitious as they have always been, and as were the wandering tribes of the Arabs, believed in magic—a belief that even yet obtains in the East. Moses is said to have executed miracles and prodigies; that is, he produced natural phenomena which the priests of Egypt, by long study and happy chance, discovered the means of executing. It is impossible to account by natural means for the miracles which Moses is said to have performed; but it is plain that the writers who described them exaggerated and corrupted the facts, with the design of magnifying the acts of their prophet, priest, and king.

30.—*Dogma of an Only God.*

The Jews, the Christians, and the Mussulmans, founding their belief upon the same books, all admit the existence of a first man, who ruined the whole human race by eating an apple. The principal difference between them consists in this, that after having admitted one indivisible God, the Christians divided the same into three persons, each of whom they maintained was a God entire and complete, without ceasing to form, with the others, an identical whole. And they maintained, further, that this being who filled the universe, assumed the form of an individual man, with a body composed of like perishable materials, without ceasing to be immortal, eternal, and infinite. The Mussulmans, who can not comprehend these *mysteries*, notwithstanding they believe in the mission of their prophet, reject the Christian doctrine as the fruit of an unsound mind; and among the Christians themselves the disagreement widens by as much as the problems upon which they differ is impossible of demonstration, and inaccessible to the approach of common sense and human reason.

Thus, while they admit that God is an incomprehensible and unknown being, they nevertheless dispute as to his essence, the causes of his actions, and his attributes; admitting his transformation into a human body to be an enigma beyond their comprehension, they dispute about the confusion or the distinction of the two natures, upon the change of substance, or- transubstantiation, the real or fancied presence, and upon the manner of the incarnation, etc.; and from these differences innumerable sects have sprung up, and, to the extent of two or three hundred, have become extinct, while two or three hundred others yet exist. The Bible, which is the common authority of all these sects, in substance, says that God (after having passed an eternity doing nothing) conceived the design of producing the world out of nothing; and, having accomplished this labor and completed his creation in six days, he rested upon the seventh; that having, as the crowning part of his creation, made a pair of human beings, the first of their kind, he placed them in a garden very delicious, to the end that they might be perfectly happy, but prohibiting them, however, from eating a certain fruit which he placed within easy reach of their hands; that this first pair having disobeyed this prohibition, all their kind, none of which were yet born, were condemned to expiate a fault which, as they had no existence, they could not commit; that after having allowed the human race to be thus condemned during four or five thousand years, this God of mercy, goodness, and justice proposed to his only begotten yet co-existent and well-beloved son to assume the form of a man, by being born of a woman upon the earth, to the end that he should suffer death to save man from eternal death; that having accomplished these things, and thus saved all men who had existed upon the earth, from the fall of the first pair until his death, this only-begotten son, co-existent with the Father, ordained, at his last supper upon earth, a plan by which those who should be born after his death might be saved, and for this purpose he instituted a sacrament, named after that event, and by which a little bread is said to compose the body of this sacrificed God, and be endowed, for the benefit of its consumer, with all the efficacy of the real body, and become the oblation or atonement for the sins of future men.

Now, is it not enough to upset all ideas of justice or reason to admit that a God, just and holy, should have condemned the whole human race because a man and a woman, four or five thousand years before, ate an apple? Was there ever a tyrant who made the children suffer for their parents' crimes? What man can atone for the crimes of another man?

The following picture, extracted from their sacred books, proves, in fact, that it is not God who has made man to his image, but, upon the contrary, it is man who has made God to that image and in that likeness which most satisfies himself and suits his purposes.

The God of the Israelites, their Jehouh, or Jehovah, as Moses distinguished the You-piter of the Egyptians, is, if we judge from the manner in which he is represented in the Bible, a despot, a revengeful God, and exterminator of the peoples. The human race was perverted, and he repents of having created the species, he speaks, he deliberates, he decides upon a violent means of destroying all that has life, thus involving not only the offending race, but all others in a common death; he has pity upon but a single family of man, which he saves. After the execution of this decision, this same God, who then had entered into an alliance with all the living, is stated to have said to the Hebrew people (See Exodus, chap. xxvi): "I will not exterminate the Canaanites before your face in one single year, for fear that the country should be reduced to a desert." It will be observed that his reason for exterminating the Canaanites at all was, that he is said to have promised their land to the Hebrews. Subsequently this same God, through the mouth of their prophet Samuel, ordered the Jews to exterminate all the people of Amalek, sparing neither man, woman, child, or beast for food or burden; and why? Because, four hundred years previously, the Amalekites opposed the passage of the Hebrews through their country. Then the same God, furious at the temerity of five thousand persons who look upon the ark of the covenant, strikes them all dead. Elsewhere this same God, among many other trifling acts, dictates to Moses the wood with which he shall make the ark; he has interviews with the prophets, speaking to them in their chambers, and repenting one day of what he ordered done the day previous. This is the God of the Jews. But where are the witnesses and proofs of these things which are alleged and reasserted in the Old Testament? There are none.

Now, observe what are the qualities of the God of the Christians. This God was at first a God of peace, goodness, and charity. Christ exhibits him to us as a being the most holy and perfect, and, at the same time, as the most affectionate father of all mankind; but Christ dies, and immediately the priests, who preach what they call Christ's doctrine, change God into a despot, burning with revenge for man's incorrigible wickedness. While assuming to be the successors of Christ, unlike him they preach neither liberty, toleration, nor peace; but, in his name, and with the emblem of his death upraised in their hands, they have led crusades against Arianism, Manicheanism, and Protestantism, under the assertion that the peoples who defended and indulged these doctrines were heretics, and, consequently, accursed of God. It is in the name of their God that the aboriginal people of America have been exterminated, Mexico and Peru have been conquered, and their inhabitants destroyed; that Africa has been devastated, and its inhabitants sold like beasts; and, in the same name, that the priests of the "Holy Inquisition" persecuted the sects of the Christian church in Europe until nearly a million of persons were destroyed, over thirty thousand of whom were roasted to death.

Now take the Koran, and see what is the god of the Mussulmans. Their god, as created by Mahomet, his prophet, and called Allah, is, according to the holy books of Islamism, a god opposed in many things to the god of the Jews and the Christians. This god, they say, after having sent twenty-four thousand prophets to the nations which had become idolatrous, finally sent a last prophet, the most perfect of all, Mahomet, *upon whom should be impressed the salutation of peace.* Then, in order that the infidel should not change the divine word, *supreme clemency itself* traced the leaves of the Koran, and thus it became immortal, uncreated, eternal as the source from which it emanated; page by page and leaf by leaf, as it was composed, was it sent by the angel Gabriel to the prophet, and was entirely delivered to him in twenty-four thousand nocturnal visits. These visits were announced by a cold sweat seizing upon the prophet. That in the vision of a night he reached the nineteenth heaven, seated upon the back of the animal Barak, half horse and half woman; that, owing to the gift of miracles, he reached the sun without protection from the intensity of his light, made trees grow with a single word, filled cisterns with water, split the disk of the moon in two; and, *charged with the commission of God, sword in hand,* Mahomet propagated a religion the most worthy of God by reason of its sublimity, and the most suitable for man by reason of its simplicity, since it consists of but nine points, viz.: 1. To profess the oneness of God. 2. To recognize Mahomet for his only prophet. 3. To pray five times a day. 4. To fast one month in the year. 5. To go to Mecca once in a lifetime. 6. To give the tenth of your property to the faithful. 7. To drink no wine.. 8. To eat no pork. 9. To make continual war upon the infidels. By practicing these precepts during life, all Mussulmans would, like himself, enjoy this world with great satisfaction, and at their death, also, like him, become apostles and martyrs, whose souls, borne in the balance of their works, and absolved by the two black angels, after having traversed hell, by crossing that bridge which is straight as a hair and sharp as a saber, would be received into a place the most delicious—a land flowing with milk and honey—where, embalmed with all the perfumes of India and Araby, chaste virgins, celestial houris, would minister constantly to their pleasure, and, with them, continue forever young.

Here we behold the god Allah of the Ishmaelites, and the paradise promised to the believers of his prophet and those who obey his laws, the first precept of which is murder and war. It is under the banner of this doctrine that, during twelve centuries, its fanatical partisans have spread the horrors of war and carnage among the neighboring nations. It is Islamism that has plunged the people of Asia, once flourishing and intelligent, into the realm of barbarism and ignorance.

It is thus that these self-styled prophets and priests of God have elevated themselves into doctors of the peoples, and opened the ways of wickedness and iniquity. Attaching merit to practices inconsequent and, in fact, ridiculous, their virtue consists in gesticulating in certain postures, in the expression of certain words, in articulating certain names, in eating and drinking certain kinds of food and drink, and refraining from others. How low are man's ideas of the most elevated of beings! It would seem, in hearkening to the priests of these different religions, that their god, whimsical and capricious, eats and drinks like a man; that, in turn, he loves and hates, casts down and uplifts; that, weak as wicked, he nurses his hate; that, contradictory as perfidious, he sets snares for the unwary; that, after permitting evil, he punishes it; that, foreseeing crime, he permits it; that, a venal judge, he is propitiated by bribes; that, an imprudent despot, he makes laws which he immediately revokes; that, ferocious tyrant, he holds or confers his favors without a cause, and bends but to the strength of meanness!

Now that we have seen, as exhibited by their priests and prophets, the God of the Jews, of the Christians, and the Mussulmans, let us examine him who is revered by Freemasons. Here is their idea of a Supreme Being. From at first they have called him the Grand Architect of the Universe, regarding the universe as that house not made with hands, eternal in the heavens, and, conformably to this idea, they comprehend under this denomination a universal and eternal intelligence, gifted with all power, all science, all love; ruling the worlds and the beings which compose the universe by regular and uniform laws to the close of their existence. It is this God, that they reverence as the Only Master, who is seen and made manifest in all the wonders of his works, which they behold amazed; and, as the author and father of all men, he gives to all intelligence and life. Thus regarding the Supreme Being, the religion of Masonry can be but a summary of human wisdom—of all those perfections the practice of which render man nearly divine; and it is, in a word, that universal morality which attaches to the inhabitants of every country—to the man of every worship. This morality is more extended and more universal than that of any national religion, for these, always exclusive, class those who do not believe nor worship at their shrines as unbelievers, as idolaters, schismatics, sectarians, and infidels, while Masonry sees nothing in religionists of every kind but brethren, to whom she opens her temple and admits them, to be therein freed from the prejudices of their country or the errors of the religion of their fathers, by learning to love one another, and to sustain each other. Bearing on high her torch, she would have it shed its pure beams to enlighten and not to destroy; but while she flies from error she neither hates nor persecutes: her object being, in fine, to blend the whole family of man into one band of brothers, united by love, science, and labor.

This being the true Masonic doctrine, it becomes necessary that masonry should open its temples to all men—to the Jew as to the Mohammedan, to the adorer of Bhulda or Fot as to the adorer of God in Christ; and this without seeking to identify itself with the rites of any of these religionists, or to follow the standard of any prophet. Without permitting herself to descend to such an adoption, Freemasonry can select from their best doctrines, and cull from their commandments all that conforms to the rule of her existence; that is, the practice of *universal morality.*

31.—*The Worship of the Stars.*

The worship of the sun has given to the Jewish and Roman Catholic priests the tonsure, which represents the disk of the sun, of which the stole is the zodiac, and the chaplets are the emblems of the stars and planets; the miter of the pontiff, together with the crozier and mantle, are those of Osiris; and the cross, the mysteries of which are extolled without being understood by the priests, is the cross of Serapis, traced by the hand of the Egyptian priests upon their symbolic plan of the world, which, passing by the equinoxes and the tropics becomes the emblem of the resurrection and a future life.

32.—*The Essenians.*

This religious and philosophic sect, of which Christ had been a member, was composed of learned Jews who lived in the form of a society similar to that of Pythagoras. Love of labor, sobriety, love of truth, the absence of all oaths, fidelity, love of peace, horror of violence, complete equality in all social relations, property in common, (of which the first Christian community of Jerusalem affords an example,) or, at the least, disinterested aid afforded to those members who were in need; in general, love to God and man, made manifest by intense honesty—these were the principles which distinguished the Essenians. It was in this celebrated philosophical sect that, among numbers of ancient traditions, that of a future savior—a great mediator who would reëstablish the nation in all its ancient glory—was conserved and principally propagated. This prediction was founded as follows:

After the Assyrians had destroyed the kingdom of Samaria, some prudent persons, foreseeing the same destiny for Jerusalem, predicted and announced it, and their predictions had all the appearance of prophecies. The hierophants, in their enthusiasm, had conceived a kingly liberator, who would reëstablish the nation in its ancient glory, and the Hebrew people again become a powerful people, conquering and to conquer, with Jerusalem the capital of an empire. coëxtensive with the whole earth.

Events having realized the first of these predictions, viz., the ruin of Jerusalem, the people attached to the second much more implicit belief than accorded with the event; and the afflicted Jews looked with an impatience corresponding with their need for the coming of that victorious king and liberator who should rebuild the nation fashioned by Moses and reëstablish the empire of David.

Otherwise, the sacred mythological traditions of the previous time had spread over all Asia an entirely analogous dogma. They had spoken of a Great Mediator, a final Judge, a future Savior, who, as God, king, and legislator, should bring the golden age to earth, deliver his empire from evil, and render to man the reign of blessing, peace, and happiness. These ideas found place in the hearts of the people the more as they became oppressed by successive devastation and saddened by the barbarism of their despotic governments; and this conformity between the oracles of other nations and the prophets of their own excited the attention of the Jews. There is little doubt that those prophets had been artful enough to calculate their events after the manner employed in the pagan mysteries; for in Judea general attention had been attracted to the coming of a final savior, when a singular circumstance determined the period of his advent.

It was written in the sacred books of the Chaldeans and Persians that the world, composed of a total revolution of *twelve thousand*,[1] was divided into two partial revolutions, one of which, *the age and reign of good*, terminated at the close of the first six thousand, and the other, *the age and reign of evil*, terminated at the close of the second six thousand. By these recitals, the first authors had extended the annual revolution of the celestial orbit called the world, and the two systematic periods of each year, viz., winter and summer, each divided into six thousand parts. These expressions, in which the *thousands* were taken in the sense of years, instead of parts, and the whole taken in a literal rather than in an astrological sense, together with the fact that in these latter days the Jews were unhappily situated, sub-

---

[1] This, it will be remembered by the reader, was the division of the zodiac of Zoroaster into twelve thousands; or twelve months, of a thousand parts each.

ject to and severely taxed by the Roman power, induced them to believe that the age of evil was about to close, and be succeeded by the age of good.

Now, in the calculations of the Jews, they commenced to count their first six thousand years from their (fictitious) creation of the world. This time was certainly about to close, and this coincidence produced an agitation in the minds of leading men among them. They talked of nothing but the approaching time; they interrogated the hierophants and their mystic books; they expected the advent daily of that restorer of their ancient greatness. Jesus Christ, educated among the Essenians, appears and preaches his doctrine. It is not satisfactory to those in power; he is arrested, tried, condemned, executed. After his death, his disciples and partisans, deprived of their chief by an incident, true, without doubt, gave place by their recitals to a rumor which gradually grew into a history, and immediately all the circumstances of the mythological traditions have place, and afford us a system authentic and complete, and which we can not doubt.

These mythological traditions set forth that, " In *the beginning* a *woman* and a *man* having, by their disobedience and consequent *fall*, introduced sin into the world." (Take an ancient celestial globe, and follow the explanation.) Here we perceive the astronomical fact that the virgin harvester and the cowherd (Bootes), occupying positions obliquely to the equinox of autumn, seem to deliver the heavens to the constellation of winter, and, falling under the horizon, introduces into the world the genius of evil, Ahrimane, symbolized by the constellation of the *serpent*.

The traditions continue : " That the woman, having fallen, seduced the man ;" and, in fact, the *virgin*, descending first, seems to drag *Bootes* toward her. "That the woman, *holding him, presents him with fruits beautiful to look upon and good to eat,* and which impart the knowledge of good and evil ;" and, in fact, the *virgin* holds in her hand a branch of fruit, which she seems to be extending toward *Bootes*, while the bough or branch, emblem of autumn, placed in the zodiac of Mithra upon the frontier of winter and of summer, seems to open the door and bestow science, which is the key of good and evil.

The traditions continue : " That this *couple had been chased from the celestial garden*, and that a cherubim, with a flaming sword, had been placed at the gate to keep them from returning ;" and, in fact, when the *virgin* and *Bootes* fall under the horizon, *Perseus* rises upon the other side, with a sword in his hand, and seemingly chases them from the heaven of summer, the garden and reign of fruits and flowers.

The traditions continue : "That of this virgin would be born—put forth a shoot—an infant who would crush the head of the serpent, and who would deliver the world from sin ;" and by this figure they designated the movement of the sun, which, in fact, at the time of the summer solstice—at the precise moment when the magi of the Persians cast the horoscope of the new year—is found resting in the bosom of the *virgin* and obliquely with the eastern horizon, and which, on this account, was symbolized in their astrological pictures under the form of a suckling infant resting in the bosom of a virgin, and became afterward, at the equinox of spring-time, the *ram* or lamb, conqueror of the constellation of the *serpent*, which at this time disappears from the heavens.[1]

These mythological traditions further state: "That in his infancy, this *restorer*, of *divine* or *celestial nature*, lived *humble, obscure, cast down,* and *indigent;*" and thus may be seen the sun of winter low in the horizon, and the first of these four ages or seasons, winter, a time of consequent obscurity, want, fasting, and privations. Further: "That, put to death by wicked ones, he was *gloriously resurrected;* that he went up from *hell* to *heaven,* where he reigns eternally;" and thus they retraced the way of the sun, who, closing his career at the solstice of winter, while Typhon ruled and the angels rebelled, he seems to be put to death by them, but immediately after reappearing, he mounts toward the vault of heaven, where he remains.

Finally, these traditions, in citing the astrological and mysterious names of this infant, say that he was sometimes called *Cris*—that is to say, the preserver—and sometimes *Iésus*. Can a closer analogy be traced between the leading features of two accounts of any event which has ever had place than this which we have just recounted, when compared with the Scriptures detailing the birth, life, and death of Christ?

Like Osiris, Adonis, or Mithra, Christ came upon the earth to destroy death and darkness, and, like them, he was born on the 25th of December. This is the solstice of winter, the moment when the sun passes from the inferior to the superior signs; and, in the cosmogony of the ancients, he enters Taurus; but, by reason of the precession of the equinoxes, he began, about the year 330 before the birth of Christ, to enter by the sign of the ram or lamb, and through which he opened the year effectually at the time when Christ appeared preaching his doctrine in Judea. Thus Christ calls himself the lamb who removeth the sins of the world.

With the sphere of Coronelli in his hand, let the reader now observe what takes place at the time of the birth of Christ.

On the 25th December, to a minute, the sun is at *Capricorn*, in

---

[1] In the explanation of the Persian sphere spoken of by Ben-Ezra, in the *Poetical Heaven* of Blaeu. p. 71, occurs this sentence: "The first square represents this beautiful virgin with long hair, seated on a lounge, with two swords in one hand, suckling an infant, called Jesus by some nations and Christ in Greek."

the stable of Ægeus, son of the sun; at the highest meridianal point is the *ass* of Bacchus and the *crib* or manger; behind him is the *water bearer* or cherubim; before him is the *eagle of St. John*. In the superior hemisphere is the *bull* and the celestial *lion;* in the east the *virgin* reposes, holding an infant in her arms, and under her feet is the *dragon*. Near her is *Bootes*, the foster-father of Horus, and near him Janus, with his key in his hand and mounted upon his *ship*—chief of the twelve months Janus appears; and upon the same line, toward the horizon, is the star *Stephen*. The *lamb* is couching, and in front of him is that constellation composed of three beautiful stars which Christian astronomers call the *Magi*.

This is the condition on the 25th December in the astronomical cosmogony. In the Christian cosmogony, upon the 25th December, at the same moment, Christ is born of a *virgin*, in a *stable*, between an *ox* and an *ass;* he is laid in a *manger*, and is called Jesus, because he is to deliver his people; then an *angel* appears, who announces the birth of Christ, whom he styles *Lord;* on the eighth day he is called Savior; near Jesus and his mother is the foster-father Joseph, the carpenter. Upon the next day is celebrated the feast of St. Stephen by the Catholic church, and upon the day following that of St. John the Evangelist, whom the sacred books represented accompanied by an eagle. Peter, chief of the twelve apostles (months), is represented carrying the keys of heaven, and, afterward Jesus is known as the Lamb of God who redeems the world. The analogy, it will be observed, is striking. Let us complete it.

No sooner is Christ born than three kings, or *magi*, guided by the star in the East, come to salute and bring him presents, which, according to immemorial usage were consecrated to the sun. Three months after the solstice of winter occurs the solstice of summer, viz.: on the 25th of March. At this instant the sun triumphs, and day and night becomes of equal length. At the moment when Gabriel, upon this day, salutes Mary, in the Christian cosmogony, Osiris, in the Egyptian, was reputed to salute the moon, to the end that she might fructify the earth. On the 24th of June, feast of St. John, and precise period of the solstice of summer, St. John the Baptist should have baptized Christ to fit him for his work. This St. John—the Latin *Janua* means gate or door—has his peer in the St. John of the 27th of December, whose feast opens the solstice of winter. Here it is plain that the St. Johns are no other than the *Janua inferi* and *Janua cœli* of the Romans, the doors to the inferior and superior places. These are, in fact, the two precise points when the sun, having arrived at the culminations of his ascending and descending courses, pass from the superior signs into the inferior, and from the latter return into the former.

We come to the death of Christ. Following the Evangelists, it took place on Good or Holy Friday; and he arose three days afterward. From the 25th December, the sun having entered the superior signs, remains insensible to our horizon until the 21st March. Well, at that instant, upon the 25th March, when he crossed the line, was celebrated by the Jews the feast of the Passover; for then this feast was not as it is to-day, a moveable one; on the contrary, it occurred invariably at the instant of the vernal equinox. Now equinox signifies equal days as nights; for during the three days which elapse from the 21st to the 25th March, the nights over all the earth are of equal length with the days—before the 21st the nights are longer; afterward they are shorter. The same phenomenon occurs at the autumnal equinox. At these two periods of the year the equator is found perpendicularly under the sun.

Now what is the result of this examination? That the disciples of Christ have surrounded his birth, life, and death with miracles which never took place, but which are, rather, symbolized under solar appearances. That the doctrine of Christ, which is a summary and code of all the truths which were known at this period, is similar to that of the Essenian school from which he graduated, as it is similar to that of the hierophants of Egypt and the gymnosophists of India. In a word, that the Christian religion came out from the mysteries of initiation; and that the creation, the gods, the angels, the occurrences, dogmas, and ceremonies, such as we find them in the sacred books, are nothing but resemblances, more or less faithful, of the ancient gods, angels, dogmas, and ceremonies of the Brahmins, the magi, and the Egyptian priests.

During the first three centuries of our era the Christian religion existed but in anarchy and chaos. Opinions as fanciful as ridiculous divided those who assumed the direction of it, and their opinions were sustained by their supporters with fervor, and an abiding faith that caused the destruction of myriads, because they were based upon traditions equally as ancient and equally as sacred as those which were offered to replace them. After three hundred years the government became associated with one of these sects, and made its doctrines the religion of the State, to the exclusion of all the others; and these, consequently, became *heresies* and their holders heretics, to be cursed and destroyed by the dominant party.

33.—*Christianity.*

This religion, having gone forth out of Judea, spread rapidly upon the earth. At first propagated by men whose only object was to reform and simplify the worship of nature, and to make universal morality the basis of that worship, by blotting out forever the numerous and horrible sacrifices which every-where inundated the altars with blood, under a solar allegory they exhibited a single victim, worthy of divinity, immolated each year for the preservation and regeneration of nature. This religion was subsequently perpetuated by priests, who altered its simple and natural forms, and substituted therefor certain mysteries, ceremonies, and above all, assumed a sacerdotal power totally unknown to its first ministers, the disciples of Christ, whose only power consisted in appeals to the consciences of men. In its primitive condition, this religion formed the allegorical complement to the worship of nature—a worship which of itself was at first nothing more than a grand and beautiful allegory.

In the earlier times, and after the death of Christ, the priests of his religion were strangers to all thought of human dominion. Entirely animated by that idea to which he gave expression in the words, "He who devotes himself most diligently to my service here shall be greatest in my kingdom hereafter," they were humble, modest, charitable, and constant in their endeavors to imbue those to whom they preached with a similar spirit. Their early meetings were devoid of either parade or show, being nothing but spontaneous reunions of all the Christians resident in any certain locality. A pure and simple morality marked their religious enthusiasm, and excited even the admiration of their persecutors. They shared every thing in common—property, joys, and sorrows. In the silence of night they met in secret to teach and pray. The *agapes*, or fraternal repasts, terminated these meetings, in which differences of social rank and position were effaced by the belief of a paternal divinity being present. It was thus that Christianity prepared two changes which gradually found place in the manners and customs of all those countries into which this religion extended. Women obtained the rank and importance to which, as the mothers of families, they are justly entitled; and the slaves, as participants at the *agapes*, were gradually elevated above that oppression under which one half of the whole human race, anterior to the advent of Christianity, had bowed itself.

34.—*The Mysteries of Christianity.*

At the beginning Christianity was an initiation similar to that of the pagans. None were admitted but upon certain determined conditions, and, these conditions complied with, they were received and a complete knowledge of the doctrine and mysteries conveyed to them in three degrees of instruction. The initiates were, consequently, divided into three classes: The first class was composed of the *hearers*, the second of the *catechumens*, or those who, having taken the first degree, were in possession of the rudiments of the Christian doctrine, and the third class was composed of *the faithful*. The *hearers* constituted the novices who, prepared by certain practices, and after having listened and assented to certain instructions, were initiated into the rudimentary degree, and brought to a knowledge of a part of the degrees of Christianity. Having attained, in this manner, to the condition of a *catechumen*, the initiate, having purified himself by the practice of certain ordinances, was baptized, or initiated into the degree of divine generation; and subsequently a knowledge of the mysteries of Christianity, viz., the incarnation, nativity, passion, death, and resurrection, were conveyed to him, and this instruction composed his initiation into the class of *the faithful*. The mysteries were divided into two parts; the first part was called the mass of the catechumens, and corresponded to the *low mass* of the Catholic Church of the present day, and the second part was called the mass of the faithful, corresponding to the *high mass* of the same church. Of these mysteries the celebration of the holy sacrament of the Eucharist, beyond all others, was held as the most inviolable secret, and known only to the faithful. All the mysteries and ceremonies which constituted the early Christian worship are to be found in the worship of Mithra, or solar worship, and the celebration of these mysteries was likewise called *the mass*.

35.—*Eleusis, Athens.*

Of all the magnificent monuments which ornamented " beautiful Athens," among those possessing any merit there now remains but the ruins of the Pantheon, the temples of Jupiter, Olympus, Theseus, the Winds, and Victory; the theaters of Bacchus and Herodus Atticus; the gate of Adrian, and the Erechtheum.

36.—*The Temple of Balbek.*

Balbek signifies city of Baal, or city of the sun, and corresponds with the Greek term *Heliopolis*. Of this ancient city time has spared but the ruins of a few temples, which may be seen at some distance from anti-Libanus. Of these two are very remarkable, being, in their dimensions, colossal, and erected with huge stones which surpass in the extent of their superficial measurement any thing to be found among the monolithic works of Egypt; while, scattered about may be found the remains of masterpieces of masonic art.

37—*The Temple of Tadmor (Palmyra).*

The edifices of Palmyra surpass in beauty and grandeur even those of Heliopolis. According to the historian, Josephus, this city was founded by Solomon, who gave it the name of Tadmor, or city of Palms. It is situated in the desert of Arabia, between Syria and the Euphrates. Having fallen into the possession of the Romans, it was considerably aggrandized by them, under the reign of the Emperor Aurelian (275 A. D.), who ordered the colleges of Roman architects to construct therein, among other monuments, many temples of such surpassing beauty and colossal dimensions, that they exceeded all of that character which had ever been erected in previous time.

From the remains of the temple of Helios it is apparent that it was supported by four hundred and sixty-four columns, of fifty feet high, which sustained the long galleries and porches on either side to the extent of seven hundred feet. Other columns, each composed of a single block of marble, were arranged in four ranks and formed superb avenues. Westwardly is found another temple, which is connected with that which has been described by a long street of columns, making, as it were, a continuous temple, or two temples connected by a colonnade, which it is evident, contained in all one thousand four hundred and fifty columns of from forty to fifty feet high each, something over a hundred of which yet exist in more or less perfection, and brokenly mark the outlines of this magnificent work of art. These ruins have been known to European travelers since 1691.

38.—*Janus.*

When the worship of idols was abandoned and that of Christ erected upon its ruins, many of the pagan divinities were appropriated by the priests of Christianity, and became saints, more or less distinguished, in the Christian calendar. For instance, Dionysius merged into St. Denis, and Bacchus into St. Demetrius. Of Perpetua and Felicitas were made St. Perpetua and St. Felicity. Saints Rogation, Donatian, Floris and Lucius, also St. Apollonarius, were all of pagan origin. Of Janus, with his double face and bearing the keys, significant of the duty assigned him by the Romans—that of opening the inferior and superior places, otherwise opening and closing the year—the Christians made that St. John who represents the summer solsticial feast, which the pagans celebrated on the 24th of June, and that other St. John, who represents the winter solsticial feast, which the pagans celebrated on the 25th of December. To favor the mechanism of the new dispensation, two Saints John, instead of one Janus, became necessary; and thus was a saint provided for the members of the corporations of Roman builders, when, forsaking paganism, they attached themselves to and became members of the Christian religion. Hitherto, and as pagans, these colleges had invariably celebrated those feasts, in common with all ancient peoples; and the transition from a pagan to a Christian festival was, as we have shown, made remarkably easy. It was this motive that induced the Fraternity to adopt the Saints John as patron saints, and not, as is generally supposed and declared, because they were the forerunner and best beloved of Christ.

APPENDIX.

Recapitulation

In the introduction to this, our work, we went back to the first ages of the human race, to the source of all religions, to the origin of hieroglyphics and symbols, and to the mysteries of antiquity, because not only were many of the truths of the sciences which were cultivated in those mysteries transmitted to the colleges of Roman builders, but because they were intimately connected with architecture, and, in that manner, allied to the history of the human race. Subsequently, in unfolding before the reader the history of the Masonic institution in so succinct a manner as we have done, we paused, in the recital, but at that period of its development in England when the colleges of architects and builders were established and consolidated with a particular character, and, pure and intact, their original privileges and freedom were guaranteed to them. In our statements concerning the foundation of this institution, and in those concerning its organization, its object, its labors, its vicissitudes, and its days of glory, we were forced to pass by all that does not really belong to its history; for this condition we religiously engaged to comply with when we began this our task. Adhering to this condition has been, we believe, as well our merit as our salvation; for, unlike most authors who have entered this field of investigation, we have not been befogged by the obscurity that must ever attend a search for the origin of Freemasonry among the Hindoos, Persians, or Egyptians, nor have we rendered our history ridiculous by ornamentation borrowed from the history, manners, or customs of these peoples or, instead of a history, transformed it into a romance, as is commonly done by those who have heretofore produced what they are pleased to offer us as the veritable history of ancient Free masonry. The road that we have followed was in part already opened by many historians, and in pursuing it, as we have indicated, it led us to the cradle of this institution; but until now, and it is with some degree of pride we make the assertion, no author before us has ever had the courage to approach this vast subject, and in treating it historically, deliver it from the body of that enchantment with which they have, on the contrary, sought to envelope it.

In presenting, for the first time in a history of Freemasonry, the works of this singular association, and in enumerating the most remarkable monuments erected by them, from their foundation to the sixteenth century, we have constantly followed the course of time and events. We have accompanied the colleges of constructors, the free corporations, and the Freemasons, into which the former successively merged, through and across centuries, revolutions, invasions, and international wars; we have traversed the ashes of ancient cities and nations, the remains of thrones and of empires, to the more calm era of the middle ages, when art, and that creative spirit of the human mind elevated towards the heaven of its hopes and desires those sublime edifices consecrated and forever the admiration of posterity. We have evoked from their tombs not only the philosophers and civilizers of the ancient peoples which have passed from earth, and the sages who have enlightened them, but also the statesmen, the warriors, the philosophers who have made Freemasonry their boast and their pride, and whom, in its turn, Freemasonry has rendered illustrious.

The epitome of the worships and mysteries with which we have closed our history, accompanied by the list of the philosophers, reformers, and founders of this worship and those mysteries, from the highest antiquity, proves conclusively that India is the cradle of the human race, and source of all the religions of the world; while, at the same time, these worships and mysteries present us with a curious museum where are found arranged, so to say, in chronological and exact order, the doctrines, ideas, and institutions of centuries, and among which we discern the origin of what we now estimate as our most useful teachings. In the notes which serve to explain and illustrate these mysteries we have extended our quotations and reflections, to the end that

Freemasons would have an opportunity of comparing the religious ideas which they may possess with those which were held by the men who for thousands of years have preceded them; and also for the purpose of accounting to them for the very evident connection which they must see exists between Freemasonry and these ancient religious beliefs and mysteries.

This examination will demonstrate to them that, because the members composing the colleges of builders were initiated into the mysteries of Greece or of Egypt, and introduced into the new institution certain forms and doctrines borrowed from these mysteries, it is not therefore necessary to conclude that these colleges of builders became the successors of the hierophants of Egypt or the gymnosophists of India. If certain truths have been conserved and transmitted to us by these colleges, they otherwise have no peculiar merit, for the Greek and Hebrew philosophers, as also the primitive Christians, have likewise propagated and transmitted such truths and many ceremonies. We repeat, therefore, that which we have more than once already asserted, that the ancient initiation was instruction in all the then known science and philosophy, while that which was practiced in the colleges was confined mainly, if not entirely, to the study and the secrets of all the branches of architecture.

Moral architecture, or Modern Freemasonry, the issue of the Masonic corporations of Britain, is, without doubt, more closely allied by its object to the ancient initiations than was that practiced among the colleges of builders; but it can never become a school of science and philosophy, seeing that science and philosophy have become the common attainment of all who are now situated and disposed to their study. While, however, this position is happily denied it, Freemasonry should be grander, more sublime, than any form of ancient mysteries, inasmuch as while they were exclusive and confined to classes and peoples, it may embrace the whole race of man, and transform that race into a society of brothers, united by love, science, and labor. It is to such an object every phase of the Freemasonry of to-day should tend, and for the accomplishment of which each of its initiates should solemnly engage his efforts and influence.

The Commandments of the Ancient Sages, as contrasted with the Precepts of Modern Freemasonry.

Having thus retraced the general history of Freemasonry, we do not consider our task completed unless we furnish, for the benefit of our younger, and, mayhap, some of our older brethren, a list of the commandments of the wise men of the past ages, and contrast the same with what is known to us as the precepts of Modern Freemasonry. These precepts, being based upon morality and virtue, it is the study of the one and the practice of the other that will render a Mason's life irreproachable. The good of humanity being the principal object of Masonry, disinterestedness is one of the first virtues imposed upon its members; for this is the source of justice and benevolence.

To contribute to the happiness of others; to be humble without degradation; to abjure all sentiments of hate and vengeance; to exhibit magnanimity and liberality without ostentation or dissipation; to be the enemy of vice; to render homage to wisdom and virtue; to respect innocence; to be constant and patient in adversity and modest in prosperity, to avoid all irregularity which may stain the soul or dishonor the body: such are the precepts which, when followed, will make of every Freemason a good citizen, a faithful husband, a tender father, submissive son, and true brother.

COMMANDMENTS OF THE ANCIENT SAGES.

1. God is eternal wisdom, omnipotence, immutable and supreme intelligence.
2. By the practice of virtue, honor thyself. Thy religion should be to do good as a pleasure, and not as a duty. In observing their precepts, become the friend of the wise. Thy soul being immortal, do nothing to dishonor it. Cease not to make war upon vice.
3. Do to others that which thou wouldst desire them to do to thyself. In submitting to fortune, thou but followest the light of the wise.
4. Thou shouldst honor thy parents and aged persons. Thou shouldst enlighten the young and protect children.
5. Thou shouldst cherish thy wife and little ones. Thou shouldst love thy country and obey her laws.

6. Thy friend being to thee as a second self, see that thou bringest no misfortune upon him. Thou shouldst regard his memory as thou wouldst his life.

7. Thou shouldst shun false friendships, avoid all excesses, and fear to stain thy good name.

8. Thou shouldst subdue thine own passions and utilize the passions of others. Be indulgent to error.

9. Hear much, speak little, and weigh well that which thou speakest.

10. Forget injuries; render good for evil, and abuse not power or authority intrusted to thee.

11. Thou shouldst learn the nature of man, to the end that thou learnest thine own nature.

12. Seek the truth. Be just. Avoid idleness.

Precepts of Modern Freemasonry.

1. Be just; because equity sustains the human race.

2. Be good; because goodness enchains all hearts.

3. Be indulgent; because, feeble thyself, thou shouldst bear with the feebleness of others.

4. Be kind; because kindness secures affection.

5. Be grateful; because gratitude is the food that nourishes liberality.

6. Be modest; because pride is offensive to your fellow-beings.

7. Pardon injuries; because vengeance perpetuates hate.

8. Render good for evil; because in this way you will rise superior to the evil-doer and make him your friend.

9. Be forbearing, temperate, chaste; because voluptuousness, intemperance, and sensuality are destructive of thy existence, and will render it miserable.

10. Be a citizen; because thy country is necessary for thy security, thy happiness, and thy well-being.

11. Defend thy country with thy life; because it is her who secures thee in thy property, and in the possession of all those beings dear to thy heart; but never forget that humanity has rights.

12. If thy country wrong thee—if she refuse thee happiness, and suffer thee to be oppressed—leave her in silence; but never trouble her. Support adversity with resignation.

REMARKS on the Views maintained by Bro. Rebold, as exhibited in his Notes to his Epitome of the Worships and Mysteries of the Ancient Eastern World.

In his explanation of the origin of Christianity, in Note 32, Bro. Rebold has adopted views not in accordance with the belief of Christians, as comprised in the Nicene Creed. He would lead us to believe that the accepted legends concerning the birth and death of Jesus can be explained by astronomical data, and that no miraculous intervention need attach to those occurrences—that his birth was but the birth of any man; his death that of one who had offended the laws of his country, and his life, at least during the term of his itinerant pastorship, alone worthy of our admiration, as fruitful with preaching the most acceptable to mankind, because expressive of all that can ennoble the human race. In this regard, the translation and publication of some of Bro. Rebold's "Notes" have given offense, and a few of those who have felt themselves offended by Bro. Rebold's views being introduced into a history of Freemasonry, have expressed their dissatisfaction in some of the Masonic newspapers of the country, as also their desire that the circulation and sale of the "*General History of Freemasonry in Europe*" should be suppressed by all who think with them, as a book dangerous to the Church and subversive of the teachings of the Holy Scriptures.

To all such brethren, and we believe few but Freemasons purchase this book, we would respectfully recommend the fact that the incidental allusions in it, expressive of its author's religious belief, can do no harm to those who do not believe as he does, and certainly they can not be regarded as hurtful to any other person. If Bro. Rebold has discovered what he conceives to be the true meaning of certain legends, expressions, and assertions contained in the Scriptures, and denies the existence of miracles, he but asserts his own individuality without depriving any other brother of that condition, and at the same time, as a historian, he takes his position among the members of that advanced school who, as to miracles, argue as follows:

"It is an absolute rule of criticism to deny a place in history to narratives of miraculous circumstances; nor is this owing to a metaphysical system, but is simply the dictation of observation No miracle has ever been really proved. All the pretended miracles near enough to be examined are referable to illusion or imposture. If a single miracle had ever been proved, we could not reject those of ancient history; for, admitting that very many of the last were false, we might still believe that some of them were true. But it is not so. Discussion and examination are fatal to miracles at the present day, and therefore we are authorized to believe that those miracles which date many centuries back, and regarding which there are no means of framing a contradictory debate, are also without reality. In other words, miracles only exist when people believe in them. The supernatural is but another term for faith. Catholicism, in yet maintaining that it possesses miraculous powers, subjects itself to the influence of this law. The miracles of which it boasts never occur where they would be most effective. Why should not this fact be brought more prominently forward? A miracle at Paris, London, or New York, for instance, performed to the satisfaction of learned men, would put an end to all doubt. But, alas for miracles! such a thing never happens. A miracle never takes place before skeptical or incredulous people, who are the most in need of such a convincing proof of the supernatural. Credulity on the part of the witnesses is the essential condition of a miracle."

There is not a solitary exception to the rule that miracles are never produced before those who are able or permitted to discuss and criticise them. Cicero, with his usual good sense and penetration, asks, in his *De Divinatione*, "Since when has this secret force disappeared? Has it not been since men have become less credulous?"

In support of the reality of miraculous agency, appeal is made to phenomena outside of natural laws, such, for instance, as the creation of man. This creation, it has been said, could only have been compassed by the direct intervention of God; and why could not this intervention be manifested at other decisive crises, and after the development of the universe? Without at all entering upon the domain of theology, it is easy to show how defective is this argument. It is equivalent to maintaining that every thing which does not happen in the ordinary conditions of nature, every thing that can not be explained by science, or performed by man upon scientific or philosophic principles, is a miracle, or, in other words, a direct intervention of Deity. While we heartily acknowledge that God may be permanently in every thing, particularly in every thing that lives, we deny the reality of the supernatural until we are cognizant of a demonstrated fact of this nature. In far distant epochs there occurred without doubt phenomena which, on the same scale at least, are not repeated in the world of to-day. But there was at the time they happened a cause for those phenomena. In geological formation may be met a great number of minerals and precious stones which nature seems no longer to produce. Yet they have all been artificially produced by manufacturers of minerals and precious stones. If life can not be artificially produced, it is because the reproductions of the conditions in which life commenced (if it may be said ever to have *commenced*) are beyond human knowledge to attain. The formation of humanity, if we think of it as a sudden, instantaneous thing, is of all things in the world the most shocking and absurd; but if it is viewed as the result of a long continued progress, lasting through incalculable ages, it maintains its place in general analogies without losing its mystery. The laws of natural life are not applicable to embryotic life. The embryo develops all its organs one after another. It creates no more, because it is no longer at the creative age; just as language is no longer invented, because there is no more to invent.

But why continue an argument wherein the adversary but begs the question? We ask for a proven miracle, and are told that such took place anterior to history. Certainly if any proof were wanting of the necessity of belief in the supernatural to certain conditions of the soul, it would be found in the fact that many minds gifted in all other points with due penetration have reposed their entire faith in an argument as desperate as this.

The objectors to Bro. Rebold's views are further content to reject what nearly all of its readers have acknowledged to be the most reasonable and apparently correct history of the origin of Freemasonry that has ever been published, because, in those "Notes," he evinces a disbelief in the accepted legends of the origin of Christianity. In view of this condition, Bro. R. may exclaim as did John Huss on sight of an old woman whom he observed perspiring under the weight of a faggot she was dragging to his stake, "*O sancta simplicitas!*" Let these good brothers repress their breath and their heat, however, for, according to a beautiful expression of Scripture, *God is not in the wind, nor in the fire.* If the annoyance which they have experienced, in reading what they object to, proved instrumental in aiding the cause of truth, there would be something of consolation in it. But Truth is not for the angry or passionate man. She reserves herself for those who, free from partisan feeling, from persistent affections, and enduring hates, seek her with entire liberty, and with no mental reservation referring to human affairs. These problems form only one of the innumerable questions with which the world is crowded and which the curious are fond of studying; and their introduction into Notes explanatory of the Mysteries and Worships of Antiquity is certainly not improper. No one should be offended by the announcement of a mere theoretical opinion. Those who would guard their faith as a treasure can defend it very easily by ignoring all works written in an opposing spirit. The timid would do better by dispensing with reading altogether.

In writing the works which he has produced, Bro. Rebold, it must be acknowledged, has been influenced by a desire to find the truth, and to make the events of the past of Freemasonry known with the greatest possible exactness. In doing so we do him but justice to believe he had no thought of shocking the religious preferences of any one. He has written with no desire to proselytize, except for truth, and evidently in the conviction that every concession made to the scruples of those who had written on this subject before him was a derogation from the dignity and culture of truth. It can at once be seen that, when conducted in such a spirit, any writer must sink his individuality in his compositions.

The first principle of the critical school is the allowance, in matters of faith, of all that is needed, and the adaptation of beliefs to individual wants. Why should we concern ourselves about things over which no one has any control? If any person should adopt the principles of Bro. Rebold, as evinced in his "Notes," it is because that person has the mental tendency and the culture adapted to those principles; and all that Bro. R. or any brother might write during the term of their natural lives could not impart this tendency and this culture to those who do not naturally possess them. Philosophy differs from faith in this: that faith is believed to operate by itself, independently of the intelligence acquired from dogmas. Bro. Rebold, on the contrary, holds that truth only possesses value when the order of its ideas is comprehended. He does not consider himself obliged to maintain silence in regard to those opinions which may not be in accord with the belief of some of his readers. He makes no sacrifices to the exigencies of differing orthodoxies, but, instead of attacking them, he evidently does not allow them to influence him in any manner. To use his own language (at pp. 423-4), he has "extended his quotations and reflections to the end that Freemasons would have an opportunity of comparing the religious ideas which they may possess with those which were held by the men who, for thousands of years, have preceded them; and also for the purpose of accounting to them for the very evident connection which they must see exists between Freemasonry and these ancient religious beliefs and mysteries" which those quotations and reflections merely serve to illustrate.

The men who believe Bro. Rebold has offended in the first instance, and his American translator in the second, evidently are unfamiliar with the speculative tendencies of Freemasonry, and do not comprehend that such tendencies lead to the study of that which those men believe should not be questioned. They would repel, yea, excommunicate those who dare to think outside of the accepted groove of their own thoughts. The Heavenly Father, upon the contrary, only excommunicates the selfish and narrow-minded. The spirit of liberty in the realm of thought, like the wind, bloweth where it listeth. Theory is not practice. Do those who freely speak when they believe duty dictates equal, after all, in merit, those who in secret cherish and restrain the doubts known only to God?

In the language of an eloquent modern writer,* we say "Peace, then, in the name of God! Let the different orders of men live and pass their days, not in doing injustice to their own proper spirits by making concessions, but in mutually supporting each other. It is well known what follows when orthodoxy succeeds in overpowering free thought and science. Stupidity and mediocrity are the bane of certain Protestant countries where, under the pretense of maintaining the spirit of Christianity, art, science, and freedom of opinion are degraded. Lucretia of Rome and Saint Theresa, Aristophanes and Socrates, Voltaire and Francis of Assissi, Raphael and Saint Vincent de Paul, all enjoyed to an equal degree the right of existence in the world, and humanity would have been lessened had a single one of their individual elements been wanting." J. F. B.

---

* Ernest Renan author of the "Origins of Christianity," etc.

www.ingramcontent.com/pod-product-compliance
Lightning Source LLC
Chambersburg PA
CBHW051732300426
44115CB00007B/530